GUINNESS®
WORLD RECORDS
2001

www.guinnessworldrecords.com

GUINNESS WORLD RECORDS LTD
338 EUSTON ROAD
LONDON
NW1 3BD
UNITED KINGDOM

TEL: +44 (0) 20 7891 4567
FAX: +44 (0) 20 7891 4501
E-MAIL: info@guinnessrecords.com

Managing Director: Christopher Irwin
Director of Print Media: Tim Footman
Director of Intellectual Property: Rosemary Seagrief
Director of Sales & Marketing: Malcolm Roughead
CEO, guinnessworldrecords.com: Stephen Nelson
Director of Television: Michael Feldman

All North American sales inquiries to Guinness World Records at Mint Publishers Inc.
TEL: (914) 244 1685
FAX: (914) 244 1737

ABBREVIATIONS & MEASUREMENTS

GUINNESS WORLD RECORDS uses imperial measurements.
The only exception to this rule is for some scientific data, where metric measurements only are universally accepted, and for some sports data.

'GDR' (the German Democratic Republic) refers to the East German state which unified with West Germany in 1990. The abbreviation is used for sporting records broken before 1990.

The Union of Soviet Socialist Republics split into a number of parts in 1991, the largest of these being Russia. The Commonwealth of Independent States replaced it and the abbreviation 'CIS' is used mainly for sporting records broken at the 1992 Olympic Games.

ACCREDITATION

Guinness World Records Ltd has a very thorough accreditation system for records verification. However, whilst every effort is made to ensure accuracy, Guinness World Records Ltd cannot be held responsible for any errors contained in this work. Feedback from our readers on any points of accuracy is always welcomed.

GENERAL WARNING

Attempting to break records or set new records can be dangerous. Appropriate advice should be taken first and all record attempts are undertaken entirely at the participant's risk. In no circumstances will Guinness World Records Ltd have any liability for death or injury suffered in any record attempts. Guinness World Records Ltd has complete discretion over whether or not to include any particular records in the book.

GUINNESS®
WORLD RECORDS
2001

www.guinnessworldrecords.com

Introduction

Welcome to *Guinness World Records 2001,* a completely new edition of the world's best-selling copyright book, including the first records of the new millennium.

It's been another astonishing year for record breaking. **Khalid Khannouchi** became the first man to run a marathon in under 2 hours 6 minutes (see page 209). Can it be long before someone runs the race in less than two hours? **The PlayStation 2** became the fastest-selling games console in history (page 120). **Sherpa Babu Chhiri** reached the summit of Everest in under 17 hours (page 32). A team of Chinese and Japanese students toppled **2,751,518 dominoes**, breaking the previous record by over 280,000 (page 76). The unlikeliest celebrities were honored, as **Harry Potter, Pikachu,** and even the inhabitants of **South Park** found themselves Guinness World Record holders for the first time.

And Guinness World Records is continuing to expand in all areas. Apart from the success of our TV show – a total audience of over 100 million people in 35 countries – we also have a mind-boggling new website. See page 256 for the full story, or you can check it out at **www.guinnessworldrecords.com** right now.

We're sure that *Guinness World Records 2001* offers plenty to fascinate, stimulate, amaze, amuse, revolt, and inspire you. And if you think you've got what it takes to join the select ranks of the record breakers, go to the website or take a look at page 252. Who knows? You too might be a Guinness World Record holder one day...

Contents

8 ● Early Starters 🏃 ⚕️
10 ● Golden Oldies 🏃 ⚕️
12 ● Big Stuff ⚕️ ☺
14 ● Strength ⚕️
16 ● Speed ⚕️ ═
18 ● Skill 1 ⚕️ 🏃
20 ● Skill 2 ⚕️ 🏃
22 ● Endurance 1 ⚕️ 🏃
24 ● Endurance 2 ⚕️ 🏃
26 ● Teamwork 1 ⚕️ 🏃 ☺
28 ● Teamwork 2 ⚕️ 🏃 ☺
30 ● Adventures & Journeys 1 ⚕️ ☠ 🌐
32 ● Adventures & Journeys 2 ⚕️ ☠ 🌐
34 ● Disasters ☠
36 ● Survivors & Lifesavers ☠ ⚕️
38 ● Space Heroes ☠ ⚕️ 🪐
40 ● Human World 1 🏃
42 ● Human World 2 🏃
44 ● World Leaders 🏃 ✊
46 ● Campaigns 🏃 ✊

48 ○ Religion 🏃 ✊
50 ○ War & Peace ✊ ☠
52 ○ Crime ✊ ☠ $
54 ○ Super Rich 🏃 $
56 ○ Big Business 1 $ ⚕️
58 ○ Big Business 2 $ ⚕️
60 ○ Charities & Gifts $ ⚕️
62 ○ Valuables 1 $
64 ○ Valuables 2 $
66 ○ Valuables 3 $
68 ○ Shopping 1 $
70 ○ Shopping 2 $
72 ○ Food & Drink 1 $ 🪶
74 ○ Food & Drink 2 🏃 ⚕️ ☺
76 ● Games & Gambling ☺ $
78 ● Toys ☺
80 ● Collectors ☺ 🏃
82 ● Clubbing & Parties ☺ 🏃
84 ● Organizations 🏃
86 ● Theme Parks & Rides ☺
88 ● Fashion ☆ 📖 $
90 ● Movies 1 ☆ 📖 $
92 ● Movies 2 ☆ 📖 $
94 ● Cartoons 📖
96 ● TV 1 ☆ 📖 $
98 ● TV 2 ☆ 📖 $
100 ● Music ☆ 📖 $
102 ● Dance, Rap & R&B ☆ 📖
104 ● World Music ☆ 📖
106 ● Classical Music & Jazz ☆ 📖
108 ● Performance & Theater ☆ 📖

110 ● Print Media 📖
112 ● Awards ☆ 📖 🏅
114 ● Body Beautiful ☆
116 ● Stunts & Special Effects 💻 📖
118 ● Computers 💻
120 ● Computer Games 💻 ☺
122 ● Internet 1 www. 💻
124 ● Internet 2 www. 💻 ☺
126 ● Robots 💻
128 ● Gadgets 1 💻 ☺
130 ● Gadgets 2 💻 ☺
132 ● Lethal Weapons 💻 ☠
134 ● Cars 💻 🏢 ═
136 ● Trucks, Trains & Buses 💻 🏢 ═
138 ● Bicycles & Motorcycles 💻 🏢 ═
140 ● Ships, Boats & Submarines 💻 ═
142 ● Aircraft 💻 ═

144 ● Spacecraft

146 ● Buildings & Structures 1

148 ● Buildings & Structures 2

150 ● Travel & Transportation

152 ● Science 1

154 ● Science 2

156 ● Planet Earth

158 ● Human Body

160 ● Animal World 1

162 ● Animal World 2

164 ● Animal World 3

166 ● Plant World

168 ● Prehistoric World

170 ● Astronomy

172 ● Weather

174 ● Diseases & Parasites 1

176 ● Diseases & Parasites 2

178 ● Medical Marvels

180 ● Environment & Ecology 1

182 ● Environment & Ecology 2

184 ● Natural Disasters

186 ● Soccer 1

188 ● Soccer 2

190 ● Basketball

192 ● Rugby

194 ● Football

196 ● Golf

198 ● Tennis

200 ● Baseball

202 ● Cricket

204 ● Ball Sports 1

206 ● Ball Sports 2

208 ● Track-and-field 1

210 ● Track-and-field 2

212 ● Gymnastics & Weight Lifting

214 ● Water Sports

216 ● Hockey

218 ● Winter Sports 1

220 ● Winter Sports 2

222 ● Combat Sports 1

224 ● Combat Sports 2

226 ● Extreme Sports 1

228 ● Extreme Sports 2

230 ● Auto Sports

232 ● Bike Sports

234 ● Horse Sports

236 ○ Sports Reference

252 ○ So You Want To Set A Record...?

254 ○ Guinness World Records: Primetime

256 ○ guinnessworldrecords.com

258 ○ Indexes

288 ○ Guinness World Records – The Story

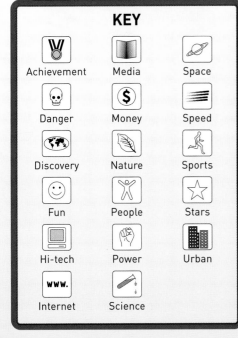

KEY

Achievement	Media	Space
Danger	Money	Speed
Discovery	Nature	Sports
Fun	People	Stars
Hi-tech	Power	Urban
www. Internet	Science	

Early Starters

YOUNGEST OLYMPIC GOLD MEDALISTS

The youngest winner of Olympic gold was a French boy – named possibly Marcel Depaillé – who coxswained the Netherlands pair in Paris, France, in 1900. He was not more than 10 years old and may have been as young as seven when he took part as a substitute for the original coxswain.

The youngest female champion was Kim Yoon-mi of South Korea, who competed in the 1994 women's 3,000-m. short-track speed-skating relay event at the age of 13 years, 85 days.

The youngest winner of an individual Olympic event was Marjorie Gestring (USA), who took the springboard diving title at the age of 13 years, 268 days at the Games in Berlin, Germany, on Aug. 12, 1936.

YOUNGEST PHYSICIAN

Balamurali Ambati of Hollis Hills, New York, USA, became the youngest doctor on May 19, 1995, graduating from the Mount Sinai School of Medicine in New York City, USA, aged 17.

YOUNGEST GRADUATES

Michael Kearney started studying for an Associate of Science degree at Santa Rosa Junior College, California, USA, in Sept. 1990, when he was just 6 years, 7 months old. He became the world's youngest graduate in June 1994, when he obtained a B.A. in anthropology from the University of South Alabama, USA, at the age of 10 years, 4 months.

Tathagat Avatar Tulsi of New Delhi, India, obtained an M.Sc. in physics from Patna University, India, at the age of 12 years, 2 months on Nov. 28, 1999.

YOUNGEST JUDGE

John Payton was 18 years, 11 months old when he took office as a Justice of the Peace in Plano, Texas, USA, in Jan 1991.

YOUNGEST PERSON TO PUBLISH RESEARCH

The youngest person to have had serious research published in a scientific or medical journal is Emily Rosa of Colorado, USA. She was 11 years old when an article she coauthored appeared in the *Journal of the American Medical Association* on April 1, 1998. The article reported on an experiment that she had conceived at the age of eight and carried out for a school project aged nine.

YOUNGEST UN AMBASSADOR

Laura Sweeting from Watford, Hertfordshire, England, became the UN's youngest Goodwill Ambassador on June 9, 2000, aged 16. Her role is to help raise awareness and funds for the Water4Life Appeal/Children Helping Children campaign.

⊙ YOUNGEST SUPERMARKET CONSULTANT

On April 15, 2000, supermarket chain Tesco announced that it had hired seven-year-old Laurie Sleator from Hertfordshire, England, to advise senior executives on the Pokémon craze currently sweeping the globe. Laurie receives Pokémon products in return for his services.

⊙ YOUNGEST DJ

Llewellyn Owen from King's Cross, London, England, also known as DJ Welly, headlined at the London club The Warp on May 1, 2000, when he was 8 years, 70 days old. He was paid $180) per hour, the standard rate for headlining DJs. As of June 2000, he was scheduled to play a number of sites in both the UK and Paris, France.

YOUNGEST HAUTE COUTURE DESIGNER

French fashion designer Yves Saint-Laurent (b. 1936) became Christian Dior's assistant at the age of 17 and was named head of the House of Dior in 1957. In 1962, he opened his own fashion house and in the 1970s expanded into ready-made lines, household linens, and fragrances.

YOUNGEST OPERA SINGER

US opera singer Ginetta La Bianca was 15 years, 316 days old when she sang the role of Gilda in Verdi's *Rigoletto* in Velletri, Italy, on March 24, 1950. She appeared as Rosina in *The Barber of Seville* at the Teatro dell'Opera, Rome, Italy, 45 days later.

⊙ YOUNGEST HOLE-IN-ONE GOLFER

The youngest golfer to have achieved a hole-in-one is Matthew Draper (UK). He was 5 years, 212 days old when he set this record at the 122-yd. fourth at Cherwell Edge Golf Club, Oxfordshire, England, on June 17, 1997.

YOUNGEST DRIVER

Andrzej Makowski (Canada) was issued with a driver's license at Namyslow, Poland, on April 10, 1974. He had passed his test on March 27, 1974, aged 14 years, 235 days.

← YOUNGEST WORLD DIVING CHAMPION

Fu Mingxia (China) was 12 years, 141 days old when she won the women's world platform diving title at Perth, Western Australia, on Jan. 4, 1991.

YOUNGEST AUTHOR

Dennis Vollmer of Grove, Oklahoma, USA, was six years old when he wrote and illustrated the book *Joshua Disobeys*. It was published by Landmark Editions, Inc. of Kansas City, Missouri, USA, after Dennis won a national contest for students in 1987.

YOUNGEST MOVIE DIRECTOR, WRITER, AND PRODUCER

The 1973 thriller *Lex the Wonderdog* was written, produced, and directed by Sydney Ling when he was just 13 years old, making him the youngest director of a professionally made, feature-length movie.

YOUNGEST NOBEL PRIZE WINNER

Professor Sir Lawrence Bragg (UK) was 25 years old when he won the 1915 Nobel Prize in physics.

YOUNGEST SOLDIERS

The Brazilian military hero and statesman Luís Alves de Lima e Silva, Marshal Duke of Caxias, entered his infantry regiment at the age of five in 1808. He was promoted to the rank of Captain in 1824 and made Duke in 1869.

Fernando Inchauste Montalvo, the son of a major in the Bolivian air force, went to the front with his father on his fifth birthday in 1935, during the 1932–1935 war between Bolivia and Paraguay. He had received military training and was subject to military discipline.

YOUNGEST MARRIED COUPLE

In 1986, an 11-month-old baby boy was married to a three-month-old baby girl at Aminpur, near Pabna, Bangladesh. The marriage took place in order to end a 20-year feud between the children's families over a farm.

YOUNGEST PROFESSOR

Colin Maclaurin was 19 years old when he was elected Professor of Mathematics at Marischal College, Aberdeen, Scotland, on Sept. 30, 1717. He went on to become Professor of Mathematics at Edinburgh University, Scotland, in 1725, on the recommendation of Sir Isaac Newton.

Golden Oldies

◉ OLDEST FEMALE MARATHON FINISHER

Jenny Wood-Allen from Dundee, Scotland, was 87 years old when she completed the 1999 London Marathon with a time of 7 hrs. 14 min. 46 sec. She has now completed more than 30 marathons, raising over $44,600 for charity in the process. The world's oldest male marathon finisher was Dimitrion Yordanidis of Greece, who set the record aged 98 on Oct. 10, 1976, in Athens, Greece. His time was 7 hrs. 33 min.

OLDEST DRIVERS

Layne Hall of Silver Creek, New York, USA, was issued with a license on June 15, 1989, when, according to the license, he was 109 years old. He died on Nov. 20, 1990, but according to his death certificate he was then only 105.

Maude Tull of Inglewood, California, USA, began driving at the age of 91 after her husband died. She was issued with a replacement driver's license on Feb. 5, 1976, when she was 104.

OLDEST QUALIFIED PILOT

The world's oldest pilot is Burnet Patten of Victoria, Australia. He obtained his flying license at the age of 80 on May 2, 1997.

◉ OLDEST PERSON TO SKI TO THE NORTH POLE

In April 1999, Jack MacKenzie (Canada), then aged 77, joined a ski expedition to the North Pole as part of celebrations to mark the International Year of Older Persons. He and the other eight members of his team skied 62 miles in five and a half days, reaching the pole on April 28, 1999.

OLDEST AIRPLANE PASSENGER

The oldest person to fly as a passenger was Charlotte Hughes of Redcar, Cleveland, England, who was given a flight on Concorde from London, England, to New York City, USA, as a 110th birthday present in Aug. 1987. She flew again in Feb. 1992, when she was 115.

OLDEST PARACHUTISTS

Hildegarde Ferrera became the oldest ever parachutist when she made a tandem jump over Mokuleia, Hawaii, USA, at the age of 99 on Feb. 17, 1996.

The oldest male parachutist is George Salyer, who made a tandem jump from an altitude of 12,001 ft. aged 97 at Harvey Airfield, Snohomish, Washington, USA, on June 27, 1998.

Sylvia Brett (UK) became the oldest female solo parachutist when she jumped at Cranfield, Bedfordshire, England, at the age of 80 on Aug. 23, 1986.

OLDEST HOT-AIR BALLOONIST

Florence Laine of New Zealand was 102 years old when she flew in a hot-air balloon at Cust, New Zealand, on Sept. 26, 1996.

OLDEST OLYMPIC GOLD MEDALIST

Oscar Swahn (Sweden) was in the winning Running Deer shooting team at the age of 64 in 1912. He was a silver medalist in the same event in 1920, aged 72.

OLDEST ATHLETE

Baba Joginder Singh was believed to have been 105 years old when he competed in the discus event at the 1998 Indian National Athletics Meet for Veterans, held in Thane, Mumbai (Bombay). He was the only competitor aged over 100.

OLDEST GROOM

Harry Stevens was 103 years old when he married 84-year-old Thelma Lucas at the Caravilla Retirement Home, Wisconsin, USA, on Dec. 3, 1984.

OLDEST BRIDE

Minnie Munro became the world's oldest bride when she married Dudley Reid at the age of 102 in Point Clare, NSW, Australia, on May 31, 1991. Reid was 83 years old.

LONGEST MARRIAGE

Canadian hunter and trapper Joseph Henry Jarvis (b. June 15, 1899) and his wife Annie (b. Oct. 10, 1904) have been married for 79 years – a record for a living couple. The pair wed on July 15, 1921, at Mooshide, Yukon, Canada, and have 12 children.

OLDEST DIVORCED COUPLE

The oldest divorcing couple on record are Simon and Ida Stern of Milwaukee, Wisconsin, USA. When they divorced in Feb. 1984, she was 91 and he was 97.

OLDEST TIGHTROPE WALKER

William Ivy Baldwin became the world's oldest ever tightrope walker when he crossed South Boulder Canyon, Colorado, USA, on his 82nd birthday on July 31, 1948. The wire he walked across was 320 ft. long and the drop was 125 ft.

OLDEST PLAYWRIGHT

George Bernard Shaw started his career as a dramatist at the age of 36 and subsequently wrote 57 plays. His last play, *Buoyant Billions*, was written in 1949, when he was 93.

OLDEST DESIGNER

British designer Sir Hardy Amies, who was born in 1909, is still actively involved in the fashion industry. Sir Hardy joined the fashion house Lachasse in Farm Street, London, England, in 1934, and founded his own business in nearby Savile Row in 1946. He is currently dressmaker by appointment to Queen Elizabeth II.

OLDEST TUBA PLAYER

Jack Hogg of Wirral, England, has been a regular member of the Heswall Concert Band since joining at the age of 94 in 1998.

OLDEST OPERA SINGER

Mark Reizen (Ukraine) sang in Tchaikovsky's *Eugene Onegin* at the Bolshoi Theater, Moscow, Russia, aged 90 in July 1990.

← OLDEST RACING DRIVER

US actor Paul Newman was 75 years old when he took part in the Rolex 24 at Daytona International Speedway, Florida, USA, from Feb. 6 to 7, 2000. His team, which included 17-year-old co-driver Gunnar Jeannette, competed in a Champion Racing Porsche 996-GT3.

Big Stuff

BIGGEST STONE SCULPTURE
The mounted figures of Jefferson Davis, Robert E. Lee, and General Thomas Jonathan (Stonewall) Jackson are 90 ft. high and cover 1.33 acres on the face of Stone Mountain near Atlanta, Georgia, USA.

BIGGEST COTTON SCULPTURE
Between May 1998 and April 1999, Anant Narayan Khairnar of Jalagon, India, created a 7-ft. 6-in. sculpture of Mahatma Gandhi out of cotton wool. It weighed 44 lbs.

BIGGEST REVOLVING GLOBE
Eartha, a sphere with a diameter of 41 ft. 18 in. and a weight of 5,600 lbs., was built by the DeLorme publishing company in Yarmouth, Maine, USA, in 1998.

BIGGEST RUBBER-BAND BALL
In April 1998, John Bain of Delaware, USA, created a 2,000-lb. rubber-band ball from rubber bands he had collected while working in his office's mail room. The ball had a circumference of 12 ft. 8.5 in.

BIGGEST PADLOCK
A mild steel padlock hand-made in 1955 by Muhammad Rafique of Pakistan is 12 in. wide, 21.5 in. high, and 4 in. thick. It weighs 111.6 lbs.

BIGGEST FLAG
The world's largest flag is the US "Superflag," owned by "Ski" Demski of Long Beach, California, USA. It measures 505 ft. x 225 ft. and weighs 1.34 tons. It was made by Humphrey's Flag Co. of Pottstown, Pennsylvania, and was unfurled at the Hoover Dam on the Colorado River, Arizona/Nevada border, USA, on June 14, 1992.

The largest flag flown from a flagstaff is a Brazilian national flag in Brasilia, Brazil. It measures a record 229 ft. 8 in. x 328 ft. 1 in)

BIGGEST CHRISTMAS CRACKER
The largest functional Christmas cracker (a paper party-favor that pops when pulled) ever constructed was 181 ft. 11 in. long and 11 ft. 9 in. in diameter.

⊙ BIGGEST DISCO BALL
A disco ball at the Mayan Club, Los Angeles, California, USA. has a diameter of 7 ft. 11.25 in. and weighs 304 lbs. Made by Big Millennium Balls of Santa Clarita, California, it consists of 6,900 mirrored squares, each measuring 2 in. x 2 in.

It was made by ex-international rugby league player Ray Price for Markson Sparks! of New South Wales, Australia, and was pulled in the parking lot of Westfield Shopping Town, Chatswood, Sydney, NSW, Australia, on Dec. 16, 1998.

BIGGEST CANDLE
A record 80-ft.-high candle with a diameter of 8 ft. 6 in. was exhibited at the 1897 Stockholm Exhibition, Sweden, by the firm Lindahls.

BIGGEST PLAYABLE GUITAR
The largest playable guitar in the world is 38 ft. 2 in. tall and 16 ft. wide, with a weight of 1,865 lbs. Modeled on the Gibson Flying V, it was made by students of Shakamak High School in Jasonville, Indiana, USA. It was unveiled on May 17, 1991, when, powered by six amplifiers, it was played simultaneously by six members of the school.

BIGGEST RECORDER
The world's largest fully functional recorder, made from specially treated stone pine, with a length of 16 ft. 5 in., was constructed in Iceland by Stefán

⊙ BIGGEST DRUM
The Ireland Millennium Drum, designed by Brian Fleming and Paraic Breathnac and constructed by Bill Wright and Seamus Purcell, has a diameter of 15 ft. 6 in. and a depth of 6 ft. 3 in. Made from birch plywood and sailcloth, it was first played at the St. Patrick's Festival in Dublin, Ireland, on March 13, 1999, to mark the launch of Ireland's Millennium Festivals.

Sane Sports Wear, Vadodara, India, built the world's largest suitcase. It measured a record 13.33 ft. x 8.75 ft. x 4.16 ft.

BIGGEST TRASH CAN
On Oct. 22, 1998, a galvanized-steel trash can with a height measuring 18 ft. and a diameter of 12 ft. was made by BRESCO of Baltimore, Maryland, USA. The

trash can had a capacity of 15,228 gal.

BIGGEST BED NET
The world's largest mosquito-repelling bed net measures 65 ft. 7.5 in. x 65 ft. 7.5 in. x 9 ft. 10 in. This is 225 times the size of a normal bed net. It was displayed at Eagle Square, Abuja, Nigeria, on April 18, 2000, to mark the

World Health Organization's African Summit on Roll Back Malaria.

BIGGEST GOLF TEE
In Sept. 1999, Des Sawa Jr. of Tobermory, Ontario, Canada, made a maple-wood golf tee that was 7 ft. 4 in. long. It had a head width of 18.5 in. and a shaft width of 7.9 in.

⊙ LONGEST WEDDING DRESS TRAIN

The world's longest wedding dress train measured a record 670 ft. Made by Hege Solli (Norway) for the wedding of Hege Lorence and Rolf Rotset on June 1, 1996, it was carried by 186 bridesmaids and page boys.

Geir Karlsson in 1994. Each of the recorder's holes is 3.3 in. in diameter.

BIGGEST SUITCASE
From Feb. 7 to 15, 1999, a team of eight people from

→ BIGGEST MUG

The world's largest mug was made by Parnassus Events of India in 1998. It is 20 ft. high, with a diameter of 14 ft. and a weight of 3.5 tons. The giant mug was unveiled at Bangalore Palace, India, on Aug. 14, 1998.

TATA Kaapi INSTANT PRESENTS THE WORLD'S BIGGEST COFFEE MUG

Strength

GREATEST AIRPLANE PULLS

On July 6, 1999, a team of 60 men from Hampshire, England, pulled a 220-ton Boeing 747 a distance of 328 ft. (100 m.) in 59.13 seconds, at Gatwick Airport, England. The stunt was performed by the team so that they could raise money for the Romsey Hospital Appeal.

A team consisting of 10 Ohakea Air Force personnel pulled a 36-ton Boeing 737-300 a distance of 328 ft. (100 m.) in 47 seconds, at Palmerston North Airport, New Zealand, on May 17, 1998.

David Huxley (Australia) pulled a 184-ton Boeing 747-400 a distance of 298 ft. 6 in. (91 m.) in 1 min. 27.7 sec., at Sydney, NSW, Australia, on Oct. 15, 1997.

On Dec. 9, 1998, a team made up of eight members of the Suffolk Braves Wheelchair Basketball, UK, pulled a 3.9-ton Cessna 421 Eagle executive aircraft a distance of 1,640 ft. (500 m.) in 16 min. 20 sec., at Cambridge Airport, England.

LONGEST AIRPLANE RESTRAINT

On June 20, 1997, Otto Acron (Australia) prevented two Cessna 300-h.p. airplanes from taking off in opposite directions for more than 15 seconds. The record was set at Hervey Bay, Queensland, Australia.

GREATEST TRAIN PULLS

Juraj Barbaric (Slovakia) single-handedly pulled a 354-ton train a distance of 25 ft. 3 in. along a railroad track at Košice, Slovakia, on May 25, 1996.

Grant Edwards (Australia) single-handedly pulled a 198-ton train a distance of 120 ft. 9 in. along a railroad track at Thirlmere, NSW, Australia, on April 4, 1996.

OLDEST PERSON TO PULL A PASSENGER VESSEL

Maurice Catarcio (USA) was 69 years, 6 months old when he pulled the 43-ton boat *Silver Bullet*, with 125 passengers on board, a distance of 300 ft. The record was set at Sunset Lake, New Jersey, USA, on Sept. 12, 1998.

⊙ MOST PUSH-UPS ON BACKS OF HANDS IN ONE HOUR

On March 5, 2000, Paddy Doyle (UK) completed a record 660 push-ups on the backs of his hands in one hour.

LONGEST FIELD GUN PULL

In 24 hours from April 2 to 3, 1993, three teams of eight men from the British Army's 72 Ordnance Company (V) pulled a 3,968-lb. (1,800-kg.) 25-pounder field gun a distance of 110.6 miles at Donnington, England.

GREATEST TRUCK PULL

On Nov. 10, 1999, Harold "Chief Iron Bear" Collins (USA) pulled a 22.51-ton truck a distance of 100 ft. in less than 40 seconds. Collins performed this feat in New York City, USA.

⊙ GREATEST WEIGHT PULLED WITH TEETH

On June 9, 1996, Walter Arfeuille (Belgium) pulled eight railway passenger coaches with a combined weight of 493,563 lbs. a distance of 10 ft. 6 in. along a track, with his teeth. The record was set at Diksmuide, Belgium.

MOST WEIGHT SUSTAINED

On Aug. 13, 1999, Kahled Dahdouh of Lowell, Massachusetts, USA, sustained a record weight of 3,045 lbs. on his chest for five seconds, on the set of *Guinness World Records: Primetime*. The weight was made up of three bodybuilders standing on cinder blocks.

HEAVIEST CAR BALANCED ON HEAD

John Evans (UK) balanced a 352-lb. gutted Mini on his head for 33 seconds at The London Studios, England, on May 24, 1999.

GREATEST WEIGHT LIFTED WITH TEETH

On March 31, 1990, Walter Arfeuille (Belgium) lifted weights totaling 620.6 lbs. a distance of 6.7 in. off the ground with his teeth. The record was set in Paris, France.

MOST BEER KEGS BALANCED

John Evans (UK) balanced 11 empty beer kegs on his head for the required 10 seconds on *Guinness World Records: Primetime* on June 17, 1998.

MOST BRICKS BALANCED ON HEAD

John Evans (UK) balanced a record 101 bricks, weighing a total of 416 lbs., on his head for 10 seconds at BBC TV Centre, London, England, on Dec. 24, 1997.

HEAVIEST WEIGHT JUGGLED

Yuri Scherbina (Ukraine) threw a 35.28-lb. (16-kg.) weight ball from hand to hand 100 times on the eastern summit of Mount Elbrus, Russia (altitude 13,800 ft.), on July 27, 1995.

MOST MILK CRATES BALANCED ON HEAD

John Evans (UK) balanced 95 milk crates, each of which weighed 3 lbs., on his head for 10 seconds at Kerr Street Green, County Antrim, Northern Ireland. He set the record on July 18, 1997.

MOST MILK CRATES BALANCED ON CHIN

Terry Cole (UK) balanced 29 milk crates on his chin for the minimum specified time of 10 seconds on May 16, 1994.

GREATEST DISPLAY OF LUNG POWER

On Sept. 26, 1994, Nicholas Mason (UK) inflated a 2.2-lb. (1-kg.) balloon to a diameter measuring 8 ft. in only 45 min. 2.5 sec.

STRONGEST HOD CARRIER

On Nov. 20, 1993, Russell Bradley of Worcester, England, carried bricks with a combined weight of 582 lbs. (264 kg.) in a hod weighing 105.8 lbs. (48 kg.) for 16 ft. 5 in. (5 m.) on flat ground, before ascending a ramp to a height of 8 ft. 2 in. (2.49 m.). This gave a total weight of 687.9 lbs. (312 kg.).

FASTEST BEER KEG LIFTER

Tom Gaskin (UK) raised a 137.8-lb. (62.5-kg.) beer keg above his head 902 times in the space of six hours at Liska House, Newry, Northern Ireland, on Oct. 26, 1996.

MOST BALLS BALANCED ON HEAD

The greatest number of soccer-sized PVC balls balanced on the head is 548, by John Evans (UK) at Leeds, W. Yorkshire, England, on June 28, 1998. The balls were contained inside a goal.

← GREATEST WEIGHT LIFTED WITH ONE EAR

On Dec. 17, 1998, Li Jian Hua of Jiangshan, China, lifted a 110.1-lb. (50-kg.) column of bricks hanging from a clamp joined to his ear on *Guinness World Records: Primetime*. He held the weight for 9.3 seconds.

Speed

FASTEST HALF MARATHON PUSHING A BABY BUGGY
The fastest time in which anyone has completed a half marathon while pushing a baby buggy is 1 hr. 49 min. 18 sec., by Peter Taylor (UK). He came 72nd out of 95 finishers in the East Yorkshire Marathon at Driffield, England, on May 11, 1997.

FASTEST BATHTUB RACER
The record time for completing a 36-mile bathtub race on water is 1 hr. 22 min. 27 sec., by Greg Mutton at the Grafton Jacaranda Festival, NSW, Australia, on Nov. 8, 1987. The bathtubs can not be longer than 75 in.

FASTEST TRASH CAN RACERS
The men's large, wheeled trash can race record is held by Shaun and Aaron Viney, who completed a 361-ft. course in 31.1 seconds at Westfield Devils Junior Soccer Club, Launceston, Tasmania, Australia, on Feb. 21, 1999. The competitors sprint 32.8 ft. to their stationary trash cans before taking turns being pulled over 164-ft. stretches of the course.

The women's record is 48.84 seconds, by Olivia and Karla Jones at the same location on the same day.

⊙ FASTEST POLE CLIMB
Jeremy Barrell (UK) climbed up an 80-ft.-high pole in 10.75 seconds during the 1999 World Poleclimbing Championship, held at the Hampshire County Show, England, on July 28, 1999. He broke his own record of 11.36 seconds, set on July 28, 1998, at the same show.

FASTEST STILT WALKERS
The fastest long-distance stilt walker on record was M. Garisoain (France), who stilt walked 4.97 miles from Bayonne to Biarritz, France, in 42 minutes in 1892 – an average speed of 7.10 m.p.h.

The fastest stilt walker over short distances is Roy Luiking (Netherlands). On May 28, 1992, he covered 328 ft. in a record 13.01 seconds while wearing 1-ft. stilts, at Didam, Netherlands.

FASTEST POGO STICK UP THE CN TOWER
Ashrita Furman (USA) pogo sticked up the 1,899 steps of the CN Tower, Toronto, Canada, in 57 min. 51 sec. on July 23, 1999.

FASTEST SACK RACER
Ashrita Furman completed a 6.2-mile sack race in 1 hr. 25 min. 10 sec. at Mount Rushmore National Park, South Dakota, USA, on Aug. 6, 1998.

FASTEST TREETOPPER
Guy German climbed a 100-ft. lumber spar pole with a circumference of 39 in. and sawed off the top in a record 53.35 seconds at Albany, Oregon, USA, on July 3, 1989.

FASTEST KNOT-TIER
The fastest recorded time in which anyone has tied the six *Boy Scout Handbook* knots (square knot, sheet bend, sheepshank, round turn and two half hitches, clove hitch, and bowline) on individual ropes is 8.1 seconds, by Clinton Bailey, Sr. of Pacific City, Oregon, USA, on April 13, 1977.

FASTEST SPIKE DRIVER
On Aug. 11, 1984, Dale C. Jones of Utah, USA, drove six 7-in. railroad spikes in a time of 26.4 seconds at the World Championship Professional Spike Driving Competition, held at the Golden Spike National Historic Site, Utah.

FASTEST TAP DANCER
The fastest rate ever measured for tap dancing is 38 taps per second, achieved by James Devine at the MCM recording studios, Sydney, NSW, Australia, on May 25, 1998.

⊙ FASTEST WINDOW CLEANER
Terry Burrows of South Ockendon, Essex, England, cleaned three standard 45-in. x 45-in. office windows, set in a frame, in 11.34 seconds at AJ Beveridge, Edinburgh, Scotland, on July 22, 1999. He used an 11.8-in. squeegee and 2.4 gal. of water.

FASTEST FLAMENCO DANCER

Solero de Jérez attained a rate of 16 heel taps per second in a routine in Brisbane, Queensland, Australia, in Sept. 1967.

FASTEST YODELER

Thomas Scholl of Munich, Germany, achieved 22 tones (15 falsetto) in one second on Feb. 9, 1992.

EMPIRE STATE BUILDING RUN-U

⊙ FASTEST TIME TO RUN UP THE EMPIRE STATE BUILDING

The fastest time in which anyone has completed the annual race up the 1,576 steps of the Empire State Building, New York City, USA, is 9 min. 53 sec., by Paul Crake (above) of Canberra, Australia, on Feb. 23, 2000. The women's record is 12 min. 19 sec., by Belinda Soszyn (Australia, top) in 1996.

FASTEST TALKER

Steve Woodmore of Orpington, Kent, England, spoke 595 words in 56.01 seconds – a rate equivalent to 637.4 words per minute – on the ITV television program *Motor Mouth* on Sept. 22, 1990. Few people are able to speak articulately at a sustained speed of over 300 words per minute.

FASTEST BED MAKER

The fastest time in which one person has made a bed is 28.2 seconds, by Wendy Wall of Sydney, NSW, Australia, on Nov. 30, 1978.

FASTEST COCONUT TREE CLIMB

The fastest time in which anyone has climbed a 29-ft. 6-in. coconut tree barefoot is a record 4.88 seconds, by Fuatai Solo (Fiji) at the annual Coconut Tree Climbing Competition in Sukuna Park, Fiji, on Aug. 22, 1980. Solo was so pleased with his win – the third in succession – that he climbed the tree again, clutching the prize money of $100 in his mouth.

FASTEST HORSE IMPERSONATORS

On Aug. 3, 1999, Geoff Seale and Stuart Coleman (both UK) ran a distance of 328 ft in a time of 16.7 seconds while wearing a horse costume. The record was set at St. Andrew's School, Cobham, Surrey, England.

FASTEST KITE SPEED

On Sept. 22, 1989, Pete DiGiacomo flew a kite at a speed of 120 m.p.h. at Ocean City, Maryland, USA.

Skill 1

MOST COINS BALANCED
Aleksandr Bendikov of Mogilev, Belarus, stacked a pyramid of 880 coins on the edge of a vertically standing coin on Nov. 15, 1995.

The most coins stacked in a single column on the edge of a vertically standing coin is 253, by Dipak Syal of Yamuna Nagar, India, on May 3, 1991. He balanced Indian one-rupee pieces on top of a five-rupee piece. He has also balanced 10 one-rupee coins and 10 10-paise coins in a single column, alternating them horizontally and vertically.

MOST DOMINOES STACKED
Ralf Laue of Leipzig, Germany, successfully stacked 555 dominoes on a single supporting domino on July 2, 1999. The stack remained standing for an hour.

MOST MATCHSTICKS BALANCED
The greatest number of matchsticks balanced on the neck of a bottle is 8,146, in 351 layers, by Peter Both on March 2, 1995. The matchsticks reached a height of 2 ft. 6 in., beating Both's previous record by 7.9 in.

MOST BOWLING BALLS BALANCED
The most bowling balls stacked vertically, without the use of adhesives, is 10, by Dave Kremer of Waukesha, Wisconsin, USA, on the US TV show *Guinness World Records: Primetime* on Nov. 19, 1998.

MOST GOLF BALLS BALANCED
Don Athey of Bridgeport, Ohio, USA, stacked nine golf balls vertically, without the use of adhesives, on Oct. 4, 1998.

MOST BEER MATS FLIPPED
Dean Gould (UK) flipped a pile of 111 beer mats – each of which was 0.04 in. thick – through an angle of 180° and caught them, in Edinburgh, Scotland, on Jan. 13, 1993.

MOST BEER MATS CAUGHT
Dean Gould (UK) stacked 2,224 beer mats on his elbow and forearm, then caught them in one hand with a downward swipe, on a ferry between Felixstowe, Suffolk, and Harwich, Essex, both England, on March 15, 1998.

LONGEST BEER-GLASS PUSH
The greatest distance that a 0.88-pint glass of beer has been pushed by the handle down a bar no wider than 19.7 in. is 110 ft. 7 in., by Gerrit Hesselink (Netherlands) at the Summer Festival, Saasveld, Netherlands, on June 27, 1998.

⊙ **MOST CLOTHESPINS CLIPPED ON FACE AND NECK**
Kevin Thackwell of Stoke-on-Trent, Staffordshire, England, attached 116 clothespins to his face and neck in five minutes at the Horseshoe Inn, Church Lawton, Cheshire, England, on Sept. 27, 1999.

⊙ **MOST SCISSORS USED TO CUT HAIR**
Dani Abergel (professionally known as Dani Figaro) of Dimona, Israel, can style hair using seven pairs of scissors in one hand, controlling each pair independently. Abergel started to use multiple pairs of scissors in 1997, and now regularly uses seven at a time in his Dimona salon. He claims that the technique allows him to create a "more interesting" look.

FASTEST SHEEPSHEARER
Godfrey Bowen (New Zealand) sheared a Cheviot ewe in 46 seconds at the Royal Highland Show in Dundee, Scotland, in June 1957.

MOST PEOPLE SHAVED
Denny Rowe shaved a record 1,994 men in one hour with a retractor safety razor at Herne Bay, Kent, England, on June 19, 1988. He averaged 1.8 seconds per volunteer and drew blood four times.

On Nov. 10, 1993, Tom Rodden of Chatham, Kent, England, shaved 278 volunteers in one hour with a cutthroat razor. He averaged 12.9 seconds per person and drew blood seven times.

MOST HAIR SPLITS
Alfred West (UK) has split a human hair 17 times – i.e., into 18 parts – on eight occasions.

MOST WORMS CHARMED

Tom Shufflebotham charmed 511 worms out of the ground at the first World Charming Championship, held in Willaston, Cheshire, England, on July 5, 1980. Entrants charm worms on a 32.3 ft.^{2} lot in 30 minutes.

MOST MOSQUITOES KILLED

The record is 21 in five minutes, by Henri Pellonpää at the 1995 World Mosquito Killing Championships in Pelkosenniemi, Finland.

← MOST HULA HOOPS SPUN

The most hula hoops spun simultaneously between the shoulders and the hips is 82, by Lori Lynn Lomeli (USA) at the Atlantis Casino Resort, Reno, Nevada, USA, on Aug. 5, 1999. Each of the hoops completed three full revolutions.

Skill 2

LONGEST BARREL JUMP
The longest barrel jump on record is 29 ft. 5 in. over 18 barrels, by Yvon Jolin at Terrebonne, Québec, Canada, on Jan. 25, 1981. To gain the speed needed to jump these sorts of distances, barrel-jump record attempts are performed on ice using ice-skates.

The women's record is 22 ft. 4 in. over 13 barrels, by Marie-Josée Houle at Lasalle, Québec, Canada, on March 1, 1987.

MOST MILK MILKED IN ONE DAY
On Aug. 25, 1992, Joseph Love of Kilifi Plantations Ltd, Kenya, hand-milked a record 117 gal. of milk from 30 cows.

MOST SNAKES MILKED
Over a 14-year period from 1951 to 1965, Bernard Keyter, a supervisor at the South African Institute for Medical Research in Johannesburg, South Africa, milked a record 780,000 venomous snakes, obtaining 870 gal. of venom. He was never bitten.

MOST NUMBERS MEMORIZED
On Nov. 6, 1999, Gert Mittring (Germany) successfully recited 27 random digits from memory, in the correct order, after the numbers had been flashed up on a screen for three seconds. The record was set in Cologne, Germany.

FASTEST STAMP LICKER
Diane Sheer of London, England, licked 225 stamps and stuck them onto envelopes in five minutes at the Normandie Hotel, Bournemouth, Dorset, England, on Aug. 3, 1997.

FASTEST RUBIK'S CUBE COMPLETION
Vietnamese refugee Minh Thai won the 1982 World Rubik Cube Championship in Budapest, Hungary, with a time of 22.95 seconds.

LONGEST TIME TOP SPUN
Hall Graham (USA) spun a spinning top for 2 hrs. 52 min. 11 sec. before its rim made contact with the ground at Woodstock High School, Georgia, USA, in Dec. 1998.

MOST CARDS HELD IN A FAN
On March 18, 1994, Ralf Laue (Germany) held 326 standard playing cards in a fan in one hand, with the value and color of each one visible, at Leipzig, Germany.

LONGEST CARD THROW
Jim Karol of North Catasauqua, Pennsylvania, USA, threw a standard playing card a record distance of 67 yds. at Mount Ida College, Massachusetts, USA, on Oct. 18, 1992.

LONGEST PIECE OF FRENCH KNITTING
Ted Hannaford of Sittingbourne, Kent, England, has produced the world's longest piece of French knitting. It was 8.48 miles long when measured in April 1999; he started knitting it more than 10 years ago.

LONGEST PEANUT THROW
On Feb. 21, 1999, Adrian Finch of Tasmania, Australia, threw a 0.14-oz. peanut a distance of 37.3 yds. at Westfield Devils Junior Soccer Club, Launceston, Tasmania, Australia.

⊙ HOUSE OF CARDS WITH MOST STORIES
Between May 15 and 27, 1999, Bryan Berg of Spirit Lake, Iowa, USA, built a 24-ft. 4-in., 127-story freestanding house of cards from 1,200 packs of standard playing cards, without using adhesives. The record was set at the College of Design, Iowa State University, Ames, Iowa, USA.

⊙ GREATEST DISTANCE RUBBER BAND SHOT
Leo Clouser (USA) shot a rubber band a record-breaking distance of 99 ft. at the Wyomissing Area High School Gym, Wyomissing, Pennsylvania, USA, on June 18, 1999.

GREATEST DISTANCE MILK SQUIRTED FROM EYE
On Nov. 20, 1998, Jim Cichon of Milford, Pennsylvania, USA, squirted milk from his eye a record distance of 6 ft. 7 in. He performed this feat on the set of *Guinness World Records: Primetime* in Los Angeles, California, USA.

GREATEST DISTANCE CRICKET SPAT
The greatest distance that anyone has spat a dead cricket from their mouth is 10 yds., by Danny Capps of Madison, Wisconsin, USA, on the set of

Guinness World Records: Primetime on June 26, 1998.

GREATEST DISTANCE PUMPKIN SHOT

On Sept. 19, 1998, the *Aludium Q-36 Pumpkin Modulator*, an air cannon built and manned by Matt Parker, Chuck Heerde, Rod Litwiller, Steve Young, and James Knepp, shot a pumpkin a record distance of 1,496 yds. at the Morton Pumpkin Festival, Illinois, USA.

MOST HAMBURGERS STUFFED IN MOUTH

Johnny Reitz (USA) managed to stuff three regulation-sized hamburgers (including buns and condiments) into his mouth at the same time on the set of *Guinness World Records: Primetime* in Los Angeles, California, USA, on June 17, 1998. He was not allowed to swallow any part of the hamburgers.

MOST M&Ms FLIPPED AND CAUGHT

The record for flipping peanut M&Ms from the back of the ear into another person's mouth is 16 in one minute, established by Mark Needem

---

→ **LONGEST ROLL IN A ZORB BALL**

The greatest distance travelled in a Zorb ball in a single roll is 353 yds., by Rich Eley (UK, center) near Glynde, E. Sussex, England, on May 10, 1999. The ball reached a record speed of 31 m.p.h.

(USA), who flipped the candy to his brother Ben on the set of *Guinness World Records: Primetime* in Los Angeles, California, USA, on Aug. 18, 1998.

MOST WORMS EATEN

Mark Hogg of Louisville, Kentucky, USA, holds the record for swallowing the most live worms in 30 seconds, having eaten 62 earthworms on the set of *Guinness World Records: Primetime* in Los Angeles, California, USA, on Nov. 19, 1998.

GREATEST DISTANCE SPAGHETTI SHOT FROM NOSE

On Dec. 16, 1998, Kevin Cole of Carlsbad, New Mexico, USA, ejected a spaghetti strand from his nose a record distance of 7.5 in. He performed this feat on the set of *Guinness World Records: Primetime* in Los Angeles, California, USA.

MOST YO-YO TRICKS

On July 22, 1999, "Fast Eddie" McDonald completed a world record 35 yo-yo tricks in only one minute at the Paulson Street Parket, Toronto, Ontario, Canada.

Endurance 1

LONGEST TIME SPENT IN TREE
Bungkas climbed up a palm tree in the Indonesian village of Bengkes in 1970 and has been there ever since, living in a nest that he made from branches and leaves. Repeated efforts to persuade him to come down have failed.

LONGEST STATIC WALL SIT
Rajkumar Chakraborty (India) stayed in an unsupported sitting position against a wall for 11 hrs. 5 min. at Panposh Sports Hostel, Rourkela, India, on April 22, 1994.

LONGEST TIME SPENT STANDING
The greatest length of time that anyone has spent continuously standing is more than 17 years, by Swami Maujgiri Maharaj (India) between 1955 and 1973, while performing *tapasya* (penance). He would lean against a plank when he was sleeping.

LONGEST TIME SPENT ON TIGHTROPE
The world tightrope endurance record of 205 days was set by Jorge Ojeda-Guzmán from Orlando, Florida, USA, from Jan. 1 to July 25, 1993. The 36-ft.-long wire was 35 ft. above the ground. Ojeda-Guzmán entertained the crowds of spectators by walking, balancing on a chair, and dancing. He had a 3-ft. x 3-ft. wooden cabin at one end of the tightrope.

MOST HOPSCOTCH GAMES IN 24 HOURS
In 24 hours from Jan. 12 to 13, 1998, Ashrita Furman (USA) successfully completed 434 games of hopscotch. The record was set at the Westin Regina Hotel, Cancun, Mexico.

MOST RATTLESNAKES SAT WITH IN BATHTUB
The record for sitting in a bathtub with the most live rattlesnakes is held jointly by Jackie Bibby of Fort Worth, Texas, USA, and Rosie Reynolds of Granbury, Texas, USA. They sat in two separate bathtubs with 75 Western Diamondback rattlesnakes each, on the set of *Guinness World Records: Primetime* in Los Angeles, California, USA, on Sept. 24, 1998.

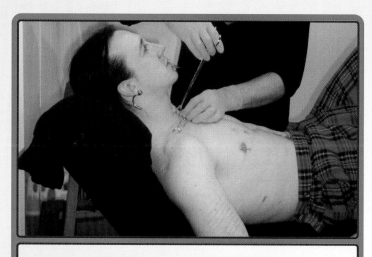

⊙ MOST BODY PIERCINGS IN ONE SESSION
On Sept. 19, 1999, Quille DeSade (New Zealand) received 90 new body piercings in one continuous session, without anesthetic, at the Absolution Body Piercing Studio, Christchurch, New Zealand.

LONGEST MOVIE MARATHON
From July 23 to 25, 1999, Hajnalka Bulla, Gabor Lantai, Tamas Puska, Krisztian Galla, Mark McMenemy, and Zoltan Belebyi watched feature-length movies continuously for 37 hrs. 25 min. at the Hollywood Multiplex, Budapest, Hungary. The 20 movies viewed included *Armageddon* (USA, 1998), *Taxi* (France, 1998), *Face/Off* (USA, 1997), and 107 minutes of *Titanic* (USA, 1997).

⊙ MOST FORWARD-THINKING RAIL TRAVELLER
On Jan. 19, 2000, Fakhruddin Takulla (India) travelled from Mumbai (Bombay) to New Delhi, both India, using a ticket he had purchased on July 15, 1973 – 26 years, 6 months earlier. Takulla used the unlimited reservation service offered by the Indian Railway Authority so that he could attend the celebrations marking the 50th anniversary of Indian Independence.

LONGEST RADIO DJ MARATHON

DJ Albert Vierhuis (Netherlands), who works for LOE Radio, played records in Elburg, Netherlands, for a total of 60 hours from midnight on April 24, 2000, to 12 p.m. on April 26, 2000.

LONGEST ARCADE MACHINE DANCE MARATHON

Mark e.t. of London, England, danced on Konami's *Dancing Stage* arcade machine for a record eight hours at the Trocadero, London, England, on March 10, 1999.

LONGEST DANCE MARATHON

The world's most taxing marathon dance ever staged as a public spectacle was performed by Mike Ritof and Edith Boudreaux, who logged 5,148 hrs. 28 min. to win $2,000 at the Merry Garden Ballroom, Chicago, Illinois, USA, from Aug. 29, 1930, to April 1, 1931. Their rest periods were progressively cut from 20 minutes per hour to 10, to 5, to no rest periods at all. Their dance steps were required to be at least 10 in. long, and they were only allowed to close their eyes for 15 seconds at a time.

LONGEST CPR MARATHON

The world's longest cardiopulmonary resuscitation marathon took place from Sept. 20 to 26, 1998, at Merry Hill Shopping Centre, West Midlands, England. Two teams of two – Ben Albutt and Phil Watson, and Robert Cole and Daren Fradgley – performed CPR (15 compressions alternating with two breaths) on a dummy for 144 hours. The men were all members of the West Midlands Ambulance Service.

LONGEST CLAPPING SESSION

The record for continuous clapping (sustaining an average of 160 claps per minute, audible from 120 yds. away) is a record 58 hrs. 9 min., by V. Jeyaraman of Tamil Nadu, India, from Feb. 12 to 15, 1988.

LONGEST LESSON

A Hungarian language and literature lesson taught at Leõwey Klára Grammar School, Pécs, Hungary, by Szabolcs Zalay lasted for a record 24 hours from June 18 to 19, 1999. It was attended by 34 students.

← LONGEST KISS

On April 5, 1999, Karmit Tsubera (left) and Dror Orpaz kissed for a record 30 hrs. 45 min. to win a kissing contest held in Rabin Square, Tel Aviv, Israel. A total of 107 couples took part in the event.

23

Endurance 2

LONGEST UNICYCLE RIDE
Hanspeter Beck (Australia) unicycled 3,876 miles across Australia from Port Hedland, Western Australia, to Melbourne, Victoria, from June 30 to Aug. 20, 1985.

LONGEST HORSE RIDE IN ARMOR
The greatest distance ridden while wearing armor is 208 miles, by Dick Brown (UK). He left Edinburgh, Scotland, on June 10, 1989, and arrived in his hometown of Dumfries four days later. His ride lasted for a total of 35 hrs. 25 min.

LONGEST WALK ON HANDS
The greatest distance covered by a person walking on their hands is 870 miles, by Johann Hurlinger (Austria) in 1900. He walked from Vienna, Austria, to Paris, France, in 55 daily 10-hour stints, averaging a speed of 1.58 m.p.h.

LONGEST BACKWARD WALK
From April 15, 1931, to Oct. 24, 1932, Plennie Wingo (USA) walked backward from Santa Monica, California, USA, to Istanbul, Turkey – a record backward-walking distance of 8,000 miles.

LONGEST BACKWARD RUNS
Arvind Pandya (India) ran backward across the USA from Los Angeles, California, to New York City in 107 days between Aug. 18 and Dec. 3, 1984. He also ran backward from John O' Groats, Scotland, to Land's End, England, in 26 days 7 hrs. between April 6 and May 2, 1990, covering a total distance of 940 miles.

LONGEST CRAWLS
The longest continuous crawl on record (defined as progression with one or other of the knees in unbroken contact with the ground) is 31.4 miles, by Peter McKinlay and John Murrie. They covered 115 laps of a running track at Falkirk, Scotland, on March 28–29, 1992.

From Dec. 1983 to March 1985, Jagdish Chander (India) crawled 870 miles from Aligarh to Jammu, India. He made the journey in order to appease the Hindu goddess Mata.

GREATEST DISTANCE RIDDEN ON ESCALATORS
Arulanantham Suresh Joachim (Sri Lanka) travelled a total distance of 140 miles on escalators at the Westfield Shopping Centre, Barwood, NSW, Australia, from May 25 to 31, 1998. His ride lasted for 145 hrs. 57 min.

LONGEST LEAPFROG
The longest leapfrog is 996.2 miles, by 14 students from Stanford University, California, USA. They began on May 16, 1991, and stopped 244 hrs. 43 min, later, on May 26, 1991.

GREATEST DISTANCE COVERED WHILE CARRYING A BRICK
The greatest distance over which a brick weighing 9 lbs. (4 kg.) has been carried in a nominated ungloved hand in an uncradled downward pincer grip is 82.2 miles, by Manjit Singh (UK) on Nov. 6–7, 1998.

The women's record is 22.5 miles, by Wendy Morris (UK) on April 28, 1986.

GREATEST DISTANCE TRAVELLED IN A BATHTUB
The greatest distance covered in 24 hours by paddling a bathtub on still water using the hands is 90.5 miles, by 13 members of the Aldington Prison Officers Social Club, Kent, England, from May 28 to 29, 1983.

⊙ **LONGEST TIME BALANCED ON FOOT**
Arulanantham Suresh Joachim (Sri Lanka) balanced on one foot for a record 76 hrs. 40 min. at Uihara Maha Devi Park Open Air Stadium, Sri Lanka, from May 22 to 25, 1997.

LONGEST BATHTUB PUSH
The record for the greatest distance covered in 24 hours while pushing a wheeled bathtub with a passenger inside is 318.97 miles, by a team of 25 people from the Tea Tree Gully Baptist Church, NSW, Australia, between March 11 and 12, 1995.

⊙ **LONGEST TIME SPENT IN AN ATTIC**
Stephan Kovaltchuk spent 57 years in his attic in Montchintsi, Ukraine, before emerging at the age of 75 in Sept. 1999 because his sister, who had looked after him, had died. Having originally gone into hiding from the Nazis, who occupied Ukraine in 1942, he remained in isolation to avoid the draft by the Russians after the Red Army's victory over the Germans.

⊙ LONGEST NONSTOP OCEAN SWIM BY A WOMAN

In 1998, Susie Maroney (Australia) became the first person to swim from Mexico to Cuba, also setting the record for the greatest distance swum without flippers in open sea. She swam 122 miles from Isla Mujeres, Mexico, to Cabo San Antonio, Cuba, in 38 hrs. 33 min., arriving on June 1, 1998.

LONGEST BARREL ROLL

In 24 hours from Nov. 28 to 29, 1998, a team of 10 people from Groningen, Netherlands, rolled a 140-lb. barrel a record distance of 164.1 miles. The event occurred at Stadspark, Rotterdam, Netherlands.

LONGEST KITE FLIGHT

From Aug. 21 to 29, 1982, a team from Edmonds Community College (USA), led by Harry Osborne, flew a kite for a record time of 180 hrs. 17 min. at Long Beach, Washington State, USA.

LONGEST CAR PUSH

The greatest distance that a car has been pushed in 24 hours is 32.6 miles, by Sangion Daniele and Valente Giorgio (both Italy). The record was set in Venice, Italy, from Oct. 17 to 18, 1998. The car was a Fiat Uno 60.

↓ LONGEST TYPEWRITING MARATHON

Les Stewart of Mudjimba Beach, Queensland, Australia, spent 16 years typing the numbers 1 to 1,000,000 on 19,990 sheets of paper. Starting in 1982, he made the final keystroke on Dec. 7, 1998.

Teamwork 1

BIGGEST GAME OF PASS-THE-ORANGE
The biggest ever game of "pass-the-orange" was played on the Granada TV program *This Morning* (UK) on March 25, 1999. A record 92 people took part.

BIGGEST GAME OF MUSICAL CHAIRS
The biggest game of musical chairs was played at the Anglo-Chinese School, Singapore, on Aug. 5, 1989. It started with 8,238 participants and ended with pupil Xu Chong Wei on the last chair.

BIGGEST "RING-O'ROSES"
On Aug. 4, 1999, 1,296 people joined hands to enact the nursery rhyme "Ring-A-Ring-O'Roses" at Sutton-in-Ashfield, Nottinghamshire, England.

⊙ BIGGEST HUMAN LOGO
On July 24, 1999, a total of 34,309 people gathered at the National Stadium of Jamor, Lisbon, Portugal, to create the Portuguese Euro 2004 logo as part of the country's successful bid to host the soccer tournament.
The event was organized by Realizar Eventos Especias.

⊙ MOST PEOPLE BLOWING BUBBLES
On May 16, 1999, before a soccer match at West Ham United's Boleyn Ground, London, England, a total of 23,680 people blew bubbles for one minute. West Ham's anthem is "I'm Forever Blowing Bubbles."

LONGEST PAPER-CLIP CHAIN
The world's longest ever paper-clip chain had a record length of 19.62 miles. It was made in 24 hours by 60 people in an event organized jointly by Wall's Ice Cream and the Care Community Services Society, and was displayed in the atrium of Plaza Singapura, Singapore, on April 3, 1999.

LONGEST PAPER CHAIN
A paper chain with a length of 51.8 miles, consisting of 584,000 links, was made in 24 hours by 60 people at Alvin Community College, Alvin, Texas, USA, on Oct. 23, 1998.

LONGEST DAISY CHAIN
The world's longest ever daisy chain was a record 1.32 miles in length. It was made in seven hours by a team of 16 villagers from Good Easter, near Chelmsford, Essex, England, on May 27, 1985.

LONGEST BUCKET CHAIN
On Aug. 5, 1997, a total of 6,569 boys representing Boy Scouts of America made a fire department bucket chain that stretched for a record 2.6 miles at the National Scout Jamboree, Fort AP Hills, Virginia, USA. The scouts started with 140 gal. of water and ended with 126 gal.

BIGGEST CLEANUP OF LITTER
The greatest number of volunteers involved in collecting litter in one location on one day is 50,405. The cleanup took place along the coastline of California, USA, on Oct. 2, 1993.

MOST TREES PLANTED IN A DAY
On May 18, 1999, a total of 34,083 year-old native white spruce seedlings were planted in the Blackfoot Provincial

Recreation Area, Alberta, Canada. The record was set by 293 members of staff, students, and parents from Fultonvale Elementary and Junior High School, Alberta.

MOST KISSING COUPLES
The greatest number of couples to have kissed in the same location at the same time is 1,588, at the Sarnia Sports and Entertainment Center, Ontario, Canada, on Feb. 13, 1999.

BIGGEST HUMAN CENTIPEDE
The biggest human centipede to have moved 30 m. (98 ft. 5 in.), with its members' ankles tied firmly together and without falling over, consisted of 1,719 students and volunteers from the Sixth Form College, Colchester, Essex, England. They set the record on Nov. 20, 1997.

BIGGEST HUMAN CONVEYOR BELT
The world's largest human conveyor belt was formed Sept. 7, 1998, by 1,000 students from the University of Guelph, Ontario, Canada. The "belt" carried a surfboard along its entire length.

BIGGEST HUMAN RAINBOW
On Nov. 9, 1997, a record 6,444 people, each of them wearing a hat and a T-shirt in one of the colors of the rainbow, formed a "human rainbow" at Transco Tower Park, Houston, Texas, USA.

BIGGEST FRIENDSHIP CIRCLE
On Nov. 7, 1998, a grand total of 6,244 Girl Scouts and their guests linked their hands, crossing their right arm over their left, made a wish, and sang a song for 9 min. 3.9 sec. at Six Flags AstroWorld, Houston, Texas, USA.

BIGGEST COFFEE MORNING
On Oct. 4, 1996, a record 513,659 people attended 14,652 coffee mornings held simultaneously throughout the UK as part of Macmillan Cancer Relief's Macmillan Appeal. The event raised a total sum $28.46 million for the charity.

BIGGEST EASTER EGG HUNT
The world's largest ever Easter egg hunt took place on March 20, 1999, during the Vision Australia Foundation's annual Easter Fair at Kooyong, Victoria, Australia. A total of 150,000 solid chocolate eggs were found by 3,000 volunteers.

⊙ MOST PEOPLE GUNGED
On March 12, 1999, two tanks, each containing 184 gal. of "gunge," were emptied over 731 people at the National Exhibition Centre, Birmingham, England, to raise money for the charity Comic Relief.

BIGGEST BUNNY HOP
On March 28, 1999, a record total of 1,241 participants put on bunny ears, formed a continuous line, and hopped along like rabbits for the required five minutes. The record was set at Walt Disney World, Orlando, Florida, USA.

↓ BIGGEST MOTORCYCLE PYRAMID
The world's biggest motorcycle pyramid was formed by Shwet Ashwas, the Motorcycle Display Team of the Corps of Military Police, India, on Oct. 15, 1999. The pyramid consisted of 151 men riding for 235 yds. on 11 motorcycles.

Teamwork 2

BIGGEST TAP DANCE
A record 6,776 tap dancers performed a two-minute routine to the tune of "Puttin' On The Ritz" outside Macy's department store, New York City, USA, on Aug. 17, 1997.

LONGEST TAP DANCE
On July 11, 1994, Rosie Radiator led an ensemble of 12 tap dancers through the streets of San Francisco, California, USA, in a choreographed routine. The group covered a total distance of 9.61 miles.

BIGGEST "YMCA" DANCE
On Nov. 1, 1997, a record 6,907 students from Southwest Missouri State University, Springfield, Missouri, USA, danced to the song "YMCA" for five minutes while it was being performed live by the group Village People at the university's Plaster Stadium.

BIGGEST CHICKEN DANCE
An estimated 72,000 people took part in a Chicken Dance staged during the Canfield Fair, Canfield, Ohio, USA, on Sept, 1, 1996.

⊙ **BIGGEST HUG**
On Dec. 18, 1998, a total of 462 people, including students, teachers, parents, and guests of Brock Corydon School, Winnipeg, Manitoba, Canada, took part in the world's biggest hug. The event was staged as part of a citizenship program being run at the school, and was intended to teach the children respect and tolerance for other people.

BIGGEST COUNTRY LINE DANCE
On Jan. 29, 2000, a total of 6,275 people took part in a country line dance in Tamworth, NSW, Australia. They danced to Brooks and Dunns' extended play version of "Bootscooting Boogie," which lasts for 6 min. 28 sec.

BIGGEST SCOTTISH COUNTRY DANCE
The largest genuine Scottish country dance on record was a 512-some reel staged in Toronto, Canada, on Aug. 17, 1991. The reel was organized by the Toronto branch of the Royal Scottish Country Dance Society.

LONGEST CONGA
The world's longest conga was the Miami Super Conga, which was formed on March 13, 1988, and consisted of 119,986 people. The record was set in conjunction with *Calle Ocho*, a Cuban-American celebration of life in Miami, Florida, USA.

⊙ **BIGGEST AEROBICS DISPLAY**
The world's largest ever aerobics display was Capital Aeróbica, which was organized by the University of Guadalajara, Mexico, and took place at Metropolitan Park, Mexico, on June 6, 1998. A record 38,633 people took part.

MOST HEADS SHAVED IN 24 HOURS

In 24 hours from April 16 to 17, 1999, 1,786 people had their heads shaved at various locations across Australia. The event was staged in support of the Leukaemia Foundation of Australia and raised $571,738.

BIGGEST CUSTARD PIE FIGHT

On April 11, 2000, a total of 20 people threw a record 3,312 custard pies in three minutes at the Millennium Dome, London, England.

MOST TEETH CLEANED SIMULTANEOUSLY

On April 19, 1999, a total of 1,365 people participated in the Healthy Smiles Partnership Brush-off in Phoenix, Arizona, USA, by brushing their teeth simultaneously for 3 min. 3 sec.

MOST BABIES BREAST-FED SIMULTANEOUSLY

A total of 388 women breast-fed their babies at the same time at the Greater Union Megaplex Marion Cinema, Adelaide, South Australia, on Aug. 5, 1999. The record was set as part of Breastfest '99: The Great Challenge, organized by the South Australian College of Lactation Consultants.

MOST PEOPLE USING SIGN LANGUAGE SIMULTANEOUSLY

On May 8, 1999, a record 1,336 elementary school students and their teachers took part in the largest sign language session, at Stevens Point, Wisconsin, USA. They all hand signed "America the Beautiful."

MOST SHOES SHINED

The greatest number of shoes shined "on the hoof" by four people in eight hours is 14,975, by members of the London Church of Christ at Leicester Square, London, England, on June 15, 1996.

LOUDEST SCREAM BY A CROWD

A scream registering a record 126.3 decibels was measured by Trevor Lewis of CEL Instruments at The Party in the Park pop concert, Hyde Park, London, England, on July 5, 1998. The concert featured stars such as Robbie Williams, Boyzone, and All Saints.

LOUDEST APPLAUSE

An audience at the BBC's *Big Bash* event, held from Oct. 24 to 27, 1997, at the National Exhibition Centre, Birmingham, England, registered applause of a record 100 decibels. The audience was not allowed to add to the noise level by stamping their feet or screaming.

BIGGEST GATHERING OF TWINS

On Nov. 12, 1999, a record 3,961 pairs of twins gathered at Taipei City Hall, Taiwan.

BIGGEST FAMILY REUNION

On June 28, 1998, a total of 2,369 members of the Busse family attended a reunion at Grayslake, Illinois, USA. The gathering celebrated the 150th anniversary of the arrival of Friedrich and Johanna Busse, the designated founders of the family, in the USA.

FASTEST BARE-HANDED HOUSE DEMOLITION

On May 11, 1996, a total of 15 members of the Aurora Karate Dojo demolished a 10-room house in Saskatchewan, Canada, using their bare hands, in 3 hrs. 6 min. 50 sec.

↓ LONGEST DANCING DRAGON

On Feb. 19, 2000, a record 3,333-yd.-long Chinese dancing dragon was brought to life by 3,200 people at the Great Wall of China, near Beijing. The record was set to celebrate the Chinese Year of the Dragon.

Adventures & Journeys 1

FASTEST CIRCUMNAVIGATION

The fastest flight under the FAI (Fédération Aéronautique Internationale) rules, which permit flights that exceed the length of the Tropic of Cancer or Capricorn (22,859.4 miles), was one of 31 hrs. 27 min. 49 sec. Captains Michel Dupont and Claude Hetru (both France) flew an Air France Concorde from JFK airport, New York, USA, eastbound via Toulouse, Dubai, Bangkok, Guam, Honolulu, and Acapulco, from Aug. 15 to 16, 1995. There were 80 passengers and 18 crew onboard flight AF1995.

FASTEST CIRCUMNAVIGATION ON SCHEDULED FLIGHTS

The fastest circumnavigation under FAI regulations using scheduled flights is 44 hrs. 6 min., by David J. Springbett of Taplow, Buckinghamshire, England. His route took him from Los Angeles, California, USA, eastbound via London, Bahrain, Singapore, Bangkok, Manila, Tokyo, and Honolulu, over a course of 23,069 miles, from Jan. 8 to 10, 1980.

David J. Springbett has, with brother Michael Bartlett (also UK), completed an antipodal circumnavigation of the globe, finishing in 62 hrs. 15 min. between March 18 and 21, 2000. In total they covered 25,484 miles on their journey between London, Seoul, Auckland, Palmerston North, Ti Tree Point (the point exactly opposite Madrid), Palmerston North, Auckland, Los Angeles, Chicago, Madrid, and London.

FASTEST CIRCUMNAVIGATION BY HELICOPTER

Ron Bower and John Williams (both USA) flew around the world in a Bell 430 helicopter in just 17 days 6 hrs. 14 min. 25 sec., at an average speed of 57.02 m.p.h. They left Fair Oaks, Chobham, Surrey, England, on Aug. 17, 1996, and flew westbound, arriving back at Fair Oaks on Sept. 3, 1996.

Jennifer Murray became the first female to fly around the world in a helicopter with co-pilot Quentin Smith (both UK).

⊙ LONGEST LAWN MOWER RIDE

Brad Hauter of Lake in the Hills, Illinois, USA, rode a lawn mower 4,039 miles through 16 states in 51 days. Hauter began the journey on April 7, 1999, in Atlanta, Georgia, and finished, despite sustaining a fractured arm, at Santa Monica, California, USA, on May 29, 1999.

⊙ MOST POLAR ADVENTURES IN A DAY

Ivan André Trifonov (Austria) has been under, on, and over the North Pole in the space of a day. He dived 42.7 ft. under, stood upon, and flew for 21.8 miles over the pole in an *OE-KZT* balloon, at an altitude of 4,921 ft., on April 27, 1999. The record was set as part of a 16-nation expedition to the North Pole in which six balloons took part.

They set the record in a Robinson R44 Astro at an average speed of 13.94 m.ph.. They left Denham, Buckinghamshire, England, on May 10, 1997, and flew eastbound, arriving back at Denham on Aug. 8, 1997.

FIRST BALLOON CIRCUMNAVIGATION

Brian Jones (UK) and Bertrand Piccard (Switzerland), piloting the *Breitling Orbiter 3*, passed the "finishing line" of 9.27° over Mauritania, North Africa, to become the first balloonists to circle the world nonstop, on March 20, 1999. They took 19 days 1 hr. 49 min. to fly 26,602 miles, setting off from Chateau d'Oex, Switzerland, on March 1, 1999. They conquered one of the last great aviation challenges –

to balloon nonstop around the globe.

FASTEST MICROLIGHT CIRCUMNAVIGATION
On July 21, 1998, Brian Milton landed at Brooklands, Surrey, England, having completed a 121-day trip around the world in a microlight. On March 22, 1998, he took off from Brooklands and flew via western Europe, Turkey and the Middle East, India, Southeast Asia, Hong Kong, Japan, Russia, North America, Greenland, and Iceland.

FASTEST CIRCUMNAVIGATION IN A POWER VESSEL
On July 3, 1998, the *Cable & Wireless Adventurer* circumnavigated the world in 74 days 20 hr. 58 min. 30 sec. The 38.33-yd.-long boat travelled more than 26,000 miles, breaking the 38-year-old record set by *USS Triton*, a submarine that circumnavigated the globe in 83 days 9 hrs. 54 min.

FASTEST TRANSATLANTIC FLIGHT
The transatlantic flight record is 1 hr. 54 min. 56.4 sec., set by Majors James Sullivan and Noel Widdifield (both USA), flying a Lockheed SR-71A Blackbird eastbound, on Sept. 1, 1974. The average speed for the 3,461.63-mile-long New York–London journey, reduced by refueling from a Boeing KC-135 tanker aircraft, was 1,807 m.p.h.

FASTEST PACIFIC CROSSING
The 50,315-ton container ship *Sea-Land Commerce* crossed the Pacific in just 6 days 1 hr. 27 min., covering a distance of 4,840 nautical miles (5,570 miles). The ship travelled from Yokohama, Japan, to Long Beach, California, USA, making the journey from June 30 to July 6, 1973, at an average speed of 33.27 knots (38.26 m.p.h.).

⊙ FASTEST CAPE-TO-CAIRO RUN
Nicholas Bourne (UK) set off from Cape Town, South Africa, on Jan. 21, 1998, arriving at the Great Pyramids, Cairo, Egypt, on Dec. 5, 1998. He ran over 7,500 miles.

LONGEST HOVERCRAFT JOURNEY
The longest hovercraft journey was 4,971 miles, achieved by the British Trans-African Hovercraft Expedition, under the leadership of David Smithers (UK). The team went through eight West African countries in a Winchester class SRN6, between Oct. 15, 1969, and Jan. 3, 1970.

MOST SUCCESSFUL MOUNTAINEER
Reinhold Messner (Italy) was the first person to successfully scale all 14 of the world's highest mountains (over 6,247 ft. or 8,000 m.), all without oxygen. He was also the first to climb the world's three highest mountains when, having reached the summits of Everest and K2, he ascended Kanchenjunga in 1982.

FIRST SOLO EXPEDITION TO SOUTH POLE
The first person to reach the South Pole, solo and unsupported, was Erling Kagge (Norway), after an 870-mile 50-day trek from Berkner Island, Antarctica, on Jan. 7, 1993.

FIRST SOLO EXPEDITIONS TO NORTH POLE
Naomi Uemura (Japan) became the first person to reach the North Pole in a solo trek across the Arctic sea-ice at 4:45 am GMT on May 1, 1978. He had travelled 450 miles, setting out on March 7 from Cape Edward, Ellesmere Island, Canada.

Dr. Jean-Louis Etienne of France was the first person to reach the North Pole solo without dogs, after 63 days, on May 11, 1986.

FASTEST ANTARCTIC CROSSING
The 2,600-mile Trans-Antarctic leg, from Sanae to Scott Base, of the 1980–2 Trans-Globe Expedition was achieved on snowmobiles in 67 days – from Oct. 28, 1980, to Jan. 11, 1981. The three-man expedition, which reached the South Pole on Dec. 15, 1980, as part of its journey, comprised Ranulph Fiennes, Oliver Shepard, and Charles Burton (all UK).

LONGEST ANTARCTIC TREK
The longest unsupported trek in Antarctica was by team-leader Ranulph Fiennes, with Mike Stroud (both UK), who set off from Gould Bay on Nov. 9, 1992, reaching the South Pole on Jan. 16, 1993. They finally abandoned their walk on the Ross ice shelf on Feb. 11, after covering 1,348 miles over their 94-day trek.

LONGEST SNOWMOBILE JOURNEY
Tony Lenzini of Duluth, Minnesota, USA, drove his 1986 Arctic Cat Cougar snowmobile a total of 7,211 miles, in 60 riding days, between Dec. 28, 1985, and March 20, 1986.

Adventures & Journeys 2

MOST TRAVELLED MAN
John Clouse from Evansville, Indiana, USA, has visited all of the independent countries and all but two of the non-independent or other territories that existed in early 1999. He began his travels 40 years ago.

MOST TRAVELLED COUPLE
The world's most travelled couple are Robert and Carmen Becker of Pompano Beach, Florida, USA. They have both visited all of the independent countries and all but seven of the non-independent or other territories.

LONGEST WALKS
The greatest distance that has been walked is 33,152 miles, by Arthur Blessitt of North Fort Myers, Florida, USA. He began his travels on Dec. 25, 1969, and has since visited 277 countries on all seven continents. Blessitt has carried a 12.1-ft. wooden cross with him throughout, preaching as he goes.

The first person reputed to have walked around the world was George Schilling (USA), who achieved this feat between Aug. 1897 and 1904. The first verified around-the-world walk was made by David Kunst (USA), who travelled 14,450 miles across four continents between June 20, 1970, and Oct. 5, 1974.

The greatest distance ever walked by a woman is 18,841 miles, by Ffyona Campbell (UK), who trekked around the world in five phases, through four continents and 20 countries. Campbell originally set off from John O' Groats, Scotland, on Aug. 16, 1983. She returned there on Oct. 14, 1994.

LONGEST WHEELCHAIR JOURNEY
Rick Hansen (Canada), who was paralyzed from the waist down in 1973 following a traffic accident, travelled a record 24,902.23 miles by wheelchair

⊙ FASTEST ASCENT OF MOUNT EVEREST
Babu Chhiri (Nepal, front of picture) reached the 29,029-ft. summit of Mount Everest in 16 hrs. 56 min. on May 21, 2000. He took over three hours off the previous record, set by Kaji Sherpa (behind Chhiri) in 1998. It was the 10th time Chhiri had scaled the world's highest peak.

through four continents and 34 countries between March 21, 1985, and May 22, 1987.

LONGEST CAR JOURNEY
Since Oct. 1984, Emil and Liliana Schmid (Switzerland) have travelled a record distance of 316,195 miles in a Toyota Landcruiser. Their journey has taken them through 127 countries.

LONGEST MOTORCYCLE JOURNEY
Emilio Scotto of Buenos Aires, Argentina, travelled a distance of over 456,720 miles by motorcycle between Jan. 17, 1985, and April 2, 1995, visiting 214 countries.

FASTEST MOTORCYCLE CIRCUMNAVIGATION
Nick Sanders (UK) motorcycled around the world in a record 31 days 20 hrs. from April 18 to June 9, 1997, covering a distance of 19,930 miles. Sanders started and finished in Calais, France.

FASTEST CAR CIRCUMNAVIGATIONS
Garry Sowerby, Colin Bryant, and Graham McGaw circumnavigated the world in a Vauxhall Frontera in 21 days 2 hrs. 14 min. between Oct. 1 and Dec. 11, 1997. They travelled a total distance of 18,345 miles, starting and finishing in Greenwich, London, England.

The record for the first and fastest circumnavigation of the world by car, made under the rules applicable in 1989 and 1991, embracing more than an equator's length of driving (24,901.41 road miles), is held by Mohammed Salahuddin Choudhury and his wife Neena of Calcutta, India. Their journey took 69 days 19 hrs. 5 min. from Sept. 9 to Nov. 17, 1989. The Choudhurys drove a Hindustan "Contessa Classic" 1989 car, starting and finishing in New Delhi, India.

⊙ LONGEST WINDSURFING JOURNEY
In 1997, Steve Fisher (USA) crossed the Pacific Ocean from California, USA, to Hawaii, USA, on *Da Slipper II,* a highly modified 17.7-ft. Windsurfer. The 2,612-mile journey took him 47 days, and he arrived on Maui Beach, Hawaii, on Sept. 3, 1997.

LONGEST BICYCLE JOURNEYS

Walter Stolle (Germany) bicycled a distance of more than 402,000 miles between Jan. 24, 1959, and Dec. 12, 1976, visiting 159 countries.

Tal Burt (Israel) circumnavigated the world in 77 days 14 hrs. from June 1 to Aug. 17, 1992. He travelled a total distance of 13,254 miles, starting and finishing in Paris, France.

The greatest distance ever covered on a tandem bicycle is 23,701 miles, by Phil and Louise Shambrook (NZ). They set out from Brigg, Lincolnshire, England, on Dec. 17, 1994, and returned there on Oct. 1, 1997.

GREATEST DISTANCE KITE SURFED

On Sept. 17, 1999, Chris Calthrop, Jason Furness, and Andy Preston, all representing the kite manufacturer Flexifoil International (UK), crossed the English Channel on kite surfers, custom-made boards attached to blade traction kites that have an area of 52.7 ft.^{2} They covered the 26.7 miles from Hythe, England, to Wissant, France, in times which ranged from 2 hrs. 30 min. to 3 hrs.

FASTEST TRANS-AMERICA SKATEBOARD CROSSINGS

Jack Smith (USA) skateboarded across the USA twice: in 1976 and 1984. The first trip, which he made with two companions, took 32 days to complete, and the second trip, made with three other people, took 26 days.

MOST COUNTRIES TRAVELLED THROUGH BY TRAIN IN 24 HOURS

On May 1–2, 1993, Alison Bailey, Ian Bailey, John English, and David Kellie travelled through a record 11 countries by train. They started their journey in Hungary and continued through Slovakia, the Czech Republic, Austria, Germany, Switzerland, Liechtenstein, France, Luxembourg, and Belgium before arriving in the Netherlands 22 hrs. 10 min. after they set off.

LONGEST HORSE-DRAWN JOURNEY

The Grant family (UK) travelled more than 17,181 miles during an around-the-world trip in a horse-drawn trailer. They began their journey in the Netherlands on Oct. 25, 1990, and ended it in the UK in early 1998.

☉ FIRST FEMALE TEAM TO REACH BOTH POLES

Caroline Hamilton, Ann Daniels, Pom Oliver, Rosie Stancer, and Zoe Hudson (all UK) completed a trek to the South Pole on Jan. 24, 2000, having reached the North Pole in 1997. They were raising funds for the charity Special Olympics, UK.

→ FASTEST SOLAR-POWERED PACIFIC CROSSING

In 1996, Kenichi Horie (Japan) made the fastest ever crossing of the Pacific in a solar-powered boat when he travelled 10,000 miles from Salinas, Ecuador, to Tokyo, Japan, in 148 days.

Disasters

WORST TRAIN DISASTER
Over 800 people died when the train they were travelling on plunged off a bridge into the Bagmati River at Samastipur, Bihar, India, on June 6, 1981. Some reports put the death toll as high as 900.

WORST UNDERGROUND TRAIN DISASTER
Approximately 300 people were killed, and at least 250 injured, when their underground train caught fire in a tunnel between two stations in Baku, Azerbaijan, on Oct. 28, 1995.

WORST FERRYBOAT DISASTER
In the early hours of Dec. 21, 1987, the ferryboat *Doña Paz*, which was sailing from Tacloban to Manila, Philippines, collided with the tanker *Vector*. Both vessels sank within minutes. The *Doña Paz* was officially carrying 1,550 passengers, but overcrowding is common in the region and it may actually have held as many as 4,000.

WORST EXPLOSION ON BOARD A SHIP
On Dec. 17, 1917, the French freighter *Mont Blanc*, which was packed with 5,000 tons of explosives and combustibles, collided with the Belgian ship *Imo* in Halifax Harbour, Nova Scotia, Canada. The resulting blast killed a total of 1,635 people, and could be felt at a distance of more than 59 miles.

WORST YACHT RACING DISASTER
During the 28th Fastnet Race, held from Aug. 13 to 15, 1979, a total of 19 people died when 23 yachts sank or were abandoned in a Force 11 gale.

WORST SUBMARINE DISASTER
On Jan. 30, 1945, a total of 7,700 people were killed when the 25,484-ton German liner *Wilhelm Gustloff* was torpedoed by a Soviet S-13 submarine off Danzig (now Gdansk), Poland.

WORST ROAD TUNNEL DISASTER
Approximately 176 people died when a gas tanker exploded inside the Salang Tunnel, Afghanistan, on Nov. 3, 1982.

WORST AIR DISASTER
The world's worst ever air disaster took place on March 27, 1977, when two Boeing 747s, operated by Pan-Am and KLM, collided on the runway at Los Rodeos Airport, Tenerife, Canary Islands. A total of 583 people were killed.

WORST MIDAIR COLLISION
On Nov. 12, 1996, a total of 351 people died when a Saudi Boeing 747 scheduled flight collided in midair with a Kazakh Illushin 76 charter flight 50 miles southwest of New Delhi, India.

WORST HELICOPTER DISASTER
A Russian military helicopter carrying 61 refugees was shot down near Lata, Georgia, on Dec. 14, 1992. Everyone on board was killed.

WORST BALLOONING DISASTER
The hot-air balloon accident that has resulted in the greatest loss of life took place on Aug. 13, 1989, when two passenger balloons, launched a few minutes apart for a sightseeing flight over Alice Springs, Northern Territory, Australia, collided at a height of 2,000 ft. The basket of one of the balloons tore a hole in the fabric of the other, which then collapsed, sending the pilot and 12 passengers to their deaths.

WORST SKI LIFT DISASTER
The world's worst ever ski lift accident occurred in the resort of Cavalese, Italy, on March 9, 1976. A total of 42 people died when a lift cable ruptured and the lift tumbled to the valley floor.

⊙ WORST SPACE DISASTER
On Jan. 28, 1986, all seven people on board *Challenger 51L* were killed when the craft exploded 73 seconds after liftoff from the Kennedy Space Center, Florida, USA.

WORST MOUNTAINEERING DISASTER
On July 13, 1990, a total of 43 climbers were killed in a massive snow and ice avalanche on the slopes of Peak Lenin, on the border between Tajikistan and Kyrgyzstan (formerly USSR). Only two members of the group survived.

WORST FIRE DISASTER
During the sack of Moscow, Russia, in May 1571, approximately 200,000 people were reported to have perished as a result of fires started by invading Tartars.

⊙ WORST ELEVATOR ACCIDENT
A total of 105 people were killed when an elevator operating at the Vaal Reefs gold mine, South Africa, fell 1,608 ft. on May 11, 1995.

⊙ WORST SINGLE-AIRCRAFT DISASTER

A total of 520 people were killed when a JAL Boeing 747, flight 123, crashed between Tokyo and Osaka, Japan, on Aug. 12, 1985.

WORST FIREWORK DISASTER

In May 1770, approximately 800 people died in an accident that took place during a fireworks display held beside the River Seine in Paris, France.

WORST SPORT DISASTERS

An estimated 604 people were killed when the stands at the Hong Kong Jockey Club racecourse, Hong Kong, collapsed and caught fire on Feb. 26, 1918.

A total of 1,112 spectators were killed when the upper tiers of the Circus Maximus, Rome, Italy, collapsed during a gladiatorial combat held during the reign of Antoninus Pius (138–161 A.D.).

BIGGEST MASS SUICIDE

In 73 A.D., approximately 960 Jewish Zealots committed mass suicide by cutting one another's throats at the fortified palace of Masada, Israel, as it was being besieged by the Romans. The incident was recorded by the historian Flavius Josephus (ca. 37–100 A.D.).

WORST DAM DISASTER

In Aug. 1975, the Banqiao and Shimantan Dams burst almost simultaneously, flooding Henan Province, China, and causing the deaths of approximately 230,000 people. The disaster was caused by a combination of geological problems and structural weaknesses.

↓ WORST JOSS STICK DISASTER

On Nov. 2, 1998, five Buddhist worshipers were killed when three giant ceremonial joss sticks collapsed at the Phra Pathom Jedi Temple, 36 miles northwest of Bangkok, Thailand. The 79–89-ft. joss sticks had been built in April 1998 to commemorate the 84th anniversary of the construction of an image of Buddha at the temple. Although the cause of the accident is unclear, the joss sticks could have collapsed under their own weight as they had soaked up a substantial amount of rain.

WORST THEATER FIRE DISASTER

A total of 1,670 people were killed in a fire at The Theatre, Guangzhou, China, in May 1845.

WORST CIRCUS FIRE DISASTER

A total of 168 people died in a fire which broke out during a circus performance in Hartford, Connecticut, USA, on July 6, 1944.

Survivors & Lifesavers

⊙ LONGEST MOUNTAIN FALL SURVIVED

In Jan. 2000, Flight Lieutenant Jeanine Godfrey, an officer with the British Royal Air Force, fell 1,299 ft. down a Scottish mountain, landing on snow-covered rocks. She sustained severe head and spinal injuries, but is expected to make a full recovery.

LONGEST ELEVATOR FALL SURVIVED

On Jan. 25, 2000, US office workers Shameka Peterson and Joe Mascora fell 40 floors (397 ft.) in four seconds in an elevator at the Empire State Building, New York City, USA. The elevator stopped just four floors from the ground, thanks to its safety mechanism, and Peterson and Mascora escaped with minor bruising.

LONGEST TIME TRAPPED IN AN ELEVATOR

Kiveli Papaioannou (Cyprus), then aged 76, was trapped in the elevator of her apartment block for six days from Dec. 28, 1997, to Jan. 2, 1998. She survived by rationing the fruit, vegetables, and bread that was in her shopping bag.

LONGEST FALL SURVIVED WITHOUT A PARACHUTE

Vesna Vulovic, a flight attendant from Yugoslavia, survived a fall from a height of 33,333 ft. when the DC-9 in which she was travelling blew up over Srbskà Kamenice, Czechoslovakia (now Czech Republic), on Jan. 26, 1972. The other 27 passengers on board the plane were killed.

HIGHEST PARACHUTE ESCAPE

Flight Lieutenant J. de Salis and Flying Officer P. Lowe (both UK) escaped at an altitude of 56,102 ft. over Derby, England, on April 9, 1958.

LOWEST PARACHUTE ESCAPE

Squadron Leader Terence Spencer (UK) made the lowest ever parachute escape, at 30–39 ft. over Wismar Bay, Germany, on April 19, 1945.

HIGHEST-SPEED MOTORCYCLE CRASH SURVIVED

During time trials at El Mirage Dry Lake, California, USA, on July 12, 1998, Ron Cook (USA) survived a motorcycle crash while he was travelling at an estimated 200 m.p.h.

YOUNGEST PERSON TO SURVIVE A CAR CRASH

On Feb. 25, 1999, Virginia Rivero from Misiones, Argentina, went into labor at her home and walked to a nearby road in order to hitchhike to hospital. Offered a ride by two men, she then gave birth to a baby girl on the back seat of their car. When she told them she was about to have a second baby, the driver passed the car in front, only to collide with a third vehicle. Virginia and her newborn daughter were ejected through the back door of the car, suffering minor injuries, but Virginia was able to stand up and flag down another car, which took them to the hospital. Once there, she gave birth to a baby boy.

MOST LIGHTNING SURVIVORS

A record 38 people survived a lightning strike at Castalia, North Carolina, USA, on July 4, 1995.

MOST LIGHTNING STRIKES SURVIVED

The only person to have survived seven lightning strikes is park ranger Roy Sullivan from Virginia, USA. He committed suicide in Sept. 1983, reportedly after being rejected in love.

LONGEST TIME SURVIVED ADRIFT IN A FISHING BOAT

On Jan. 4, 1999, *Yadira I*, a drifting Nicaraguan fishing boat with a crew of seven, was found by Norwegian oil tanker *Joelm* 497 miles southwest of San Juan del Sur, Nicaragua. The boat had been lost at sea for 35 days after its engine stopped working.

MOST LABOR CAMP ESCAPES

Tatyana Russanova, a former Soviet citizen now living in Israel, escaped from Stalinist labor camps in the former Soviet Union on 15 occasions between 1943 and 1954. She was recaptured and sentenced 14 times.

LONGEST FALL SURVIVED BY AN INFANT

In Nov. 1997, an 18-month-old baby named Alejandro fell 65 ft. 7 in. from the seventh-floor kitchen window of his parents' apartment in Murcia, Spain. His only injuries were a broken tooth, a split lip, and bruising.

LONGEST ELEVATOR SHAFT FALL SURVIVED

In May 1998, Stuart Jones (New Zealand) survived a 230-ft. fall down an elevator shaft. He fell while carrying out structural work on the roof of a temporary elevator car at the Midland Park Building, Wellington, New Zealand.

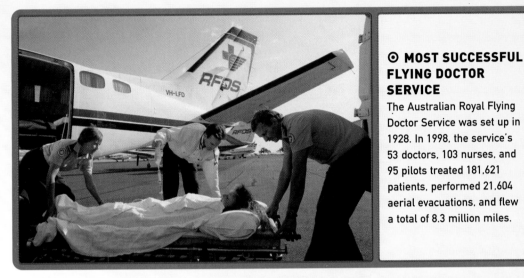

⊙ MOST SUCCESSFUL FLYING DOCTOR SERVICE

The Australian Royal Flying Doctor Service was set up in 1928. In 1998, the service's 53 doctors, 103 nurses, and 95 pilots treated 181,621 patients, performed 21,604 aerial evacuations, and flew a total of 8.3 million miles.

MOST LIVES SAVED BY A SEAT BELT INNOVATION

The three-point safety belt, invented by Swedish engineer Nils Bohlin, was patented by Volvo in 1959. Inertia-roll technology was developed by the same company in 1968. The US National Highway and Traffic Safety Administration estimates that seat belts have prevented 55,600 deaths and 1.3 million injuries in the last decade in the USA alone, saving $105 billion in medical costs.

MOST ARTISTS SAVED

Varian Fry, "The Artists' Schindler," journeyed from the USA to France in 1940 with a list of 200 prominent artists and intellectuals known to be in parts of Nazi-occupied Europe. He subsequently helped to save around 4,000 people from the Gestapo, including Max Ernst, Marc Chagall, and André Breton.

BIGGEST PRESENT-DAY WAR HOSPITAL

The International Committee of the Red Cross (ICRC) hospital in Lopiding, Kenya, is the world's largest war hospital, with a capacity of 560 beds. Founded in 1987 with just 40 beds, it has treated around 17,000 victims of the long-running civil war in Sudan, fitting 1,500 patients with artificial limbs.

MOST PEOPLE RESCUED BY ONE DOG

Barry, a St. Bernard, saved more than 40 people during his 12-year career in the Swiss Alps.

OLDEST LIFEGUARD

The world's oldest lifeguard is Stephen Dicheck of North Carolina, USA, who works at the Triangle Sportsplex in Hillsborough, North Carolina. Born on Jan. 13, 1923, he has been a lifeguard since Nov. 1995.

BIGGEST RESCUES

On May 8, 1942, a record 2,735 people were rescued from the aircraft carrier *USS Lexington* after it was sunk during the Battle of the Coral Sea.

All 2,689 people aboard the *Susan B. Anthony* were rescued when the ship sank off the coast of Normandy, France, on June 7, 1944.

⊙ LONGEST POST-EARTHQUAKE SURVIVAL BY A CAT

On Dec. 9, 1999, 80 days after an earthquake struck Taiwan, killing an estimated 2,400 people, a cat was discovered alive in a collapsed building in Taichung, Taiwan. It was taken to a veterinary hospital, where it made a full recovery.

Space Heroes

FIRST WOMAN IN SPACE
Valentina Vladimirovna Tereshkova (USSR) was launched into Space aboard *Vostok 6* from the Baikonur Cosmodrome, Kazakhstan, on June 16, 1963. *Vostok 6* returned to Earth on June 19, 1963, having completed 48 orbits – a total distance of 1.225 million miles – in 2 days 22 hrs. 50 min.

FIRST PEOPLE ON THE MOON
On July 20, 1969, Neil Armstrong (USA), the command pilot of the *Apollo 11* mission, became the first person to set foot on the Moon. Armstrong was followed out of the lunar module *Eagle* by Buzz Aldrin (USA), while the command module *Columbia*, piloted by Michael Collins (USA), orbited above. *Eagle* lifted off on July 21 after a stay of 21 hrs. 36 min.

GREATEST ALTITUDES ATTAINED
The crew of *Apollo 13* – Jim Lovell, Fred Haise, and Jack Swigert, all USA – were a record distance of 248,661 miles from the Earth's surface on April 15, 1970.

The greatest altitude ever attained by a woman is 380 miles, by Kathryn Thornton (USA) during the *STS-61 Endeavour* mission. Thornton set this record on Dec. 10, 1993, following an orbital engine burn.

FASTEST SPEEDS ATTAINED
The record for the greatest speed at which a human being has ever travelled is 24,792 m.p.h., or 6.88 miles/sec., by the crew of the command module of *Apollo 10* (Thomas Stafford, Eugene Cernan, and John Young, all USA). The record was set on the command module's trans-Earth return flight on May 26, 1969.

Kathryn Sullivan (USA) achieved a women's record speed of 17,761 m.p.h. on April 29, 1990, at the start of reentry at the end of the *STS-31 Discovery* shuttle mission. It is possible that this speed could have been exceeded by Kathryn Thornton on Dec. 10, 1993, after an orbital engine burn during the *STS-61 Endeavour* mission.

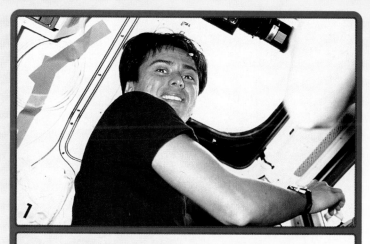

⊙ MOST SPACE MISSIONS
Franklin Chang-Díaz (Costa Rica, above) has flown on a record six missions (1986–1998), as have Americans Story Musgrave (1983–1996), Shannon Lucid (1985–1996), and John Young (1965–1983).

LONGEST STAY ON THE MOON
During the *Apollo 17* mission, which lasted for 12 days 13 hrs. 51 min. 59 sec. from Dec. 7 to 19, 1972, Eugene Cernan and Harrison Schmitt (both USA) spent a total of 74 hrs. 59 min. 40 sec. on the Moon's surface.

LONGEST STAY IN ORBIT AROUND A CELESTIAL BODY
Ronald Evans (USA) orbited the Moon for 147 hrs. 41 min. 13 sec. during the *Apollo 17* mission. He stayed on board the mission's command module while Cernan and Schmitt explored the Moon.

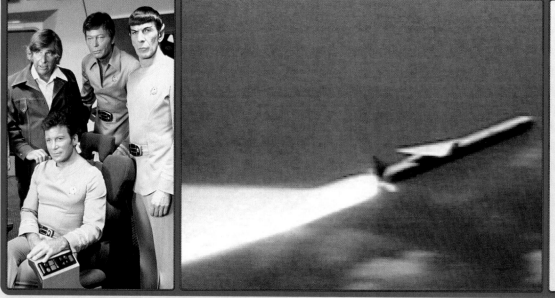

⊙ FIRST SPACE FUNERAL
On April 21, 1997, the ashes of 24 Space pioneers and enthusiasts, including *Star Trek* creator Gene Roddenberry and counter-culture guru Timothy Leary, were sent into orbit on board Spain's *Pegasus* rocket at a cost of $4,920 each. Roddenberry is seen here with *Star Trek* actors William Shatner, DeForest Kelly, and Leonard Nimoy (left to right).

FIRST SPACE WALKS
The first ever space walk was made on March 18, 1965, by Aleksey Leonov (USSR) of *Voskhod 2.*

The first woman to perform a space walk was Svetlana Savitskaya (USSR) from *Soyuz T12/Salyut 7.* She set the record on July 25, 1984.

LONGEST SPACE WALKS
On May 13, 1992, Pierre Thuot, Rick Hieb, and Tom Akers (all USA) of *STS-49 Endeavour* made a space walk that lasted for a record 8 hrs. 29 min.

Kathryn Thornton of *STS-49 Endeavour* made a 7-hr. 49-min. spacewalk on May 14, 1992.

The longest space walk by Russian cosmonauts lasted for 7 hrs. 16 min. It was made by Anatoly Solovyov and Aleksandr Balandin of *Soyuz TM9* outside the *Mir* space station on July 1, 1990.

MOST SPACE WALKS
Aleksandr Serebrov (USSR) has made a record 10 space walks: five during the *Soyuz TM8* mission in 1990, and five during the *Soyuz TM17* mission in 1993.

FIRST UNTETHERED SPACE WALK
The first untethered space walk was made by Bruce McCandless (USA) of the space shuttle *Challenger* on Feb. 7, 1984, at an altitude of 164 miles above Hawaii, USA. He wore a $15-million backpack.

LONGEST SPACEFLIGHT BY A WOMAN
The longest spaceflight ever made by a woman lasted for 188 days 4 hrs. 14 sec. Shannon Lucid (USA) was launched to the *Mir* space station aboard the US space shuttle *STS-76 Atlantis* on March 22, 1996, and returned to Earth on Sept. 26, 1996, on *STS-79 Atlantis.* She was awarded the Congressional Space Medal of Honor by US president Bill Clinton or her achievement.

← MOST SHUTTLE-FLIGHT LANDINGS BY A WOMAN
Eileen Collins (USA) has made a record two shuttle-flight landings. In Feb. 1995, she became the first woman to land a space shuttle as a pilot, on the *STS-63* mission; and in July 1999, on the *STS-93* mission, she became the first ever female shuttle commander.

Human World 1

◉ MOST POPULOUS CITY
The most populous city in the world is Tokyo, Japan. According to the United Nations, it had an estimated population of 26.4 million in March 2000.

MOST POPULOUS COUNTRY
China is the world's most populous country, with an estimated population of 1.24 billion in 1998. Its annual rate of natural increase (births minus deaths) is 1.3% per year, or 44,100 people a day. More people now live in China than inhabited the whole world 150 years ago.

LEAST POPULOUS COUNTRY
The independent state with the smallest population is Vatican City, which had an estimated 870 inhabitants in July 1999.

MOST DENSELY POPULATED COUNTRIES
In 1997, the Chinese special administrative region of Macau, which has a total area of 7.5 miles^2, had an estimated population of 421,000, giving it a population density of 56,133/mile^2.

The most densely populated country with an area of more than 965 miles^2 (2,500 km.^{2}) is Bangladesh. In 1997, it had a population of 125.3 million living in a 56,977-mile^2 area, giving it a population density of 2,199.8/mile^2.

The world's most densely populated island is Java, Indonesia, which in 1997 had a population of 118.7 million living in an area of 51,037 miles^2 – a population density of 2,326/mile^2.

MOST SPARSELY POPULATED COUNTRY
The most sparsely populated independent country in the world is Mongolia. In 1997 it had a population of 2.37 million in an area of 604,800 miles^2, giving it a population density of 3.9/mile^2.

HIGHEST LIFE EXPECTANCY
According to the results of a 1998 World Bank census, the country with the highest life expectancy is Japan, where life expectancy at birth is 83.9 years for women and 77.3 years for men.

LOWEST LIFE EXPECTANCY
In Sierra Leone, life expectancy at birth is 39.8 years for women and 35.9 years for men.

GREATEST DIFFERENCE IN LIFE EXPECTANCY
In 1995, life expectancy for males in the Russian Federation was 58.27 years, compared with a figure of 71.7 years for females – a record difference of 13.43 years.

BIGGEST SHORTAGE OF WOMEN
The country with the biggest recorded shortage of women is Qatar, where 67.2% of the population is male. Worldwide, there are estimated to be 1,015 males for every 1,000 females.

BIGGEST SHORTAGE OF MEN
The country with the largest recorded shortage of men is Ukraine, where 53.7% of the population is female.

HIGHEST BIRTH RATE
According to a United Nations estimate, Niger's birth rate was 54.5 births per 1,000 population in 1996.

LOWEST BIRTH RATE
Excluding Vatican City, where the rate is negligible, the world's lowest current birth rate is 6.5 births per 1,000 population, for Bosnia-Herzegovina in 1995–96.

HIGHEST DEATH RATES
The highest estimated current death rate is 25.1 deaths per 1,000 population, for Sierra Leone in 1995–96.

East Timor had a death rate of 45 deaths per 1,000 population between 1975 and 1980, although this figure subsided to 17.4 deaths per 1,000 population from 1990 to 1995.

⊙ MOST TELEPHONES PER CAPITA

Monaco is the country with the most telephones per capita, with 1,994 for every 1,000 people.

The country with the most doctors per capita is Monaco, where there is one doctor for every 169 people.

FEWEST DOCTORS

Malawi has the fewest doctors per capita, with one for every 49,118 people.

MOST NURSES

The country with the greatest number of nurses is the USA, which had 2.044 million in 1995.

HIGHEST UNEMPLOYMENT

In 1996, a total of 75% of the labor force in Bosnia-Herzegovina was unemployed.

LOWEST UNEMPLOYMENT

In 1997, just 2.7% of Liechtenstein's work force was unemployed.

LOWEST DEATH RATE

The lowest estimated current death rate is 2.2 deaths per 1,000 population, for Kuwait in 1995–1996.

HIGHEST RATE OF NATURAL INCREASE

Between 1992 and 1997 Afghanistan's rate of natural increase was 7.4% per year.

HIGHEST MARRIAGE RATES

The marriage rate in the US Virgin Islands is 35.1 per 1,000 population.

The independent country with the highest marriage rate is The Maldives, with 19.7 marriages per 1,000 population.

HIGHEST DIVORCE RATE

There were just over 1.15 million divorces in the USA in 1997, giving it a divorce rate of 4.3 per 1,000 population. In 1998, a total of 9.8% of all US adults – 19.4 million people – were divorced.

HIGHEST SUICIDE RATE

The highest suicide rate on record is 47 per 100,000 population, for Sri Lanka in 1991.

LOWEST SUICIDE RATE

The lowest suicide rate ever recorded is 0.04 per 100,000 population, for Jordan in 1970, where just one case of suicide was reported.

MOST DOCTORS

The country with the greatest number of physicians is China, which had 1.918 million in 1995. This total includes dentists and those practicing traditional Chinese medicine.

↓ MOST PHARMACISTS

The country with the greatest number of pharmacists is China, with 418,000 in 1995. The Chinese have relied on traditional herbal cures dispensed by pharmacists for over 2,000 years.

Human World 2

HIGHEST TAXATION
Denmark is the highest-taxed country in the world. Its highest rate of income tax is 68%, with the basic rate starting at 42%. As a result, the Danes enjoy some of the world's best health care and welfare benefits.

WORST INFLATION
The world's worst inflation occurred in Hungary in June 1946, when the 1931 gold pengó was valued at 130 million trillion paper pengós. Notes were issued for *Egymillárd billió* (1,000 trillion) pengós on June 3 and withdrawn on July 11 the same year. Vouchers for 1 billion trillion pengós were issued for taxation payment only.

Zaire (now The Democratic Republic of Congo) experienced the highest inflation rate in 1996, at 650%.

LOWEST INFLATION
In 1998, the latest year for which comparable data is available, eleven countries experienced deflation: Barbados, Belize, the Central African Republic, China, The Maldives,

⊙ LEAST TAXED COUNTRY
The independent countries with the least income tax are Bahrain and Qatar, where the rate, regardless of income, is zero. For both nations, oil is the backbone of the economy, providing over half of government revenues.

Oman, Saudi Arabia, Singapore, Sweden, Syria, and Uganda. Of these countries, the Central African Republic had the most favorable figures, with a deflation of -1.89%.

LOWEST HEALTH BUDGET
In 1996, the last year for which comparable figures are available, Somalia had the lowest health expenditure as a percentage of gross domestic product (GDP).

The Somali health budget was estimated to be 1.5% of GDP. As the government infrastructure of Somalia has since collapsed, the figure is no longer meaningful.

HIGHEST HEALTH BUDGET
The USA is the country with the highest health expenditure as a percentage of GDP. The US health budget was 12.7% of GDP in 1996, the last year for which comparable figures are available.

LARGEST GOLD RESERVES
The US Treasury had approximately 262 million fine troy oz. of gold during 1996, equivalent to $100 billion at the June 1996 price of $382 per fine oz. The US Bullion Depository at Fort Knox, 30 miles southwest of Louisville, Kentucky, USA, where 147 million fine troy oz. are currently stored, has been the principal federal depository

⊙ CHEAPEST CITIES
In the Economist Intelligence Unit's biannual survey, Indian cities New Delhi and Mumbai (Bombay) finished with the lowest and cheapest ranking in a survey of the cost of living in 126 cities. With New York City, USA, used as a median (ranked at 100), Mumbai and New Delhi rated only 42 and 41 respectively.

of US gold since Dec. 1936. Gold's peak price was $850 on Jan. 21, 1980.

HIGHEST GNP PER CAPITA
The country with the highest gross national product (GNP) per capita in 1998 was Luxembourg, according to the World Bank, with $45,100.

LOWEST GNP PER CAPITA
Ethiopia, with a GNP per capita of $100, had the lowest of 260 countries for which figures were available to the World Bank in 1998.

LEAST VALUABLE CURRENCY
In May 2000, there were 615,290 Turkish lira to the US dollar (927,123 Turkish lira to the pound sterling and 571,810 to the euro).

HIGHEST COST OF LIVING
For the ninth year running, Tokyo, Japan, topped a survey of the most expensive cities in the world. Using New York City, USA, as a median, Tokyo rates at 64% more expensive than the US city. The Economist Intelligence Unit publishes the biannual survey to help companies calculate salary packages for employees they plan to relocate overseas.

MOST INDUSTRIALIZED COUNTRIES
Equatorial Guinea is the world's most industrialized country, with 66.4% of its GDP derived from industry in 1998, of which a major proportion comes directly from extractive industries.

Belarus derives the highest amount of its GDP from its manufacturing sector, with 39.2% in 1998, according to the

World Development Report 2000.

MOST RENTED HOUSING
The country with the greatest percentage of rented housing is Estonia where, in 1995, 81.5% of property was rented. The British Crown Colony of Gibraltar had a higher rate: at the 1991 census, 84.8% of housing was rented.

MOST PRIVATE HOUSING
The country with the greatest percentage of private housing is Mongolia where, in 1997, 100% of property was occupied by the owner.

MOST DWELLING UNITS
China has the greatest number of dwelling units, with 276,947,962 at the time of the most recent census in 1990.

MOST HOSPITALS
The country with the greatest number of hospitals is China, with 67,807 in 1995.

MOST HOSPITALS PER CAPITA
Monaco has the most hospital beds per person, with 163 for every 10,000 people.

FEWEST HOSPITALS PER CAPITA
Benin and Nepal have the fewest hospital beds, with three per 10,000 people.

← MOST RURAL COUNTRY
According to a 1998 World Bank survey, agriculture contributed to 62.8% of Guinea-Bissau's GDP. One of the 20 poorest countries in the world, it depends mainly on farming and fishing.

World Leaders

YOUNGEST QUEEN
Queen Margrethe II of Denmark was 31 years old when her coronation took place on Jan. 14, 1972.

YOUNGEST PRESIDENT
The youngest head of state of a republic is Lt. Yaya Jammeh, who became president of the Provisional Council and head of state of the Gambia at the age of 29 on July 26, 1994, following a military coup. He was elected president on Sept. 27, 1996, after a return to civilian government.

OLDEST PRESIDENT
The world's oldest republican head of state is 83-year-old Kiro Gligorov, president of the Former Yugoslav Republic of Macedonia.

YOUNGEST PRIME MINISTER
Ljupco Georgievski was 32 years old when he became prime minister of the FYR of Macedonia

⊙ FIRST LADY OF MOST COUNTRIES
Graca Machel was married to Samora Machel, the president of Mozambique, from 1975 to Oct. 19, 1986, when he was killed in a plane crash. On July 18, 1998, she married Nelson Mandela, president of South Africa, making her the first woman to be "first lady" of two different countries.

on Nov. 30, 1998. He leads the Internal Macedonian Revolutionary Organization-Democratic Party of Macedonian National Unity (VMRO-DPMNE).

OLDEST PRIME MINISTER
Sirimavo Bandaranaike was 78 years old when she was elected prime minister of Sri Lanka in Nov. 1994, the third time she had held the office. She had become the world's first ever woman prime minister in July 1960. Her daughter, Chandrika Bandaranaike Kumaratunga, is the country's president.

SHORTEST HEAD OF STATE
The shortest head of state is Frederick Chiluba, who became president of Zambia in 1991. He is 5 ft. tall.

LONGEST-SERVING HEADS OF STATE
Omar Bongo has been president of the central African republic of Gabon since Dec. 2, 1967. He was reelected, unopposed, at presidential elections held every seven years under a single-party system until 1993, when he was returned with a narrow majority following the restoration of a multiparty system.

The longest-serving ruler of a republic is Fidel Castro, who became prime minister of Cuba

on July 26, 1959, following the overthrow of the dictator Fulgencio Batista. Castro has been president and head of government of the country since Dec. 3, 1976, when the post of premier was abolished.

LONGEST REIGNS
Bhumibol Adulyadej (Rama IX), the King of Thailand, is the world's longest-reigning monarch. He succeeded to the throne on June 9, 1946, following the death of his older brother.

The most durable monarch is Norodom Sihanouk, the King of Cambodia. He became king for the first time on April 16, 1941, abdicated on March 2, 1955, and returned to the throne on Sept. 24, 1993, aged 70.

LONGEST-SERVING WOMAN PRIME MINISTER
The world's longest-serving woman premier was Indira Gandhi. She was prime minister of India for a total of 15 years 11 months, in two periods: from Jan. 1966 to March 1977, and from Jan. 1980 until her assassination in Oct. 1984.

⊙ YOUNGEST MONARCH
The world's youngest monarch is King Mswati III of Swaziland (right). He was crowned on April 25, 1986, aged 18 years, 6 days.

MOST WOMEN MINISTERS
The country which has the highest number of women ministers is Sweden, where, following the country's March 1996 general election, a cabinet consisting of 11 female and 11 male ministers was formed.

HIGHEST-PAID PRIME MINISTER
Yoshiro Mori, the Japanese prime minister, has a salary of $676,000 per year, a total that includes monthly allowances and bonuses.

LONGEST UN SPEECH
A UN speech made by President Fidel Castro of Cuba on Sept. 26, 1960, lasted for 4 hrs. 29 min.

MOST HEADS OF STATE TOGETHER
To mark the 50th anniversary of the United Nations, a Special Commemorative Meeting of the General Assembly was held at the UN headquarters in New York City, USA, from Oct. 22 to 24, 1995. It was attended by a record 128 heads of government and of state.

PRESIDENT WITH MOST FAMILY MEMBERS IN POWER
Until 1995, Barzan Ibrahim, a half-brother of Iraqi president Saddam Hussein, was ambassador to the UN and controlled much of the family fortune. Another of Saddam's half-brothers, Watban Ibrahim, was minister of the interior, and a third half-brother, Sabaoni Ibrahim, was chief of general security. Saddam's sons, Udday and Qusay, hold various state and other offices. The latter was head of security services, but was replaced by one of Saddam's in-laws.

⊙ HIGHEST PERSONAL MAJORITY
Boris Yeltsin had a personal majority of 4,726,112 in parliamentary elections held in the Soviet Union on March 26, 1989. Yeltsin, who became president of the Russian Federation, received 5,118,745 of the 5,722,937 votes cast in his Moscow constituency.

← HEAVIEST MONARCH
King Taufa'ahau Tupou IV of Tonga, who is 6 ft. 3 in. tall, weighed 462 lbs. in Sept. 1976. By 1985, he was reported to have slimmed down to 308 lbs.; in early 1993, he was 280 lbs.; and by 1998, he had lost further weight as a result of a fitness program.

Campaigns

BIGGEST DEMONSTRATION
A total of 2.7 million people were reported to have taken part in a demonstration against the USSR in Shanghai, China, from March 3 to 4, 1969, following border clashes.

LONGEST CIVIL-DISOBEDIENCE MARCH
On March 12, 1930, Mohandas Karamchand Gandhi led 78 followers on a 241-mile march from Sabarmati Ashram to Dandi, Gujarat, India, to protest against British India's levy of a tax on salt. The protesters arrived in Dandi on April 5, 1930. Gandhi picked up a lump of salt that was being harvested on the seashore, only to be arrested immediately for producing salt illegally.

BIGGEST ANTIWAR RALLY
On Nov. 15, 1969, an estimated 600,000 people gathered in Washington, D.C., USA, to protest against continued US involvement in the Vietnam War.

BIGGEST RACIAL EQUALITY RALLY
On Aug. 28, 1963, US civil rights campaigner Martin Luther King led more than 250,000 protesters on a march in Washington, D.C., USA, to demand equal rights for all Americans, irrespective of their race or color.

LONGEST HUMAN CHAIN
On Aug. 23, 1989, approximately 2 million people joined hands to form a 370-mile human chain across Estonia, Latvia, and Lithuania. The event took place to mark the 50th anniversary of the signing of a nonaggression treaty between the USSR and Nazi Germany.

LONGEST CIVIL COURT CASE
The longest civil court case led by the same individual lasted for a record 32 years from 1965 to 1997. Prof. Saburo Ienaga, who taught history at the now-defunct Tokyo University of Education, Japan, had challenged a ruling by the Japanese Ministry of Education that his textbook *The New History Of Japan* should be altered. The Ministry objected to passages in the book which stated that the Japanese government had committed atrocities during World War II, and that they had glamorized war. Ienaga was finally awarded $4,000 damages by the Japanese Supreme Court.

⊙ BIGGEST ENVIRONMENTAL PETITION
A petition launched by Greenpeace in 1995, calling for President Chirac of France to end nuclear testing near the French Polynesian island of Mururoa, was signed by a record 8.5 million people. The tests finally came to an end in Jan. 1996.

BIGGEST SEX-DISCRIMINATION SETTLEMENT
On March 22, 2000, the US government agreed to pay $508 million to settle a sex-discrimination suit brought by 1,100 women against the US Information Agency.

YOUNGEST PRISONER OF CONSCIENCE
Three-year-old Thaint Wunna Khin was one of 19 people, including her mother, who were arrested in Burma (Myanmar) from July 19 to 24, 1999. She was released on July 29, 1999.

⊙ BIGGEST GAY RIGHTS MARCH
Approximately 300,000 people took part in the March on Washington for Lesbian, Gay, and Bi Equal Rights and Liberation, held in Washington, D.C., USA, on April 25, 1993. The event was planned to show support for legislation granting equal rights to homosexuals in American society, such as an end to the ban on gays in the military.

LONGEST-HELD PRISONER OF CONSCIENCE
Woo Yong-gak (North Korea) was held in Taejon Prison, South Korea, for 40 years following his arrest for espionage in 1958. He spent much of his sentence in solitary confinement.

BIGGEST BOOK OF SIGNATURES
During their year-long Get Up Sign Up campaign, organized to show support for the Universal Declaration of Human Rights, Amnesty International collected the signatures of over 10 million people. These were then compiled in a book, which was presented to Kofi Annan, the UN Secretary-General, in Paris, France, on Dec. 10, 1998.

BIGGEST PETITION
Between June 1, 1993, and Oct. 31, 1994, a total of 21,202,192 people, most of whom were from South Korea, signed a petition protesting against the partition of Korea and the forced separation of families that resulted from this.

BIGGEST CONSERVATION ORGANIZATION
The World Wide Fund For Nature (WWF) is the world's largest independent conservation organization. Registered as a charity on Sept. 11, 1961, it has around 5 million supporters in some 100 countries. The aim of the WWF is to protect nature and conserve biological diversity.

BIGGEST HUMAN RIGHTS ORGANIZATION
Amnesty International has more than 1.2 million members and supporters in 160 countries and territories, with national offices in 50 countries and over 5,300 local groups on every continent except Antarctica.

LONGEST-RUNNING ENVIRONMENTAL CAMPAIGN
The environmental pressure group Greenpeace was founded in 1971 and has been campaigning against nuclear testing ever since. Its first protest was against testing off the coast of Alaska, USA.

GREATEST DISTANCE COVERED BY CAMPAIGN VESSELS
Greenpeace's campaigning flagships, *Rainbow Warrior 1* and its replacement, *Rainbow Warrior 2*, have covered an estimated total of 575,780 miles. *Rainbow Warrior 1* was sunk by the French secret service in 1985.

→ MOST INTERNATIONAL PETITION
A petition launched in April 1997 as part of the campaign by the antidebt movement Jubilee 2000, had been signed by 17 million people from 160 countries and territories by April 4, 2000. Pictured are two of the campaign's most high-profile supporters, Bono of U2 (left) and boxing legend Muhammad Ali.

Religion

BIGGEST RELIGION
Christianity is the world's predominant religion, with some 2 billion adherents in 1999, or 33% of the world's population. However, religious statistics are necessarily only tentative, as the test of adherence to religion varies widely in rigor.

BIGGEST RELIGIOUS DENOMINATION
The world's largest religious denomination is Roman Catholicism, which had 1.045 billion adherents (17.4% of the world's population) as of Feb. 2000.

BIGGEST NON-CHRISTIAN RELIGION
The largest non-Christian religion is Islam, with some 1.16 billion followers in 1999. The biggest Muslim denomination is Sunni, which is adhered to by 85% of the world's Muslim population.

BIGGEST BUDDHIST TEMPLE
Borobudur, near Jogjakarta, Indonesia, is 103 ft. tall and covers an area of 162,853 ft.^{2}

BIGGEST HINDU TEMPLES
The Srirangam Temple complex in Tiruchirappalli, Tamil Nadu, India, covers an area of 156 acres, with a perimeter of 693.5 miles.

The largest Hindu temple outside India is the Shri Swaminarayan Mandir, London, UK, which covers an area of 65,344 ft.^{2}

BIGGEST SYNAGOGUE
Temple Emanu-El on Fifth Avenue at 65th Street, New York City, USA, has an area of 37,922 ft.^{2} When the adjoining Beth-El Chapel and the Temple's other three sanctuaries are in use, 5,500 people can be accommodated in the synagogue.

⊙ BIGGEST MOSQUE
The Shah Faisal Mosque near Islamabad, Pakistan, can accommodate 100,000 worshippers in the prayer hall and courtyard and a further 200,000 in the adjacent grounds. The total area of the complex is 47 acres, with the covered area of the prayer hall taking up 1.19 acres.

⊙ HIGHEST PILGRIMAGE
The world's highest-altitude pilgrimage ends at Mount Kailas, Tibet, which has a height of 22,000 ft. Also known as Mount Meru, the mountain attracts the followers of four religions: Hinduism, Buddhism, Jainism, and Bon-po, a pre-Buddhist shamanistic religion practiced in Tibet.

BIGGEST CHURCH
The largest church in the world is the Basilica of Our Lady of Peace in Yamoussoukro, Côte d'Ivoire (Ivory Coast). Completed in 1989, it has a total area of 323,000 ft.^{2}, with seating for 7,000 people.

BIGGEST ORTHODOX CATHEDRAL
The Cathedral Church of Christ the Savior, Moscow, Russia, is 335 ft. high. Built to commemorate Russia's dead in the Napoleonic Wars, it was completed in 1883, partially destroyed by Stalin in 1931, and restored between 1995 and 1997.

BIGGEST MORMON TEMPLE
The Salt Lake City Temple, Utah, USA, dedicated on April 6, 1893, has a total floor area of 253,000 ft.^{2}

BIGGEST RELIGIOUS CROWD
The highest recorded number of people known to have assembled with a common

purpose is an estimated 20 million Hindu pilgrims who gathered at the "half" Kumbha Mela festival in Prayag, Allahabad, Uttar Pradesh, India, on Jan. 30, 1995. The festival, which lasts for one and a half months, is held every three years at one of four different sites: Prayag, Nasik, Ujjain, and Haridwar.

BIGGEST GATHERING OF SIKHS

From April 13 to 17, 1999, more than 8 million Sikhs gathered at the Anandpur Sahib temple, Punjab, India, to celebrate the 300th anniversary of the Sikh Khalsa, one of the orders of the Sikh religion.

BIGGEST PAPAL CROWD

On Jan. 15, 1995, Pope John Paul II offered Mass to an estimated 4–5 million people at Luneta Park, Manila, Philippines.

MOST COMPLETE MODERN PURDAH

Since the Islamic fundamentalist Taliban movement took control of Afghanistan's capital, Kabul, in 1996, Afghan women have been subjected to the most complete purdah in the modern world. Forced to wear an all-covering garment, they are denied access both to education and employment in Taliban-controlled areas of the country.

FASTEST-GROWING MODERN CHURCH

The Kimbanguist Church, which was founded in 1959 by Baptist student Simon Kimbangui, had over 6.5 million members by 1996.

SMALLEST KORAN

A miniature Koran owned by Narendra and Neera Bhatia from Faridabad, India, measures just 0.8 in. x 0.6 in. x 0.4 in. An unabridged Arabic-language version, it is 572 pages long.

⊙ LONGEST-SERVING ALTAR BOY

Tommy Kinsella of Bray, Co. Wicklow, Republic of Ireland, served as an altar boy in the Church of the Holy Redeemer, Bray, for a record 81 years between April 1917 and Oct. 1998. He died on April 1, 1999.

↓ BIGGEST RELIGION WITHOUT RITES

The Baha'i faith, which is practiced by approximately 6 million people worldwide, has no ceremonies, no sacraments, and no clergy. Baha'ism emphasizes the importance of all religions and the spiritual unity of humanity. It emerged through the teaching of the 19th-century Persian visionary Baha'ullah, and is now adhered to in over 70 countries. Pictured is the Baha'i House of Worship (Lotus Temple) in Kalkaji, New Delhi, India.

War & Peace

⊙ BIGGEST ARMY

According to *Jane's World Armies*, China's People's Liberation Army had 2.2 million service personnel as of May 2000.

LONGEST WARS

The longest continuous war was the Thirty Years War, fought between various European countries from 1618 to 1648.

The *Reconquista* – the series of campaigns to recover the Iberian Peninsula from the Moors – began in 718 and continued intermittently for 774 years until 1492, when Granada was finally recaptured by the Spanish.

SHORTEST WAR

The shortest war was fought between the UK and Zanzibar (now part of Tanzania). It lasted for just 45 minutes, from 9:00 to 9:45 a.m., on Aug. 27, 1896.

MOST EXPENSIVE WAR

The material cost of World War II (1939–45) has been estimated at $1.5 trillion – more than the cost of all other wars put together.

BIGGEST MILITARY EVACUATION

The largest evacuation in military history was that carried out by 1,200 Allied naval and civil craft from the beachhead at Dunkirk, France, between May 26 and June 4, 1940. A total of 338,226 British and French troops were evacuated.

BIGGEST CIVILIAN EVACUATION

In 1945, an estimated 2 million Germans were evacuated from East Prussia when the region was ceded to the Soviet Union under the terms of the Potsdam Agreement.
The Germans were replaced by Russians, Belorussians, Ukrainians, and other Soviet citizens. Although some military personnel were moved, the overwhelming majority of evacuees were civilians.

BLOODIEST WARS

The costliest war in terms of human life was World War II, in which the total number of military and civilian deaths is estimated to have been 56.4 million. Poland suffered the largest number of fatalities: 6.028 million people, or 17.2% of its prewar population, were killed.

In Paraguay's war against Brazil, Argentina, and Uruguay from 1864 to 1870, Paraguay's population was reduced from 407,000 to 221,000. Fewer than 30,000 of the war's survivors were adult males.

OLDEST ARMY

The oldest military unit is the Vatican's 80–90-strong Swiss Guard, which dates back to Jan. 21, 1506. Its origins, however, predate 1400.

BIGGEST NAVY

The largest navy in the world in terms of human resources is the US Navy, with 570,400 serving personnel, including Marines, as of Jan. 2000.

The US Navy is also the largest in terms of warships, with 315 principal battle vessels. As of May 2000, 98 of these were deployed.

BIGGEST AIR FORCE

The largest air force in the world in terms of human resources is China's, with 470,000 service personnel as of Jan. 2000.

The largest air force in terms of aircraft is that of the USA, which had 4,413 combat aircraft as of Sept. 1999. This total includes 179 bombers, 1,666 fighter and attack aircraft, and 1,279 trainer aircraft.

⊙ MOST PEOPLE KILLED BY AN ATOMIC BOMB

On Aug 6, 1945, 155,200 people were killed when an atomic bomb was dropped on Hiroshima, Japan. This figure includes deaths from radiation sickness within a year of the explosion.

⊙ LONGEST-RUNNING PEACEKEEPING OPERATION

The longest-running UN peacekeeping mission is UNTSO (United Nations Truce Supervision Organization), which has been in place since June 1948. UNTSO's headquarters are in Jerusalem, Israel, but it maintains military observation posts throughout the Middle East.

BIGGEST PEACEKEEPING DEPLOYMENT

The UN peacekeeping mission with the largest deployment was UNPROFOR (United Nations Protection Force), which took place in former Yugoslavia from Feb. 1992 to March 1995. The mission attained a maximum strength of 39,922 military personnel in Sept. 1994, including a rapid reaction force.

OLDEST TREATY

The oldest treaty still in force is the Anglo-Portuguese Treaty, which was signed in London, England, on June 16, 1373.

MOST INDIVIDUALS KILLED IN A TERRORIST ACT

On June 23, 1985, a total of 329 people were killed when a bomb that was believed to have been planted by Sikh extremists exploded on board an Air India Boeing 747. The plane was flying over the Atlantic Ocean, southwest of Ireland, at the time.

MOST MULTINATIONAL ARMY

As of March 2000, the French Foreign Legion had 8,200 men from 120 different countries serving in its ranks. Most new recruits come from former Eastern Bloc nations. After months of intensive training at the Legion's barracks in Castelnaudary, 200 miles west of Marseilles, France, the new Legionnaires are presented with the *kepis blanc*, the regimental cap.

BIGGEST CONTRIBUTORS TO PEACEKEEPING

Canada and Fiji have taken part in the most United Nations peacekeeping operations to date, having each participated in approximately 40 out of 49 missions.

↓ YOUNGEST GUERRILLA LEADERS

"God's Army," a renegade ethnic group from Burma (Myanmar) led by 12-year-old twins Johnny (left) and Luther Htoo, who are said to possess mystical powers, took 700 people hostage for 24 hours at a hospital in Ratchaburi, Thailand, on Jan. 24, 2000. The guerrilla faction was formed when a splinter group left the Karen National Union (KNU) insurgent army.

Crime

MOST PROLIFIC MURDERERS

It was established at the trial of Behram, the Indian thug, that he had strangled at least 931 victims with his yellow and white cloth strip, or *ruhmal*, in the Oudh district (now in Uttar Pradesh, India) between 1790 and 1840.

The most prolific female murderer was Elizabeth Bathory (1560–1615) of Transylvania (now Romania). She is alleged to have killed around 650 girls in order to drink their blood and bathe in it, an act that she believed would preserve her youth.

MOST PROLIFIC MODERN SERIAL KILLER

Pedro Lopez (Colombia) raped and killed a total of 300 young girls in Colombia, Peru, and Ecuador. The "Monster of the Andes" was sentenced to life imprisonment in Ecuador in 1980, on 57 charges.

BIGGEST JEWEL ROBBERY

The costliest jewel theft on record took place at the Carlton Hotel, Cannes, France, on Aug. 11, 1994. Gems with an estimated value of $45 million were stolen from the jewelry shop by a three-man gang.

BIGGEST ROBBERY BY A MUGGER

Treasury bills and certificates of deposit worth $525.6 million were stolen when a money-brokers' messenger was mugged in the City of London, England, on May 2, 1990.

BIGGEST OBJECT STOLEN

On June 5, 1966, armed only with an axe, William Kennedy slashed free the mooring lines of the 10,639-dwt *SS Orient Trader*, owned by Steel Factors Ltd. of Ontario, at Wolfe's Cove, St. Lawrence Seaway, Canada. The vessel drifted to a waiting

⊙ MOST VALUABLE OBJECT STOLEN

Leonardo da Vinci's *Mona Lisa*, which has never actually been valued, is probably the most valuable object ever stolen. It was taken from the Louvre, Paris, France, on Aug. 21, 1911, and recovered in Italy in 1913, when Vincenzo Perugia was charged with its theft.

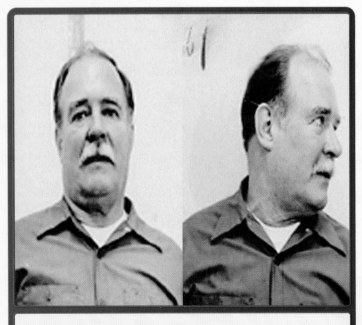

⊙ MOST PRISON TRANSFERS

Over a period of 27 years, between 1971 and his death on Sept. 12, 1998, Lawrence Doyle Conklin (USA) was transferred 117 times between 53 different prison facilities in the USA.

blacked-out tug, thus evading a ban on any shipping movements during a waterfront strike. It then sailed for Spain.

BIGGEST CRIMINAL ORGANIZATION

According to Interpol, the centuries-old Six Great Triads of China form the world's largest organized criminal association, with an estimated 100,000 members scattered around the world.

MOST PROFITABLE CRIMINAL ORGANIZATION

The most profitable organized crime syndicate is believed to be the Mafia. In March 1986,

Rudolph Giuliani, then US Attorney for the Southern District of New York, estimated their profits at $75 billion.

LONGEST CRIMINAL TRIAL

The longest criminal trial in the world took place in Hong Kong and lasted from Nov. 30, 1992, to Nov. 29, 1994. The High Court sat for a record 398 days to hear charges against 14 South Vietnamese boat people accused of murdering 24 North Vietnamese adults and children who died in a blazing hut during a riot at a refugee camp in Hong Kong in Feb. 1992. All the defendants were eventually acquitted of murder.

LONGEST SENTENCES

Chamoy Thipyaso and seven of her associates were each jailed for 141,078 years by the Bangkok Criminal Court, Thailand, on July 27,1989. They had been swindling the public through a multimillion-dollar deposit-taking business.

The longest sentence given to a mass murderer was the 21 life sentences imposed on John Wayne Gacy, who killed 33 people between 1972 and 1978 in Illinois, USA. He also received 12 death sentences at his trial in Chicago, Illinois, in 1980, and was executed on May 10, 1994.

GREATEST MASS ARREST

The greatest mass arrest reported in a democratic country was that of 15,617 demonstrators rounded up by South Korean

⊙ MOST SECURE PRISON

The Administrative Maximum Facility "Supermax" Prison, west of Pueblo, Colorado, USA, is equipped with motion detectors, 1,400 remote-controlled steel doors, laser beams, pressure pads, and silent attack dogs. Inmates include Oklahoma City bomber Timothy McVeigh, Theodore Kaczynski (the "Unabomber"), and Mafia don John Gotti.

police on July 11, 1988. This was to ensure tight security for the 1988 Olympic Games in Seoul.

MOST ARRESTS

Tommy Johns of Brisbane, Queensland, Australia, faced his 2,000th conviction for drunkenness on Sept. 9, 1982. By the time he died, in 1988, his total had reached nearly 3,000, stretching back to 1957.

MOST EXECUTIONS

China executes more people than the rest of the world put together. Over 17,500 people were executed there between 1990 and the end of 1999.

MOST EXECUTIONS PER CAPITA

Saudi Arabia executed 103 people in 1999, or one for every 208,772 residents. A total of 1,163 people have been executed in the country since 1980, many of them foreign nationals and migrant workers.

BIGGEST PRISON POPULATION

In Feb. 2000, the prison population in the USA reached two million. This accounts for 25% of the world's prison population, although the country has only 5% of the world's total population.

← BIGGEST CRIMINAL GANG

The Yamaguchi-gumi gang of the *yakuza*, the Japanese criminal organization, has 30,000 members. Hiroyuki Suzuki (left), a former gangster who is now a priest, has typical *yakuza* characteristics, such as tattoos and cut-off fingertips.

Super Rich

RICHEST PERSON OF ALL TIME

The estimated wealth of oil magnate and philanthropist John D. Rockefeller (USA) was $900 million in 1913, which is equivalent to $189.6 billion today. Having made his fortune in oil, Rockefeller retired in 1897; by 1922 he had given away $1 billion to his family and to charity. Rockefeller kept a total of just $20 million for himself.

RICHEST LIVING PERSON

According to *Forbes* magazine, Bill Gates (USA), the founder and chairman of Microsoft Corporation, is the richest person in the world, with an estimated fortune of $60 billion. In 2000, Gates was briefly knocked off the No. 1 spot by both Lawrence Ellison (USA), the founder of Oracle, and Masayoshi Son (Japan), the president of Softbank.

RICHEST WOMAN

Liliane Bettencourt (France), the heiress to the L'Oréal fortune, has an estimated net worth of $15.2 billion. Her wealth has increased from $13.9 billion in 1999, thanks to L'Oréal's double-digit growth – and because she's worth it.

RICHEST MEDIA TYCOON

Kenneth Thomson (Canada), the head of publishing and information group Thomson Corp., has a fortune of $16.1 billion. The company currently owns 55 North American newspapers, including Canada's *Globe & Mail*, but is now focusing more on electronic information, having agreed as of June 2000 to buy rival information provider Primark Corp. for $1 billion.

RICHEST COSMETICS TYCOONS

The wealthiest cosmetics tycoons are Leonard and Ronald Lauder (USA). They and their family have a combined fortune of $8.8 billion. Leonard runs Estée Lauder, the cosmetics company founded by his mother.

RICHEST ROYAL

According to *Forbes* magazine, King Fahd Bin Abdulaziz Alsaud of Saudi Arabia has an estimated fortune totaling $30 billion. He has overtaken Hassanal Bolkiah, the Sultan of Brunei, who is now worth $16 billion.

RICHEST LUXURY GOODS TYCOON

Bernard Arnault (France), the chairman of luxury goods company LVMH, is worth an estimated $12.6 billion. The strength of the luxury goods market led to a doubling of his fortune from 1999 to 2000. LVMH owns brands such as Christian Dior, Givenchy, Kenzo, and Louis Vuitton, and had total sales of $8 billion in 1999.

RICHEST BAND

The Rolling Stones (UK) are the world's richest music group, with a combined fortune of $683 million. In 2000, according to *The Sunday Times*, lead singer Mick Jagger had an estimated worth of $241 million, guitarist

⊙ HIGHEST ANNUAL EARNINGS BY A FILM PRODUCER

Hollywood producer-director George Lucas (USA) topped the 2000 *Forbes* Celebrity 100 List, having earned $400 million in 1999 following the release of *Star Wars: Episode 1 – The Phantom Menace*.

⊙ HIGHEST ANNUAL EARNINGS BY A FASHION DESIGNER

According to the 2000 *Forbes* Celebrity 100 List, Giorgio Armani (Italy) earned an estimated $135 million in 1999.

⊙ HIGHEST ANNUAL EARNINGS BY A BAND

The Backstreet Boys (USA) earned an estimated $60 million in 1999, according to the 2000 *Forbes* Celebrity 100 List.

RICHEST BUSINESSMAN IN LATIN AMERICA

Carlos Slim Helú, the head of Mexican conglomerate Grupo Carso, is Latin America's richest man, with a combined family fortune totaling $7.9 billion. The group has interests in a number of different fields, including technology, telecommunications, financial services, and retailing, with stakes in US companies CompUSA and CDNow and a controlling interest in internet service provider Prodigy.

RICHEST BUSINESSMAN IN AFRICA

Nicky Oppenheimer (South Africa), the chairman of the diamond and mining empire De Beers, has a family fortune estimated at $2.8 billion.

Keith Richards was worth $209 million, drummer Charlie Watts was worth $104.5 million, guitarist Ronnie Wood was worth $88.3 million, and former bassist Bill Wyman was worth an estimated $40.2 million.

RICHEST MUSIC PRODUCER

Master P, the Chief Executive Officer of No Limit Records, based in New Orleans, Louisiana, USA, has an estimated net worth of $56.5 million. Born Percy Miller, Master P has stayed out of the East Coast/West Coast rap feud and is currently the world's most successful rap star.

YOUNGEST BILLIONAIRE

Jerry Yang (USA), who is the cofounder of internet search engine Yahoo! Inc., became the youngest billionaire in the world in 1998, aged 29. Yang is now worth an estimated $4 billion.

RICHEST BUSINESSMEN IN EUROPE

Theo and Karl Albrecht (Germany) and their family have a combined fortune of $20 billion. They own the Aldi discount store group, which had revenues of $26 billion in 1999, as well as the Trader Joe's chain and a 7% share in Albertson's supermarkets.

RICHEST BUSINESSMAN IN ASIA

The fortune of Prince Alwaleed Bin Talal Alsaud (Saudi Arabia) was estimated at $20 billion in May 2000. An investor, mostly in US and European blue-chip stocks, his major holding is Citigroup.

→ HIGHEST-PAID BOXER

Oscar de la Hoya (USA) is the world's highest-paid boxer, with estimated earnings of $43.5 million in 1999, according to the 2000 *Forbes* Celebrity 100 List.

Big Business 1

⊙ BIGGEST CHANGE IN SHARE PRICE IN A DAY

On March 27, 2000, the price of one share in Yahoo! Japan stood at $1.12 million. By the end of trading on March 28, 2000, this had dropped to $518,200 – a fall of $610,100, or 54.07%. A total of 51.2% of Yahoo! Japan, the country's dominant information portal, is owned by Japanese company Softbank, with US-based Yahoo! owning 34.2%.

BIGGEST FLOTATION
The stock market launch of ENEL, Italy's state-owned electricity generator and distributor, became the world's largest ever initial public offering after the Italian government sold shares worth $19.26 billion on Oct. 31, 1999.

BIGGEST AGM ATTENDANCE
A record total of 20,109 shareholders attended the AGM of American Telephone and Telegraph Company (now AT&T Corp.) in April 1961.

HIGHEST-PAID CEO
Charles B. Wang, the founder and Chief Executive Officer of Computer Associates International, earned $650,048,000 in the financial year 1999/2000 – a figure that includes salary, bonus, and stock gains. His total earnings over the period 1996–2000 were $713,452,000.

HIGHEST INVESTMENT CONSULTANCY FEES
Harry D. Schultz, an investment consultant who lives in Monte Carlo, Monaco, charges a record $2,400 on weekdays and $3,400 at weekends for a standard consultation of 60 minutes. His *International Harry Schultz Letter*, which was instituted in 1964 and has subscribers in 90 different countries, sells at $50 per copy, while a life subscription to the publication costs $2,400. He has written a total of 22 books, which are mostly about investing.

BIGGEST GOLDEN HANDSHAKE
The largest golden handshake in business history was one of $53.8 million given to F. Ross Johnson, who left his post as chairman of the food company RJR Nabisco in Feb. 1989.

RICHEST INVESTOR
Warren Buffett, the head of Berkshire Hathaway, is the world's richest investor, with an estimated worth of $28 billion.

MOST INVESTORS
The record number of investors in a single share issue is 5.9 million, for the Mastergain '92 equity fund, floated by the Unit Trust of India in April and May 1992.

OLDEST FAMILY BUSINESS
The Hoshi Ryokan in Japan dates back to 717 A.D. and is a family business spanning 46 generations.

OLDEST STOCK EXCHANGE
The Stock Exchange in Amsterdam, Netherlands, was founded in the Oude Zijds Kapel in 1602, for dealings in printed shares of the United East India Company of the Netherlands.

⊙ BIGGEST RECORD COMPANY
Warner EMI Music, the $20-billion joint venture between Time Warner and EMI that was announced on Jan. 30, 2000, is the world's largest record company. Artists with the company include Madonna (above), Quincy Jones, Garth Brooks, and the Rolling Stones.

BIGGEST MARKET CAPITALIZATION

In May 2000, over 3,025 companies had stock listed on the New York Stock Exchange, with global market capitalization worth more than $16 trillion. The 2.089 billion shares were worth a total of $12.3 trillion.

BIGGEST DAILY TRADING VOLUME

On Jan. 7, 2000, a total of 136,846,600 shares in Lucent Technology were traded on the New York Stock Exchange – a record for a single stock in one day.

BIGGEST TRADING LOSS SUSTAINED

In 1996, Japan's fourth largest trading company, Sumitomo Corporation, revealed that they had suffered $2.6-billion copper trading losses as a result of unauthorized dealings by one of their top traders, Yasuo Hamanaka. The dealings had taken place on the London Metal Exchange over a 10-year period.

HIGHEST LECTURE FEES

Dr. Ronald Dante was paid $3,080,000 for lecturing students on hypnotherapy at a two-day course held in Chicago, Illinois, USA, on June 1–2, 1986.

→ LOWEST-PAID CEO

Steve Jobs, Chief Executive Officer and cofounder of Apple Computer Inc., receives a salary of $1 per year. However, in Jan. 2000, he was given a Gulfstream luxury airliner and 10 million stock options for agreeing to stay with Apple as its permanent CEO.

Big Business 2

BIGGEST COMPANIES

The world's largest company is General Electric Co. (USA), which had a market capitalization of $532.2 billion in May 2000 and total profits of $10.7 billion in 1999.

General Motors (USA) had total sales of $189 billion in 1999.

BIGGEST BANK

The world's largest bank is Citigroup (USA), with a market capitalization of $207.1 billion in May 2000.

BIGGEST TELECOMMUNICATIONS COMPANY

The Nippon Telegraph and Telephone Corporation (NTT) of Japan had a market capitalization of $207 billion in May 2000 and revenues of $75.9 billion in 1998.

BIGGEST LAW FIRM

Clifford Chance LLP (USA) employs a total of 3,100 legal advisers (630 of whom are partners) in 29 offices around the world. The company was formed after the merger of Clifford Chance, Rogers & Wells LLP, and Pünder, Volhard, Weber & Axster in Jan. 2000.

The three companies had a combined revenue of $986 million in 1998.

BIGGEST INSURANCE COMPANY

AXA (France) had revenues of $78.7 billion in 1998 and a market capitalization of $49.7 billion in May 2000.

BIGGEST OIL COMPANY

Exxon Mobil (USA) is the biggest oil and energy company in the world, with a total market capitalization of $280.8 billion in April 2000.

BIGGEST ADVERTISING AGENCY

WPP Group plc, based in London, England, became the world's largest advertising agency in May 2000, following its $4.7-billion takeover of US firm Young & Rubicam. In 1999, the companies had a combined revenue of $5.2 billion, and earnings before interest and tax of $704 million.

BIGGEST PR COMPANY

The world's largest public relations company is Burson-Marsteller, which was founded by Harold Burson and Bill Marsteller in New York City, USA, over 40 years ago.

⊙ BIGGEST EMPLOYER

The world's largest commercial or utility employer is Indian Railways. In 1997, it had a record 1,583,614 regular employees.

The PR firm had worldwide revenues of more than $275 million in 1995.

BIGGEST PHARMACEUTICAL COMPANY

Merck and Co., Inc., a research-driven pharmaceutical company which is based at Whitehouse Station, New Jersey, USA, develops, manufactures, and markets a broad range of human and animal health products. On March 30, 2000, its market capitalization stood at $148.4 billion, while its sales for the year ending Dec. 31, 1999, were $32.71 billion.

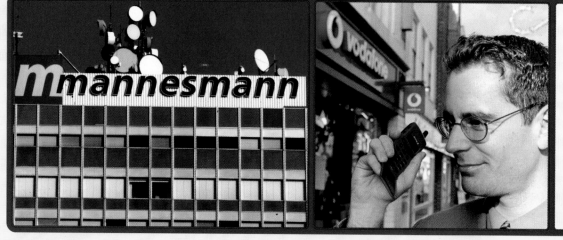

⊙ BIGGEST CELL PHONE COMPANY

The world's largest cell phone company is Vodafone AirTouch Group (UK). The firm was created on Feb. 5, 2000, when a $171.1-billion merger between British cell phone giant Vodafone AirTouch and rival company Mannesmann (Germany) took place.

BIGGEST TOBACCO COMPANY

The world's largest tobacco company is Philip Morris (USA), which had a market capitalization of $50.9 billion in April 2000.

BIGGEST SOAP AND COSMETICS COMPANY

The largest soap and cosmetics firm in the world is Procter & Gamble, based in Cincinnati, Ohio, USA. It had a market capitalization of $79.3 billion in May 2000 and revenues of $38.1 billion in 1999.

BIGGEST CHIPS COMPANY

Frito-Lay (USA), part of the PepsiCo Group, is the world's largest producer of salty snacks, responsible for brands such as Doritos, Cheetos, and Ruffles. At the end of 1999, the company had a 30% share of the world's salty snack market, and accounted for up to two-thirds of PepsiCo's sales.

BIGGEST LIVE ENTERTAINMENT COMPANY

SFX Entertainment is the largest producer and promoter of live entertainment events such as concerts, Broadway shows, and motor sports meets. It also provides sports marketing and management and talent representation services. It owns, leases, or manages about 125 sites in the USA.

BIGGEST PUBLISHING COMPANY

The largest publishing and printing company is Bertelsmann AG (Germany). In the financial year ending June 1999, it had sales of $14.16 billion.

Charities & Gifts

WEALTHIEST CHARITABLE FOUNDATION

The Bill And Melinda Gates Foundation is the world's biggest and wealthiest charitable foundation, with an asset base of $21.8 billion. The organization, which comprises two separate charities – The Gates Learning Foundation and The William H. Gates Foundation – donates money to global health care programs, education initiatives, libraries, and community causes in the Seattle region of Washington, USA. The foundation's largest donation to date, made on Sept. 16, 1999, is $1 billion, which will be used over 20 years to fund scholarships for students from ethnic minorities.

BIGGEST SINGLE PRIVATE CHARITABLE DONATION

Bill Gates and his wife Melinda donated a record $6 billion to The Bill And Melinda Gates Foundation in Aug 1999.

BIGGEST SINGLE BEQUEST

On March 12, 1991, US publishing tycoon Walter Annenberg announced his intention to leave his art collection, valued at $1 billion, to the Metropolitan Museum of

⊙ BIGGEST FUNDRAISING CHARITY

From 1991 to 1998 (the last year for which figures are available) the US arm of the Salvation Army raised more funds annually than any other charity. Its total for 1998 was $1.2 billion. The organization was founded by William Booth in London, England, in 1878.

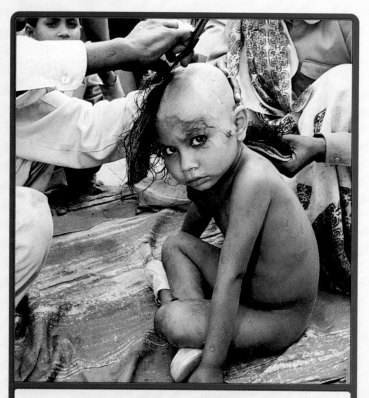

⊙ BIGGEST DONATION OF HAIR

Pilgrims to the Tirupathi Temple in Andhra Pradesh, India, which attracts an average of 30,000 visitors per day, donate their hair as a form of sacrifice. The 600 barbers employed by the temple shave the pilgrims' heads 24 hours a day, and more than $2.2 million a year is raised through the auction of the hair.

Art in New York City, USA – the largest single bequest by an individual ever.

MOST MONEY RAISED BY A SINGLE SPORTING EVENT

The London Marathon, which has been run through the streets of London, England, since 1981, raises more money for charity than any other single sporting event in the world. An estimated record $31.6 million was raised at the most recent event, held on April 16, 2000.

The greatest amount of money raised by one person in a charity walk or run is a record $16,629,749, by Terry Fox (Canada). Fox, who was suffering from cancer and had an artificial leg, ran a total distance of 3,339 miles in eastern Canada. The run took place from April 12 to Sept. 2, 1980.

MOST MONEY RAISED BY A MARATHON RUNNER

Retired advertising executive John Spurling (UK) raised a record-breaking $1.87 million for charity by running in the London Marathon on April 18, 1999.

⊙ BIGGEST WEDDING BANQUET

Jayalalitha Jayaram (center), a movie star and former chief minister of Tamil Nadu, India, hosted and paid for a luncheon for over 150,000 guests at the wedding of her foster son, V.N. Sudhakaran (right), to N. Sathyalakshmi (left). The banquet was served by the coast in the state capital, Chennai, on Sept. 7, 1995.

← BIGGEST GIFT

The Statue of Liberty (officially called "Liberty Enlightening the World") was a gift from the people of France to the USA. Completed in 1886, the statue, sculpted by Auguste Bartholdi and engineered by Gustave Eiffel, stands 151 ft. 1 in. tall and weighs 225 tons.

MOST SUCCESSFUL SPONSORED SWIMS

The greatest amount of money raised in a charity swim is $194,498, in "Splash '92," organized by the Royal Bank of Scotland Swimming Club. The event was held at the Royal Commonwealth Pool, Edinburgh, England, on Jan. 25–26, 1992, and attracted 3,218 participants.

The record amount for an event staged at several different pools is $964,490.80, by "Penguin Swimathon '88." A total of 5,482 swimmers participated in the event, which was held at 43 pools throughout London, England, from Feb. 26 to 28, 1988.

BIGGEST SIMULTANEOUS BLOOD DONATION

A one-day blood donation drive organized jointly by the American Red Cross and the University of Missouri, and held at the Hernesh Center Field House, Columbia, Missouri, USA, on April 7, 1999, attracted a record 3,539 donors.

The drive yielded a total of 3,155 productive units of blood – just over 328 gal.

MOST MONEY RAISED BY A TELETHON EVENT

On Sept. 5-6, 1998, the Jerry Lewis MDA (Muscular Dystrophy Association) Telethon, which was broadcast on 200 US TV stations and shown live on the web, raised $53,116,417 in pledges and contributions. The telethon has made a record $954 million since it first aired in 1966.

MOST OSCAR DRESSES SOLD AT A CHARITY AUCTION

On March 18, 1999, a record 56 dresses and evening gowns that had been worn to Academy Awards ceremonies by actresses such as Elizabeth Taylor, Sharon Stone, and Uma Thurman were auctioned at "Unforgettable: Fashion of the Oscars" at Christie's, New York City, USA. A total of $786,120 was raised for the American Foundation For AIDS Research (AmFAR).

Valuables 1

MOST VALUABLE PIECES OF JEWELRY

On Nov. 14, 1980, a record-breaking $7.2 million was paid for two pear-shaped diamond drop earrings, one of 58.6 carats and the other of 61 carats, at Sotheby's, Geneva, Switzerland. They were bought and sold anonymously.

MOST VALUABLE DIAMOND

A 100.10-carat pear-shaped "D" flawless diamond was sold for $16,548,750 at Sotheby's, Geneva, Switzerland, on May 17, 1995. It was bought by Sheikh Ahmed Fitaihi for his chain of jewelry shops in Saudi Arabia.

MOST VALUABLE JEWELRY BOX

A Cartier jeweled vanity case set with a fragment of Egyptian steel was sold at Christie's, New York City, USA, for $189,000 on Oct. 19, 1993.

MOST VALUABLE COIN

An 1804 silver dollar, one of only 15 in existence, fetched a record $1.815 million at an auction held in New York City, USA, on April 8, 1997. The coin was part of the collection of banker Louis Eliasberg from Baltimore, Maryland, USA – the only person to possess a complete set of US coins.

MOST VALUABLE MISSING ART TREASURE

The Amber Room, presented to Catherine the Great of Russia by King Friedrich Wilhelm I of Prussia in 1716, was installed in the Catherine Palace near St. Petersburg, Russia. It consisted of intricately carved amber panels, together with richly decorated chairs, tables, and amber ornaments. In 1941, invading Germans dismantled the room and took it back to Germany, where it was reassembled in Königsberg castle, East Prussia (now Kaliningrad, Russia). The Amber Room was later put into storage, and much of it disappeared, but fragments were returned to Russia by Germany on April 29, 2000.

MOST VALUABLE CLOCK

On July 8, 1999, a Louis XVI clock, part of the collection of the Barons Nathaniel and Albert von Rothschild, was sold at Christie's, London, England, for a record $3,001,290.

MOST VALUABLE PEN

In Feb. 1988, a Japanese collector paid $218,007 for the "Anémone" fountain pen, made by French company Réden. Encrusted with 600 precious stones, including emeralds, amethysts, rubies, sapphires, and onyx, it took craftsmen over a year to complete.

⊙ MOST VALUABLE TYPEWRITER

Ian Fleming's gold-plated typewriter, which he commissioned from the Royal Typewriter Company, New York City, USA, in 1952, was sold for $89,229 at Christie's, London, England, in May 1995.

MOST VALUABLE PIECE OF FURNITURE

On July 5, 1990, the 18th-century Italian Badminton Cabinet, owned by the Duke of Beaufort, was sold at Christie's, London, England, for $15.1 million – a record price for a single piece of furniture.

MOST VALUABLE CHAIRS

A pair of chairs designed by Robert Adam and built by Thomas Chippendale were sold to an anonymous buyer at Christie's, London, England, for $2,762,330 on July 3, 1997.

MOST VALUABLE CARPET

A 16th-century tabriz medallion carpet, part of the Rothschild collection, was sold for $2,488,943 at Christie's, London, England, on July 8, 1999.

MOST VALUABLE SKULL

The skull of Emanuel Swedenborg, the Swedish philosopher and theologian, was bought in London, England, by the Royal Swedish Academy of Sciences for $10,560 on March 6, 1978.

MOST VALUABLE TOOTH

In 1816, a tooth belonging to Sir Isaac Newton was sold in London, England, for $3,241. It was purchased by a nobleman, who had it set in a ring.

MOST VALUABLE HAIR

On Feb.18, 1988, a lock of hair belonging to the British naval hero Lord Nelson sold for a record $10,035 at an auction

⊙ MOST VALUABLE DINKY TOY

A very rare green 1937 Dinky Bentalls store delivery van with yellow upper side panels and a white roof was sold for $19,355 at Christie's, London, England, on Oct. 14, 1994.

in Crewkerne, Somerset, England. It was bought by a bookseller who was from Cirencester, Gloucestershire, England.

MOST VALUABLE STAMP COLLECTION
On Nov. 3, 1993, Japanese engineer–industrialist Hiroyuki Kanai bought a 183-page collection of classic Mauritian stamps for a record $10,135,134, at an auction held in Geneva, Switzerland.

MOST VALUABLE SINGLE STAMP
A Swedish treskilling was sold for $2.3 million in Geneva, Switzerland, in Nov. 1996.

MOST VALUABLE PAPERWEIGHT
On June 26, 1990, $258,500 was paid for a glass paperweight – a mid-1840s Clichy Millefiori basket with no handle – at Sotheby's, New York City, USA.

MOST VALUABLE THIMBLE
On Dec. 13, 1992, a late-16th-century gold jeweled thimble was sold for $31,359 at Phillips, Solihull, W. Midlands, England. It was reputed to have belonged to Queen Elizabeth I.

MOST VALUABLE CELLO
On June 22, 1988, a Stradivarius cello was sold for a record $1,213,960 at Sotheby's, London, England. The cello, known as "The Cholmondeley," was made in Cremona, Italy, ca. 1698.

MOST VALUABLE PIANO
The highest price ever paid for a piano is $1.2 million, for a Steinway created under the direction of Sir Lawrence Alma-Tadema. It sold at Christie's, London, England, on Nov 7, 1997.

MOST VALUABLE GUITAR
A 1956 Fender Stratocaster, known as "Brownie" and belonging to Eric Clapton, sold for $497,500 at Christie's, New York City, USA, on June 24, 1999.

⊙ MOST VALUABLE WRISTWATCH
A 1922 18-karat gold gentleman's wristwatch, produced by Patek Phillippe, sold for $1,918,387 at Antiquorum Auctioneers, Geneva, Switzerland, on Nov. 14, 1999. It was bought by a Middle Eastern collector.

→ MOST VALUABLE POP STAR CLOTHING
An outfit worn by Geri Halliwell for the Spice Girls' 1997 Brit Awards performance was sold for a record $66,112 at Sotheby's, London, England, on Sept. 16, 1998. It was bought by Peter Morton, the owner of the Hard Rock Hotel in Las Vegas, Nevada, USA.

Valuables 2

⊙ MOST VALUABLE FILM POSTER
A poster for the Universal film *The Mummy* (USA, 1932), which starred Boris Karloff, sold for a record $453,500 at Sotheby's, New York City, USA, on March 7, 1997.

MOST VALUABLE PAINTING
Portrait Of Dr. Gachet by Vincent Van Gogh sold at Christie's, New York City, USA, for a record $82.5 million on May 15, 1990.

MOST VALUABLE PRINT
Diehard by US artist Robert Rauschenberg was sold at Sotheby's, New York City, USA, for a record $1.6 million on May 2, 1989.

MOST VALUABLE SCULPTURE
The Three Graces by Antonio Canova was jointly purchased by the Victoria & Albert Museum, London, England, and the National Gallery of Scotland, Edinburgh, for $11.5 million in 1994.

The highest price fetched by a sculpture at auction is $11,250,000, paid for Edgar Degas' *Petite Danseuse De Quatorze Ans* at Sotheby's, New York City, USA, on Nov. 11, 1999.

MOST VALUABLE PEN AND INK DRAWING
Oliviers Avec Les Alpilles Au Fond by Vincent Van Gogh was sold at Sotheby's, London, England, for a record $8,578,740 on Dec. 7, 1999.

MOST VALUABLE POSTER
A poster designed by Charles Rennie Mackintosh to advertise an art exhibition at the Glasgow Institute of Fine Arts, Glasgow, Scotland, in 1895, sold for a record $103,357 at Christie's, London, England, in Feb. 1993.

MOST VALUABLE FILM PROP
The *Maltese Falcon,* a vital prop in the 1941 Humphrey Bogart film of the same name, was sold for $398,500 at Christie's, New York City, USA, in 1994. In Jan. 1995, it was resold to a secret buyer for an undisclosed price.

MOST VALUABLE OSCAR
David O. Selznick's Oscar for *Gone With The Wind* (USA, 1939) was bought by Michael Jackson for a record $1,542,000 at Sotheby's, New York City, USA, on June 12, 1999.

MOST VALUABLE TELEGRAM
A telegram sent by former Soviet president Nikita Khrushchev to Yuri Gagarin on April 12, 1961, which congratulated him on being the first person in Space, sold for $68,500 at Sotheby's,

New York City, USA, on Dec. 11, 1993. It was bought by Alberto Bolaffi of Turin, Italy.

MOST VALUABLE BOOK
An original four-volume subscriber set of J.J. Audobon's *The Birds of America* was sold for $8,802,500 at Christie's, New York City, USA, on March 10, 2000.

MOST VALUABLE LETTERS
A letter written and signed by Abraham Lincoln on Jan. 8, 1863, in which he answers criticisms made of the Emancipation Proclamation, was sold for a record $748,000

⊙ MOST VALUABLE FILM COSTUME
Both the blue and white gingham dress and the red slippers worn by Judy Garland for her role as Dorothy in *The Wizard Of Oz* (USA, 1939) reached record prices at auction. The former was sold for $324,188 at Christie's, London, England, on Dec. 9, 1999, and the latter fetched $666,000 at Christie's, New York City, USA, on May 24, 2000.

⊙ MOST VALUABLE PHOTOGRAPH

Grande Vague - Séte, taken by French photographer Gustave Le Gray in around 1855, was sold at Sotheby's, London, England, for $832,300 on Oct. 27, 1999. It was bought by an anonymous bidder.

MOST VALUABLE COMIC

A first-edition copy of *Action Comics*, published in June 1938 and featuring the first appearance of Superman, was sold for $100,000 in 1997.

MOST VALUABLE ILLUMINATED MANUSCRIPT

A 16th-century prayer book, part of the collection of the Barons Nathaniel and Albert von Rothschild, was sold at Christie's, London, England, for $13,547,614 on July 8, 1999.

MOST VALUABLE LYRICS

In Feb. 1998, the lyrics to *Candle In The Wind 1997*, signed by their writer Bernie Taupin and the song's composer Elton John, were sold for $442,500 in Los Angeles, California, USA. The song was performed at the funeral of Diana, Princess of Wales in Sept. 1997.

MOST VALUABLE CAMERA

An 1882 Enjalbert Pocket Revolver camera, made with real revolver parts, was sold at Christie's, London, England, for $87,275 on Aug. 31, 1995.

MOST VALUABLE MUSIC BOX

A Swiss music box, made for a Persian prince in 1901, was sold for a record $27,128 at Sotheby's, London, England, on Jan. 23, 1985.

at Christie's, New York City, USA, on Dec. 5, 1991.

A letter written by Ronald Reagan in which he praises Frank Sinatra was sold for $12,500 at the Hamilton Galleries, California, USA, on Jan. 22, 1981 – a record price for a letter signed by a living person.

MOST VALUABLE ATLAS

A 1492 version of Ptolemy's *Cosmographia* was sold for a record $1,925,000 at Sotheby's, New York City, USA, on Jan. 31, 1990.

↓ MOST VALUABLE TEDDY BEAR

A Steiff bear named "Teddy Girl" was sold for $170,830 – more than 18 times the guide price – at Christie's, London, England, on Dec. 5, 1994. It was bought by Japanese businessman Yoshihiro Sekiguchi.

Valuables 3

⊙ MOST VALUABLE PAIR OF JEANS

In March 1997, Levi Strauss & Co. paid a vintage denim dealer in New York City, USA, a record $25,000 for a pair of Levi 501 jeans that are believed to have been made between 1890 and 1901.

MOST VALUABLE SOCCER PROGRAM

A program for the 1908 FA Charity Shield replay between Manchester United and Queens Park Rangers was sold at Old Trafford stadium, Manchester, England, for $12,759 on April 10, 2000. It was bought by the Manchester United Museum.

MOST VALUABLE CRICKETING MEMORABILIA

A first edition of *Wisden Cricketers' Almanack*, dating from 1864, was sold at Phillips, London, England, for $11,989 in June 1999.

MOST VALUABLE BASEBALL

The highest price paid for a baseball is $3,054,000, by Todd McFarlane at Guernsey's, New York City, USA, on Jan. 12, 1999. The baseball had been hit by Mark McGwire of the St. Louis Cardinals in Sept. 1998, for a major league record of 70 home runs in a season.

MOST VALUABLE BASEBALL GLOVE

The baseball glove worn by Lou Gehrig for his final baseball game on April 30, 1939, was sold for a record $389,500 at Sotheby's, New York City, USA, on Sept. 29, 1999.

MOST VALUABLE TENNIS RACKET

A Slazenger lawn tennis racket used at Wimbledon by Fred Perry sold at Christie's, London, England, for $37,724 in June 1997.

MOST VALUABLE BICYCLE

A diamond-frame safety bicycle dating from 1891 was sold at Phillips, London, England, for $170,310 in Aug. 1999, beating the previous record price for a bicycle by over 200%.

MOST VALUABLE ITEM OF HEAD WEAR

In Nov. 1981, a Native North American Tlingit Kiksadi ceremonial frog helmet dating from approximately 1600, was sold for $66,000 in New York City, USA. It was bought by the Alaska State Museum, Juneau, Alaska, USA.

MOST VALUABLE DRESS

The flesh-colored beaded Jean Louis gown worn by Marilyn Monroe when she sang "Happy Birthday" to President Kennedy in May 1962, sold for $1.15 million

⊙ MOST VALUABLE PEZ DISPENSERS

A Mickey Mouse softhead, a one-piece shiny gold elephant, and a headless dispenser embossed with the words PEZ-HAAS were sold for $6,000 each – a total of $18,000 – by David Welch, an author and Pez dealer, in May 1998.

at Christie's, New York City, USA, on Oct. 27, 1999. It was bought by Robert Schagrin and Peter Siegel of Gotta Have It! Collectibles, New York City.

MOST VALUABLE POP MEMORABILIA

John Lennon's 1965 Phantom V Rolls-Royce was sold for $2,229,000 at Sotheby's, New York City, USA, on June 29, 1985.

MOST VALUABLE ZIPPO LIGHTER

An original 1933 Zippo lighter was sold for $10,000 by Ira Pilossof on July 12, 1998. The lighter was an early 1933 model without any slash marks on the two corners – all later models had these corner marks. This is the first Zippo model ever produced (formerly referred to as a 1932) and is the most sought after by Zippo collectors.

⊙ MOST VALUABLE SOCCER SHIRT

A red No. 6 soccer shirt, taken by Bobby Moore (second from left) as a spare to the 1966 World Cup final between England and West Germany, sold for a record $71,650 at Wolverhampton Wanderers' Molineux stadium, W. Midlands, England, on Sept. 21, 1999. The shirt was auctioned as part of a collection belonging to ex-England trainer Harold Shepherdson.

⊙ MOST VALUABLE BOXING MEMORABILIA

A black and white robe worn by Muhammad Ali before the 1974 "Rumble in the Jungle" fight against George Foreman fetched $157,947 at a sale in Beverly Hills, California, USA, in Oct. 1997.

MOST VALUABLE MICKEY MOUSE TOY

A rare clockwork Mickey Mouse motorcycle, made in approximately 1939, sold for a record $83,650 at Christie's, London, England, in June 1997.

MOST VALUABLE WAX DOLL

A rare Lucy Peck wax doll modeled as the young Queen Victoria sold for $13,879 at Christie's, London, England, in May 1999.

MOST VALUABLE KALEIDOSCOPE

An English kaleidoscope in a mahogany case, made in approximately 1830, sold for $74,934 at Christie's, London, England, in Nov. 1999.

MOST VALUABLE GI JOE

On Aug. 19, 1994, at an auction held at Christie's, New York City, USA, to commemorate the 30th anniversary of GI Joe,

a unique GI Joe fighter pilot action figure sold for a record-breaking $5,750.

MOST VALUABLE CHRISTMAS CARD

A Christmas card hand-drawn by John Lennon and addressed to Brian Epstein, the Beatles' then manager, sold for a record $8,502 at Christies, London, England, on April 27, 2000. The card featured two ink cartoon emus.

MOST VALUABLE ILLUSTRATED MANUSCRIPT

The *Codex Leicester*, an illustrated manuscript in which Leonardo da Vinci predicted the invention of the submarine and the steam engine, was sold to Bill Gates for a record 30.8 million at Christie's, New York City, USA, on Nov. 11, 1994. It is the only da Vinci manuscript in private hands.

→ MOST VALUABLE BIKINI

A hand-sewn, diamond-encrusted bikini made by Prestons of Windsor, Berkshire, England, has been valued at a record $194,458.97. It was unveiled on March 22, 2000, during Windsor Fashion Week, when a diamond and setting worth $3,150 were being offered to the first person to guess its value correctly. Here, the bikini is modeled by Susan Sangster.

Shopping 1

⊙ BIGGEST SHOPPING CENTER

The world's largest shopping center is the $1.1-billion West Edmonton Mall in Alberta, Canada, which was opened on Sept. 15, 1981, and was finally completed four years later. Covering an area of 5.2 million ft.², it encompasses over 800 stores and services, as well as 11 major department stores. The mall also has the world's biggest parking lot, with room for 20,000 vehicles and overflow facilities for another 10,000.

LONGEST MALL
A mall inside the Milton Keynes, Buckinghamshire, England, shopping center is 2,360 ft. long.

BIGGEST UNDERGROUND SHOPPING COMPLEX
The PATH Walkway, which is in Toronto, Canada, has a record 16.8 miles of shops with 4 million ft.² of retail space.

OLDEST SHOPPING ARCADE
The Galleria Vittorio Emanuele in Milan, Italy, which was designed in 1861, was first opened to the general public in 1867.

BIGGEST OPEN-AIR MARKET
The San Jose flea market sits on 120 acres of land in the heart of Silicon Valley, California, USA. It was officially opened in 1960 on an abandoned cattle feed lot, when it had 20 booths and about 100 customers. Today it averages more than 6,000 booths and 80,000 visitors each week, and has a management staff of 150.

BIGGEST WHOLESALE MARKET
The Dallas Market Center on Stemmons Freeway, Dallas, Texas, USA, covers an area of nearly 6.9 million ft.² in five separate buildings. It houses some 2,580 permanent showrooms displaying the merchandise of more than 50,000 manufacturers, and attracts 800,000 buyers each year to its 50 markets and trade shows.

BIGGEST DEPARTMENT STORE
Macy's, an 11-story building occupying an entire block in Herald Square, New York City, USA, covers an area of 2.15 million ft.² The company has a chain of department stores across the USA and was one of the first major retailers to place such stores in shopping centers.

MOST SHOPPERS IN A DAY
The largest number of visitors to a single department store in one day is an estimated 1.07 million, to the Nextage Shanghai, China, on Dec. 20, 1995.

GREATEST SALES PER UNIT AREA
The record for the greatest number of sales in relation to area of selling space is held by Richer Sounds plc, a British hi-fi retail chain. Sales at its branch in London Bridge Walk, England, reached a peak of $27,830/ft.² in the year ending Jan. 31, 1994.

BIGGEST FASHION RETAIL CHAIN
Gap Inc. has almost 2,900 stores selling its clothing in the USA, the UK, Canada, France, Germany, and Japan. Founded in San Francisco, California, USA, in 1969, the company had sales of $11.6 billion in 1999.

BEST-SELLING CLOTHING BRAND
Levi Strauss is the world's biggest brand-name clothing manufacturer. Its Levis, Dockers, and Slates brands are sold in more than 30,000 retail outlets in 60 countries, and its sales totaled $6 billion in 1999.

⊙ BIGGEST RETAILING FIRM
The world's largest retailing firm is Wal-Mart Stores, Inc., founded by Sam Walton in Bentonville, Arkansas, USA, in 1962. The company had revenues of $165 billion and profits of $8.419 billion in the year ending Jan. 31, 2000, and by March 2000 had 4,003 retail outlets in 10 countries, employing 1.14 million people.

→ BIGGEST SPORTSWEAR COMPANY

The sportswear giant Nike was founded in 1972 in Oregon, USA, by Bill Bowerman and Phil Knight. The company had revenues of $8.78 billion in 1999, making it the 197th largest company on the *Fortune* 500 list. Nike currently controls more than 45% of the US sportswear market.

BIGGEST FASHION FRANCHISE

The Benetton Group (Italy) operates in 120 countries through its 7,000 franchised stores and company-owned megastores. Its clothing consists primarily of knitwear and sportswear, and it is the largest consumer of wool in the garment sector. Today it has nine factories in different parts of the world. Its sales totalled $1.9 billion in 1999.

BIGGEST ELECTRONICS RETAILER

Best Buy Co., Inc. (USA) is the world's biggest retailer of consumer electronics, audio-visual equipment, entertainment software, and domestic appliances, with 1999 sales topping $10 billion.

MOST ELECTRONICS RETAIL OUTLETS

Radio Shack has more than 6,900 stores and franchises selling electronics and computers across the USA.

BIGGEST BOOKSTORE

The world's biggest bookstore is the Barnes & Noble Bookstore on Fifth Avenue, New York City, USA. It covers an area of 154,250 ft.^{2} and has 12.87 miles of shelves.

BIGGEST MENSWEAR STORE

Slater Menswear in Glasgow, Scotland, covers an area of 28,000 ft.^{2} and has about 14,000 suits in stock at any one time.

BIGGEST RUMMAGE SALE

The White Elephant Sale at the Cleveland Convention Center, Ohio, USA, raised a record $427,935.21 over two days from Oct. 18 to 19, 1983.

The greatest amount of money ever raised at a one-day rummage sale is $214,085.99, at the 62nd one-day rummage sale organized by the Winnetka Congregational Church, Winnetka, Illinois, USA, on May 12, 1994.

MOST EXPENSIVE SHOPPING STREET

Fifth Avenue in New York City, USA, is the most expensive shopping street in the world on which to rent store space, at $580/ft.^{2} It is followed in cost by 57th Street, also in New York City ($500/ft.^{2}), and Oxford Street in London, England ($400/ft.^{2}).

MOST CREDIT CARDS

Walter Cavanagh of Santa Clara, California, USA, has 1,397 individual credit cards, which together are worth more than $1.65 million in credit. He keeps them in the world's longest wallet, which is 250 ft. in length and weighs 38 lbs. 8 oz.

⊙ BIGGEST TOY RETAILER

The world's largest toy retailer is Toys "R" Us Inc., based in Paramus, New Jersey, USA. It currently has 1,552 stores in 27 countries.

Shopping 2

⊙ MOST EXPENSIVE PHOTOGRAPHIC BOOK

A first edition hardback of *Sumo*, a 480-page book of photographs by Helmut Newton (Australia), retails for a record $1,500. The book is published by Taschen-Verlag (Germany) and contains 400 photographs, including images of Elizabeth Taylor (far left) and Faye Dunaway. It weighs 66 lbs. and measures 20 in. x 28 in., being so large that it needs its own stand. Newton is seen on the right of the black and white picture, along with publisher Benedikt Taschen.

MOST EXPENSIVE WATCH

In 1999, Gianni Vive Sulman of London, England, produced a watch that cost more than $520,000. Only five are to be made every year.

MOST EXPENSIVE SWATCH WATCH

A limited edition Swatch – one of only 120 made – designed in 1985 by French artist Christian Chapiron (known as Kiki Picasso), sold at auction at Sotheby's, Milan, Italy, for $45,000 in 1989. When they were first released, the watches were given away for free.

MOST EXPENSIVE MAGAZINE

Visionaire magazine, created by Stephan Gan (USA), is the most expensive magazine in the world. Prices for each copy start at $100, with one issue, available in its own Louis Vuitton case, selling for $5,000 on the black market. The most sought-after edition of all is No. 20, which was edited by designer Rei Kawakubo of Comme des Garçons and became an instant collector's item as it came with a free toile (muslin copy) of one of her frocks. For the second issue, designer Martin Margeila contributed 1,000 bags of confetti as a giveaway.

MOST EXPENSIVE SWISS ARMY KNIFE

An 18-karat gold Swiss army knife, produced by Swiss jeweler Luzius Elmer, currently retails for $4,299.

MOST EXPENSIVE WOOL

The highest price ever paid for wool is $3,629.70 per lb., a record set on Jan. 11, 1995, when Aoki International Co., Ltd. of Yokohama, Japan, bought a bale of extra superfine wool with an average fiber diameter of 13.8 microns, at an auction in Geelong, Victoria, Australia.

MOST EXPENSIVE WALLET

The world's most expensive wallet is a platinum-cornered, diamond-studded crocodile creation made by Louis Quatorze of Paris, France, and Mikimoto of Tokyo, Japan. It sold for $75,000 in Sept. 1984.

MOST EXPENSIVE PERFUME

A cologne called Andron, which contains a trace of the attractant pheromone androstenol, was marketed by Jovan of Chicago, Illinois, USA, for $2,750 per oz. in March 1984. Retail prices of fragrances tend to be fixed with an eye to public relations rather than the market cost of ingredients and packaging.

MOST EXPENSIVE PINBALL MACHINE

Aaron Spelling, a pinball machine named after the US TV producer, was made in Feb. 1992 and was reported to have been sold for $120,000 in Los Angeles, California, USA.

MOST EXPENSIVE LOUDSPEAKERS

Wilson Audio Modular Monitor (WAMM) system speakers cost a record $405,512) per set. They are specially created by a Wilson designer, who visits the buyer and develops the speakers in accordance with their needs.

MOST EXPENSIVE CELL PHONE

A cell phone designed by David Morris International of London, England, sold for a record $110,604 in 1996. Made entirely from 18-karat gold, it has a keypad encrusted with pink and white diamonds.

MOST EXPENSIVE ANIMAL

Racehorses are by far the most expensive animals. The record price paid for a yearling is $13.1 million, by Robert Sangster and partners for Seattle Dancer on July 23, 1985, in Kentucky, USA.

⊙ MOST EXPENSIVE PEN

"La Modernista Diamonds," a pen made by Swiss company Caran d'Ache, went on sale in Harrods, London, England, for $265,000 in 1999. Created in memory of architect Antonio Gaudí, the rhodium-coated solid silver pen has an 18-karat gold pen point and is pavé-set with 5,072 diamonds and 96 half-cut rubies.

MOST EXPENSIVE CAT

Cato, a generation two Bengal cat, was bought for a record price of $41,435 by Cindy Jackson of London, England, in Feb. 1998. The cat was sold by breeder Lord C Esmond Gay of Bedfordshire, England.

MOST EXPENSIVE INSECT

On Aug. 19, 1999, a 3-in. stag beetle (*Dorcus hopei*) was sold for a record $90,000 at a store in Tokyo, Japan. The beetle is believed to have been bought by a 36-year-old company president, but he has refused to be identified for fear of being targeted by thieves.

MOST EXPENSIVE TREE

The highest price ever paid for a tree is $51,000, for a single Starkspur Golden Delicious apple tree from Yakima, Washington, USA. The tree was bought by a nursery in 1959.

↓ MOST EXPENSIVE MINI

The Mini Limo, a one-of-a-kind commissioned by Rover Group and built by John Cooper Garages (UK), was sold for a record $80,000 in Sept. 1997. The two-door car boasts a $12,836 Alpine Mini-Disc sound system and has seats worth $9,627.

MINI

Food & Drink 1

MOST EXPENSIVE LIQUOR
On Dec. 9, 1996, an anonymous Scottish businessman paid a record $24,600 for a bottle of 60-year-old Macallan whiskey after taking part in a sealed-bid auction. The distillery rarely produces whiskey of this age and, when it does, only releases 10 bottles, one of which it keeps. Another is earmarked for charity, and the rest are sold by the bidding method.

MOST EXPENSIVE WINE
The world's most expensive commercially available wine is 1787 Chateau d'Yquem Sauternes, which costs between $56,000 and $64,000 per bottle.

STRONGEST ALCOHOL
When Estonia was independent between the two world wars, the Estonian Liquor Monopoly marketed 98% (196 proof) alcohol distilled from potatoes.

STRONGEST BEERS
Samuel Adams Triple Bock, brewed by the Boston Beer Company, Massachusetts, USA, has an alcohol volume of 17.5%.

Baz's Super Brew, which is brewed by Barrie Parish and sold in one-third measures at The Parish Brewery, Somerby, Leicestershire, England, has an alcohol volume of 23%. However, it is rarely brewed these days.

MOST EXPENSIVE SPICE
Prices for wild ginseng from China's Chan Pak Mountain area peaked at a record $23,000/oz. in Nov. 1979, in Hong Kong. Total annual exports of the spice – believed by many to be an aphrodisiac – from Jilin Province do not exceed 8.75 lbs.

HOTTEST SPICE
The world's hottest spice is Red Savina Habanero, which was developed by GNS Spices

⊙ BIGGEST BAGEL
On July 23, 1998, Lender's Bagels of Mattoon, Illinois, USA, made a blueberry bagel that was 13.75 in. high, had a diameter of 59 in., and weighed a record 714 lbs.

of Walnut, California, USA. It has a rating of 350,000–570,000 on the Scoville scale (an index for measuring the hotness of hot peppers), compared with a rating of 30,000–50,000 for cayenne pepper and one of 2,500–5,000 for jalapeño.

BIGGEST PUMPKIN
A pumpkin weighing 1,131 lbs. was grown from Atlantic Giant seed stock by Gerry Checkon of Altoona, Pennsylvania, USA. It was weighed at the Pennsylvania Pumpkin Bowl on Oct. 2, 1999.

BIGGEST PANCAKE
The world's biggest pancake ever was 49 ft. 3 in. in diameter and 1 in. deep, with a weight of 2.95 tons. It was made and flipped at Rochdale, Greater Manchester, England, on Aug. 13, 1994, as part of celebrations to mark the 150th anniversary of the Co-operative movement.

LONGEST SUSHI ROLL
On Oct. 12, 1997, a sushi roll with a total length of 3,281 ft. was made by 600 members of the Nikopoka Festival Committee in Yoshii, Japan.

LONGEST SAUSAGE
The longest continuous sausage on record extended a distance of 28.77 miles. It was made by MM Meat Shops in partnership with J.M. Schneider Inc. at Kitchener, Ontario, Canada, on April 28–29, 1995.

BIGGEST PIZZA
A pizza with a diameter of 122 ft. 8 in. was baked at Norwood Hypermarket, Norwood, South Africa, on Dec. 8, 1990.

BIGGEST PAELLA
A paella with a record diameter of 65 ft. 7 in. was made by Juan Carlos Galbis and a team of helpers in Valencia, Spain, on March 8, 1992. It was eaten by 100,000 people.

⊙ BIGGEST SANDWICH
In Aug. 1999, representatives from Marks & Spencer and from McVities Prepared Foods, UK, created a prepacked tuna and cucumber sandwich that measured a record 7 ft. x 7 ft. x 9 ft. 11 in.

BIGGEST OMELETTE
On March 19, 1994, representatives of Swatch cooked a 160,000-egg omelette with an area of 1,383 ft.^{2} in Yokohama, Japan.

BIGGEST LOLLIPOP
A peppermint-flavored lollipop that weighed 1.35 tons was made by the staff of BonBon, Holme Olstrup, Denmark, on April 22, 1994.

BIGGEST ICE CREAM SUNDAE
The largest ice cream sundae on record weighed 24.5 tons. The sundae was made by Palm Dairies Ltd. under the supervision of Mike Rogiani in Edmonton, Alberta, Canada, on July 24, 1988.

BIGGEST CHINESE DUMPLING
The Hong Kong Union of Chinese Food and Culture Ltd. and the Southern District Committee made a 1,058-lb. dumpling on July 5, 1997, to celebrate the return of Hong Kong to China.

BIGGEST CURRY
On May 17, 1998, a curry weighing 5,849 lbs. was made by a team from The Raj Restaurant, Maldon, Essex, England, under the supervision of Mafiz Ali. It was divided into 13,500 portions.

LONGEST STRING OF GARLIC
A record 171-ft.-long string of garlic was made by a team of women from the village of Cornellá Del Terri, Spain, at the Second Fair of Garlic in Cornellá on Oct. 12, 1997.

MOST CANDLES ON A CAKE
On Oct. 27, 1996, staff at the Polish daily newspaper *Express Ilustrowany* produced a cake with 900 candles on it, to celebrate the 900th goal scored by Polish soccer club Widzew Lódz.

BIGGEST COOKIE
A giant chocolate chip cookie with a diameter of 81 ft. 8 in. and an area measuring 5,241.5 ft.^{2} was made by Cookie Time in Christchurch, New Zealand, on April 2, 1996.

BIGGEST TACO
The world's biggest taco was 15 ft. long, 29 in. wide, and weighed a massive 747 lbs. The taco was created on May 5, 1999, in Houston, Texas, USA, by employees of La Ranchera Food Products Inc. and La Tapatia Taquería. It was filled with 559 lbs. of meat, 46 lbs. of tomatoes, 37 lbs. of onions, and 18 lbs. of cilantro.

→ MOST POPULAR FRUIT
The banana (*Musa sapientum*), together with its relative the plantain (*Musa paradisiaca*), is the most consumed fruit in the world. It is also the fifth most important agricultural commodity in terms of international trade, coming after cereals, sugar, coffee, and cocoa.

Food & Drink 2

⊙ BIGGEST SANCOCHO

The world's biggest sancocho (a Latin American meat and vegetable stew) was made in Puerto Plata, Dominican Republic, on Jan. 1, 2000, by staff from the Playa Dorada hotel complex. The sancocho, which took seven hours to cook, was divided into 10,020 portions, each weighing 8 oz.

MOST EXPENSIVE MEAL PER HEAD

In Sept. 1997, three diners at Le Gavroche, London, England, spent a record $20,945.92 on one meal. Only $345.92 went on food; cigars and liquor accounted for $1,352 and the remaining $19,248 went on six bottles of wine. The most expensive bottle, a 1985 La Romanée-Conti costing $7,920, proved "a bit young," so the diners gave it to the restaurant staff.

MOST RESTAURANTS VISITED

The record for the greatest number of restaurants visited is held by restaurant grader Fred E. Magel of Chicago, Illinois, USA, who over a period of 50 years dined out 46,000 times in 60 different countries. His favorite dishes were South African rock lobster and fresh English strawberry mousse.

BIGGEST BREAKFAST

On April 17, 1998, a total of 13,797 people took part in a breakfast of cereal and milk at Dubai Creekside Park, Dubai, United Arab Emirates. The event was organized by Kellogg's, who provided all the participants with miniature boxes of cereal.

BIGGEST TOAST

At 11 p.m. E.S.T. on Feb. 26, 1999, a record-breaking 197,648 people gathered simultaneously in pubs, restaurants, and bars in 74 metropolitan areas of the USA for The Great Guinness Toast.

⊙ BIGGEST RESTAURANT

The Mang Gorn Luang (Royal Dragon) restaurant in Bangkok, Thailand, can seat up to 5,000 customers and is manned by a staff of 1,200. Opened in Oct. 1991, its service area of 4 acres is worked by 541 waiters, who wear roller skates to enable them to serve up to 3,000 meals an hour.

BIGGEST TEQUILA SLAM

On Nov. 26, 1999, 132 people performed a "Mexican-wave"-style tequila slam at Bar Madrid, London, England. The event was started by Chris Greener, the UK's tallest man, and took 5 min. 14 sec. to complete.

BIGGEST BARBECUE

A record 44,158 people attended a barbecue at Warwick Farm Racecourse, Sydney, NSW, Australia, on Oct. 10, 1993.

BIGGEST BAR

The Mathäser in Munich, Germany, seats 5,500 people and sells 84,470 pints of beer a day. It was established in 1829, demolished during World War II, and reopened in 1955.

LONGEST BAR

The bar in the Beer Barrel Saloon, Ohio, USA, is 405 ft. 10 in. long. Put up in 1989, it is fitted with 56 beer taps and is surrounded by 160 bar stools.

LONGEST-DISTANCE PIZZA DELIVERY

In March 1998, Eddie Fishbaum, the owner of Broadway's Jerusalem 2 in New York City, USA, was asked to hand-deliver a plain pizza base to TV presenter Eiji Bando in Tokyo, Japan – a distance of 6,753 miles. The request was made on the Japanese TV show *Unbelievable*, shown on the Fuji network. The total cost of the pizza, including Fishbaum's expenses, came to $7,000.

FASTEST RICE EATER

Using chopsticks, Dean Gould of Felixstowe, Suffolk, England, ate 51 grains of rice, one by one, in three minutes. The record was set at Bombay Nite, Walton, Essex, England, on March 10, 1998.

FASTEST SODA CRACKER EATER

On April 20, 2000, during filming for the TV show *Guinness World Records*, Vic Kent (UK) ate three soda crackers in 2 min. 6 sec.

FASTEST BAKED BEAN EATER

The greatest number of baked beans eaten with a swizzle stick in five minutes is 226, a record set by Andy Szerbini (UK) at London Zoo, London, England, on Nov. 18, 1996.

LONGEST LINE OF CANDY

In 24 hours on Dec. 5 and 6, 1998, 60 scouts constructed a continuous line of 306,250 Mintie candies, covering a distance of 9.4 miles. This world record was set at Goldfields Leisure Nestle Centre, Maryborough, Victoria, Australia.

LONGEST NOODLE

The longest Chinese-style noodle ever made was 181 ft. in length, with a diameter of 0.28 in. It was created at the Pasir Panjang Family Fun Day, Singapore, on May 30, 1999.

HEAVIEST CHOCOLATE MODEL

A 13.8-ft. x 13.8-ft. x 6.6-ft. chocolate model of a house, weighing a record 5 tons, was made by José Rafael Palermo in Córdoba, Argentina, between March 8 and 23, 1997.

⊙ TALLEST CHAMPAGNE FOUNTAIN

From Dec. 28 to 30, 1999, Luuk Broos, director of Maison Luuk-Chalet Fontaine, constructed a 56-story champagne fountain at the Steigenberger Kurhaus Hotel, Scheveningen, Netherlands. It was made from 30,856 traditional long-stem glasses.

→ BIGGEST SERVING OF FISH AND CHIPS

The largest serving of fish and chips was produced by Somerfield Stores Ltd. in Bristol, England, on Feb. 25, 2000. The fish, fried by David Morgan (right), weighed 8 lbs. and the chips weighed 7 lbs.

Games & Gambling

BIGGEST HOPSCOTCH GRID
On Sept. 5, 1998, Liz Barr, Rebecca Woodle, and Blain Littlefield of Hinsdale, Illinois, USA, created a 15-yd.-long hopscotch grid consisting of 30 squares, each with an area of 22 in.[2]

BIGGEST GAME OF PASS-THE-PARCEL
The largest ever game of pass-the-parcel involved 3,918 students removing 2,200 wrappers from a 4.9-ft. x 4.9-ft. x 1.6-ft. parcel in two and a half hours. The record was set at Nanyang Technological University, Singapore, on Feb. 28, 1998.

LONGEST TIDDLEDYWINKS JUMP
A jump of 31 ft. 3 in. was achieved by Ben Soares of the St. Andrew's Tiddlywinks Society at Queen's College, Cambridge, England, on Jan. 14, 1995.

HIGHEST TIDDLEDYWINKS JUMP
The high-jump record is 11 ft. 5 in., by Adrian Jones, David Smith, and Ed Wynn of the Cambridge University Tiddlywinks Club, all on Oct. 21, 1989.

FASTEST GAME OF SOLITAIRE
On Aug. 2, 1991, Stephen Twigge completed a game of solitaire in 10 seconds at Scissett Baths, W. Yorkshire, England.

FASTEST-BUILT JENGA TOWER
The fastest time in which a 30-story Jenga tower has been built, within the rules of the game, is 12 min. 27 sec., by Simon Spalding and Ali Malik at Highclere Castle, Hampshire, England, on Aug. 17, 1997.

HIGHEST SKITTLE SCORES
The highest table skittle score in a 24-hour period is 116,047, by 12 players at the Castle Mona, Newcastle, Staffordshire, England, on April 15–16, 1990.

The highest long-alley score is 94,151, by a team from the Carpenters Arms, Leigh, Dorset, England, on March 10–11, 1995.

HIGHEST SCRABBLE SCORES
The highest competitive game score is 1,049, by Phil Appleby of Lymington, Hampshire, England, on June 25, 1989, in Wormley, Hertfordshire, England. His opponent scored 253, giving Appleby a record 796-point margin of victory.

The highest single-turn score is 392. Dr. Saladin Karl Khoshnaw, in Manchester, England, in April 1982, laid down the word "CAZIQUES" – "native chiefs of West Indian aborigines."

MOST CHECKERS OPPONENTS
On April 26, 1998, Ronald "Suki" King (Barbados) played

⊙ BIGGEST LOTTERY WIN BY A TOWN
On Dec. 22, 1999, the Spanish National Lottery *El Gordo* ("The Fat One") was particularly kind to the people of the southeastern town of Elche. All of the lottery's 1,450 first-prize coupons were bought there, giving its citizens a record total of $262 million in prize money.

⊙ BIGGEST DOMINO TOPPLE
At 11:22 p.m. Chinese time on Dec. 31, 1999, a record 2,751,518 dominoes were toppled in 32 min. 22 sec. at the Gymnasium of Beijing University, Beijing, China. The dominoes had been set up over 40 days by a team of 53 Chinese and Japanese students. The attempt was jointly organized by Tokyo Broadcasting System, Japan, and Beijing TV, China.

2815, by the current world champion Gary Kasparov (Russia) in 1993.

The highest-rated woman chess player is Judit Polgar (Hungary), who achieved a peak rating of 2675 in 1996.

MOST BRIDGE WORLD TITLES
Italy's Blue Team (Squadra Azzura) won 13 Bermuda Bowl world titles and an additional three team Olympiads between 1957 and 1975. Giorgio Belladonna played in all the team's winning games.

MOST BRIDGE HANDS
During the 1989 World Championships, held in Perth, Western Australia, Marcel Branco and Gabriel Chagas (both Brazil) played a record 752 out of a possible 784 boards.

BIGGEST LOTTERY JACKPOT
The Big Game Lottery, run by seven US states (Georgia, Illinois, Maryland, Massachusetts, Michigan, New Jersey, and Virginia), offered a jackpot of $350 million on May 9, 2000. Two ticket holders shared the prize. The odds of a player picking the winning numbers were 76 million to one – the same odds as a random name picked from a USA-wide phone book being that of a living US ex-president.

BIGGEST SLOT-MACHINE JACKPOT
Cindy Jay (USA), a 38-year-old cocktail waitress, won a record $34,959,458 on a Megabucks game at the casino of the Desert Inn Hotel, Las Vegas, Nevada, USA, on Jan. 26, 2000.

BIGGEST GAME OF BINGO
The largest "house" in Bingo history was one of 15,756 at the Canadian National Exhibition, Toronto,

Canada, on Aug. 19, 1983. Organized by the Variety Club of Ontario Tent Number 28, the event offered total prize money of $167,723, with a record one-game payout of $67,089.

BIGGEST HORSE-BETTING PAYOUT
On April 19, 1987, Anthony Speelman and Nicholas Cowan (both UK) won a record-breaking $1,627,084 – after federal income tax of $406,768 had been deducted –

on a $64 nine-horse accumulator at Santa Anita Racecourse, California, USA. The jackpot had been built up for 24 days.

MOST ROLLS-ROYCES RAFFLED
In March 2000, a record 31 Rolls-Royce cars – one for every day of the month – were raffled in Dubai, United Arab Emirates. The raffle was part of the Dubai Shopping Festival.

⊙ MOST PLAYED BOARD GAME
By June 2000, Monopoly had been played by 500 million people worldwide. The game was invented by Charles B. Darrow (above) of Pennsylvania, USA, in 1934, and has now sold over 200 million units.

385 simultaneous games of checkers at the Houston International Festival, Houston, Texas, USA. King donned roller skates to move more quickly between his 385 opponents.

MOST CHECKERS WORLD TITLES
Walter Hellman (USA) won a record eight checkers world titles between 1948 and 1975. He was World Champion for two stretches – from 1948 to 1955, and from 1963 until his death in July 1975.

HIGHEST CHESS RATINGS
The highest rating ever attained on the officially adopted Elo System – devised by Arpad E. Elo (Hungary, later USA) – is

↓ MOST WAGERED ON FLAT RACING
Of the $40 billion wagered on flat racing worldwide, $17.2 billion, or 43%, is placed in Japan. The biggest flat race in the Japanese racing calendar is the annual Japan Cup, which usually attracts bets of around $306.3 million.

Toys

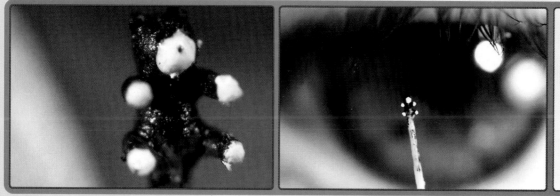

⊙ **SMALLEST
TEDDY BEAR**
In 1999, Japanese artist
Hiromu Morine from Sapporo,
Japan, created a resin teddy
bear less than 0.04 in. in
height. Morine, a member
of the Japan Doll House
Association, has had his work
exhibited around the world.

**MOST VALUABLE
MONOPOLY SET**
A $2-million Monopoly set was
created by jeweler Sidney Mobell
(USA) in 1988. Its board is made
of 23-karat gold, the chimneys
of the gold houses and hotels are
topped with rubies and sapphires,
and the dice's spots are diamonds.

**MOST EXPENSIVE
BOARD GAME**
The most expensive commercially
available board game is the
deluxe version of Outrage!,
produced by Imperial Games
(UK). The game, which is based
around the theme of stealing the

Crown Jewels from the Tower
of London, currently sells for
a record $6,200.

BIGGEST BOARD GAME
The world's biggest
commercially available board
game is Galaxion, created by
Cerebe Design International
of Hong Kong, China.
The game's board measures
33 in. x 33 in.

BIGGEST TWISTER SHEET
The world's largest single
sheet for the game Twister
measured 60 ft. x 20 ft. The
sheet was made by Vision

International of Salt Lake City,
Utah, USA, in Feb. 1998.

**BIGGEST PACKS OF
PLAYING CARDS**
In 1998, Naipes Heraclio
Fournier of Vitoria, Spain,
printed 150 packs of the
world's biggest playing
cards. Each card measured
3 ft. 1 in. x 2 ft. 2.5 in.

SMALLEST JIGSAW PUZZLES
The 99-piece "Nano" wooden
jigsaw puzzle, made by World
of Escher, Texas, USA,
measures 2.6 in. x 2.2 in.
The smallest commercially

available 1,000-piece jigsaw
measures 18.1 in. x 11.8 in.
It is manufactured by Educa
Sallent of Barcelona, Spain.

BIGGEST JIGSAW PUZZLES
The largest ever jigsaw puzzle
measured 51,485 ft.² and
consisted of 43,924 pieces.
It was assembled in Marseille,
France, on July 8, 1992.

The largest commercially
available jigsaw puzzle is
manufactured by Educa
Sallent of Barcelona, Spain.
It measures 35.5 ft.² and
contains 10,000 pieces.

⊙ **LONGEST FLIGHT
OVER WATER BY A
MODEL HELICOPTER**
On Dec. 18, 1999, Michael
Farnan (Australia) flew his
JR Vigor model helicopter
a distance of 39.8 miles
across Port Philip Bay,
Victoria, Australia. The
helicopter was controlled
from a full-size helicopter
flying alongside it, and took
40 minutes to complete the
distance. It had a total takeoff
weight of 18 lb. 12 oz.

⊙ BIGGEST KITE FLOWN

The largest kite ever flown is the Megabite, which is 210 ft. long (including tails) and 72 ft. wide, with a total flat area of 10,043 ft.² Designed by Peter Lynn (New Zealand), it was flown for 22 min. 57 sec. at the Bristol International Kite Festival, England, on Sept. 7, 1997.

BIGGEST TEDDY BEAR

On May 6, 1999, Omni Toys Oy of Turku, Finland, created a traditional stitched teddy bear that was 25 ft, 3 in. long and weighed 1,764 lbs.

LONGEST STUFFED TOY

Pupils of Veien School in Hønefoss, Norway, created a 1,377-ft.-long stuffed snake in June 1994.

BIGGEST YO-YO

A 896-lb yo-yo with a diameter of 10 ft. 5 in. was devised by JN Nichols (Vimto) Ltd. and made by students at Stockport College, Greater Manchester, England. It was launched by crane from a height of 189 ft. on Aug 1, 1993, and yo-yoed about four times.

TALLEST LEGO STRUCTURE

A Lego tower built by more than 2,000 children in Moscow, Russia, from July 14 to 19, 1998, reached a record height measuring 80 ft .11 in. It was made from 387,903 bricks.

LONGEST LEGO STRUCTURE

On May 31, 1998, 20,000 people built a 1,895-ft.-long Lego millipede in the Old Town Square, Prague, Czech Republic, using 1,500,834 bricks.

SMALLEST KITE FLOWN

A kite built by Nobuhiko Yoshizuni (Japan) and flown in Seattle, Washington, USA, on April 18, 1998, measured just 0.39 in. x 0.31 in.

LONGEST KITE FLOWN

On Nov. 18, 1990, Michel Trouillet flew a 3,394-ft.-long kite at Nîmes, France.

LENGTHIEST FLIGHT BY A PAPER AIRPLANE

Ken Blackburn flew a paper plane for 27.6 sec. at the Georgia Dome, Atlanta, USA, on Oct. 8, 1998.

BIGGEST LITE-BRITE PICTURE

Lori Kanary (USA) created a 4-ft. x 6-ft. version of Monet's *Impression Sunrise* using 62,856 Lite-Brite pegs. It was exhibited on Nov. 5, 1999, in Denver, Colorado, USA.

Collectors

BIGGEST CLOTHING TAG COLLECTION
Angela Bettelli of Modena, Italy, had collected a total of 2,180 different cardboard clothing tags by 1990. Her collection includes tags from French, German, and Italian designers. The oldest one is 40 years old.

BIGGEST PARKING METER COLLECTION
Lotta Sjölin of Solna, Sweden, had accumulated a collection of 292 different parking meters by July 1996. She obtains the disused meters from local authorities all over the world, and started her collection in 1989.

BIGGEST KEY RING COLLECTION
Jeremy Demchuck of Kent, Washington, USA, has collected a total of 21,513 different key rings since 1993. Each one was obtained from a lost-and-found office or purchased at a rummage sale.

BIGGEST GOLF BALL COLLECTION
Ted Hoz of Baton Rouge, Louisiana, USA, has collected 46,778 different golf balls since 1986.

BIGGEST CHAMBER POT COLLECTION
Manfred Klauda has collected 9,400 chamber pots, the earliest one dating from the 16th century. His collection can be seen at the Zentrum für Aussergewöhnliche Museum, Munich, Germany.

BIGGEST GNOME AND PIXIE COLLECTION
Since 1978, Anne Atkin of West Putford, Devon, England, has collected a total of 2,010 gnomes and pixies. They live in a 4-acre gnome reserve, which has been visited by over 25,000 people to date.

BIGGEST FRUIT STICKER COLLECTION
Antoine Secco of Bourbon-Laancy, France, has collected over 20,500 different fruit stickers.

BIGGEST REFRIGERATOR MAGNET COLLECTION
Louise Greenfarb of Spanaway, Washington, USA, has collected over 29,000 refrigerator magnets.

BIGGEST CIGARETTE LIGHTER COLLECTION
Francis Van Herle of Beringen, Belgium, has a collection of 58,259 different lighters.

BIGGEST ROBIN CHRISTMAS CARD COLLECTION
Joan Gordon of Kent, England, has collected a total of 10,677 Christmas cards with pictures of robins on them. She uses them to decorate her house each Christmas, a process that starts in November.

BIGGEST BOTTLE OPENER COLLECTION
Dale Deckert of Orlando, Florida, USA, started his collection of bottle openers after being discharged from the US Army in 1945. They come from 136 different countries and total 20,884, excluding duplicates.

BIGGEST BUS TICKET COLLECTION
Yacov Yosipovv of Tel Aviv, Israel, has over 14,000 used bus tickets, every one different in some way.

BIGGEST BEER MAT COLLECTION
Leo Pisker of Langenzersdorf, Austria, has collected a record 152,860 different beer mats from 185 countries to date. The largest in his collection measures 2 ft. 6 in. x 2 ft. 6 in., and the smallest measures just 1 in. x 1 in.

BIGGEST BARBIE DOLL COLLECTION
Tony Mattia of Brighton, E. Sussex, England, has a collection of 1,125 Barbie dolls – about half the models produced since Mattel launched the doll in the USA in 1959. This total includes many versions of Barbie's boyfriend Ken.

BIGGEST AIRPLANE SICK BAG COLLECTION
Nick Vermeulen of Wormerveer, Netherlands, has collected 2,112 different airplane sick bags from 470 airlines around the world.

BIGGEST NAIL CLIPPER COLLECTION
André Ludwick of Parys, South Africa, has collected 505 different nail clippers since 1971. His favorite set are the oldest, which were handmade by a blacksmith in approximately 1935.

BIGGEST FAKE MASTERPIECE COLLECTION
Christophe Petyt of France owns over 2,500 fake paintings representing some of the most famous works in art history. Widely considered to be one of the world's best forgers, he created the collection with the help of 82

⊙ BIGGEST CHIP PACK COLLECTION
Frank Ritter (USA), who lives in Nottingham, England, has collected 683 individual chip packs, from 15 different countries, since 1993.

other painters. He founded the L'Art du Faux foundation in Paris, France, in 1992.

BIGGEST *BOTIJO* COLLECTION

Since 1991, Jesús Gil-Gilbernau del Río of Logroño, Spain, has collected over 2,500 *botijos* – traditional Spanish drinking vessels with two spouts and a handle. His collection includes *botijos* made of porcelain, crystal, wood, and pottery.

BIGGEST SHOT GLASS COLLECTION

Brad Rogers of Las Vegas, Nevada, USA, has a collection of 8,411 shot glasses.

BIGGEST THERMOMETER COLLECTION

John Thynne of Southwick, W. Sussex, England, has collected 240 thermometers since 1989.

BIGGEST GUM COLLECTION

Since 1980, Steve Fletcher of London, England, has collected a record total of 5,100 packs of chewing gum and bubble gum.

BIGGEST SIGNED BOOK COLLECTION

Michael Silverbrooke and Pat Tonkin of Vancouver, Canada, have collected a total of 318 books that have been signed by their authors.

BIGGEST MUG COLLECTION

Marlene Williamson of Charleston, South Carolina, USA, has been collecting mugs since 1996, and has amassed a record total of 1,419.

→ BIGGEST ANGEL COLLECTION

Joyce and Lowell Berg from Beloit, Wisconsin, USA, have a collection of 12,037 angel and cherub figurines, music boxes, and even an angel smoke alarm.

Clubbing & Parties

BIGGEST MILLENNIUM PARTIES

The largest millennium parties held on Dec. 31, 1999/Jan. 1, 2000, took place in London, England, New York City, USA, and Rio de Janeiro, Brazil.

In London, 3.5 million people lined 7.5 miles of the River Thames at midnight to watch a 15-minute fireworks display that took place on 16 barges moored along the river. The fireworks were covered by 54 television networks from around the world, and were the largest display of their kind ever, requiring over 30 tons of pyrotechnics. The all-day celebrations, which began at 11 a.m. and lasted until 2 a.m., drew an estimated 5 million people in total and included two amusement parks, an arts festival, four performance stages, 50 live music acts, and three giant video screens.

The celebrations in New York drew a crowd of 3 million people in and around Times Square, who watched a 6-ft.-wide, 1,070-lb. Waterford crystal ball drop down

a 77-ft. flagpole, triggering fireworks and 4 tons of confetti. The festivities ran for 24 hours, with a different show every hour representing the arrival of the millennium in each of the world's time zones. The event was the longest continuously running performance in the city's history, and featured live music, giant puppets, video broadcasts from around the globe, and over 500 performers. It was estimated to have cost $7 million, and produced 30 tons of litter.

Rio de Janeiro, Brazil, hosted fireworks displays on a number of its beaches, attracting an overall crowd estimated at 4 million people. The largest of the displays took place at Copacabana, where 3 million people turned up along an 8-mile stretch of beach to join in the celebrations. Fireworks were launched from an offshore barge, five locations on the sand, and two forts at either end of the beach. Three giant sound stages were erected, as well as a 328-ft. high-resolution screen, and the proceedings were broadcast around the world.

BIGGEST CARNIVALS

Salvador Carnival, Bahia, Brazil, attracts 2 million people, including 800,000 tourists, every year and generates $254 million in business. The six-day carnival takes place on 16 miles of road through the town center, with 100 carnival groups called *blocos* entertaining the crowds. The 1999 Mardi Gras celebrations in the French Quarter of New Orleans, Louisiana, USA, also drew an estimated 2 million people.

BIGGEST ROCK FESTIVAL

The highest attendance at a rock festival was a record 670,000, for Steve Wozniak's 1983 US Festival at Devore, near San Bernardino, California, USA. It lasted from May 28 to 30, with a fourth day for country music on June 4. The event's headline artists were The Clash, Van Halen, David Bowie, and Willie Nelson.

BIGGEST ANNUAL FOOD FIGHT

On the last Wednesday of every August, the town of Buñol, Spain, holds its annual tomato festival, known as the Tomatina. At the 1999 event, 25,000 people spent one hour hurling about 123 tons of tomatoes at each other. The fruit is dumped in streets for participants to scoop up and throw.

⊙ BIGGEST INDOOR NIGHTCLUB

Privilege in Ibiza, Spain, can accommodate 10,000 clubbers on its 69,968 ft.^{2} of dance space, spread over three floors. One end of the club is made from sheet glass to allow the morning sun to shine through. A swimming pool, fountains, gardens, trees, and plants add to the ambience of the club, the site of the legendary Manumission all-nighters.

⊙ LONGEST DANCE PARTY

The longest dance party on record was hosted by MTV India and took place at the Fireball club, Gurgaon, India, from Nov. 26 to 29, 1999. It featured 56 participants who danced continuously for 50 hours.

↓ BIGGEST GAY FESTIVALS

The Lesbian Gay Bisexual Transgender Pride Parade in San Francisco, California, USA, and the Sydney Gay and Lesbian Mardi Gras in Sydney, NSW, Australia (pictured), each attracted 600,000 people in 1999.

BIGGEST GARLIC FESTIVAL

The three-day Gilroy Garlic Festival, held each summer in Gilroy, California, USA, attracts 130,000 people, who can sample garlic-flavored food ranging from meat to ice cream.

BIGGEST BIRTHDAY PARTY

The largest birthday party for someone who actually attended the event took place in Louisville, Kentucky, USA, on Sept. 8, 1979, to celebrate the 89th birthday of Kentucky Fried Chicken founder Col. Harland Sanders. A total of 35,000 guests turned up.

BIGGEST CHILDREN'S PARTY

A party to celebrate the International Year of the Child, held in Hyde Park, London, England, on May 30–31, 1979, was attended by 160,000 children.

BIGGEST TEDDY BEARS' PICNIC

On June 24, 1995, 33,573 bears (and their owners) attended a teddy bears' picnic at Dublin Zoo, Ireland.

⊙ SMALLEST NIGHTCLUB

The Miniscule of Sound, London, England, is 8 ft. long, 4 ft. wide, and 8 ft. high, with a 21.5-ft.^{2} dance floor. It can accommodate a maximum of 14 people, including the DJ.

Organizations

BIGGEST SCHOOL
In 1999, the City Montessori School, Lucknow, India, had an enrollment of 22,612 pupils.

BIGGEST LABOR UNION CONGLOMERATE
In March 2000, the Federation of Independent Labor Unions of Russia had 38 million members.

BIGGEST STAMP-COLLECTING ORGANIZATION
With over 55,000 members in more than 110 countries, the American Philatelic Society is the largest nonprofit society in the world for stamp collectors and postal historians. It is supported entirely by membership dues, gifts, and the sale of its publications and services. The APS was founded in 1886.

OLDEST MAGIC SOCIETY
The Society of American Magicians is the oldest magic society in the world. It was founded in Martinka's famous magic shop in New York City, USA, on May 10, 1902, with only 24 members.

OLDEST ROTARY CLUB
Chicago, USA, lawyer Paul Harris, together with three friends, started the first Rotary Club on Feb. 23, 1905. The club had a total of 30 members by the end of the year.

COUNTRY WITH MOST ROTARY CLUBS
Rotary International consists of 29,500 clubs in 162 countries. The USA boasts 7,485 clubs, while Japan is in second position with 2,280.

OLDEST MASONIC LODGES
The oldest written records for a Masonic lodge belong to Aitchison's Haven in Musselburgh, Scotland. They date back to Jan. 9, 1599.

The oldest written records for a Masonic lodge that is still in existence today are from The Lodge of Edinburgh (Mary's Chapel), No. 1, Scotland. They date back to July 31, 1599.

SMALLEST LABOR UNION
The Sheffield Wool Shear Workers Union, S. Yorkshire, England, has only 10 members.

The Jewelcase and Jewellery Display Makers' Union (JJDMU), founded in 1894, was dissolved by its general secretary Charles Evans on Dec. 31, 1986. The motion was seconded by Fergus McCormack, the union's only other surviving member.

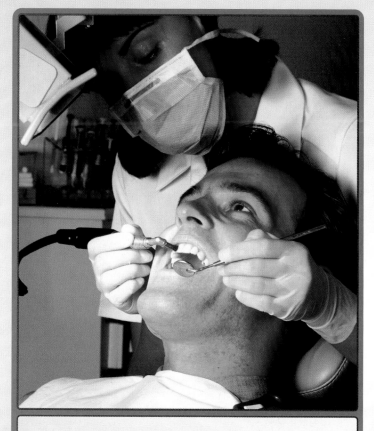

⊙ BIGGEST DENTAL ASSOCIATION
As of March 2000, the American Dental Association had 155,400 registered members.

⊙ BIGGEST MAGIC SOCIETY
The International Magicians' Society, founded in New York City, USA, in 1968, has 23,000 members worldwide. These include David Copperfield (left), the highest-paid magician in the world.

BIGGEST ASSOCIATION OF PSYCHOLOGISTS
The registered membership of the American Psychological Association was 159,000 in March 2000.

LONGEST-RUNNING FAN CLUB FOR A GROUP
The Official Queen Fan Club was set up by EMI after the launch of the band's first album, *Queen*, in 1973, because of the unprecedented number of fan letters the group was receiving. At its peak, the club had more than 20,000 members, although this number has now dropped to 9,500.

LONGEST-RUNNING FAN CLUB FOR A SOLO ARTIST

The Club Crosby, founded in 1936, celebrates the work of Bing Crosby and currently has 450 members worldwide. Its official magazine is published twice a year.

OLDEST LIFESAVING ORGANIZATION

The Royal National Lifeboat Institution (RNLI), a British lifesaving society, was formed by royal edict in March 1824 and celebrated its 175th anniversary in 1999. By April 1999, the organization had saved 132,500 lives.

BIGGEST VOLUNTEER AMBULANCE ORGANIZATION

Abdul Sattar Edhi (Pakistan) began his ambulance service in 1948, ferrying injured people to the hospital. Today, his radio-linked network includes 500 ambulances all over Pakistan, and attracts funds of $5 million a year. He has also set up 300 relief centers, three air ambulances, 24 hospitals, three drug rehabilitation centers, women's centers, free dispensaries, and soup kitchens.

BIGGEST NEWS ORGANIZATION

Founded in 1848, the Associated Press is the world's oldest and largest news organization, with 3,500 employees working in 240 bureaus in 72 countries. AP supplies 20 million words a day to subscribers and agencies in 112 countries worldwide.

OLDEST INTERNATIONAL HUMAN RIGHTS ORGANIZATION

The oldest international human rights organization still in existence today is the UK-based Anti-Slavery, founded in 1839 as the British and Foreign Anti-Slavery Society (BFASS). It continues to fight exploitation and all forms of forced labor around the world.

← MOST FAN CLUBS

There are more than 613 active Elvis Presley fan clubs worldwide, with a total membership of 510,489. The longest-running of these is the French *La Voix d'Elvis* ("The Voice of Elvis"), founded in Jan. 1956 by Evelyne Bellemin. It currently has 30 members.

Theme Parks & Rides

MOST VISITED THEME PARK
In 1999, Tokyo Disneyland in Japan attracted a record 17.46 million visitors – an increase of 4.6% on the previous year. The park also holds the record for the highest theme park attendance for the period 1990–99, when it drew a total of 162.6 million people.

BIGGEST INDOOR THEME PARK
The world's largest indoor amusement park is Galaxyland, located inside the West Edmonton Mall, Alberta, Canada. The park covers an area of 44,444 yds.^{2} and contains 30 skill games and 27 rides and attractions. These include *The Mindbender*, a 14-story, triple-loop roller coaster that exerts a record G-force of 6.5 on its passengers, and *Drop Of Doom*, a 13-story free-fall ride.

BIGGEST INDOOR WATER PARK
The Ocean Dome is part of a leisure complex in Miyazaki, Kyushu, Japan. The park is 984 ft. 3 in. long, 328 ft. 1 in. wide, and 124 ft. 8 in. high, with a 459-ft. 3-in.-long beach made from crushed marble. It also contains the biggest wave-making machine in the world, capable of creating waves 8 ft. 2 in. high.

MOST RIDES IN A THEME PARK
Cedar Point in Sandusky, Ohio, USA, has a total of 67 different rides – the most of any theme park in the world today. These include traditional wooden-track roller coasters such as *Blue Stack*, which was built in 1961, and *Woodcock Express*, a steel-track coaster that opened in 1999.

COUNTRY WITH MOST ROLLER COASTERS
There are a record 427 roller coasters in the USA. The UK is second, with 114, and Japan third, with 66.

FASTEST ROLLER COASTER
Superman The Escape, located at Six Flags Magic Mountain, Valencia, California, USA, is the fastest roller coaster in the world. Riders are taken up to a height of 415 ft. in 15-seater gondolas before falling back along the tracks at a speed of 100 m.p.h. They experience a record 6.5 seconds of "airtime," or negative G-force.

LONGEST ROLLER COASTER
The Ultimate roller coaster at Lightwater Valley Theme Park, Ripon, N. Yorkshire, England, is 1.42 miles long. The average ride lasts for 5 min. 50 sec.

⊙ OLDEST AMUSEMENT PARK
The world's oldest operating amusement park is Bakken, located in Klampenborg, Denmark. Opened in 1583, it has a 98-ft. wooden roller coaster, a flume, and various other thrill rides.

TALLEST GRAVITY-BASED ROLLER COASTER
The steel-track *Millennium Force* at Cedar Point, Sandusky, Ohio, USA, reaches a record height of 310 ft. Designed by Intamin Ag of Switzerland and opened on May 12, 2000, the roller coaster's highest drop – one of 300 ft. – allows riders to experience speeds of up to 92 m.p.h.

TALLEST GYRO DROP RIDE
Drop Zone, designed by Ride Trade of Liechtenstein and located at Paramount's Kings Island Theme Park, Ohio, USA, is the world's tallest gyro drop ride. Riders fall a record distance of 262 ft. 6 in. from a 300-ft.-high lift-tower, experiencing speeds of up to 65 m.p.h. in the process.

⊙ LONGEST HORROR HOUSE WALK-THROUGH
Jikei General Hospital, located at the Fujikyu Highland Amusement Park, Yamanashi Prefecture, Japan, is a horror house with a record 547-yd.-long walk-through. Completed on May 25, 1999, the attraction was designed by hospital architects in order to give it an authentic feel, and is laid out just like a typical Japanese hospital. *Jikei* means "bloodcurdling" in Japanese.

MOST ROLLER COASTERS RIDDEN IN 24 HOURS

From Sept. 12 to 13, 1999, a team of six people from Sun Microsystems, Bracknell, Berkshire, England, rode 29 different roller coasters at five theme parks.

BIGGEST OBSERVATION WHEEL

The British Airways London Eye, designed by architects David Marks and Julia Barfield (both UK), is 446 ft. 7 in. tall with a 443-ft. diameter. Located in Jubilee Gardens, London, England, it made its first "flight" on Feb. 1, 2000.

BIGGEST BOUNCY CASTLE

The biggest inflatable castle is 39 ft. tall and 62 ft. wide. Designed by Dana Caspersen and William Forsythe, it was built by Southern Inflatables, Hampshire, England.

← BIGGEST AMUSEMENT PARK

Disney World, located 20 miles southwest of Orlando, Florida, USA, covers an area of 30,000 acres. It was opened on Oct. 1, 1971, and cost an estimated $400 million to develop.

Fashion

⊙ **LONGEST CAREER MODELING FOR ONE COMPANY**
Shima Iwashita (Japan) has been a house model for the Japanese cosmetics company Menard for 28 years. She first signed a contract on April 1, 1972.

MOST EXPENSIVE SHOES
For his self-coronation on Dec. 4, 1977, Emperor Bokassa of the Central African Empire (now Central African Republic) commissioned pearl-studded shoes from the House of Berluti, Paris, France, that cost a record $85,000.

The most expensive shoes ever marketed were mink-lined golf shoes with 18-karat gold embellishments and ruby-tipped spikes, made by Stylo Matchmakers International of Northampton, England, and costing a record $20,400. They were last made in 1993.

MOST EXPENSIVE DESIGNER HAT
In 1977 UK, designer David Shilling created a straw-colored hat valued at $34,833. A chain of diamonds covering the crown of the hat could be worn as a necklace, a rose decoration as a brooch, and a dewdrop design as a pair of earrings. The hat would now be worth $109,776.

MOST EXPENSIVE TIARA
The world's most expensive tiara was designed by Gianni Versace and had an estimated retail value of $5 million in 1996. Set in yellow gold and decorated with 100-carat diamonds, it weighed approximately 10.5 oz.

MOST EXPENSIVE JEANS
In Oct.1998, Gucci launched a range of jeans retailing at $3,113. They were sold complete with African beading, tribal feather trims, and strategically placed rips, silver metal buttons, and rivets.

RICHEST DESIGNER
Ralph Lauren has a personal fortune estimated at $1.7 billion. The Ralph Lauren empire, which began with a tie shop in the 1960s, is now valued at around $3 billion.

FASTEST-GROWING DESIGNER LABEL
In the fiscal year 1999, the Tommy Hilfiger company had sales of $1.637 billion – an increase of just over 93% on the previous year. Hilfiger clothes are sold in about 1,500 specialized retail shops around the world.

OLDEST ATHLETIC SHOE ENDORSEMENT
Converse's basketball shoes, cross-training casual shoes, and children's shoes are sold under the Chuck Taylor Converse All-Star brand, named after Chuck Taylor (USA), who became the first athletic shoe endorser in 1923. Taylor's name was added to the shoes' ankle patch to honor his contribution to basketball.

⊙ **MOST DESIGNERS AT ONE FASHION SHOW**
A total of 89 designers took part in Paris Fashion Week in 1999, including Jean-Paul Gaultier (above), Vivienne Westwood, and Yves Saint Laurent.

MOST EXPENSIVE WEDDING DRESS
A wedding dress created by Hélène Gainville, with jewels by Alexander Reza, was valued at a record $7.3 million in March 1989. The dress was embroidered with diamonds mounted on platinum.

MOST EXPENSIVE SHAWLS
Shahtoosh shawls, which are made from the soft underbelly hair of the rare Tibetan antelope, have a retail value of $7,500–$15,000. Up to five antelope are killed to make each shawl, and trade in the garments is illegal.

⊙ BEST-SELLING SKATE SHOES

Vans is the ninth largest footwear manufacturer in the USA and, according to *Sporting Goods Intelligence*, leads the market in alternative footwear. The company had sales of $205.1 million in 1999. Vans shoes are distributed in 90 countries.

BIGGEST SURF WEAR MANUFACTURER

In 1999, Quiksilver had a revenue of approximately $444 million, making it the largest manufacturer of surf wear in the world.

BEST-SELLING UNDERPANTS

Marks & Spencer (UK) sells 50 million pairs (counting multipacks as a pair) of its own brand women's underpants globally each year, or nearly 137,000 pairs a day.

→ MOST EXPENSIVE BRA

The $10-million "Millennium Bra," modeled here by Heidi Klum, is produced by US company Victoria's Secret. Covered in 3,024 stones, including 1,988 sapphires, it is made to order and is delivered to the customer under armored car and guard.

Movies 1

HIGHEST BOX OFFICE GROSS
Paramount's *Titanic* (USA, 1997) has grossed a record total of $1.835 billion worldwide. This figure includes a record 10-week gross of $918.6 million.

Rising ticket prices mean that the world's top-grossing movies are nearly all recent releases. However, the receipts for *Gone With The Wind* (USA, 1939) – $393.4 million – add up to $3.79 billion when adjusted for inflation.

MOST PROFITABLE MOVIE SERIES
The 20 Bond movies, the first of which was *Dr No* (UK, 1962), have grossed a total of over $3.2 billion worldwide.

BIGGEST BOX OFFICE LOSS
MGM's *Cutthroat Island* (USA, 1995), starring Geena Davis and directed by her then husband Renny Harlin, cost over $100 million to produce and promote, but reportedly earned back just $11 million.

MOST EXPENSIVE FEATURE MOTION PICTURE
Titanic (USA, 1997) cost just over $200 million to make, a total partly accounted for by the lengthy delays incurred at the postproduction stage.

In terms of real costs adjusted for inflation, the most expensive movie ever made was *Cleopatra* (USA, 1963). Its $44-million budget would be equivalent to $306.9 million today.

LEAST EXPENSIVE FEATURE MOTION PICTURE
Victorian Film Productions' *The Shattered Illusion* (Australia, 1927), a silent movie written and directed by A.G. Harbrow, cost just $1,458 to make.

BIGGEST PUBLICITY BUDGET
Universal and its licensed merchandisers spent a record total of $68 million promoting Steven Spielberg's *Jurassic Park* (USA, 1993) in the US alone. This was $8 million more than the cost of the film.

⊙ TOP BUDGET:BOX OFFICE RATIO
The Blair Witch Project (USA, 1999), directed by Daniel Myrick and Eduardo Sánchez, cost $22,000 to make. It grossed $240.5 million – a budget:box office ratio of 1:10,931.

TOP-GROSSING ACTRESS
The box office gross of the 22 movies Carrie Fisher has appeared in is $1.41 billion. Her most profitable movies have been *Star Wars* (USA, 1977), *The Empire Strikes Back* (USA, 1980), and *Return Of The Jedi* (USA, 1983), each of which made over $200 million.

BIGGEST MOVIE STUDIO
The largest movie studio complex in the world is at Universal City, Los Angeles, California, USA. Called The Back Lot, it has an area of 420 acres and includes 561 buildings and 34 sound stages.

BIGGEST MOVIE SET
The largest movie set on record was the 437-yd. x 251-yd. re-creation of the Roman Forum used in Samuel Bronston's production of *The Fall Of The Roman Empire* (USA, 1964). Designed by Veniero Colosanti and John Moore, it was built on a 55-acre site outside Madrid, Spain. A total of 1,100 workmen spent seven months laying its surface with 170,000 cement blocks and erecting 7,327 yds. of concrete stairways, 601 columns, 350 statues, and 27 full-sized Roman buildings.

⊙ TOP-GROSSING ACTOR
The 24 movies Harrison Ford (left, in *Air Force One*) has starred in have a combined box office gross of $3.01 billion. Ten of them have grossed over $200 million. Ford's movies include the original *Star Wars* trilogy (USA, 1977–83), the Indiana Jones movies (USA, 1981–89), *The Fugitive* (USA, 1993), and *Air Force One* (USA, 1997).

MOST COSTUMES IN ONE MOVIE
A record 32,000 costumes were worn in *Quo Vadis* (USA, 1951).

LONGEST MOVIE
The longest movie ever made was the 85-hour *The Cure For Insomnia* (USA, 1987), directed by John Henry Timmis IV and premiered in its entirety at The School of The Art Institute in Chicago, Illinois, USA, from Jan. 31 to Feb. 3, 1987.

MOST LEADING ROLES
John Wayne appeared in 153 movies, from *The Drop Kick* (USA, 1927) to *The Shootist* (USA, 1976). He played the lead role in all but 11 of them.

GREATEST AGE RANGE PORTRAYED BY AN ACTOR IN ONE MOVIE
Dustin Hoffman was 33 years old when he played the role of Jack Crabbe in *Little Big Man* (USA, 1970). In the course of the movie his character ages from 17 to 121.

LONGEST SCREEN CAREER
German actor Curt Bois (1901–1991) made his debut in *Der Fidele Bauer* (Ger., 1908) at the age of eight. His final movie appearance was 79 years later, in Wim Wenders' *Wings Of Desire* (Ger., 1987).

LONGEST SCREEN PARTNERSHIP
Indian stars Prem Nazir and Sheela played opposite each other in 130 movies. Sheela retired in 1975.

BIGGEST MOVIE THEATER
The largest movie theater is the Radio City Music Hall, New York City, USA, which opened on Dec. 27, 1932, with 5,945 seats. It now has 5,910 seats.

→ HIGHEST OPENING-DAY GROSS
Star Wars Episode 1: The Phantom Menace took $28,542,349 from 2,970 movie theaters in North America on its opening day, May 19, 1999.

Movies 2

BIGGEST MOVIE OUTPUT
India produces more feature-length movies than any other country, with a peak output of 948 in 1990. In 1994, the last year for which figures are available, 754 movies in 16 languages were produced at India's three major centers of production, Mumbai (Bombay), Calcutta, and Chennai (Madras).

BIGGEST MOVIE THEATER ATTENDANCE
In 1988, there were 21.8 billion movie theater visits in China.

HIGHEST-GROSSING COMEDIES
Home Alone (USA, 1990), starring Macaulay Culkin and directed by Chris Columbus, took a record $533.8 million at the international box office.

Austin Powers: The Spy Who Shagged Me (USA, 1999), starring Mike Myers, grossed $54.92 million June 12–13, 1999, the weekend following its release.

⊙ SHORTEST ACTOR
Verne Troyer, seen here as Mini-Me in *Austin Powers: The Spy Who Shagged Me* (USA, 1999) with Mike Myers, is 2 ft. 8 in. tall. His other movies include *Men In Black* (USA, 1997) and *How The Grinch Stole Christmas* (USA, 2000).

HIGHEST-GROSSING WESTERN
Dances with Wolves (USA, 1990), directed by and starring Kevin Costner, grossed $424.2 million at the international box office.

MOST EXPENSIVE SILENT MOVIE
Ben Hur (USA, 1925) cost a record total of $3.9 million to film. This figure is equivalent to $33 million today.

HIGHEST-GROSSING SILENT MOVIE
The Big Parade (USA, 1925), which starred John Gilbert, grossed a record total of $22 million during its worldwide release.

LONGEST MOVIE SERIES
A total of 103 movies have been made about the 19th-century martial arts hero Huang Fei-Hong. The first in the series was *The True Story Of Huang Fei-Hong* (1949) and the most recent was *Once Upon A Time In China 5* (1995). All the movies were made in Hong Kong.

The 48 *Tora-San* comedy movies, made by Shochiku Studios, Japan, between Aug. 1969 and Dec. 1995, all starred Kiyoshi Atsumi in the role of Torajiro Kuruma, making this the longest movie series with the same leading actor.

MOST FILMED STORY
There have been a record 95 movies based on the classic fairy tale *Cinderella*, including cartoon, ballet, operatic, and parody versions. The first ever version was *Fairy Godmother* (UK, 1898) and the most recent was *Ever After* (USA, 1998).

MOST FILMED FICTIONAL CHARACTER
The fictional character most frequently portrayed on the big screen is Sherlock Holmes, the detective created by Sir Arthur Conan Doyle. He has been portrayed by 75 actors in more than 211 movies since 1900.

⊙ LONGEST SHOOT
Stanley Kubrick's *Eyes Wide Shut* (USA, 1999), starring Tom Cruise and Nicole Kidman, was in production for over 15 months, a period that included an unbroken shoot of 46 weeks. Kubrick, who died before the film was released, also held the record for the most retakes of one scene, with 127 for a scene in *The Shining* (USA, 1980).

⊙ HIGHEST-GROSSING HORROR FILM
The supernatural horror-thriller *The Sixth Sense* (USA, 1999),
starring Bruce Willis and Haley Joel Osment, had taken
$679.4 million worldwide by April 2000.

MOST FILMED
HISTORICAL FIGURE
The French emperor Napoleon
Bonaparte has been portrayed
in 177 movies since 1897.

MOST FILMED
HORROR CHARACTER
Count Dracula, who was created
by Bram Stoker (Ireland), has
been portrayed in more horror
movies than any other character.
Representations of the Count
or his immediate descendants
outnumber those of his closest
rival, Frankenstein's monster,
by 161 to 117.

MOST FILMED AUTHOR
A total of 394 feature movies and
TV movies based on plays by
William Shakespeare have been
made to date. *Hamlet* has proved
the most popular choice of play
for filmmakers, with 75 versions
made, followed by *Romeo And
Juliet* with 51, and *Macbeth* with
33. Recent adaptations include
*William Shakespeare's Romeo
And Juliet* (USA, 1996) and *O*
(USA, 2000), based on *Othello*.

↓ HIGHEST-GROSSING
FRENCH FILM
Cyrano de Bergerac
(Fr., 1990) grossed
$15.1 million worldwide,
a record for a French-
language film, and made
its leading actor Gerard
Depardieu (right) an
international star.

HIGHEST-GROSSING
INDIAN MOVIE
Hum Aapke Hain Koun..! (India,
1994) took over $63.8 million in
its first year.

HIGHEST-GROSSING
AFRICAN MOVIE
Sankofa (1993), directed by
Haile Gerima (Ethiopia), grossed
$2.691 million in the USA
alone. The movie was
shot in Germany,
Burkina Faso,
and Ghana.

HIGHEST-GROSSING
ITALIAN MOVIE
La Vita È Bella (*Life Is
Beautiful*) (It., 1997),
written by and starring
Roberto Benigni, had a
worldwide gross of $229 million.

HIGHEST-GROSSING
MOVIE IN GERMAN
Das Boot (Ger., 1981),
the story of a World War II
submarine crew,
took $84.9 million
worldwide.

93

Cartoons

LONGEST-RUNNING NEWSPAPER COMIC STRIP

The Katzenjammer Kids was first published in the *New York Journal* on Dec. 12, 1897, and is still running. Created by Rudolph Dirks, it is now drawn by Hy Eisman.

LONGEST-RUNNING COMIC STRIP BY ONE ARTIST

Jim Russell (Australia) has been drawing the comic strip *The Potts* since Jan. 1940. It was published in the newspaper *Smiths Weekly* until 1950, since when it has appeared daily in the *Melbourne Herald.*

MOST EDITIONS OF A COMIC

A total of 7,561 issues of the Mexican comic *Pepín* were published between March 4, 1936, and Oct. 23, 1956. At the height of its popularity, sales were estimated at 320,000 copies a day, with twice that number being sold on Sundays. *Pepín* finally started outselling its closest rival, *Chamaco Chico*, in the 1940s, when Yolanda Vargas Dulche joined the writing team, creating characters such as the villainess Raratonga the Jungle Queen.

MOST PROLIFIC CARTOONIST

Joe Martin (USA), the creator of *Mr. Boffo*, *Willy 'N Ethel*, *Cats With Hands,* and *Porterfield*, draws 1,300 cartoon strips and single panels a year. He has had 20,865 cartoons published since 1978.

MOST SYNDICATED LIVING CARTOONIST

The strips *The Wizard of Id* and *B.C.*, created by Johnny Hart (USA), are each syndicated to 1,300 newspapers worldwide.

MOST FILMED CARTOON CHARACTER

Zorro has been portrayed in 69 films to date. Created by Johnston McCulley, he was also the first comic strip character to be the subject of a major motion picture, *The Mark of Zorro* (USA,1920), starring Douglas Fairbanks. The most recent Zorro film, *The Mask Of Zorro* (USA, 1998), saw the identity of the masked avenger pass from Anthony Hopkins to Antonio Banderas.

MOST EXPENSIVE ANIMATED FILM

DreamWorks' *The Prince of Egypt* (USA, 1998) cost $60 million to make. Directed by Brenda Chapman and Steve Hickner, it was in production for four years and was worked on by 350 artists and animators. It contains 1,192 special effects, one of which – the four-minute Red Sea sequence – took an estimated 350,000 hours to complete.

MOST CONSECUTIVE OSCAR NOMINATIONS

Aardman Animation, based in Bristol, England, received six Oscar nominations for Best Short Animated Film between 1991 and 1997. Three of the nominations, *Creature Comforts*, *The Wrong Trousers,* and *A Close Shave*, all directed by Aardman founder Nick Park, went on to win Oscars.

LONGEST-RUNNING PRIMETIME ANIMATED SERIES

The Simpsons, created by cartoonist Matt Groening (USA), is the longest-running primetime animated TV series, with a total of 242 episodes shown on the Fox network to March 15, 2000. Originally developed in 1987 as a set of 30-second inserts for Fox's *The Tracey Ullman Show*, *The Simpsons* has featured the voices of 240 celebrities – a record number for an animated series.

EARLIEST FULL-LENGTH ANIMATED MOVIE

The first full-length feature cartoon was *El Apóstol* (Argentina, 1917), which was made by Don Federico Valle.

PEANUTS

Dear Friends,

I have been fortunate to draw Charlie Brown and his friends for almost 50 years. It has been the fulfillment of my childhood ambition.

Unfortunately, I am no longer able to maintain the schedule demanded by a daily comic strip, therefore I am announcing my retirement.

I have been grateful over the years for the loyalty of our editors and the wonderful support and love expressed to me by fans of the comic strip.

Charlie Brown, Snoopy, Linus, Lucy...how can I ever forget them....

Charles M. Schulz

1-3-00

© 1999 United Feature Syndicate, Inc.

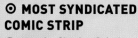

⊙ MOST SYNDICATED COMIC STRIP

Peanuts by Charles Schulz (USA) appears in 2,620 different newspapers in 75 countries. Schulz published his last strip on Jan. 3, 2000, and died on Feb. 12.

EARLIEST ANIMATED TV SERIES

Alex Anderson and Jay Ward's syndicated cartoon series *Crusader Rabbit* was produced in San Francisco, California, USA, from 1949 to 1951. The show, each episode of which ran for five minutes, was made in color, despite the fact that there was no color television at this time.

MOST CONVULSIONS CAUSED BY A TV SHOW

On Dec. 16, 1997, more than 700 children in Japan had to be rushed to hospital when an episode of the TV show *Pokémon* caused them to have convulsions. A total of 208 children aged three and above were kept in the hospital after the broadcast. According to experts, the convulsions were caused by a sequence in which red lights flashed from the eyes of the character Pikachu.

MOST VALUABLE CARTOON CELLS

In 1989, a black-and-white drawing from Walt Disney's *Orphan's Benefit* (USA, 1934), depicting Donald Duck being punched by an orphan, raised $280,000 at Christie's, London, England.

One of the 150,000 color cells from Disney's *Snow White* (USA, 1937) was sold in 1991 for $203,000.

MOST VALUABLE CARTOON POSTER

A poster for the Walt Disney short *Alice's Day At Sea* (USA, 1924) was sold at Christie's, London, England, for a record-breaking $36,534 in April 1994.

BIGGEST CARTOON MUSEUM

The International Museum of Cartoon Art in Boca Raton, Florida, USA, has a collection of over 160,000 original animated drawings from 50 different countries. The collection also includes 10,000 books on animation and 1,000 hours of cartoons, interviews, and documentaries on film and tape.

← **MOST SWEARING IN AN ANIMATED MOVIE**
South Park: Bigger, Longer & Uncut (USA, 1999), which lasts for 81 minutes, contains 399 swear words and 128 offensive gestures.

TV 1

⊙ SHORTEST TV SITCOMS

The Gaveltons, a sitcom about a family that will sue anyone, has an air time of just 60 seconds. It has been shown on the US network TV Land since July 1998, where it has now been joined by two other 60-second "blipcoms": *All's Well* and *Spin & Cutter*.

LONGEST-RUNNING CHILDREN'S PROGRAM

The BBC's live magazine program *Blue Peter* was first aired on Oct. 16, 1958. Originally presented by Christopher Trace and Leila Williams, it had had a total of 28 presenters as of April 2000, the longest-serving being John Noakes, who fronted the show from 1965 to 1978. *Blue Peter* was first broadcast once a week, but has gone out three times a week since 1995.

LONGEST-RUNNING DRAMA

The longest-running drama serial is Granada's soap *Coronation Street*. The show ran twice weekly on the UK's ITV network from Dec. 9, 1960, to Oct. 20, 1989; since then viewers have been treated to a third weekly episode.

LONGEST-RUNNING TV SHOW

NBC's *Meet The Press* was first transmitted on Nov. 6, 1947, and has been shown weekly from Sept. 12, 1948. As of April 2, 2000, 2,605 episodes had been aired.

MOST WATCHED TV NETWORK

The state-owned station China Central Television (CCTV) is transmitted to 84% of all viewers in China. It is estimated that more than 900 million people in the country have access to television.

BIGGEST GLOBAL TV NETWORK

CNN International can be seen in over 149 million households in 212 countries and territories, through a network of 23 satellites.

MOST TV EPISODES

Since 1949, over 150,000 episodes of the TV show *Bozo The Clown* have been broadcast. The program is aired daily on 150 stations in the USA.

BIGGEST TV AUDIENCE FOR A LIVE BROADCAST

The worldwide TV audience for the funeral of Diana, Princess of Wales, on Sept. 6, 1997, was estimated at 2.5 billion.

MOST EXPENSIVE PROGRAM

In Jan. 1998, NBC agreed to pay Warner Brothers a total of $10–13 million for each one-hour episode of the hospital drama *ER*, which has a weekly audience of 33 million in the USA. They had previously paid $1.6 million per episode. The deal will run for three years, working out at $660–858 million for 66 episodes.

MOST EXPENSIVE MINISERIES

The 14-episode TV miniseries *War And Remembrance* cost $110 million to make over three years. It was aired on US network ABC in two parts, in Nov. 1988, and March 1989, and won the 1989 Best Miniseries Emmy.

MOST EXPENSIVE DOCUMENTARY SERIES

The six-part BBC documentary series *Walking With Dinosaurs* cost a total of $9.9 million, or $61,112 per minute, to produce. Filmed in various locations around the world, the show, each episode of which lasted 27 minutes, used computer graphics and animatronics to depict how dinosaurs lived, reproduced and finally became extinct.

⊙ SHORTEST MUSIC VIDEO

In 1994, US death metal band Brutal Truth produced a 2.18-second-long video to accompany their track "Collateral Damage." The video features a sequence of flash frames depicting popular US conservative cultural icons of the late 20th century, and ends with a shot of an explosion.

MOST EXPENSIVE TV RIGHTS FOR A FILM

The US network Fox paid a record $80 million for the TV rights to Steven Spielberg's *The Lost World: Jurassic Park* (USA, 1997) in June 1997, before the film's international release.

BEST-SELLING VIDEO

The world's best-selling video is Walt Disney's animated feature *The Lion King* (USA, 1994), which has sold more than 55 million copies worldwide. This includes 20 million copies in the first six days after its release.

BIGGEST VIDEO RETAILER

Blockbuster is the world's largest video retailer, with a 30% market share. The first store opened in Dallas, Texas, USA, in Oct. 1985, and the company now operates 4,438 branches in the USA and 2,005 in 26 other countries.

⊙ MOST SPIN-OFF SHOWS

The Japanese series *Ultraman*, which aired between July 1966 and April 1967, spawned 14 spin-off series and several movies. The title character (left) is seen battling Kodalar, a sea monster, in *Ultraman: The Alien Invasion* (Japan, 1993).

MOST EXPENSIVE MUSIC VIDEO

The video for Michael and Janet Jackson's hit single "Scream" (1995), directed by Mark Romanek (USA), cost a record $7 million to make.

LONGEST MUSIC VIDEO

Michael Jackson's part feature film, part music video *Ghosts* (1996), is 35 minutes long. It was based on an original concept by cult horror writer Stephen King.

MOST PARTICIPANTS IN A TV QUIZ

The All-Japan High-School Quiz Championship, which was televised by NTV on Dec. 31, 1983, had a record 80,799 participants.

MOST COST-EFFECTIVE COMMERCIAL

Macintosh, a TV commercial based on George Orwell's novel *1984*, cost $600,000 to produce and $1 million to show. Directed by Ridley Scott, its impact was so great and its recall so high, that it is considered to be the most cost-effective commercial ever made. It was shown only once – in 1984.

SHORTEST TV COMMERCIAL

An advertisement lasting only four frames (there are 30 frames in a second) was aired in the USA on KING TV's *Evening Magazine* on Nov. 29, 1993. The ad was for Bon Marche's Frango sweets.

TV 2

RICHEST ACTRESS ON TV
Helen Hunt, the star of *Mad About You*, is the world's wealthiest TV actress, with a net worth of $31 million in 1998.

HIGHEST ANNUAL EARNINGS BY AN ACTOR
Jerry Seinfeld, the former star of *Seinfeld*, earned an estimated $267 million in 1998, according to the 1999 *Forbes* Celebrity 100 List – a record for any actor in a single year.

HIGHEST ANNUAL EARNINGS BY A TALK SHOW HOST
According to the 2000 *Forbes* Celebrity 100 List, Oprah Winfrey earned more than $150 million in 1999.

HIGHEST-EARNING NEWS BROADCASTER
Barbara Walters (USA) reputedly earns in excess of $13 million a year as news correspondent and co-anchor of *ABC News Magazine*, *20/20*, *The Barbara Walters Specials* and *The View*. She has interviewed every US president since Richard Nixon and made journalistic history in Nov. 1977 by arranging the first ever joint interview of President Anwar Sadat of Egypt and Prime Minister Menachem Begin of Israel.

HIGHEST ANNUAL EARNINGS BY A TV PRODUCER
David E. Kelley (USA), the creator of *Ally McBeal* and *The Practice*, was the leading TV producer on the 2000 *Forbes* Celebrity 100 List, with earnings of $118 million in 1999. He is also the highest-earning active TV writer.

HIGHEST-EARNING TV WRITER
The highest-earning TV writer ever is Larry David (USA), co-writer of the hit comedy *Seinfeld*. He earned an estimated $242 million in 1998, coming second only to Jerry Seinfeld on the 1999 *Forbes* Celebrity 100 List. David left the show in 1996, returning to pen its final episode in 1998.

MOST POPULAR TV STAR IN JAPAN
Akashiya Sanma polled 56.8% in Video Research (Japan) Ltd.'s 1999 survey of television popularity, making him the country's most popular TV star.

⊙ MOST INTERACTIVE DRAMA-DOCUMENTARY
In the show *Big Brother*, broadcast in the Netherlands from Sept. 16 to Dec. 30, 1999, nine people's lives became a daily half-hour "live soap" after they were placed in a house fitted with 24 cameras and 59 microphones. More than 4.7 million viewers phoned and e-mailed to vote on which contestants would leave the program, and which one would remain to win $125,000.

LONGEST TIME IN ONE ROLE
William Roache has been playing the character Ken Barlow without a break since the first episode of the British soap opera *Coronation Street* on Dec. 9, 1960. Barlow, who was first seen as a student, has had three wives and 23 girlfriends and survived a suicide attempt.

⊙ BIGGEST TV CASH PRIZE
On Dec. 24, 1999, Ian Woodley (left of picture) won a record $1.6 million after correctly answering four questions in a quiz on *TFI Friday*, a British talk show hosted by Chris Evans (right). Evans had awarded the same sum to the winner of a quiz on his Virgin Radio show the previous day.

MOST APPEARANCES BY AN EXTRA
British actor Vic Gallucci has appeared in the ITV police drama *The Bill* more than 819 times since making his debut in 1989. Gallucci plays Detective Constable Tom Baker, who is often seen in the background leaning against filing cabinets and shuffling papers.

LONGEST TIME SURVIVED ON COMPETITION WINNINGS
In Jan. 1998, the Japanese program *Denpa Shonen*, shown on Nippon Television Network (NTV), challenged a viewer named "Nasubi" to win 1 million Japanese yen (the equivalent of $7,762) by taking part in magazine and radio competitions. Naked, he was locked into an apartment fitted with CCTV cameras, from where his travails were broadcast to the nation on a weekly basis.

Nasubi reached his target after 335 days, and was released back into society after a celebratory trip to South Korea.

BIGGEST TV CONTRACT
In Sept. 1998, Oprah Winfrey signed a $150-million contract with King World Productions that commits her to hosting the talk show *Oprah* through to the 2001/02 TV season. She received a check for $75 million in Oct. 1998, and another for the same amount in June 2000.

MOST PROLIFIC TV PRODUCERS
Mark Goodson, a former radio announcer who co-founded US company

Goodson–Todman Productions with Bill Todman in 1946, has produced a total of 39,312 episodes of game shows to date, totalling over 21,831 hours of air time. Goodson–Todman Productions has been responsible for a string of successful US game shows, including *Winner Takes All*, *What's My Line*, *Stop The Music*, and *The Price Is Right*.

Aaron Spelling has produced a total of 3,842 hours of television since 1956, comprising 3,578 hours of TV series and 264 hours of TV movies. His output has included *Charlie's Angels*, *Dynasty*, *Melrose Place,* and *Beverly Hills 90210*, which features his daughter Tori.

↓ BIGGEST AUDIENCE FOR A TV SERIES
Baywatch is the most widely viewed TV series in the world, with an estimated weekly audience of more than 1.1 billion in 142 countries. Since June 1996, it has been broadcast on every continent except Antarctica.

Music

BIGGEST ROCK CONCERT ATTENDANCES

An estimated 195,000 people paid $18 to attend a performance by Norwegian band A-Ha at the Rock In Rio festival, Maracanã Municipal Stadium, Rio de Janeiro, Brazil, in April 1990.

Rod Stewart's free concert at Copacabana Beach, Rio de Janeiro, Brazil, on New Year's Eve, 1994, reportedly attracted an audience of 3.5 million.

The largest paying audience attracted by a solo performer was an estimated 184,000, in the Maracanã Municipal Stadium, Rio de Janeiro, Brazil, to hear Paul McCartney on April 21, 1990.

CONCERTS ON MOST CONTINENTS IN 24 HOURS

British heavy metal band Def Leppard played concerts on three continents on Oct. 23, 1995. Each concert lasted for at least one hour and was attended by 200 or more people. The first began at 12:23 a.m. at Tangier, Morocco. The band then flew to London, England, for the second concert and finished their tour in Vancouver, Canada, at 11:33 p.m. on the same day.

BEST-SELLING ALBUM

The best-selling album of all time is *Thriller* by Michael Jackson, with global sales of over 47 million copies since 1982.

BEST-SELLING ALBUM BY A GROUP

The best-selling album in the world by a group is *Their Greatest Hits 1971–75* by The Eagles, sales of which are estimated at more than 25 million.

BEST-SELLING DEBUT ALBUM

The top-selling debut album is *Boston* by the US rock band Boston, which has sold 16 million copies since its release in 1976.

MOST NO. 1 SINGLES

The Beatles have had the most US No. 1 hits, with 20.

The Beatles and Elvis Presley had the most UK No. 1's, with 17 each.

MOST WEEKS AT NO. 1 ON THE US SINGLES CHART

"Near You" by Francis Craig topped the US chart for 17 weeks in 1947.

The longest chart-topper since 1955 has been "I Will Always Love You" by Whitney Houston, which was at No.1 for 14 weeks in 1992.

Elvis Presley's 18 No. 1 singles have occupied the top of the chart for a total of 80 weeks.

MOST WEEKS AT NO. 1 ON THE UK SINGLES CHART

Bryan Adams spent 16 straight weeks at No. 1 from July to Oct.

1991, with "(Everything I Do) I Do It For You," the theme from the film *Robin Hood: Prince Of Thieves* (USA, 1991).

⊙ BEST-SELLING SINGLE

The biggest-selling single since the charts began is Elton John's "Something About The Way You Look Tonight"/"Candle In The Wind 1997," with sales of 33 million worldwide. As of Oct. 20, 1997, it had also reached No. 1 in 22 countries. All Elton John's royalties and record company PolyGram's profits have been donated to the Diana, Princess of Wales Memorial Fund.

MOST SUCCESSFUL SONGWRITERS

The most successful songwriters in terms of No. 1 singles are John Lennon and Paul McCartney, formerly of The Beatles. McCartney is credited as writer on 32 No. 1 hits in the US, to Lennon's 26 (with 23 co-written), whereas Lennon authored 29 UK No. 1's to McCartney's 28 (with 25 co-written).

MOST COMPLETE DOMINATION OF THE US SINGLES CHART

On April 4,1964, The Beatles held the Top 5 positions on the US Hot 100 and placed a further seven titles elsewhere in the chart. The Top 5, in descending order,

⊙ LONGEST ALBUM TITLE

The album with the longest title to reach the US chart is Fiona Apple's 90-word *When The Pawn Hits The Conflicts He Thinks Like A King What He Knows Throws The Blows When He Goes To The Fight And He'll Win The Whole Thing 'Fore He Enters The Ring There's No Body To Batter When Your Mind is Your Might So When You Go Solo, You Hold Your Own Hand And Remember That Depth Is The Greatest Of Heights And If You Know Where You Stand, Then You'll Know Where To Land And If You Fall It Won't Matter, Cuz You Know That You're Right*, released on Nov. 9, 1999. The title is a poem Apple wrote after reading a bad review of her work.

BEST-SELLING ALBUM BY A TEENAGE SOLO ARTIST →

...*Baby One More Time* by Britney Spears had passed the 12 million sales mark in the USA alone by Feb. 2000. It was also a top-seller in many other countries.

were: "Can't Buy Me Love," "Twist And Shout," "She Loves You," "I Want To Hold Your Hand," and "Please Please Me."

LONGEST TOUR BY A DEAD ARTIST

"Elvis – The Concert" became the first live tour starring a dead performer when it started in the USA in the spring of 1998. During the concert, a video of Elvis Presley singing and playing was projected, while his original musicians from the 1970s performed on stage.

HIGHEST-EARNING POP STAR

In 1998, Celine Dion ranked 12th on *Forbes* magazine's list of the 40 richest entertainers. Her income of $55.5 million made her the highest-earning pop star in a single year. Her successes include "My Heart Will Go On," the theme from *Titanic* (USA, 1997).

MOST PSEUDONYMS USED BY POP STARS

John Lennon used 15 pseudonyms: Long John; Dr. Winston Booker Table & the Maître Ds; Dwarf McDougal; Rev. Fred Ghurkin; Dr. Winston O'Ghurkin; Dr. Winston O'Boogie and Los Paranois; Musketeer Gripweed; Dr. Dream; Mel Torment; Dr. Winston O'Reggae; Honorary John St John Johnson; Kaptain Kundalini; John O'Cean; Joel Nohnn; and Dad.

The record for a living star is 11. This is held jointly by Lennon's former colleague George Harrison, whose pseudonyms include The George O'Hara Smith Singers, L'Angelo Misterioso and Ohnothimagain; and Prince Rogers Nelson, known, among other names, as Prince, The Artist Formerly Known As Prince, The Artist, and ⚥ .

⊙ FIRST FIVE SINGLES IN AT NO. 1

In 1999–2000 Irish boy band Westlife became the only group to have their first five singles enter the UK chart at No. 1.

Dance, Rap & R&B

MOST DANCE CLUB PLAY SINGLES
Madonna has had a total of 22 No. 1 singles on the *Billboard* Dance Club Play chart in the USA. Her hits include "Like A Virgin," "Vogue," "Beautiful Stranger," and "American Pie."

The group with the most No. 1's is C+C Music Factory (comprising Robert Clivillés and David Cole), with eight.

The male solo performer with the most No. 1's is Prince, who has reached the top seven times.

MOST SIMULTANEOUS HITS BY A DANCE ACT
On April 20, 1996, all 10 hit singles by the UK group Prodigy were in the UK Top 100. The band, comprising Liam Howlett, Keith Flint, Leeroy Thornhill, and Maxim Reality, had their first No. 1, "Firestarter," in March, and their nine previous singles were then re-released.

MOST NO. 1 RAP SINGLES
LL Cool J (real name James Todd Smith) has had eight No. 1's on the *Billboard* Rap Chart, including "Loungin'" and "I'm That Type Of Guy." He is on

the Def Jam label, which holds the record for the company with the most rap No. 1's. Other artists on the label have included the Beastie Boys, Run DMC, and Public Enemy.

BEST-SELLING GANGSTA RAP ALBUM
Life After Death by The Notorious BIG, aka Biggie Smalls (real name Christopher Wallace), has sold 10 million copies in the USA alone. The album first charted a month after the rapper was murdered in March 1997.

OLDEST RAPPERS
Japanese twin sisters Kin Narita and Gin Kanie were born on Aug. 1, 1892. For their 100th birthdays in 1992, they recorded a "granny rap" record that reached the Japanese pop charts. Kin died at the age of 107 on Jan. 23, 2000.

FASTEST RAP ARTIST
Rebel XD of Chicago, Illinois, USA, rapped 674 syllables in 54.9 seconds at the Hair Bear Recording Studio, Alsip, Illinois, on Aug. 27, 1992. This represents an average of 12.2 syllables per second.

⊙ **BEST-SELLING BIG BEAT ALBUM**
You've Come A Long Way Baby by Fatboy Slim (real name Norman Cook) has sold over 3 million copies and was crucial in popularizing the "big beat" sound. The album, released in Oct. 1998, includes the hits "The Rockafeller Skank," "Right Here, Right Now," and "Praise You."

MOST SUCCESSFUL RAP PRODUCER
Sean "Puffy" Coombs, aka Puff Daddy, is the most successful rap producer, having been responsible for four singles that consecutively headed the US rap chart for a record 36 weeks in 1997. These hits included "I'll Be Missing You," Puff Daddy's tribute to The Notorious BIG (see "Best-Selling Gangsta Rap Album").

⊙ **BEST-SELLING HIP-HOP ALBUM**
CrazySexyCool (1994) by TLC (T-Boz, Left-Eye, and Chilli) has reached sales of 11 million in the USA, according to the RIAA. This makes it the best-selling hip-hop/rap album ever, surpassing M.C. Hammer's *Please Hammer Don't Hurt 'Em* (1990).

BEST-SELLING JAZZ-FUNK ALBUM
Travelling Without Moving by the UK band Jamiroquai has sold more than 7 million albums globally since its release in 1996. Jamiroquai, led by Jason Kay, have sold 11 million albums in total.

FIRST COMPLETELY SAMPLED ALBUM
Entroducing (1996) by D.J. Shadow (real name Josh Davis) was the first album to be recorded with nothing but sampled sounds.

LONGEST CHART SPAN (R&B)
The R&B artist with the longest span of US No. 1 pop hits is Michael Jackson. His first solo No. 1 was "Ben" in Oct. 1972, and he last topped that chart 22 years, 11 months later with "You Are Not Alone," in Sept. 1995. The latter was also the first ever single to enter the US chart at No. 1. Jackson topped the US chart as lead singer of the Jackson 5 four times before his first solo No. 1.

⊙ BEST-SELLING DRUM 'N' BASS ALBUM
New Forms by Roni Size/Reprazent has sold over 760,000 copies around the world. The album won the Mercury Music Prize in 1997.

← BEST-SELLING CLUB DANCE COMPILATION
The Ministry of Sound's *The Annual II*, mixed by Pete Tong and Boy George, has sold over 610,000 units since its release in 1996. The Ministry of Sound opened as a nightclub in London, England, in 1990, and has since expanded into fashion and publishing as well as CDs.

World Music

MOST SUCCESSFUL COUNTRY ARTISTS

Garth Brooks is the most successful country recording artist of all time, with album sales of 92 million. Despite his enormous success on the US album chart, Brooks did not have a US Top 100 single until Dec. 1998, with "It's Your Song."

Reba McEntire is the biggest-selling female country vocalist in the USA, with 13 platinum and seven gold albums to her name by Feb. 2000.

Kim Brooks and Ronnie Dunn are the most successful country duo of all time. Six of their albums have sold over 1 million copies, and 12 of their singles have reached No. 1, including "Boot Scootin' Boogie" (1992), "Little Miss Honky Tonk," (1995) and "Husbands And Wives" (1998).

BEST-SELLING COUNTRY ALBUM

Come On Over by Shania Twain had sold over 17 million copies in North America by April 2000. The album includes the hit "Man! I Feel Like A Woman."

BEST-SELLING LATIN ARTISTS

Spanish singer Julio Iglesias is the most successful Latin music star in the world, with reported global sales of more than 200 million albums. His album *Julio* (1983) was the first foreign-language album to sell more than 2 million copies in the USA.

Cuban-born singer Gloria Estefan is the most successful female Latin artist in the world. Her current total world sales stand at more than 35 million.

LONGEST SALSA CAREER

Singer Celia Cruz began her career with the Cuban band Sonora Matancera in 1950 before moving to the USA in 1960. She has recorded over 50 albums, the most recent of which include *Celia Cruz and Friends: A Night Of Salsa Live* and *Angelitos Negros* (2000).

BEST-SELLING SON ALBUM

Buena Vista Social Club (1997) has sold over 4 million copies worldwide. It brought together some of Cuba's most respected musicians, including Ruben Gonzalez, Ibrahim Ferrer and Compay Segundo.

MOST CANTO-POP AWARDS

As of April 2000, Hong Kong crooner Andy Lau had won an unprecedented 292 awards for a singing career that began in 1988. He has sold 20 million albums, 4.4 million in 1999 alone, and has cemented his popularity in the world's Mandarin-speaking areas with recordings in Putonghua, or standard Chinese. Between 1981 and 1999 he featured in 101 movies.

BEST-SELLING REGGAE ALBUM

Legend (1984) by Bob Marley is the best-selling reggae album of all time. In the UK, where it topped the chart, it has had certified sales of 1.8 million, and although it has never reached the Top 40 in the USA, it has sold more than 10 million copies there. The album's tracks include "No Woman No Cry" and "One Love."

LONGEST INTERNATIONAL SITAR CAREER

Ravi Shankar (India) celebrated his 60th year as a classical sitarist in 1999. His first concert performance took place alongside his guru Allaudin Khan in 1939, and his first international concert was in New York City, USA, in 1956. He first achieved wide international acclaim when he gave sitar lessons to George Harrison of the Beatles.

MOST SUCCESSFUL BHANGRA BANDS

Alaap, a UK-based bhangra band led by singer Channi Singh, were established in London, England, in 1977 and are still performing today. Alaap have recorded a record 11 albums and performed on five continents.

Bhujangy, based in Birmingham, W. Midlands, England, have been performing since 1967 and were pioneers of the fusion of Punjabi folk songs and dance music now known as bhangra music. Singer Balbir Singh is the only remaining original member. Their biggest hit was "Bhabiye Ankh Lad Gayi" (1975).

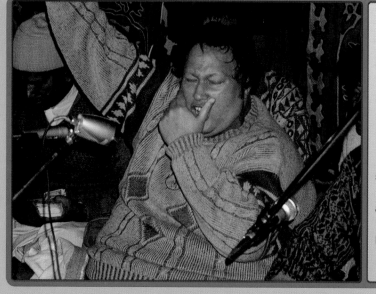

MOST QAWAALI RECORDINGS

Nusrat Fateh Ali Khan (Pakistan) recorded over 125 albums of Qawaali (the devotional music of the Sufi Muslims) before his death in 1997. He performed on several soundtracks, including *The Last Temptation Of Christ* (USA,1988) and *Dead Man Walking* (USA, 1995), on which he duetted with Eddie Vedder of Pearl Jam.

☉ BIGGEST-SELLING SALSA ARTIST

Marc Anthony (USA) is the top selling tropical salsa artist in the world. His second album, *Todo a Su Tiempo* (1995), sold over 800,000 copies in the USA and Puerto Rico. *Contra La Corriente* (1997) also earned him a gold disc, and "I Need To Know," from his fourth album, *Marc Anthony*, sold over one million copies in the USA, reaching the Top 10 there and in Canada.

MOST SUCCESSFUL SOLO BHANGRA ARTIST

Malkit Singh has recorded 19 albums under his own name or as Golden Star since he started his career in 1985 with the hit "Gur Nalo Ishq Mittha" ("Sweeter Than Sugar Is Love"). Malkit's albums have sold over 4.9 million copies.

MOST RECORDINGS BY AN AFRICAN ARTIST

Fela Kuti (Nigeria) recorded 46 albums between 1969 and 1992. In the 1960s he also made 12 albums with the band Koola Lobitos.

BEST-SELLING RAI ARTIST

Algerian singer Khaled has sold over 3 million albums worldwide, including *Khaled*, which featured his first international hit, "Didi." His live album *1,2,3 Soleils*, recorded with fellow Algerian stars Rachid Taha and Faudel in 1999, sold a further million copies.

BIGGEST INTERNATIONAL MUSIC FESTIVAL

Since being founded by singer Peter Gabriel in 1982, WOMAD (World of Music, Arts, and Dance) has presented more than 90 events on four continents, featuring artists from over 30 different countries.

↓ BEST-SELLING ALBUM BY A COUNTRY GROUP

The biggest-selling album by a country group is *Wide Open Spaces* by the Dixie Chicks (1998), which had sold 8 million copies in the USA by Dec. 1999. It is also the only album by a country group or female group to enter the US pop chart at No. 1.

Classical Music & Jazz

MOST PROLIFIC COMPOSER
Georg Philipp Telemann, a German composer of the late Baroque period, is the most prolific on record. His output included over 1,000 cantatas, masses, motets and psalms, 46 Passions, 40 operas, 600 overtures, 50 concertos, and innumerable suites, quartets and sonatas for varying instrumental combinations.

MOST PROLIFIC SYMPHONIST
Johann Melchior Molter, a contemporary of Telemann, wrote over 170 symphonies.

OLDEST ORCHESTRA
The oldest symphony orchestra still in existence is the Gewandhaus Orchestra of Leipzig, Germany. Established in 1743 as the Grosses Concert, its current name dates back to 1781.

BIGGEST AUDIENCE FOR A CLASSICAL CONCERT
On July 5, 1986, an estimated 800,000 people attended a free open-air concert given by the New York Philharmonic, conducted by Zubin Mehta, on the Great Lawn of Central Park, New York City, USA.

BEST-SELLING CLASSICAL ALBUM
In Concert, which was recorded by José Carreras, Placido Domingo, and Luciano Pavarotti during the 1990 soccer World Cup Finals, has sold over 10.5 million copies to date.

YOUNGEST PERSON AT NO. 1 IN THE CLASSICAL CHARTS
Welsh soprano Charlotte Church was just 12 years, 9 months old when her debut album *Voice of an Angel* reached No. 1 in the UK classical album charts on Nov. 9, 1998. The album was certified double platinum in the UK within four weeks of its release.

MOST RECORDINGS BY A CONDUCTOR
Austrian conductor Herbert von Karajan, who died in 1989, made over 800 recordings in the course of his career.

FEWEST NOTES IN A CLASSICAL PIECE
The 1952 piece *4'33"* by John Cage, written "for any instrument," contains no notes at all. Instead, the performer sits quietly on the concert platform for 4 min. 33 sec.,

⊙ **BIGGEST CELLO ENSEMBLE**
On Nov. 29, 1998, a total of 1,013 cellists gathered in Kobe, Japan, to take part in a mass cello concert conducted by Kazuaki Momiyama. Nine pieces were performed, the longest of which was J.S. Bach's *Suite in D Major* at 8 min. 26 sec.

while the "music" comprises any noise that comes from the audience and from outside the concert hall.

LONGEST OPERA
The seven-act *The Life and Times of Joseph Stalin* by Robert Wilson lasted for 13 hrs. 25 min. when performed at the Brooklyn Academy of Music, New York City, USA, from Dec. 14 to 15, 1973.

The longest frequently performed opera is Wagner's *Die Meistersinger von Nürnberg*. An uncut version performed by

⊙ **OLDEST JAZZ CLUB**
The Village Vanguard cellar jazz club opened in New York City, USA, in the 1930s and has been hosting mainstream jazz concerts ever since. Artists who have appeared there include John Coltrane, Miles Davis, Stan Getz, Wynton Marsalis, and Thelonious Monk.

the Sadler's Wells company in London, England, in 1968, lasted for 5 hrs. 15 min.

SHORTEST OPERA

The shortest published opera is *The Sands of Time* by Simon Rees and Peter Reynolds, which lasted for 4 min. 9 sec. when first performed by Rhian Owen and Dominic Burns at The Hayes, Cardiff, Wales, on March 27, 1993. A 3-min.-34-sec. version was performed under the direction of Peter Reynolds at BBC Television Centre, London, England, on Sept. 14, 1993.

HIGHEST NOTE

The highest vocal note in the classical repertoire is G^3 [1,568 Hz], which occurs in Mozart's *Popolo di Tessaglia*.

LOWEST NOTE

The lowest vocal note in the classical repertoire is a low D (73.4Hz). It occurs in Mozart's *Die Entführung aus dem Serail*.

BIGGEST ORCHESTRA

On Nov. 23, 1998, the world's largest orchestra, consisting of 3,503 musicians, assembled at the National Indoor Arena, Birmingham, England, in an event organized by Music for Youth. They played Malcolm Arnold's *Little Suite No. 2* in a performance conducted by Sir Simon Rattle.

MOST VALUABLE MUSIC MANUSCRIPTS

On May 22,1987, London dealer James Kirkman paid a record $4.136 million at Sotheby's, London, England, for a 508-page bound volume of nine complete symphonies in the hand of their composer, Mozart.

The highest price paid for a single music manuscript is $2 million, for the autographed copy of the *Piano Sonata in E minor* (opus 90) by Beethoven, at Sotheby's, London, England, on Dec. 6, 1991.

BEST-SELLING JAZZ ARTIST

US saxophonist Kenny G has sold an estimated 55 million albums worldwide. This includes an estimated 14 million copies of *Breathless*, the best-selling jazz album of all time.

EARLIEST JAZZ RECORDS

The first jazz record to be released was "Livery Stable Blues"/"Dixie Jazz Band One-Step," recorded by the Original Dixieland Jazz Band in Feb. 1917, and released by Victor on March 7, 1917. The band had previously recorded "Indiana"/"The Dark Town Strutters Ball" for the Columbia label, but this was not released until May 1917.

BIGGEST JAZZ FESTIVAL

The Festival International de Jazz de Montreal in Québec, Canada, is the world's largest jazz festival. Lasting 11 days, it attracts over 1.5 million people to watch around 400 concerts.

MOST VALUABLE JAZZ INSTRUMENT

A saxophone owned by Charlie Parker sold for a record $144,700 at Christie's, London, England, in Sept. 1994.

CLASSICAL CLEAN SWEEP →

In Nov. 1999, Italian tenor Andrea Bocelli became the first vocalist to hold the top three places on the US classical album charts, with his albums *Sacred Arias*, *Aria – The Opera Album*, and *Viaggio Italiano*.

Performance & Theater

OLDEST TOURING CIRCUS
The oldest touring circus in the world is Circus Krone of Germany, which was established in 1904 and has been run continuously by the same family ever since.

OLDEST CIRCUS BUILDING
The oldest circus building is Cirque d'Hiver (originally Cirque Napoléon), which opened in Paris, France, on Dec. 11, 1852.

BIGGEST CIRCUS CASTS
A total of 263 people and 175 animals took part in Barnum & Bailey Circus' 1890 US tour.

Cirque du Soleil's show *Fascination* had a cast of 61 people for its tour of Japan in 1992 – a record for a circus with no animal performers.

BIGGEST CIRCUS AUDIENCES
A performance given by Ringling Brothers and Barnum & Bailey Circus at the New Orleans Superdome, Louisiana, USA, on Sept. 14, 1975, attracted an audience of 52,385.

The largest audience for a circus show in a tent was 16,702, a record established when Ringling Brothers and Barnum & Bailey Circus performed at Concordia, Kansas, USA, Sept. 13, 1924.

BIGGEST THEATERS
The largest building used for theatrical performances is the National People's Congress Building (Renmin Dahuitang) on Tiananmen Square, Beijing, China. Completed in 1959, it covers an area of 12.8 acres and can seat an audience of 10,000.

The biggest purpose-built theater is the Perth Entertainment Centre in Perth, Western Australia, which opened on Dec. 26, 1974. It has 8,500 seats, with a main stage area of 70 ft. x 45 ft.

BIGGEST STAGE
The Hilton Theater at the Reno Hilton, Reno, Nevada, USA, has the largest stage in the world, measuring 175 ft. x 241 ft. The stage has three main elevators, each capable of carrying 1,200 performers, and two turntables, each with a circumference of 62 ft. 8 in. It is lit by up to 800 spotlights.

⊙ **MOST-WATCHED CIRCUS**
Ringling Brothers and Barnum & Bailey Circus, which comprises the two independent circus troupes of Ringling Brothers and Barnum & Bailey, is watched by an average of 12 million people every year.

SMALLEST AMATEUR THEATER
The Acorn Theatre in Seaforth, Western Australia, is the smallest theater to stage regular amateur performances, with a maximum capacity of 28 seats. The group stages four productions a year.

MOST LEAD PERFORMANCES
Kanmi Fujiyama played the lead role in 10,288 performances by the Japanese comedy company Sochiku Shikigeki from Nov. 1966 to June 1983.

MOST CONSECUTIVE PERFORMANCES IN ONE ROLE
James O'Neill (USA) gave over 6,000 consecutive performances in the title role of *The Count Of Monte Cristo* between 1883 and 1891.

MOST PERFORMANCES OF A ONE-MAN SHOW
Laxman Deshpande has performed his play *Varhad Nighalay Londonla* 1,930 times all over the world since the first production in Aurangabad, India, in Dec. 1979. The three-hour comedy is about a marriage party from India going to London for the wedding of one of their sons, and Deshpande plays all 52 parts. He is also the play's producer and director.

⊙ **MOST EXPENSIVE STAGE PRODUCTION**
The stage adaptation of Disney's 1994 film *The Lion King* is the most expensive theatrical production on record. The Broadway show cost an estimated $15 million to stage, while the West End show (left, with Josette Bushell-Mingo as Rafiki) cost over $10.4 million.

HIGHEST-GROSSING THEATRICAL PRODUCTION

By Dec. 1999, the box office takings of Andrew Lloyd Webber's musical *The Phantom Of The Opera* had topped $3.25 billion. This surpasses the box office takings of *Titanic* (USA, 1997), the highest-grossing film ever.

SHORTEST PLAY

The world's shortest play is the 30-second *Breath*, written by the Irish-born playwright and novelist Samuel Beckett in 1969.

LONGEST PLAY

The longest play is *The Non-Stop Connolly Show* by John Arden and Margaretta Darcey. It lasted 26 hrs. 30 min. at Liberty Hall, Dublin, Ireland, in 1975.

OLDEST PROFESSIONAL CHORUS LINE

The 11 dancers from the chorus line of The Fabulous Palm Spring Follies, a show staged at the Plaza Theater, Palm Springs, California, USA, have a combined age of 733. The youngest dancer is 54 and the oldest is 87.

LONGEST THEATRICAL RUN

The Mousetrap, a thriller written by Agatha Christie, opened at the Ambassadors Theatre, London, England, on Nov. 25, 1952, and moved to the adjacent St. Martin's Theatre on March 25, 1974. The show's 19,700th performance took place on March 30, 2000.

LONGEST-RUNNING MUSICAL

The off-Broadway musical *The Fantasticks*, written by Tom Jones and Harvey Schmidt, opened on May 3, 1960, at the Sullivan Street Playhouse, Greenwich Village, New York City, USA. By May 3, 2000, it had been performed a record 16,523 times.

LONGEST-RUNNING COMEDY

No Sex Please, We're British, written by Anthony Marriott and Alistair Foot and presented by John Gale, opened at the Strand Theatre, London, England, on June 3, 1971. It transferred to the Duchess Theatre, London, on Aug. 2, 1986, and had its 6,761st and final performance on Sept. 5, 1987.

BIGGEST CAST OF BLIND ACTORS

Swatantryachi Yashogatha, a Marathi-language play first staged in Pune, India, on Aug. 2, 1997, featured 88 blind actors.

BIGGEST HUMAN MOBILE

In 1996, a record-breaking 16 performers from the Circus of Horrors, which is based at Addlestone Moor, Surrey, England, were suspended from a crane to form a human mobile in Munich, Germany.

GREATEST DISTANCE FLOWN BY A HUMAN ARROW

The Bulgarian performer Vesta Gueschkova, whose stage name was "Airiana," was fired a record distance of 75 ft. from a crossbow at Ringling Brothers and Barnum & Bailey Circus, Tampa, Florida, USA, on Dec. 27, 1995.

← LONGEST SHAKESPEARE PLAY

Hamlet is the longest of the 37 plays written by William Shakespeare, with a total of 4,042 lines and 29,551 words. Actors who have played the title role in recent years include Ralph Fiennes (left), Keanu Reeves, Kenneth Branagh, and Mel Gibson.

Print Media

BIGGEST-SELLING NEWSPAPERS
The newspaper with the highest circulation is *Yomiuri Shimbun*, published in Tokyo, Japan. Established in 1874, it had a daily circulation of 14,385,464 by Jan. 2000 – 10,203,513 for the morning edition; 4,181,951 for the evening edition.

Komsomolskaya Pravda, the youth paper of the former Soviet Communist Party, reached a peak daily circulation of 21.98 million copies in May 1990.

The eight-page weekly newspaper *Argumenty i Fakty* of Moscow, USSR (now Russia), sold a record 33,431,100 copies in May 1990, when it had an estimated readership of over 100 million.

MOST SYNDICATED COLUMNIST
Columns written by US personal-problem solver Ann Landers appear in over 1,200 newspapers and have an estimated readership of 90 million. Landers' only serious rival in the problem page market is her identical twin sister Abigail Van Buren, better known as "Dear Abby."

OLDEST NEWSPAPERS
There is a surviving copy of a news pamphlet published in Cologne, Germany, in 1470.

The oldest newspaper still being produced is the Swedish journal *Post och Inrikes Tidningar*, which was established in 1645 and is published by the Royal Swedish Academy of Letters.

MOST LETTERS TO NEWSPAPER EDITORS
Hakim Syed Irshad of Gujrat, Pakistan, had 602 letters published in national newspapers over almost 40 years. In 1963 alone, he had 42 letters published.

MOST PROLIFIC CROSSWORD COMPILER
Roger Squires of Ironbridge, Shropshire, England, has compiled over 53,000 crosswords to date. Two-thirds of them were cryptic, while the remaining third were quick crosswords.

HIGHEST MAGAZINE CIRCULATIONS
The syndicated color magazine *Parade*, which is distributed with 340 different US Sunday newspapers, had a circulation of 37 million as of April 2000, the highest for any magazine in the world. With advertisements costing $629,600 per four-color page, it is also the most expensive magazine in which to advertise.

The free magazine with the highest circulation is the Danish quarterly *Idé-nyt*, which specializes in homes and gardens. It is currently distributed to a total of 2.52 million readers.

☉ SMALLEST NEWSPAPER
The Brazilian weekly journal *Vossa Senhoria*, first published in 1935, measures a minuscule 1.4 in. x 1 in. Each issue has up to 16 pages, and includes photographs, drawings, and advertising space.

☉ BIGGEST BOOK SERIES
The *Doctor Who* series, now published by BBC Worldwide, is the largest fictional series built around one principal character. Approximately 150 titles were produced between 1977 and 1997 by the series' former publisher, Target Books, with many being reprinted and reissued. Since BBC Worldwide took on the series in 1997, a further 82 titles have been published. In total, over 8 million copies have been sold. The original *Doctor Who* program ran on BBC television from 1963 to 1989.

BIGGEST MAGAZINE
The biggest single issue of a magazine was the Jan. 10, 1990 edition of *Shukan Jutaku Joho* (*Weekly Housing Information*), published in Japan by Recruit Company Ltd. The magazine, which cost $2.40, had a record 1,940 pages.

MOST COVERS FOR ONE MAGAZINE ISSUE
The inaugural issue of *DPICT*, a bimonthly magazine on camera culture, was published in the UK in April 2000 with 560 different, customized covers.

BEST-SELLING BOOKS
The world's best-selling and most widely distributed book is the Bible, with an estimated 2.5 billion copies sold since 1815. It has been translated into 2,233 languages and dialects.

Excluding noncopyright works, the best-selling book is *The Guinness Book Of Records* (now *Guinness World Records*), first published by Guinness Superlatives in Oct. 1955. Global sales in 23 languages had surpassed the 90 million mark by April 2000.

BEST-SELLING NOVELS
Three novels have been credited with sales of approximately 30 million, all of them by US female authors. They are *To Kill A Mockingbird* (1960) by Harper Lee; *Gone With The Wind* (1936) by Margaret Mitchell; and *Valley Of The Dolls* (1966) by Jacqueline Susann, which sold 6.8 million copies in the first six months after its release but is now out of print.

Alistair MacLean (UK) wrote a total of 30 novels, 28 of which have sold more than 1 million copies in the UK alone. His books have been translated into 28 languages, and 13 of them have been made into films. It is estimated that a novel by MacLean is purchased every 18 seconds.

⊙ BEST-SELLING CHILDREN'S BOOK SERIES IN ONE YEAR
In 1999, the first three books in the Harry Potter series, by J.K. Rowling (above), sold over 18.5 million copies in the USA and over 4.5 million copies in the UK and the Commonwealth. The first title in the series, *Harry Potter And The Philosopher's Stone*, sold over 1.5 million copies in the UK and the Commonwealth and 10.4 million copies in the USA (under the title *Harry Potter And The Sorcerer's Stone*), a record for a children's title in one year.

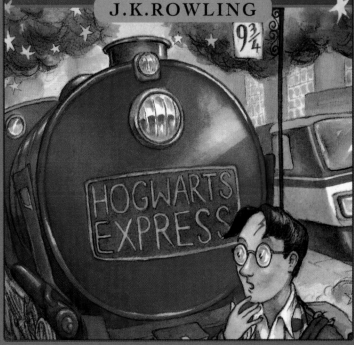

BEST-SELLING CHILDREN'S BOOK SERIES
The 80 titles in the *Goosebumps* series by R.L. Stine have sold a total of 220 million copies worldwide since the first book, *Welcome to Dead House*, was published by Scholastic Inc. in 1992.

BEST-SELLING AUTHOR
The top-selling fiction writer of all time is Dame Agatha Christie, the creator of the detectives Hercule Poirot and Miss Marple. Her 78 crime novels have sold an estimated 2 billion copies in 44 different languages, generating total royalties of around $4 million per year.

MOST PROLIFIC AUTHOR
British author Charles Hamilton (alias Frank Richards), the creator of the schoolboy character Billy Bunter, is estimated to have written between 72 and 75 million words during his career.

BEST-SELLING DIARY
The Diary Of Anne Frank, the young author's account of events that took place when her family and their friends were hiding from the Nazis in Amsterdam, Netherlands, during World War II, has been translated into 55 languages and has sold more than 25 million copies.

BIGGEST PRINT RUNS
The initial print order for the German zip code directory, published by Deutsche Bundespost on July 1, 1993, was 42,300,000 copies.

The first print run of the English-language edition of *Guinness World Records 2000*, printed in Barcelona, Spain, in 1999, was 2,402,000 copies, a record for a full-color hardback title.

Awards

⊙ MOST BEST ACTOR OSCARS
Tom Hanks is one of seven people who have won the Best Actor award twice, for *Philadelphia* (USA, 1993) and *Forrest Gump* (USA, 1994). He shares the record with Spencer Tracy, Fredric March, Gary Cooper, Marlon Brando, Jack Nicholson, and Dustin Hoffman.

MOST OSCARS
Walt Disney won a record-breaking 26 Oscar awards from 64 nominations between 1932 and 1969, the last being awarded posthumously for *Winnie The Pooh And The Blustery Day* (USA, 1968). He also holds the record for the most Oscars won in a single year, with four in 1953 for Best Cartoon (*Toot, Whistle, Plunk And Boom*), Best Documentary Short (*The Alaskan Eskimo*), Best Documentary Feature (*The Living Desert*), and Best Two-Reel Short (*Bear Country*).

OLDEST OSCAR-WINNER
Jessica Tandy won Best Actress for *Driving Miss Daisy* (USA, 1990) aged 80 years, 295 days.

YOUNGEST OSCAR-WINNER
Tatum O'Neal was 10 years, 148 days old when she was voted Best Supporting Actress for *Paper Moon* (USA, 1973).

Shirley Temple was awarded an honorary Oscar at the age of six years, 310 days in 1935.

MOST OSCARS BY A FILM
Two films have won 11 Oscars: *Ben-Hur* (USA, 1959), starring Charlton Heston; and *Titanic* (USA, 1997), which was directed by James Cameron.

MOST OSCAR NOMINATIONS FOR A FILM
All About Eve (USA, 1950) and *Titanic* (USA, 1997) both received a record 14 nominations.

MOST NOMINATIONS FOR A FILM WITHOUT AN OSCAR
Turning Point (USA, 1977) and *The Color Purple* (USA, 1986) both received 11 nominations but failed to win any Oscars.

MOST BEST DIRECTOR OSCARS
John Ford won four Oscars as Best Director, for *The Informer* (USA, 1935), *The Grapes Of Wrath* (USA, 1940), *How Green Was My Valley* (USA, 1941), and *The Quiet Man* (USA, 1952).

MOST BEST ACTRESS OSCARS
Katharine Hepburn won four Best Actress awards, for *Morning Glory* (USA, 1933), *Guess Who's Coming To Dinner* (USA, 1967), *The Lion In Winter* (UK, 1968 – award shared), and *On Golden Pond* (USA, 1981). She also had the longest award-winning career, spanning 48 years.

MOST BEST SUPPORTING ACTOR OSCARS
Walter Brennan won Oscars for Best Supporting Actor in *Come And Get It* (USA, 1936), *Kentucky* (USA, 1938), and *The Westerner* (USA, 1940).

MOST BEST SUPPORTING ACTRESS OSCARS
The record is two, shared by Shelley Winters for her roles in *The Diary Of Anne Frank* (USA, 1959) and *A Patch Of Blue* (USA, 1965); and Dianne Wiest for *Hannah And Her Sisters* (USA, 1986) and *Bullets Over Broadway* (USA, 1994).

MOST VERSATILE AWARD-WINNER
Actress/singer/director Barbra Streisand has won a total of two Oscars, five Emmys, seven Grammys, seven Golden Globes, and a special Tony in 1970 as Broadway Actress of the Decade.

LONGEST OSCAR SPEECH
The longest Oscar acceptance speech on record lasted for 5 min. 30 sec. It was made at the 1942 Academy Awards by Greer Garson, who was voted Best Actress for her role in *Mrs. Miniver* (USA, 1942).

MOST GRAMMYS
The Hungarian-born British conductor Sir Georg Solti won a record 31 Grammy awards (including a special Trustees' award presented in 1967) between 1958 and 1997.

MOST GRAMMYS BY A FEMALE ARTIST
Aretha Franklin (USA) has won a total of 15 Grammys to date, including a record 11 for Best R&B Female Vocal Performance.

⊙ MOST OSCARS FOR BEST FOREIGN LANGUAGE FILM BY ONE COUNTRY
Italy has won a total of 13 Oscars for Best Foreign Language Film. The most recent was for *Life Is Beautiful* (1997), which starred Roberto Benigni, Giorgio Cantarini, and Nicoletta Braschi (left to right).

MOST GRAMMYS BY A SOLO POP PERFORMER
Stevie Wonder has won 19 Grammys since 1973.

MOST GRAMMYS BY A POP GROUP
The most Grammys won by a pop group is eight, by 5th Dimension.

MOST EMMYS BY AN ACTRESS
Candice Bergen has won the Best Actress (Comedy) Emmy five times, for her title role in *Murphy Brown*.

MOST EMMYS BY AN ACTOR
Don Knotts won the Best Actor Emmy five times, for his part as Barney Fife in *The Andy Griffith Show*.

MOST BRIT AWARDS
Annie Lennox, formerly of the Eurythmics, has won seven Brit awards as a solo artist – more than any other artist or act. Her most recent award was Best British Female Artist in 1996.

MOST BRIT AWARDS BY A GROUP IN ONE YEAR
British band Blur hold the record for the most wins in a year, with four in 1995.

MOST CESAR AWARDS
French star Isabelle Adjani is the only person to have won four Césars, awarded by the French Académie des Arts. Her wins were for *Possession* (Fr./W. Ger., 1981), *L'Eté Meurtrier* (Fr., 1983), *Camille Claudel* (Fr., 1988), and *La Reine Margot* (Fr./Ger./It., 1994).

MOST INTERNATIONAL FILM AWARDS
Satyajit Ray, nicknamed "God" in Bombay film circles, was India's most celebrated movie director. He received a total of 34 international film awards in the course of his career, including an Oscar for Lifetime Achievement. Ray died in 1992.

MOST BOOKER PRIZE WINS
South African author J.M. Coetzee is the only person to have won the Booker Prize for Fiction twice. His wins were in 1983 for *The Life And Times Of Michael K* and in 1999 for *Disgrace*.

MOST PULITZER PRIZES
The Associated Press, founded in 1848, has received 45 Pulitzer Prizes – more than any other news organization.

↓ MOST EMMYS BY A SERIES IN ONE SEASON
Both *Hill Street Blues* and *ER* won a record eight Emmys in their first seasons, which were in 1981 and 1995 respectively. *ER's* wins included a Best Supporting Actress (Drama) award for Julianna Margulies (below), for her role as nurse Carole Hathaway.

◉ MOST GRAMMYS IN ONE YEAR
The record for the the most Grammy awards in a single year is shared by Michael Jackson, who won eight in 1984, and Carlos Santana (left), who won eight in 2000. Santana's awards were for Album Of The Year (*Supernatural*), Record Of The Year ("Smooth"), Best Pop Performance By A Duo Or Group With Vocals ("Maria, Maria"), Best Pop Collaboration With Vocals ("Smooth"), Best Pop Instrumental Performance ("El Farol"), Best Rock Performance By A Duo Or Group With Vocals ("Put Your Lights On"), Best Rock Instrumental Performance ("The Calling"), and Best Rock Album (*Supernatural*).

Body Beautiful

MOST PIERCED MAN
The most pierced man is Luis Antonio Aguero of Havana, Cuba, who has a total of 230 piercings on his body and head, including a record 175 on his face. He charges a nominal fee for photographs in order to help support his extended family.

MOST TATTOOED MAN
Tom Leppard, a retired soldier who lives on the Isle of Skye, Highlands & Islands, Scotland, has had 99.9% of his body tattooed with a leopard-skin design. The only parts of his body that remain free of tattoos are the insides of his ears and the skin between his toes.

MOST TATTOOED WOMEN
Strip artiste Krystyne Kolorful from Alberta, Canada, has had 95% of her body tattooed.

Julia Gnuse of southern California, USA, began tattooing her body in 1991 to hide the effects of the skin disease porphyria. She hopes to achieve 100% coverage in the near future.

MOST VALUABLE LEGS
In 1952, US actress Cyd Charisse had a $5-million insurance policy accepted on her legs. The previous record holder was Betty Grable, who became known as "The Girl with the Million Dollar Legs" when she insured her legs for $1,250,000 in 1937.

RICHEST SUPERMODEL
Although she no longer appears regularly on the catwalk, Elle MacPherson, also known as "The Body," is said to be worth $36.8 million.

HIGHEST-PAID SUPERMODEL
According to *Forbes* magazine, Claudia Schiffer earned $9 million in 1999.

MOST MR. OLYMPIA CONTESTANTS
In 1989, a record-breaking 26 contestants vied for the title of Mr. Olympia at Rimini, Italy. The winner was Lee Haney (USA), who equalled Arnold Schwarzenegger's then record of six consecutive titles.

FEWEST MR. OLYMPIA CONTESTANTS
In 1968, Sergio "The Myth" Oliva (USA) defended his Mr. Olympia title unopposed at the Brooklyn Academy of Music, New York City, USA. Arnold Schwarzenegger (Austria) was also unopposed when he competed in 1971 in Paris, France.

⊙ LONGEST CATWALK CAREERS
Carmen Dell'Orefici was born in 1931 and has been modelling for the Ford Agency since the 1940s. At the age of 69 she is still in demand for contracts and international shows. Daphne Self, who featured in the 1999 Laura Ashley campaign, is 71 years old but has had an on/off modelling career.

⊙ LONGEST-RUNNING BEAUTY PAGEANT
The Miss World Pageant has been held annually since 1951. It is also the world's largest global beauty pageant, with a record 94 entrants in 1999.

TALLEST MR. OLYMPIA CONTESTANT
The tallest Mr. Olympia contestant was Lou Ferrigno (USA), who took part in the 1974 competition. He stands 6 ft. 5 in. tall. Ferrigno later played the title role in the TV series *The Incredible Hulk*.

SHORTEST MR. OLYMPIA CONTESTANT
Flavio Baccanini from San Francisco, California, USA, was the shortest person to vie for the Mr. Olympia title. Baccanini, who competed in Atlanta, Georgia, USA, in 1993, is 4 ft. 10 in. tall. He weighed 160 lbs. at the time of the contest.

LONGEST TIME BETWEEN MR. OLYMPIA WINS
Arnold Schwarzenegger won the Mr. Olympia title for the sixth time in 1975 and announced his retirement immediately afterwards. In 1980, Schwarzenegger came out of retirement to win again, in Australia.

MOST MR. OLYMPIA TITLES
Lee Haney of South Carolina, USA, won the Mr. Olympia contest eight times between 1984 and 1991.

☉ HEAVIEST MR. OLYMPIA CHAMPION

Dorian Yates (UK) weighed a record 257 lbs. when he was crowned Mr. Olympia for the second year in succession at Atlanta, Georgia, USA, in 1993.

BIGGEST MS. OLYMPIA CONTEST

In 1990, 30 women competed in the Ms. Olympia contest.

OLDEST MS. OLYMPIA CONTESTANT

Christa Bauch (Germany) was 47 years old when she participated in the 1994 Ms. Olympia competition.

YOUNGEST MS. OLYMPIA CONTESTANT

Lorie Johnson (USA) was 17 years old when she took part in the first Ms. Olympia competition in 1980.

LIGHTEST MS. OLYMPIA CONTESTANT

Erika Mes (Netherlands) weighed 100 lbs. when she competed in 1984.

SHORTEST MS. OLYMPIA CONTESTANT

Michele Ralabate (USA), who competed in 1995, is only 4 ft. 11 in. tall.

HEAVIEST MS. OLYMPIA CONTESTANT

Nicole Bass (USA) weighed 204 lbs. when she participated in the 1997 contest. She was also the tallest ever contestant, at 6 ft. 2 in.

MOST FILMS MADE BY A MR. OLYMPIA

Arnold Schwarzenegger has appeared in a total of 29 feature films, including *The Terminator* (USA, 1984), *Total Recall* (USA, 1990), *Terminator 2: Judgment Day* (USA, 1991), *True Lies* (USA, 1994), *Batman And Robin* (USA, 1997), and *End Of Days* (USA, 1999).

MOST MISS WORLD WINNERS FROM ONE COUNTRY

Both Miss UK and Miss Venezuela have won the Miss World Pageant a record five times. However, the UK's 1974 winner, Helen Morgan, was forced to give up her title because of the pressures of motherhood.

↓ MOST BODY PIERCINGS

Elaine Davidson of Edinburgh, Scotland, has acquired a record 462 body piercings since Jan. 1997, 192 of which are on her head.

Stunts & Special Effects

MOST "BLOWN-UP" PERSON

US entertainer Allison Bly, better known as "The Dynamite Lady," has blown herself up more than 1,000 times inside a box she calls the "Coffin of Death," using explosives with a force equivalent to two sticks of dynamite.

LONGEST FULL-BODY BURN WITHOUT OXYGEN

Stig Günther (Denmark) endured a full-body burn without oxygen supplies for a record-breaking 2 min. 6 sec. in Copenhagen, Denmark, on March 13, 1999.

LONGEST WALL OF DEATH RIDE

The longest wall of death ride on record lasted 7 hrs. 13 sec. It was made by Martin Blume (Germany), who rode a Yamaha XS 400 more than 12,000 laps on a wall with a diameter of 32.8 ft. at Berlin, Germany, on April 16, 1983. His average speed over the 181.4 miles covered was 28 m.p.h.

OLDEST WALL OF DEATH RIDER

Jerry De Roye (UK), who was born in 1927, is the oldest wall of death rider still performing regularly. He rides a 1927 V-Twin Indian Type 101 "Scout" motorbike.

LONGEST RAMP JUMP IN A CAR

The longest ramp jump made in a car, with the car landing on its wheels and driving on afterwards, is 237 ft., by Ray Baumann (Australia) at Ravenswood International Raceway, Perth, Western Australia, on Aug. 23, 1998.

LONGEST BACKWARD MOTORCYCLE JUMP

Roger "Mr. Backward" Riddell (USA) jumped over seven cars – a distance of 60 ft. – riding backward on a 650 cc Honda motorcycle in Franklin, Indiana, USA, in May 1987.

HIGHEST ROOF-TO-ROOF MOTORCYCLE JUMP

On July 30, 1998, Super Joe Reed (USA) leaped from the roof of one 140-ft building to another on a 250 cc dirtbike in Los Angeles, California, USA. The gap between the buildings was 65 ft.

LONGEST AND HIGHEST BLINDFOLD SKYWALK

On Nov. 11, 1998, Jay Cochrane of Atlantic City, New Jersey, USA, made a blindfold tightrope walk of 600 ft. between the two 300-ft.-high towers of the Flamingo Hilton, Las Vegas, Nevada, USA.

⊙ LONGEST RAMP JUMP IN A MONSTER TRUCK

On Sept. 11, 1999, Dan Runte (USA) jumped 202 ft. over a Boeing 727 passenger jet in the monster truck *Bigfoot 14*. The record was set at Smyrna Airport, Tennessee, USA.

HIGHEST DIVE INTO AN AIR BAG

Stig Günther (Denmark) jumped from a record-shattering height of 343 ft. into a 39.4 x 49.2 x 14.8-ft. air bag on Aug. 7, 1998.

LONGEST LEAP IN A CAR BY A STUNT MAN

The longest leap made in a car that was being propelled by its own engine was performed by stunt driver Gary Davis for the film *Smokey and the Bandit II*

⊙ MOST STILL CAMERAS USED IN A FILM SEQUENCE

When shooting the "Bullet time" sequence of *The Matrix* (USA, 1999), directors Larry and Andy Wachowski used a total of 120 specially modified still cameras to achieve a panning shot of protagonist Neo (Keanu Reeves) as he dodges bullets fired by a pursuer.

Hollywood

(USA, 1981). Davis raced a stripped-down Plymouth at a speed of 80 m.p.h. up a ramp that was wedged against the back of a double-tiered car-carrier. He flew 163 ft. through the air before landing safely on the desert floor.

HIGHEST FREE-FALL BY A STUNT MAN
For the film *Highpoint* (Canada, 1979), stunt man Dar Robinson made a free-fall from the height of 1,100 ft., jumping from a ledge at the summit of the CN Tower, Toronto, Canada. The free-fall lasted for six seconds before Robinson's parachute opened just 300 ft. from the ground. He was paid $150,000 for the feat – a record for a single stunt.

HIGHEST JUMP WITHOUT A PARACHUTE BY A STUNT MAN
The highest ever jump made by a movie stunt man without a parachute is 232 ft., by A.J. Bakunus while he was doubling for Burt Reynolds in *Hooper* (USA, 1978). He fell onto an air mattress.

MOST EXPENSIVE AERIAL STUNT
Simon Crane [UK] performed one of the most dangerous aerial stunts ever when he moved between two jets at an altitude of 2.95 miles for *Cliffhanger* (USA, 1993). The stunt, performed only once because it was so risky, cost a record $1 million.

HIGHEST STUNT MAN: ACTOR RATIO
The Rookie (USA, 1990), directed by and starring Clint Eastwood, featured a total of 87 stunt men and just 37 actors.

BIGGEST FILM STUNT BUDGET
More than $3 million of the $200-million budget for *Titanic* (USA, 1997) went toward the movie's stunts. In the most complex scene, 100 stunt people leaped, fell, and slid 751 ft. as

the ship broke in half and rose out of the water at a 90° angle.

BIGGEST CAR PILE-UP IN A FILM
The climax of the film *Blues Brothers 2000* (USA, 1998) is marked by a car chase and a resulting pile-up that involves 100 police cars.

MOST PROLIFIC MOVIE STUNT MAN
Vic Armstrong (UK) has doubled for every actor playing James Bond, and in a career spanning three decades has performed stunts in more than 200 films, including *Raiders Of The Lost Ark* (USA, 1981) and *Terminator 2: Judgment Day* (USA, 1991). He has also co-ordinated stunts for movies such as *Tomorrow Never Dies* (UK/USA, 1997). He is married to stunt woman Wendy Leech.

MOST EXPENSIVE SPECIAL EFFECTS IN A MUSIC VIDEO
The video for "What's It Gonna Be?" (1999) by Busta Rhymes and Janet Jackson, directed by Hype Williams, cost a record-breaking $2.4 million to produce. State-of-the-art computer-morphing effects accounted for much of this expenditure. The track was taken from Rhymes' millennium-themed album *ELE – The Final World Front*.

MOST COMPUTER-GENERATED EFFECTS IN A MOVIE
The film *Pleasantville* (USA, 1998) contained a record 1,700 digital visual effect shots, compared with an average of 50 for most Hollywood movies.

← MOST STUNTS BY A LIVING ACTOR
Jackie Chan, the Hong Kong actor, director, producer, stunt co-ordinator, and writer, has appeared in more than 65 films, including *The Big Brawl* (USA, 1980) and *Rumble In The Bronx* (USA, 1996). No insurance company will underwrite Chan's productions, in which he performs all his own stunts.

MOST ANIMATED DUST
Toy Story 2 (USA, 1999), a computer-animated feature co-produced by Disney and Pixar Animation Studios, included a scene directed by John Lasseter in which 2 million tiny three-dimensional particles, each with an individual algorithm to define its movement, acted as "dust" – traditionally one of the most difficult substances to animate.

Computers

FASTEST COMPUTERS

The fastest general-purpose vector-parallel computer is the Cray Y-MP C-90 supercomputer, which has 2 gigabytes (2 billion bytes) of central memory and 16 CPUs (central processing units). This gives it a combined peak performance of 16 gigaflops (16 billion floating point operations, i.e., computer calculations, per second).

Intel installed an even faster supercomputer at Sandia, Texas, USA, in 1996. Using 9,072 Intel Pentium Pro processors, each running at about 200 MHz, and 608 gigabytes of memory, it will eventually perform at around 1.8 teraflops (1.8 trillion floating point operations per second).

Several suppliers now market massively parallel computers which, with enough processors, can have a theoretical aggregate performance exceeding that of the C-90. However, performances on real-life applications can often be less impressive, as it can be harder to harness effectively the power of a large number of small processors than that of a small number of large ones.

The world supercomputing speed record was set in Dec. 1994 by a team of scientists from Sandia National Laboratories and Intel Corporation, who linked together two of the largest Intel Paragon parallel-processing machines. The massively parallel supercomputer achieved a performance of 281 gigaflops on the Linpack benchmark. It also achieved 328 gigaflops when running a program used for radar signature calculations. The supercomputer made use of a total of 6,768 processors working in parallel.

MOST POWERFUL COMPUTER IN SPACE

The Mars Pathfinder is controlled by an IBM RAD6000, a radiation-hardened single board computer related to the standard PowerPC. It has a 32-bit architecture and is able to carry out 22 million instructions per second. Used to store flight software, engineering and silence data and images, as well as data from the rover vehicle, it has 128 million bytes of memory. Pathfinder landed on Mars in July 1997.

⊙ MOST SUCCESSFUL COMPUTER

Approximately 30 million Commodore 64 computers were sold between the model's launch in 1982 and its commercial decline in 1993. The computer contained 64K RAM, 16K graphics, and 16K sound.

YOUNGEST SOFTWARE DEVELOPER

Roy Narunsky (Israel), who developed Curtains 95, a commercial software program designed to help children operate the Windows 95 environment, was just 13 years old when the program was published by Makh-Shevet ML in 1998.

BIGGEST SCANNER

The SLC972C color scanner, produced by Widecom Group Inc., Brampton, Ontario, Canada, has a 6-ft. scan width. Unveiled at a California trade show in May 1999, it is targeted at people who work in industries such as automotive and aircraft manufacturing and shipbuilding, who regularly deal with huge drawings that require a scanning capacity of this size. The SLC972C first appeared on the market in Sept. 1999, and sells for $17,184.

SMALLEST KEYBOARD

The smallest computer keyboard with a full complement of alphanumeric, symbol, and command keys was patented on March 18, 1997, by David Levy, an ergonomics graduate of the Massachusetts Institute of Technology, USA. The keyboard has 64 keys, each big enough to be operated with a large thumb, yet the whole device measures just 3 in. x 1.2 in., or 60% of the size of a credit card.

⊙ BIGGEST COMPUTER HARD DRIVE

The IBM Deskstar 75GXP, which was unveiled on March 15, 2000, has 75 gigabytes of space, or more than 10 times the capacity of the hard drive found in the average PC. Operating at 7,200 r.p.m., it can store the same amount of data as 18 DVDs, 159 music CDs, or a stack of documents 2 miles high.

⊙ GREATEST STORAGE CAPACITY

US firm C3D Inc. has developed and tested a fully operational read-only disk with a storage capacity of 140 gigabytes. C3D, which first exhibited the disk in Oct. 1999, is currently looking for backers for its product. By comparison, a DVD can store up to 17 GB, and a CD-ROM a mere 650 MB.

"MOST HUMAN" COMPUTER PROGRAM

A computer running the program Albert was awarded the 1999 Loebner Prize for the "most human" computer system, winning $2,000 for its author, Robby Garner from Georgia, USA. Albert is a program that a user can communicate with using human speech.

GREATEST MEMORY DENSITY

On March 23, 2000, researchers at Seagate Technologies, Scotts Valley, California, USA, announced that they had developed a data storage disk capacity equivalent to 45 GB/in.² This would be like a 3.5-in. floppy holding 25 DVD-quality movies.

SMALLEST PERSONAL DATA ASSISTANT (PDA)

The REX PC Companion, built in 1998 by Franklin Electronic Publishers of Burlington, New Jersey, USA, measures just 3.37 in. x 2.12 in. x 0.25 in., weighing 1.4 oz.

FASTEST-SPREADING WORM

The Visual Basic Script Worm "I Love You" was first detected in Hong Kong, China, on May 1, 2000. The worm (as opposed to a virus, which requires e-mail to transmit itself) passes through Microsoft Outlook and propagates at a speed four times greater than that of the Melissa virus. By May 5, the worm had mutated into three different generations and had caused an estimated $1.54–billion worth of damage worldwide. On May 8, Trend Micro Inc. published figures showing that the worm had infected a total of 3.1 million computers worldwide: 2.5 million in North America, 325,000 in Europe, 129,000 in Asia, and 25,500 in Australia and New Zealand. On the same day, Philippine National Bureau of Investigation (NBI) officers arrested a man in the country's capital, Manila, in connection with the worm.

BIGGEST NUMBER CRUNCHED

In April 1997, it was announced that computer scientists at Purdue University, Indiana, USA, had co-ordinated researchers around the world to find the two largest numbers that, multiplied together, equal a known 167-digit number, $(3^{349}-1) \div 2$. The breakthrough came after 100,000 hours. The two factors had 80 digits and 87 digits. The previous factorization record was 162 digits.

BEST CHESS COMPUTER

In 1995, IBM's *Deep Blue* supercomputer became the first computer to beat a human chess grandmaster in a regulation game when it won against Gary Kasparov in Philadelphia, USA. The computer subsequently beat Kasparov in a six-game series on May 11, 1997.

→ YOUNGEST IT EXAM PASS

Krishan Radia (b. Oct. 26, 1991) of London, England, was 6 years, 8 months old when he obtained a grade C in his GCSE Information Technology examination in June 1998, making him the youngest person to gain an IT qualification.

Computer Games

⊙ FASTEST-SELLING CONSOLE

A total of 980,000 units of the Sony PlayStation2 (PS2) were sold in the 48 hours following its release.

BEST-SELLING COMPUTER GAMES

The Nintendo game *Super Mario Brothers* had sold a total of 40.23 million copies worldwide by April 2000.

The 26 games featuring Mario, the plumber who first appeared in the arcade game *Donkey Kong* in 1982, have sold more than 152 million copies in total.

MOST ADVANCED GAMES CONSOLE

The Sony PlayStation2, launched in Japan on March 4, 2000, is powered by a 128-bit RISC chip known as the "Emotion Engine" that runs at 294.912 MHz and is capable of generating polygons at a rate of 66 million a second. The unit supports DVD video and audio CD formats, and has a memory capacity of 32 MB. The PS2, the second 128-bit console to be released (after the Sega Dreamcast), is expected to dominate the highly competitive games console market for some time to come. Other 128-bit machines, developed by Nintendo and Microsoft, are expected to be released in late 2000 or early 2001.

FASTEST-SELLING PC GAME

Myst, which was developed by Cyan and released by Broderbrund in 1993, sold 500,000 copies in its first year. Sales of the game have now topped 4 million, and it has made a total worldwide profit of over $100 million.

MOST EXPENSIVE COMPUTER GAME DEVELOPMENT

The Dreamcast FREE (Full Reactive Eyes Entertainment) title *Shenmue* cost over $20 million to develop. The project took seven years, and was the brainchild of Yu Suzuki, the head of Sega's game-development AM2 division.

MOST ON-LINE CONSOLE SALES

Of the 980,000 consoles sold in the first 48 hours after the launch of the PS2 on March 4, 2000, 380,000 were sold on-line.

MOST SUCCESSFUL GAMES PUBLISHER

In the fiscal year ending March 1999, Electronic Arts, of California, USA, reported sales of $1.22 billion and profits of $73 million.

BIGGEST GLOBAL GAMING MARKET SHARE

As of March 2000, Sony Computer Entertainment's two consoles, the PlayStation and PlayStation2, held a 70% share of the world game console market.

BEST-SELLING HAND-HELD GAME SYSTEM

The world's most popular video game system is the Nintendo Game Boy, which sold more than 80 million units between 1989 and 1999. With its variant units – the original Game Boy, Game Boy Pocket and Game Boy Color – Nintendo currently occupies more than 99% of

⊙ BEST-SELLING DRIVING SIMULATOR

Gran Turismo Real Driving Simulator, a Sony PlayStation game, had sold 7 million units worldwide by Feb. 2000. The game was developed by Polyphony Digital, a satellite company of Sony Computer Entertainment. A sequel, *Gran Turismo 2*, was launched in 1999, and *Gran Turismo 2000* is one of the headline titles showcasing the "Emotion Engine" processor of the PS2.

⊙ OLDEST GIGA PET

The world's oldest known Giga Pet is Elvis, owned by Jessica Troiano of New Milford, Connecticut, USA. According to its manufacturer, Tiger Electronics, Elvis' "life" began on July 3, 1997. It claimed the record on Jan. 13, 1998, at the age of 194 days.

the US market. More than 1,000 Game Boy titles are now available worldwide.

BEST-SELLING SOCCER GAME

The *FIFA* series of games, developed by EA Sports, have sold more than 16 million units.

BEST-SELLING FLIGHT SIMULATOR

MS Flight Simulator was released by Microsoft in April 1992 ,and had sold a total of 21 million units by June 1999.

MOST POPULAR DJ-SIMULATION ARCADE GAME

By May 1999, Japanese company Konami had released 6,700 copies of the arcade game *Beatmania* (known as *Hiphopmania* outside Japan), a DJ-simulation game in which the player has to handle two record decks and an effects button. They are then rated on their competence at mixing effectively and timing the additional sound effects.

MOST ADVANCE ORDERS FOR A GAME

More than 325,000 US consumers put down deposits for copies of *The Legend of Zelda: Ocarina of Time*, a Nintendo 64 game, to ensure that they received their copy as soon as it went on sale on Nov. 23, 1998.

MOST RIGOROUS SOFTWARE REGULATIONS

Germany has strict regulations stipulating that blood shown on computer games be green, and that victims likely to end up getting killed be portrayed as zombies, or as far from human as possible.

↓ FASTEST-SELLING COMPUTER GAME

The Nintendo Game Boy title *Pokémon Yellow* was released in the USA on Oct. 18, 1999, and had sold 1 million copies within 10 days.

Internet 1

⊙ BIGGEST SINGLE E-COMMERCE TRANSACTION

American internet tycoon Mark Cuban (inset) from Dallas, Texas, USA, bought a Gulfstream V business jet over the internet in Oct. 1999. The jet changed hands for $40 million.

MOST QUESTIONS TO A WEBSITE

During a web event to promote his album *Flaming Pie*, held on May 17,1997, former Beatle Sir Paul McCartney received over 3 million questions from fans in 30 minutes.

MOST VISITED WEBSITES

The official website of the 1998 soccer World Cup, www.france98.com, received a total of 1,137,218,296 hits over the course of the competition, which was held between June 10 and July 12, 1998.

The website also holds the records for the most hits in a 24-hour period (73,030,828 on June 30, 1998), the most hits in one hour (10,290,429, also on June 30, 1998), and the most hits in one minute (235,356 on June 29, 1998).

According to web statisticians alexa.com, the most visited website on a day-to-day basis is www.msn.com, Microsoft Corporation's website. In March 2000, it received a total of 10.5 billion page views, 62% of which were accounted for by hotmail.com, Microsoft's free e-mail service provider.

BIGGEST INTERNET CRASH

At approximately 11:30 a.m. Eastern Standard Time on April 25, 1997, the global computer network ran into major problems and much of the system became unusable. Human error and equipment failure led to a network in Florida, USA, claiming "ownership" of 30,000 of the internet's 45,000 routes. Data packets were routed incorrectly and connections across the net failed. Although some service providers took action within 15 minutes, the problem persisted until 7 p.m.

MOST CONDOLENCES EXPRESSED ON THE NET

In Sept. 1997, the month following the death of Diana, Princess of Wales, a record 350,000 messages of condolence were left on the

⊙ MOST VALUABLE DOMAIN NAME

On Dec. 1, 1999, Texan entrepreneur Marc Ostrofsky sold the internet domain name "business.com" to US firm eCompanies for $7.5 million. An internet service provider in London, England, had sold him the name for $150,000 in 1996. However, GreatDomains.com, an auction house for internet addresses, expects this record to be broken sometime toward the end of 2000, as it claimed in April 2000 to have received a $10-million bid for the name "america.com."

memorial page of the British Monarchy's official website. The site received a total of 14 million visitors that month – a record amount for a royal website.

MOST POPULAR INTERNET SUFFIX
Of the 15.72 million internet suffixes in existence by the end of March 2000, the most popular was ".com," which was used by 9.48 million hosts.

BIGGEST COMPUTER NETWORK
The number of computers connected to the internet has doubled every year since 1987. The global figure is now approaching 300 million, although there may be many more computers hidden behind corporate "firewalls" designed to exclude electronic visitors, including hackers.

MOST COMMERCE CONDUCTED ON THE NET
US businesses exchanged an estimated $17 billion in goods and services in 1999 – more than any other country.

MOST EXPENSIVE COUNTRY CODE
Tuvalu, a tiny developing island nation located between Hawaii and Australia in the Pacific Ocean, has a population of just 10,588. In April 2000, it announced that it had made $50 million by selling its rights to the URL suffix ".tv" to California company Idealab for 10 years.

SMALLEST SERVER HARDWARE
The web page of the Wearables Laboratory at Stanford University, Palo Alto, California, USA, is supported by Jumptec's DIMM-PC, a "matchbox" server that measures just 2.7 in. x 1.7 in. x 0.25 in., making it slightly higher and wider than a box of matches. It has a volume of about 1 in.^{3} – less than a tenth the size of that of the previous record-holder.

MOST WIRED COUNTRY
The USA had over 110 million internet users at the end of 1999 – nearly 43% of the worldwide total. Japan is second, with 18.16 million users, and the UK third, with nearly 14 million.

According to the Computer Industry Almanac (www.c-i-a.com), Canada has the most internet users per capita, with 428.3 out of every 1,000 people in the country using the net.

BIGGEST DOMAIN OWNERSHIP
According to NetNames Ltd., the USA owns over 11 million of the 15,719,462 domains that exist throughout the world. Germany has the second most, with 1,483,387, and the UK is third, with 1,002,788.

BIGGEST SEARCH ENGINE
The biggest search engine is AltaVista, with 150 million indexed pages.

BIGGEST FREE E-MAIL PROVIDER
Hotmail.com, which was launched in July 1996, is the world's largest free web-based e-mail service provider. As of April 2000, it had more than 60 million subscribers.

YOUNGEST NATION IN CYBERSPACE
Palestine, which is still battling for international recognition as an independent state, acquired autonomy in cyberspace on March 22, 2000, when the Internet Corp. for Assigned Names and Numbers (ICANN), the regulatory body for net addresses, granted the Palestinian National Authority its own two-letter suffix to advertise real estate on-line. The authority will now be able to register addresses under its own domain, "ps," in line with other so-called country codes such as "fr" for France and "it" for Italy.

↑ MOST VISITED PERSONAL HOMEPAGE
The personal homepage of photojournalist Mahir Cagri from Izmir, Turkey – members.xoom.com/primall/mahir/ – had received a total of 3,173,973 page views as of April 12, 2000, with a peak of around 50,000 page views per day. Visitors to the site, which is full of kitsch photographs of Cagri playing the accordion and lying on the beach in skimpy red swimming trunks, are welcomed by the message "I kiss you!"

Internet 2

⊙ BIGGEST ONLINE GOLF TOURNAMENT

More than 11,000 players took part in the 'internet's first major' – the 1999 Jack Nicklaus Online Golf Championship. The final round of the competition was held on Dec. 10, 1999 at the Pelican Hill Golf Club, California, USA, when Chet Stone (USA) won the title 4 & 3 after 36 holes of match play on a digitally-rendered version of the Pelican Hill course. He won $5,000.

BIGGEST MULTILINGUAL WEB BROADCASTS

The opening and closing ceremonies of the Third Conference of the Parties of the United Nations Framework Convention on Climate Change, held in Kyoto, Japan, in Dec. 1997, were broadcast simultaneously via the net in seven languages – Arabic, Chinese, English, French, Japanese, Russian and Spanish.

MOST POPULAR INTERNET NEWS SERVICE

The seven sites of the international news service CNN, which is based in Atlanta, Georgia, USA, have a combined average of 55 million page views per week. They also receive more than 3,000 user comments per day via the CNN message boards. The sites currently contain more than 210,000 pages, but grow by 90–150 pages daily.

BIGGEST INTERNET CONCERT

On Dec. 14, 1999 former Beatle Sir Paul McCartney played a one-off gig at the Cavern Club, Liverpool, England, the site of the Beatles' early performances in the 1960s. In addition to the 300-strong audience, around 3 million fans watched the concert via a live webcast. Another 15,000 gathered in Chavasse Park, Liverpool, where a video screen showed the 13-song gig live. The entire performance lasted just over 40 minutes.

MOST DOWNLOADED WOMAN

Images of actress and model Cindy Margolis (USA) had been downloaded an estimated 53 million times by April 2000.

MOST CYBERSTAR VARIATIONS

There are an estimated 2,000 variations of the Dancing Baby, a cyberstar originally created as an animated 3D graphics model in Oct. 1996 by Kinetix, a subsidiary of Autodesk Inc. The Dancing Baby featured heavily in the TV show *Ally McBeal*.

MOST DOWNLOADED CYBERPET

More than 10 million people worldwide have downloaded MOPy, a lifelike pet fish screensaver, since its release on the web in Oct. 1997.

BIGGEST SAVING OF PAPER THROUGH INTERNET USE

The delivery firm Federal Express has announced that it saves approximately 2 billion sheets of paper a year in the USA by tracking packages online.

FIRST CYBERCLINIC

In March 1997 US clinical psychologist Dr Kimberly Young established the Center for On-Line Addiction, the world's first psychiatric cybercentre for internet addicts and those with related mental health problems. The clinic is situated at www.netaddiction.com.

On April 19, 2000 virtual newscaster Ananova delivered her first news broadcast from www.ananova.com. Ananova, a product of PA News Media of Leeds, England, is a complete 3D model, generated in real time and programmed to act like a human newsreader.

MOST EXPENSIVE VIRTUAL MEMORIALS

While most of the virtual cemeteries on the internet provide memorials for an average of $50, Perpetual Memorials (http://www.cleverthings.com/partners/memorials/) charges $995 for a complete multimedia package, which includes photographs and video and audio clips.

LONGEST WEB PAGE

Ralf Laue of Leipzig, Germany, created a web page 350.2 miles long, but only 21,698 Kb in size, at the Mitsubishi Electric exhibition stand at the CEBIT fair, Hannover, Germany, from March 18 to 24, 1999.

BIGGEST MASS DISMISSAL FOR E-MAIL ABUSE

In Nov. 1999 the *New York Times* newspaper dismissed a total of 23 employees who had been sending inappropriate and offensive e-mail messages, including jibes about bosses and explicit photographs. Scores of other workers at the newspaper were warned about misuse of the internet.

BIGGEST MP3 SITE

mp3.com is the world's premier online music service provider, hosting 208,000 songs by over 35,000 artists available for download.

BIGGEST ONLINE SHOP

Amazon.com, founded in 1994 by Jeff Bezos (USA), opened its virtual doors in July 1995, and has now sold products to more than 13 million people in over 160 countries. Its catalog of 4.7 million books, CDs and audiobooks makes it the largest online shop in the world.

BIGGEST VOLUNTARY WEB SAFETY ORGANIZATION

Formed in June 1995 by Colin Gabriel Hatcher (USA), the Cyber Angels (the cyber branch of the Guardian Angels) has dealt with more than 200 cases of cyberstalking.

MOST DISTANT MEDICAL TREATMENT VIA THE WEB

In Nov. 1998 Dr Daniel Carlin of Boston, Massachusetts, USA, 'treated' Russian yachtsman Victor Yazykov over the internet for a dangerous abscess. Yazykov was taking part in a solo round-the-world yacht race at the time, and was off the coast of South Africa, 7,705 miles away from Boston.

← LONGEST DOMAIN NAME

The longest domain name is http://www.llanfairpwllgwyn-gyllgogerychwyrndrobwll-llantysiliogogogoch.co.uk. It belongs to a site promoting the village of the same name in Anglesey, Gwynedd, Wales. The name means 'St Mary's Church in the hollow of the white hazel near a rapid whirlpool and the Church of St Tysilio near the red cave'.

Robots

SMALLEST ROBOT
The world's smallest robot is the Monsieur microbot, developed by Seiko Epson Corporation of Japan in 1992. This light-sensitive robot, which measures less than 0.06 in.[3] and weighs 0.05 oz., is made from 97 separate watch parts. Capable of reaching speeds of up to 0.4 in./sec. for about five minutes when charged, the Monsieur has earned a design award at the International Contest for Hill-Climbing Micromechanisms.

BIGGEST ROBOT EXHIBITION
The International Robot Show is a biennial event held in Tokyo, Japan. The 1999 show, which took place in October, attracted over 700 exhibitors.

MOST COMPLEX ARTIFICIAL BRAIN
Genobyte Corp. of Boulder, Colorado, USA, in conjunction with Advanced Telecommunications Research (ATR) of Japan, have developed a brain for a robot cat called *Robokoneko* (Japanese for "robot kitten"). The architect of this Cellular Automata Machine (CAM) is Hugo de Garis, who works at ATR's labs in Kyoto, Japan. De Garis' CAM consists of 37.7 million artificial neurons, each neuron being a group of transistors coupled as a cell. By contrast, contemporary AI "brains" contain only a few hundred neurons. When completed, *Robokoneko* will have the ability to "learn," creating new neural pathways in the process.

MOST EXPENSIVE ROBOT FISH
As a result of a four-year project costing $1 million, Mitsubishi Heavy Industries of Japan have developed a series of robotic fish so lifelike that they can only be distinguished from real fish on extremely close inspection. The first model to be produced was a robot sea bream that weighed 5.5 lbs. and had a length of 20 in. However, the company is more interested in making robotic replicas of extinct fish for use in virtual aquariums. It is hoped that future robot fish will be able to look for sources of pollution or make oceanographic maps.

BIGGEST ROBOT
The world's largest robot is Tower Belcon, designed and built by Mitsubishi Heavy Industries in 1998. A concrete-conveying robot that stands 231 ft. tall, with a 250-ft. boom, it can deliver 6,356 ft.[3] of concrete an hour via two 105-ft.[3] buckets. It is owned by Kabuki Corporation of Japan.

⊙ MOST ADVANCED VACUUM CLEANER
The Dyson DC06 vacuum cleaner is controlled by three onboard computers that prevent it from falling down stairs, bumping into children and pets, and covering areas that have already been vacuumed. It uses information from its 50 sensors to make 16 decisions every second about where it should clean next.

TOUGHEST ROBOT
Commander Manipulator, a robot developed by British Nuclear Fuels Ltd., helps to clean up contamination at Windscale Pile 1 (now Sellafield), Cumbria, England – the scene of one of the world's worst nuclear accidents in 1957. The robot is largely resistant to radiation, and its hydraulically powered arm can shift weights of 280 lbs.

⊙ MOST COCKTAILS MIXED BY A ROBOT
Cynthia's Cyberbar in London, England, which opened in Oct. 1999, is run by two cocktail-making robots named Cynthia and Rastus. Both 7 ft. tall, they each cost $410,000. They are able to mix 75 different cocktails, even choosing the correct glass and executing the final pour.

CHEAPEST ROBOT
Walkman, a 5-in.-tall robot, was built from the remains of a Sony Walkman for $1.75 at the Los Alamos National Laboratory, New Mexico, USA, in 1996.

MOST WIDELY USED INDUSTRIAL ROBOT
Puma (Programmable Universal Machine for Assembly), designed by Vic Schienman in the 1970s and manufactured by Swiss company Staubli Unimation, is the most commonly used robot on assembly lines and in university laboratories.

FASTEST INDUSTRIAL ROBOT
In July 1997, Japanese company Fanuc developed the LR Mate 100i high-speed conveyance robot, the axis speed of which is estimated to be 79% faster than previous models. The robot can carry objects for up to 1 mile 1,513 yds., and can move up and down 1 in. and back and forth 12 in. in a time of 0.58 seconds – 60% faster than previous models and an industry record.

MOST HUMANOID ROBOT
In 1997, Honda of Japan launched the 5-ft. 3-in.-tall P3 robot. The robot, which has three-dimensional sight, can turn its head, step over obstacles, change direction, and correct its balance if pushed.

MOST INTELLIGENT ROBOT
Based at the Massachusetts Institute of Technology (MIT), Cambridge, Massachusetts, USA, the Cog Project is an attempt to bring together the many different fields of artificial intelligence and robotics. When completed, Cog, the robot currently under construction, will be the ultimate in AI/robotics synergy – an "intelligent" robot that can think, hear, feel, touch and speak.

⊙ MOST DISTANT REMOTE-CONTROLLED ROBOT
On July 4, 1997, NASA's Sojourner robot rover completed its 80-million-mile journey to Mars, landing on its surface within sight of the earlier Pathfinder lander.

← FASTEST-SELLING ROBOT PET
The Artificial Intelligence roBOt, or Aibo (Japanese for "partner"), is Sony's robot dog, which retails for $2,066. When Aibo made its first appearance on Sony's website on May 31, 1999, 3,000 were sold within 20 minutes.

Gadgets 1

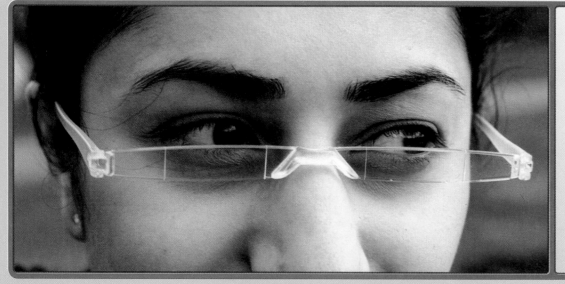

← SMALLEST WRISTWATCH PHONE

The smallest wristwatch phone is NTT's prototype Personal Handy-phone System (PHS), which has a volume of 1.83 in.³ and weighs 1.58 oz. It incorporates voice recognition. Prototypes of wristwatch phones have also been developed by Motorola, Swatch, and Samsung Electronics. Samsung's CDMA-based SPH-WP10 watch phone (left), which has a volume of 4.74 in.³, weighs 1.76 oz., and features a 250-contact phone book, is the only commercially available wristwatch phone.

FASTEST CAMERA

A camera built for research into high-powered lasers by the Blackett Laboratory at Imperial College of Science and Technology, London, England, registers images at a rate of 33 billion frames per sec.

The fastest production camera is the Imacon 675, made by Hadland Photonics Ltd. of Bovingdon, Hertfordshire, England. It operates at up to 600 million frames per sec.

SMALLEST MARKETED CAMERA

Excluding intracardiac surgery and espionage cameras, the smallest camera is the circular Japanese "Petal." With a 1.1-in. diameter and a 0.64-in. thickness, it has a focal length of just 0.5 in.

SMALLEST FILM CAMERA WITH ZOOM LENS

The world's smallest fully automatic Advanced Photo System (APS) Leaf-Shutter compact camera with 2x zoom lens (composed of two aspherical lens elements), is a Canon model, known as the IXY 320 in Japan, the ELPH 2 in the USA, and the IXUS II elsewhere. It measures 3.42 in. x 2.24 in. x 0.96 in. and weighs 6 oz., excluding the 0.39-oz. battery. The camera uses hybrid focusing with active and passive autofocusing, and a high-image-quality 2x zoom lens to deliver high-contrast images. It also has advanced APS functions, such as Mid-Roll Change and Print Quality Improvement, as well as print amount specification and three custom functions.

MOST SUCCESSFUL INSTANT CAMERA

A system of one-step photography that uses the principle of diffusion transfer to reproduce the image recorded by a camera lens directly onto a photosensitive surface, was developed by Polaroid Corporation founder Edwin Land (USA) in 1937.

⊙ LIGHTEST EYEGLASSES

The Helper Superlight glasses, manufactured by Seika Trading Company Ltd. of Osaka, Japan, and first sold in Aug. 1998, weigh just 0.16 oz. The glasses are available with lenses of seven different strengths, ranging from +1.00 to 4.00 diopters.

SMALLEST FAX MACHINE

Real Time Strategies Inc.'s hand-held device, the Pagentry, which combines various functions including the transmission of messages to facsimile machines, measures just 3 in. x 5 in. x 0.75 in. and weighs only 5 oz.

SMALLEST TELEPHONE

The smallest operational telephone was created by Jan Piotr Krutewicz of Munster, Indiana, USA, on Sept. 16, 1996. It is 1.87 in. x 0.39 in. x 0.82 in.

SMALLEST HAND-HELD CELL PHONE

The world's smallest cell phone is the Motorola V3688, which measures just 3.2 in. x 1.7 in. x 1 in. The dual-band phone is based on the clamshell design of its predecessor, the Motorola StarTAC 8500. Its battery allows for between 140 and 180 minutes of talk time and a standby time of up to 100 hours.

⊙ SMALLEST CELL PHONE TV

The SCH-M220, Korean-based Samsung Electronics' combination portable TV/cell phone unit, measures just 3.6 in. x 2 in. x 1.4 in. It provides up to 200 minutes of continuous television viewing time, with 180 and 170 minutes' standby and talk time respectively.

LIGHTEST CELL PHONE

The NTT Docomo Mova P208 cell phone unit is the lightest in the world. It weighs a mere 2 oz. and was launched on Oct. 1, 1999.

HIGHEST-RESOLUTION DIGITAL CAMERA

The Olympus Camedia C-3030 Zoom digital camera, which costs $1,265, was first sold in 1999. The camera has a picture resolution which is made up of a record 3.34 million pixels.

FINEST OPTICAL FIBERS

Physicists at the University of Bath, England, have recently produced the world's narrowest optical fibers for use in communications. Stretching to a length of 6 miles, 376 yds., with cores that measure only 0.000000002 in. in thickness, their total length-to-width ratio is equivalent to the Channel Tunnel between England and France being extended from the Earth to the planet Jupiter.

↑ SMALLEST INSTANT CAMERA

The Polaroid PopShot, the world's first disposable instant camera, measures 6.5 in. x 4.25 in. x 2.5 in. and weighs only 9 oz. The PopShot can take 10 color photographs, each measuring 4.5 in. x 2.5 in. It comes with a postage-free mailing envelope to encourage users to return it for recycling.

Gadgets 2

← BEST-SELLING ROBOT LAWNMOWER

The Robomow, designed and developed in Israel and marketed by Friendly Robotics of Thame, Oxfordshire, England, has sold over 300 units since its launch in 1999. With a length of 3 ft. and a retail price of $809, the machine uses a miniature electronic brain to map out a garden before it starts to mow. It can cut up to 6,000 yd.[2] of grass in one go – the equivalent of two tennis courts.

$399, can play continuously for 15 hours, or 26 hours with an additional battery pack. It measures just 3.1 in. x 0.7 in. x 3.1 in.

BEST-SELLING MP3 PLAYER

A total of 400,000 units of the Diamond Rio PMP300 MP3 player were sold between its release in Nov. 1998 and May 1999.

SMALLEST CAMCORDERS

The Sony CCD-CR1 Ruvi measures only 5 in. x 2.5 in. x 1.75 in. and can store 30 minutes of moving images. The camera has a 2.5-in. LCD screen and an optical zoom.

Sony's DCR-PC7, launched in 1996, weighs only 17.85 oz. and can fit into the palm of a person's hand. The camcorder has a 2.5-in. LCD screen, a conventional color finder, a swivel for its flip-out screen, and a DV OUT jack that allows individual digital images to be captured and stored on a PC without any loss of quality.

THINNEST MINI DISC PLAYER

Sony's MZ-R55 is 0.25 in. thick and weighs only 6 oz. with its lithium ion battery and alkaline AA cells.

LONGEST-PLAYING MINI DISC PLAYER

The Sharp MD-MT831H Mini Disc player, which retails for

MOST MEDIA FROM ONE COMPONENT

The JVC Victor XV-D9000 DVD player can accommodate four different playback functions: DVD video, DVD audio, video CD, and audio CD.

SMALLEST VIDEO CAMERA

The world's smallest video camera measures just 1 in. x 2 in. x 0.5 in. It is fitted with a pinhole lens produced at Oak Ridge National Laboratory, Tennessee, USA.

BIGGEST TV SET

The Sony Jumbo Tron color TV screen, exhibited in March 1985 at the Tsukuba International Exposition '85, Tokyo, Japan, measured 80 ft. x 150 ft.

The largest cathode ray tubes for color TV sets are 37-in. models which are manufactured by Mitsubishi Electric of Japan.

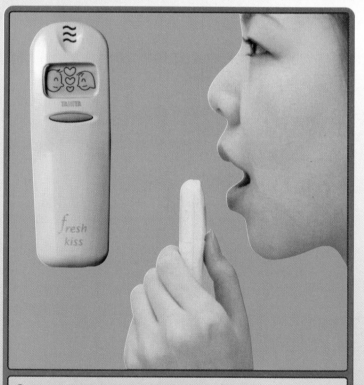

☉ BEST-SELLING HALITOSIS DETECTOR

Japanese electronics company Tanita produced the Fresh Kiss HC-201 in July 1999. Retailing at $37, it sold 800,000 units in its first year on the market. The small, hand-held device analyzes the odor of the user's breath, classifying it as anything from "undetectable" to "very strong halitosis."

MOST SOPHISTICATED TOILET

The Washlet Zoë, first sold in May 1997 by Toto of Japan, has a seat and lid that lift automatically and a flush simulator – a sound effect that serves to cover any embarrassing noises. The seat is heated and the toilet can wash and dry the user. The entire unit can be operated by remote control and it automatically freshens the air every time it is used.

PENKNIFE WITH MOST BLADES

The Year Knife had 1,822 blades when it was first made in 1822 by cutlers Joseph Rodgers and Sons, of Sheffield, S. Yorkshire, England. A blade was added every year until 1973, when there was no further space left.

MOST "INTELLIGENT" PEN

The SmartQuill, developed by British Telecom, can function as a diary, calendar, contacts database, alarm, note taker, calculator, pager, e-mail receiver, and pen.

BEST-SELLING PORTABLE BIDET

The Travel Washlet, produced by Toto of Japan, can deliver a steady stream of up to 7 fl. oz. of warm water for 30 seconds. Toto has sold more than 180,000 Travel Washlets since the product's release in 1996.

⊙ MOST ACCURATE COMMERCIALLY AVAILABLE SATELLITE PHOTOS

On Sept. 24, 1999, Space Imaging of Denver, Colorado, USA, launched a satellite, named *Ikonos*, that was equipped with a Kodak-designed camera. *Ikonos*, which orbits 400 miles above the Earth, moves at 4 miles/sec. and can be used to take photographs of any place in the world, distinguishing objects as small as 11 ft.^{2} Customers can purchase images for a minimum of $1,000 in the USA and $2,000 elsewhere. Sample photographs can be viewed at www.spaceimaging.com.

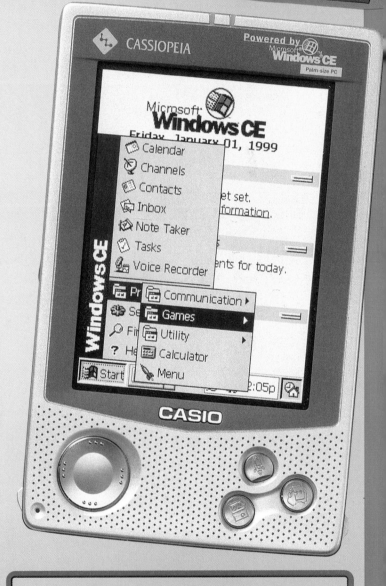

↑ MOST POWERFUL PERSONAL DIGITAL ASSISTANT

Launched in 1999, the Casio Cassiopeia E-105 has a 131-MHz processor and a back-lit TFT crystal 65,536-color display. It contains 32 MB of RAM and 16 MB of ROM, and weighs 9 oz.

Lethal Weapons

FASTEST TANKS
The fastest tracked armored reconnaissance vehicle is the British Scorpion, which can reach a top speed of 49.7 m.p.h. when carrying a 75% payload.

The British Warrior tank has a top speed of 46.6 m.p.h., which it can achieve with a full payload.

BIGGEST MORTARS
The two biggest mortars ever constructed were Mallet's mortar, built at Woolwich Arsenal, London, England, in 1857, and Little David, made in the USA during World War II. Each had a caliber of 36 in., but neither was used in action.

The heaviest mortar to be employed was the tracked German 24-in. siege piece known as "Karl," used during the Battle of Stalingrad in 1942–43.

BIGGEST GUN
Schwerer Gustav, a gun used by the German Army during the siege of Sevastopol, USSR (now Ukraine) in July 1942, had a 94-ft. 7-in.-long barrel and an 31.5-in. caliber. It weighed 1,323 tons and had a range of 13 miles for a 7.9-ton projectile and 29 miles for a 4.7-ton projectile. The remains of the gun were discovered near Metzenhof, Bavaria, Germany, in Aug. 1945.

HEAVIEST CANNON
A cannon built in Perm, Russia, in 1868 weighed a record 141.8 tons.

GUN WITH GREATEST RANGE
The German-made Paris–Geschütz (Paris Gun), which shelled Paris, France, during World War I, had a designed range of 79 miles and a caliber of 8.3 in. The greatest range it actually achieved was 75.8 miles, from the Forest of Crépy, France, in March 1918.

HIGHEST SHOT FIRED BY A GUN
On Nov. 19, 1966, the HARP (High Altitude Research Project) gun fired a 185-lb. projectile to a record-breaking altitude of 112 miles at Yuma, Arizona, USA. The gun, which consists of two barrels fused in tandem into a single 119-ft. 5-in.-long barrel, weighs 147.6 tons.

HEAVIEST NUCLEAR BOMB
The heaviest known nuclear bomb was the MK 17, which was carried by US B-36 bombers in the mid-1950s. It weighed 42,000 lbs. and was 24 ft. 6 in. long.

HEAVIEST CONVENTIONAL BOMB
The heaviest conventional bomb to be used operationally was the British Royal Air Force's Grand Slam, which weighed 22,000 lbs. The first Grand Slam bomb was dropped on Bielefeld Railroad Viaduct, Germany, on March 14, 1945.

A bomb weighing 42,000 lbs. was tested by the US Air Force at Muroc Dry Lake, California, USA, in 1949.

MOST POWERFUL NUCLEAR MISSILE
The most powerful ICBM (Intercontinental Ballistic Missile) is the former USSR's SS-18 (Model 5), which is believed to be armed with 10 750-kiloton MIRVs (Multiple Independently Targetable Re-entry Vehicles). All SS-18 ICBMs had been returned to Russia by the end of April 1995, where 150 are still operational. If the START 2 (Strategic Arms Reduction Talks 2) agreement is fully implemented, the remaining SS-18s and all other ICBMs with more than one warhead will be destroyed.

MOST POWERFUL ATOMIC BOMB
A thermonuclear device with power equivalent to approximately 57 megatons of TNT was detonated by the former USSR in the Novaya Zemlya area on Oct. 30, 1961. The resulting shock wave circled the world three times, with each circuit taking 36 hrs. 27 min. Estimates put the power of the device at between 62 and 90 megatons.

⊙ **MOST EXPENSIVE FIGHTER PLANE**
The US F22 Raptor, developed by Lockheed Martin Aeronautical Systems, Lockheed Martin Fort Worth and Boeing in the late 1990s, cost approximately $13.3 billion – twice as much as its European counterpart, the Eurofighter.

⊙ **MOST ACCURATE BOMB**
The Joint Direct Attack Munition, developed by the US Air Force and the US Navy, is the most accurate bomb in the world. After release, its location is continually monitored by seven different satellites, and it can hit targets with an accuracy of within 6 ft. 7 in.

MOST EXPENSIVE BOMBER

The world's most expensive military aircraft is the US B2 Spirit, currently priced at $1.3 billion. A long-range multirole bomber, it is capable of delivering both conventional and nuclear munitions, and can carry a total payload of 17.85 tons.

LONGEST-RANGE MISSILE

The US Atlas missile, which entered service in 1959, had a range of 10,360 miles – about 3,000 miles more than was necessary to hit any point in Soviet territory from launch sites in the West.

MOST POWERFUL TORPEDO

The Russian Type 65, a 26-in. torpedo, carries a warhead of nearly 2,016 lbs. of conventional explosive or a 15-kiloton nuclear warhead – giving it slightly less explosive power than the bombs that destroyed Hiroshima and Nagasaki in 1945.

FASTEST-FIRING MACHINE GUN

Designed in the late 1960s for use in helicopters and armored vehicles, the 0.3-in. M134 Minigun is the world's fastest-firing machine gun. Based on the multiple-barreled Gatling design, it has six barrels that are revolved by an electric motor and fed by a 4,000-round link belt. This allows for a firing rate of 6,000 rounds per minute – about 10 times that of an ordinary machine gun.

MOST ACCURATE PORTABLE ANTI-AIRCRAFT MISSILE

The Stinger missile, introduced in the early 1980s, is 5 ft. long, weighs 22 lbs. and has a range of about 3 miles and a speed of around 1,300 m.p.h.

← MOST WIDELY USED FIREARM

The Kalashnikov AK-47, along with its variants, has been used in over 75 wars – more than any other firearm. Over 100 million units of the rifle have been assembled in 25 countries, often illegally.

Cars

⊙ FASTEST ELECTRIC CAR

On Oct. 22, 1999, *White Lightning Electric Streamliner*, an electric car owned by Dempsey's World Record Associates, achieved a record speed of 245.951 m.p.h. at the Bonneville Salt Flats, Utah, USA. The car was driven by Patrick Rummerfield (USA).

HIGHEST LAND SPEED

The one-mile land speed record is 763.055 m.p.h., set by Andy Green (UK) in *Thrust SSC* in the Black Rock Desert, Nevada, USA, on Oct. 15, 1997. The car is powered by two Rolls-Royce Spey 205 jet engines, which together generate 22.32 tons of thrust.

Kitty Hambleton (USA) holds the record for the fastest land speed achieved by a woman, having reached 524.030 m.p.h. in the rocket-powered three-wheeled *SM1 Motivator* in the Alvard Desert, Oregon, USA, on Dec. 6, 1976. Her official two-way record was 512.724 m.p.h., and she is believed to have touched a scorching 600 m.p.h. for a moment. For a land speed record to be bona fide, it has to be set twice; the vehicle first travelling one way over a set course, then returning to its starting point.

FASTEST ROAD CAR

The highest speed ever reached by a standard production car is 240.3 m.p.h., by a McLaren F1 driven by Andy Wallace (UK) at the Volkswagen Proving Ground, Wolfsburg, Germany, on March 31, 1998.

FASTEST ACCELERATION

The fastest road-tested acceleration on record is 0–60 m.p.h. in 3.07 seconds, by a Ford RS200 Evolution driven by Graham Hathaway at Millbrook Proving Ground, Bedfordshire, England, on May 25, 1994.

GREATEST FUEL RANGE

The greatest distance travelled on the contents of a standard fuel tank (capacity 80.1 liters) is 1,338.1 miles, by an Audi 100 TDI diesel car. The car was driven by Stuart Bladon (UK) from John O'Groats, Highlands & Islands, Scotland, to Land's End, Cornwall, England, and back again from July 26 to 28, 1992.

⊙ HIGHEST LIMOUSINE

The world's highest limousine measures 10 ft. 11 in. from ground to roof. Built by Gary Duval of Colton, California, USA, in just over 4,000 hours, it has two separate engines and an eight-wheel independent suspension system. It sits on eight monster truck tires.

HIGHEST MILEAGE
The highest documented mileage for a car is a record 1,764,000 miles, for a 1966 Volvo P-1800S owned by Irvin Gordon of East Patchogue, New York, USA, as of Jan. 2000.

BIGGEST CAR
The biggest car ever produced for private use was the Bugatti "Royale" type 41, assembled at Molsheim, France, by the Italian designer Ettore Bugatti. First built in 1927, it has an eight-cylinder engine with a capacity of 12.7 liters, and is over 22 ft. long. Its hood alone measures 7 ft. in length.

BIGGEST CAR ENGINES
Three production cars had engines with a capacity of 13.5 liters: the US Peerless 6–60 of 1912–14, the Pierce-Arrow 6–66 Raceabout of 1912–18, and the Fageol of 1918.

MOST POWERFUL CAR
The most powerful production car on the market is the McLaren F1 6.1, which develops in excess of 627 h.p. It can accelerate to 60 m.p.h. in 3.2 seconds.

SMALLEST CAR
The smallest roadworthy car ever built was the Peel P50, constructed by Peel Engineering Co. at Peel, Isle of Man, in 1962. It was a mere 52.8 in. long, 39 in. wide, and 52.8 in. in height. It weighed only 130 lbs.

LONGEST CAR
The longest car ever built was a 100-ft.-long, 26-wheeled limousine designed by Jay Ohrberg of Burbank, California, USA. Intended mainly for use in films and exhibitions, it can be driven as a rigid vehicle or altered to bend in the middle. It has many features, including a swimming pool with a diving board, and a king-sized waterbed.

MOST EXPENSIVE PRODUCTION CAR
The world's most expensive production car is the Mercedes Benz CLK/LM, which costs $1,547,620. It has a top speed of 200 m.p.h. and can accelerate from 0–62 m.p.h. in 3.8 seconds.

CHEAPEST CARS
The 1922 Red Bug Buckboard, built by the Briggs & Stratton Co. of Milwaukee, Wisconsin, USA, went on sale for $125–$150, equivalent to around $996 today. It had a 61.8-in. wheelbase and weighed 245 lbs.

Early models of the US King Midget cars, which were made in kit form for self-assembly, sold for as little as $100 in 1948. Today, this would be equivalent to around $800.

BIGGEST CAR MANUFACTURER
The world's biggest manufacturer of motor vehicles and parts (and the largest manufacturing company in the world) is

⊙ **GREATEST FUEL EFFICIENCY**
A car designed by the Microjoule Team from Toulouse, France, achieved a performance of 9,845 m.p.g. at the Shell Eco Marathon, Silverstone, Northamptonshire, England, on July 15, 1999. It was driven by 14-year-old Julien Lebrigand (left) and 10-year-old Thibaud Maindru.

General Motors Corporation of Detroit, Michigan, USA. The giant company currently has 388,000 employees, and has produced more than 8,600,000 cars worldwide to date.

MOST POPULAR CAR
A record total of 24,208,483 Toyota Corollas have been produced since the car's launch in 1966.

MOST VALUABLE CAR
A 1931 Berline de Voyage Royale was bought for $8.1 million by Thomas Monaghan of Ann Arbor, Michigan, USA, in 1986.

← **LOWEST CAR**
Lowlife, a car produced by Perry Watkins (left) of Aylesbury, Buckinghamshire, England, measures just 23.6 in. from ground to roof, and clears the ground by just 1 in.

Trucks, Trains & Buses

LONGEST VEHICLE
The Arctic Snow Train, built by R.G. LeTourneau Inc. of Longview, Texas, USA, for the US Army, is 572 ft. long, with 54 wheels and a gross weight of 400 tons. Its fuel capacity is 6,522 gal., and it has a top speed of 20 m.p.h. It is driven by a crew of six.

LONGEST ROAD TRAIN
The world's longest road train (a line of trailers pulled by a single truck) was driven by Greg Marley on the Great Eastern Highway at Merredin, Australia, on April 3, 1999. Marley used a Kenworth Tri-Drive Cab Over Model K100G to pull 45 trailers, giving an overall length of 2,003 ft. 7 in.

BIGGEST FORKLIFT TRUCKS
In 1991, Kalmar LMV of Lidhult, Sweden, manufactured three counterbalanced forklift trucks capable of lifting loads of up to 88 tons at a load center of 7 ft. 6 in. The massive trucks were built for use in the construction of two pipelines, one running from Sarir to the Gulf of Sirte and the other running from Tazirbu to Benghazi, all Libya.

BIGGEST MONSTER TRUCK
The monster truck *Bigfoot 5* is 15 ft. 6 in. high, has 10-ft.-high tires, and weighs 38,000 lbs. It was built by Bob Chandler of St. Louis, Missouri, USA.

LONGEST TRACTOR WHEELIE
Heiner Rohrs drove a record distance of 3 miles on the back wheels of a tractor at Fintel, Lower Saxony, Germany, on Aug. 20, 1995.

LONGEST SIDE-WHEEL DRIVE IN A TRUCK
On May 19, 1991, Sven-Erik Söderman drove a 7.5-ton Daf 2800 truck a record distance of 6 miles 1,277 yds. on two side wheels at Mora Siljan Airport, Mora City, Sweden.

BIGGEST SNOWPLOW BLADE
The snowplow with the world's biggest blade was made by Aero Snow Removal Corporation of New York City, USA, in 1992, for use at JFK International Airport. Its blade is 50 ft. 2 in. long, 4 ft. 1 in. high, and can clear 1,095 ft.^{3} of snow in one pass.

⊙ BIGGEST EARTH MOVER
The L-1800 loader, developed by R.G. LeTourneau Inc., is 58 ft. 6 in. long and weighs 214 tons. It has a payload capacity of 44.6 tons and a bucket capacity of 33 yd.^{3}

BIGGEST TRAILER
The world's largest trailer is a two-wheeled, five-story model that was built in 1990 for Sheik Hamad Bin Hamdan Al Nahyan of Abu Dhabi, United Arab Emirates. It is 66 ft. long, 39 ft. wide, and weighs a record 120 tons. It contains eight bedrooms and four garages.

BIGGEST AMBULANCES
The world's largest ambulances are the 59-ft.-long articulated Alligator Jumbulances Marks VI, VII, VIII, and IX, operated by the

⊙ LONGEST BUSES
The longest rigid single bus (seen left) is 49 ft. in length. Built by Van Hool of Belgium, it can carry 69 passengers. The buses with the greatest overall length are the 105-ft. 8-in.-long articulated DAF Super CityTrain buses of the Democratic Republic of Congo. They have room for a total of 350 passengers: 250 in the first trailer and 100 in the second.

ACROSS Trust to take sick and disabled people on holidays and pilgrimages across Europe. Built by Van Hool of Belgium at a cost of $306,000, they can each carry a total of 44 patients and staff.

FASTEST RAILED VEHICLE
The highest speed attained by a railed vehicle is Mach 8 (6,121 m.p.h.), by an unmanned rocket sled over the 9.4-mile-long rail track at White Sands Missile Range, New Mexico, USA, on Oct. 5, 1982.

FASTEST MAGLEV
On April 14, 1999, the MLX01, a Maglev (manned superconducting magnetically levitated vehicle) operated by the Central Japan Railroad Company reached a record speed of 343 m.p.h. on the Yamanashi Maglev Test Line between Otsuki and Tsuru, Japan.

LONGEST PASSENGER TRAIN
The longest passenger train on record had a length of 5,686 ft. and weighed 2,742 tons. Set up as a one-shot by the National Belgian Railroad Company on April 27, 1991, it was made up of 70 coaches pulled by one electric locomotive. The train travelled the entire way from Ghent to Ostend, Belgium – a distance measuring 38 miles, 1,320 yds. – in 1 hr. 11 min. 5 sec.

LONGEST FREIGHT TRAIN
A freight train with a record length of 4 miles, 880 yds., comprising 660 freight cars, a tank car, and a caboose, travelled 535 miles on the Sishen–Saldanha railroad, South Africa, on Aug. 26–27, 1989. Moved by nine 50-kV electric and seven diesel-electric locomotives, it took 22 hrs., 40 min. to complete the journey.

OLDEST STEAM LOCOMOTIVE IN USE
The Fairy Queen, built in 1855 by Kitson, Thompson, & Hewitson of Leeds, W. Yorkshire, England, was used by the East India Railway Company until 1909. It was restored in 1966, and since Oct. 1997 has been used to haul a twin-coach train on the 89-mile trip between Delhi and Alwar, Rajasthan, India. The journey takes 5 hrs., 30 min. and is mainly made by tourists.

BIGGEST STEAM LOCOMOTIVE
The South African Railways GMA Garratt type 4–8–2+2–8–4, which was built between 1952 and 1954, weighs 184.4 tons.

FASTEST STEAM LOCOMOTIVE
The highest speed that was ever attained by a steam locomotive is 125 m.p.h., a record established by the LNER 4–6–2 No. 4468 Mallard (later numbered 60022) when it hauled seven coaches with a gross weight of 239 tons a distance of 440 yds. down Stoke Bank near Essendine, England, on July 3, 1938.

OLDEST STREETCARS
The oldest streetcars in the world still in service are Motorcars 1 and 2 of the Manx Electric Railway, which date from 1893. They regularly make the 17-mile, 1,249-yd. journey between Douglas and Ramsey, Isle of Man.

EARLIEST BUS SERVICE
The first recorded municipal motor-bus service in the world was inaugurated on April 12, 1903. It ran between Eastbourne Railway Station and Meads, both in E. Sussex, England.

↓ FASTEST RAIL SYSTEM SPEED
The highest speed recorded on any national rail system is 320 m.p.h., by the SNCF TGV (Train à Grande Vitesse) Atlantique between Courtalain and Tours, France, on May 18, 1990.

Bicycles & Motorcycles

SMALLEST BICYCLE

The world's smallest-wheeled ridable bicycle has a front wheel with a diameter of 0.43 in. and a back wheel with a diameter of 0.51 in. It was ridden by its constructor, Zbigniew Rózanek of Pleszew, Poland, for a distance of 16 ft. on Aug. 11, 1999.

BIGGEST BICYCLE

The largest bicycle in the world is *Frankencycle*, built by Dave Moore of Rosemead, California, USA, and first ridden by Steve Gordon of Moorpark, California, on June 4, 1989. It is 11 ft. 2 in. high, with a wheel diameter of 10 ft.

LIGHTEST BICYCLE

A bicycle made from titanium and carbon fiber, weighing 12 lbs. 1 oz., was built by Dionisio Coronado of San Sebastian, Spain, in 1999. It was ridden by Miguel Capelli in the Veleta Peak race, Spain, in July 1999.

BICYCLE WITH MOST GEAR COMBINATIONS

A 107-lb. bicycle constructed by Leon Chassman of Taylor, Michigan, USA, has a record 1,500 gear combinations. Made mainly from the salvaged parts of 27 other bicycles, it has two sets of 10-speed gears and one set of 15-speed gears. With a wheel size of 20 in. and a wheelbase of 56 in., it was completed in 1998.

FASTEST BICYCLIST

The world's highest speed ever achieved on a bicycle is 166.944 m.p.h., by Fred Rompelberg (Netherlands) at Bonneville Salt Flats, Utah, USA, on Oct. 3, 1995. His record attempt was greatly assisted by the slipstream from his lead vehicle.

LONGEST BICYCLE WHEELIE JOURNEY

The world's longest bicycle wheelie journey was one of 2,839 miles made by Kurt Osburn of Fullerton, California, USA. He travelled from the Guinness World of Records Museum in Hollywood, California, USA, to the Guinness World of Records Museum in Orlando, Florida, USA, between April 13 and June 25, 1999.

MOST PEOPLE ON A BICYCLE

A record of 19 people on one bicycle was set by members of Jago Sports Club, Semerang, Java, Indonesia, on June 30, 1988. They cycled a total distance of 656 ft..

⊙ **LONGEST BICYCLE WHEELIE**
On Aug. 8, 1998, Kurt Osburn (USA) rode for a record 11 hours on the back wheel of a bicycle at the Anaheim Convention Center, California, USA.

SMALLEST UNICYCLE

Peter Rosendahl (Sweden) rode an 8-in.-high unicycle with a wheel diameter of 0.71 in. a record distance of 27 ft. 10 in. at the ZDF TV Studios, Unterföhring, Germany, on March 29, 1998. The unicycle has no attachments or extensions fitted.

TALLEST UNICYCLE

The tallest ridable unicycle was 101 ft. 9 in. high. It was ridden by Steve McPeak (with a safety wire suspended from an overhead crane) for a distance of 376 ft. at Las Vegas, Nevada, USA, in Oct. 1980.

FASTEST UNICYCLISTS

Peter Rosendahl set a sprint record for 100 m. from a standing start of 12.11 sec. (18.47 m.p.h.) at Las Vegas, Nevada, USA, on March 25, 1994.

Takayuki Koike of Kanagawa, Japan, set a record for 100 miles of 6 hrs. 44 min. 21.84 sec. on Aug. 9, 1987. His average speed was 14.83 m.p.h.

SMALLEST MOTORCYCLE

Simon Timperley and Clive Williams of Progressive Engineering Ltd., Greater Manchester, England, designed and constructed a motorcycle with a wheelbase of 4.25 in., a seat height of 3.74 in., a front wheel with a diameter

⊙ **LONGEST BICYCLE**
The longest true bicycle (i.e. without a third stabilizing wheel) is 84 ft. 11 in. in length, with a weight of 3,858 lbs. Designed by Super Tandem Club Ceparana of Ceparana, Italy, it was ridden a distance of 368 ft. by 40 members of the club on Sept. 20, 1998. Not surprisingly, cornering is a problem for the bike.

of 0.75 in., and a back wheel with a diameter of 0.95 in. The tiny motorcycle was ridden a distance of 3 ft. 3 in.

LONGEST MOTORCYCLE
Douglas and Roger Bell of Perth, Western Australia, designed and constructed a record 24-ft. 11-in.-long motorcycle that weighed nearly 4,409 lbs.

MOST EXPENSIVE MOTORCYCLE
The Italian-made Morbidelli 850 V8 is the world's most expensive production motorcycle, retailing at $102,872 in 1998.

FASTEST PRODUCTION MOTORCYCLE
The Suzuki Hayabusa GSX 1300R is reported to be able to reach speeds of 194 m.p.h., making it the fastest production motorcyle in the world.

BIGGEST MOTORCYCLE MANUFACTURER
The Honda Motor Company of Japan is the largest manufacturer of motorcycles

in the world. In 1998, Honda sold a record total of 5.1 million motorcylces to retailers around the world.

FASTEST MOTORCYCLIST
On July 14, 1990, Dave Campos (USA) set American Motorcyclist Association (AMA) and Fédération Internationale de Motorcylisme (FIM) absolute speed records on the 23-ft.-long streamliner *Easyriders*, powered by two 1,491-cc Ruxton Harley–Davidson engines. Campos' overall average speed was 322.16 m.p.h. and he completed the faster run at an average speed of 322.870 m.p.h. The record was set at Bonneville Salt Flats, Utah, USA.

FASTEST MOTORCYCLE WHEELIE
The highest speed attained on the back wheel of a motorcycle is 191.3 m.p.h., by Patrick Furstenhoff (Sweden) on a Honda Super Blackbird

1,100-cc Turbo at Bruntingthorpe Proving Ground, Leicestershire, England, on April 18, 1999.

LONGEST MOTORCYCLE WHEELIE
Yasuyuki Kudo covered a record distance of 205.7 miles on the back wheel of his Honda TLM220R motorcycle at the Japan Automobile Research Institute proving ground, Tsukuba, near Tsuchiura, Japan, on May 5, 1991.

MOST EXPENSIVE PRODUCTION MOTOR SCOOTER
The Suzuki AN 400 Burgman is the most expensive motor scooter in production, costing $6,660, with an on-the-road charge of $396.

⊙ LONGEST BACKWARD UNICYCLE
Steve Gordon (USA) rode a unicycle backward for 68 miles at Southwestern Missouri State University, Springfield, Missouri, USA, on June 24, 1999.

↓ TALLEST MOTORCYCLE
The tallest ridable motorcycle is *Bigtoe*, which has a maximum height of 7.5 ft. and a top speed of 62 m.p.h. Built by Tom Wiberg (Sweden), it is powered by a Jaguar V12 engine.

Ships, Boats & Submarines

⊙ BIGGEST CRUISE LINER
The world's biggest cruise liner is *Voyager of the Sea*, which is 1,020 ft. long and 157.5 ft. wide, with a gross tonnage of 142,000. It can accommodate 3,114 passengers and 1,181 crew.

BIGGEST SAILING SHIPS
The biggest sailing vessel ever built was the 5,806-ton *France II*, which was launched at Bordeaux, France, in 1911. This steel-hulled, five-masted bark had a 418-ft. hull, and although principally designed as a sailing vessel with a stump top gallant rig, was also fitted with two auxiliary engines. These were removed in 1919, making it a pure sailing vessel. *France II* was wrecked off the coast of New Caledonia on July 12, 1922.

The largest sailing ship currently in service is the 358-ft.-long *Sedov*, which was built in Kiel, Germany, in 1921 and is now used for training by the Russian Navy. It is 48 ft. wide, with a displacement of 6,200 tons and a sail area of 45,124 ft.[2]

BIGGEST SAIL
The 157-ft. sloop *Hyperion*, built by Wolter Huisman (Netherlands), has a single sail with an area of 5,600 ft.[2] The boat was commissioned by Netscape founder Jim Clark (USA) in 1995.

FASTEST SAILING VESSEL
On Oct. 26, 1993, the trifoiler *Yellow Pages Endeavour* reached a record speed of 46.52 knots (53.57 m.p.h.) while on a timed run of 547 yds. at Sandy Point near Melbourne, Victoria, Australia.

OLDEST ACTIVE SAILING VESSEL
The oldest oceangoing sailing vessel is the 1,197-ton iron bark *Star of India*, which was built at Ramsey, Isle of Man, in 1863, as the full-rigged ship *Euterpe*. It is now preserved as a museum ship in San Diego, California, USA, but still makes occasional day trips under sail.

BIGGEST YACHT
The Saudi Arabian royal yacht *Abdul Aziz*, which was built in Denmark and completed at Vospers Yard, Southampton, Hampshire, England, in June 1984, is 482 ft. long.

BIGGEST JUNK
The oceangoing *Zheng He* had a displacement of 3,100 tons and an estimated length of 538 ft. The flagship of Admiral Zheng He's 62 treasure ships ca.1420, it is believed to have had nine masts.

LONGEST CANOE
The Maori war canoe *Nga Toki Matawhaorua*, which was shaped with adzes at Kerikeri Inlet, New Zealand, in 1940, is 117 ft. 1 in. long and 6 ft. 7 in. wide. It can carry a total of 135 people – 80 paddlers and 55 passengers.

BIGGEST CAR FERRYBOAT
In terms of tonnage, the largest car and passenger ferryboat is *Silja Europa*, which entered service between Stockholm, Sweden, and Helsinki, Finland, in 1993. Operated by Silja Line, it has a gross tonnage of 59,914, a length of 662 ft., and a beam of 107 ft. It can carry 3,000 passengers, 350 cars, and 60 trucks.

FASTEST CAR FERRYBOAT
Lucian Federico L has a top speed of 60 knots (69.1 m.p.h.) and a loaded speed of 57 knots (65.6 m.p.h.). It was designed in Australia by Advanced Multi-Hull Designs, built in Spain by Bazan, and operates on the 110-mile Rio de la Plata route from Buenos Aires, Argentina, to Montevideo, Uruguay. It can carry 52 cars and 450 passengers.

BIGGEST HOVERCRAFT
The 185-ft.-long SRN4 Mk III, a British-built civil hovercraft, weighs 305 tons and is large enough to accommodate a total of 418 passengers and 60 cars. Powered by four Bristol Siddeley Marine Proteus engines, it has a maximum speed in excess of 65 knots (75 m.p.h.), which is the permitted cross-Channel operating speed.

BIGGEST CARGO VESSEL
The oil tanker *Jahre Viking* (formerly known as *Happy Giant* and *Seawise Giant*) is 1,504 ft. long and weighs 564,763 dwt. It has a beam of 225 ft. 9 in. and a draft of 80 ft. 8 in. The tanker was almost totally destroyed during the Iran-Iraq war, but underwent a $60-million renovation in Singapore and the United Arab Emirates before being relaunched under its new name in Nov. 1991.

BIGGEST BATTLESHIPS
The Japanese battleships *Yamato* and *Musashi*, which were both sunk by the USA

⊙ BIGGEST CATAMARAN

The largest and most expensive catamaran ever built is the $6.3-million *Team Philips*, which is 120 ft. long, 70 ft. wide, 136 ft. high, and weighs 13.5 tons. Made of carbon fiber, it has two razor-sharp hulls that allow it to slice through waves rather than bounce over them, and is capable of reaching speeds of up to 40 knots (50 m.p.h.). The man behind *Team Philips* is Pete Goss from Torpoint, Cornwall, England, a former Royal Marine who received an MBE and France's Legion d'Honneur in 1996 for turning back during the Vendee Globe round-the-world race to rescue fellow competitor Raphael Dinelli.

during World War II, had an overall length of 863 ft., a beam of 127 ft., a full load displacement of 69,988 tons, and a full load draft of 35 ft. 5 in. Each was armed with nine 75-ft.-long guns, which weighed 162 tons and fired 3,200-lb. projectiles.

BIGGEST CONTAINER SHIP

The largest container vessel in the world currently in service is *Regina Maersk*, which was built at Odense, Denmark. The ship was completed in Jan. 1996, and has a gross tonnage of 81,488 and a capacity of 6,000 Twenty-foot Equivalent Units (TEUs).

GREATEST DEPTH REACHED BY A SUBMARINE

On Aug.11, 1989, the Japanese research submarine *Shinkai 6500* reached a record depth of 21,414 ft. in the Japan Trench off Sanriku, Japan.

MOST VALUABLE SHIPWRECK

The late treasure hunter Mel Fisher (USA) found the *Nuestra Señora de Atocha* off the Key West coast, Florida, USA, in 1985. The ship had been carrying 39.4 tons of gold and silver and 70 lbs. of emeralds when it went down in a hurricane in Sept. 1622.

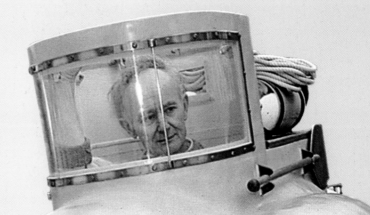

→ SMALLEST SUBMARINE

The world's smallest fully functional submarine is *Water Beatle*, which is 9 ft. 8 in. long, 3 ft. 9 in. wide, and 4 ft. 8 in. high. Built in 1991 by William Smith (right) of Bognor Regis, W. Sussex, England, it can reach depths of approximately 100 ft., remaining underwater for at least four hours. It is currently being used for locating aircraft wreckage off the Sussex coast.

Aircraft

FASTEST AIRCRAFT

The fastest combat jet is the former Soviet Mikoyan MiG-25 fighter, which NATO code-named "Foxbat." The single-seat reconnaissance "Foxbat-B" has a wingspan of 45 ft. 9 in., a length of 78 ft. 2 in., and an estimated maximum takeoff weight of 36.8 tons. It has been tracked by radar at speeds of about Mach 3.2 (2,110 m.p.h.).

The fastest propeller-driven aircraft is the former Soviet Tu-95/142, code-named "Bear" by NATO. It has four 14,795-h.p. engines driving eight-blade contra-rotating propellers, and a maximum level speed of Mach 0.82 (575 m.p.h.).

The fastest biplane was the one-shot Italian Fiat CR42B, which had a 1,010-h.p. Daimler-Benz DB601A engine. It reached a speed of 323 m.p.h. in 1941.

The highest speed achieved by a piston-engined aircraft is 528.33 m.p.h. over a 1-mile, 1,520-yd. course, by *Rare Bear*, a modified Grumman F8F Bearcat piloted by Lyle Shelton.

⊙ GREATEST PASSENGER LOAD

The greatest number of passengers carried by a single commercial airliner is 1,088, by an El Al Boeing 747 during Operation Solomon, which began on May 24, 1991. The purpose of the operation was to evacuate Ethiopian Jews to Israel following the toppling of the Ethiopian government. The figure includes two babies born during the flight.

The record was set on Aug. 21, 1989, at Las Vegas, Nevada, USA.

FASTEST AIRLINERS

The Tupolev Tu-144, first flown on Dec. 31, 1968, was reported to have reached Mach 2.4 (1,600 m.p.h.), but had a normal cruising speed of Mach 2.2. It flew at Mach 1 for the first time on June 5, 1969, and exceeded Mach 2 on May 26, 1970, being the first commercial airliner to do so. The plane started making scheduled flights on Dec. 26, 1975, when it was employed to carry freight and mail. Today it is being used in a joint venture by Tupolev and NASA to aid NASA's development of supersonic passenger aircraft. The BAC/Aérospatiale Concorde, first flown on March 2, 1969, cruises at speeds of up to Mach 2.2 (1,450 m.p.h.). On Jan. 21, 1976, it became the first supersonic airliner to be used on passenger services, and set the New York–London speed record (2 hrs. 54 min. 30 sec.) on April 14, 1990.

BIGGEST HELICOPTERS

The Russian Mil Mi-12 had a rotor diameter of 219 ft. 10 in., a length of 121 ft. 4 in., and a weight of 101.6 tons. Powered by four 6,500-h.p. turboshaft engines, the helicopter was demonstrated as a prototype at the Paris Air Show, France, in 1971, but never entered service.

The world's largest helicopter currently being produced is the 131-ft.-long Russian Mil Mi-26, which has a maximum takeoff weight of 55.1 tons and an unladen weight of 27.7 tons. Its eight-bladed main rotor has a diameter of 105 ft. and is powered by two 11,240-h.p. static HP turboshaft engines.

SMALLEST HELICOPTER

The single-seat Seremet WS-8 ultralight helicopter, which was built in Denmark in 1976, had a 35-h.p. engine and a weight of 117 lbs. when empty. Its rotor measured 14 ft. 9 in. in diameter.

⊙ BIGGEST WORKING AIRSHIP

The largest working airship is the WDL 1B, three models of which have been built at Mulheim, Germany. It is 197 ft. long and has an inflated volume of 254,232 ft.[3]

BIGGEST BALLOON

The largest balloon ever built had an inflated volume of 70 million ft.³ and a height of 1,000 ft. Manufactured by Winzen Research Inc. (now Winzen Engineering Inc.) of South St. Paul, Minnesota, USA, it was destroyed at its launch on July 8, 1975.

BIGGEST AIRSHIPS

The world's largest airships were the 210.5-ton German *Hindenburg* (LZ 129) and *Graf Zeppelin II* (LZ 130), both of which were 803 ft.10 in. long with a hydrogen gas capacity of 7,062,100 ft.³ The *Hindenburg* first flew in 1936, exploding and crashing on May 6, 1937, and the *Graf Zeppelin II* made its first flight in 1938.

GREATEST MASS ASCENT

The greatest mass ascent from a single site took place on Aug. 15, 1987, when 128 hot-air balloons took off in the course of one hour at the Ninth Bristol International Balloon Festival, Ashton Court, Bristol, England.

SMALLEST AIRCRAFT

The smallest twin-engined aircraft in the world is believed to be the Colombian MGI5 Cricri, first flown on July 19, 1973, which has a wingspan of 16 ft. and a length of 12 ft. 10 in. It is powered by two 15-h.p. JPX PUL engines.

The smallest biplane ever flown was *Bumble Bee Two*, which was designed and built by Robert H. Starr of Tempe, Arizona, USA. Capable of carrying just one person, it was only 8 ft. 10 in. long and had a wingspan of just 5 ft. 6 in. It weighed 396 lbs. when empty and was capable of attaining a speed of up to 190 m.p.h. On May 8, 1988, it crashed and was totally destroyed after flying to an altitude of 394 ft. Its pilot suffered serious injuries, but went on to make a full recovery.

Baby Bird, designed and built by Donald R. Stits, is the smallest monoplane ever flown. It is 11 ft. long, with a wingspan of 6 ft. 3 in. and a weight of 252 lbs. when empty. The monoplane is powered by a 55-h.p. two-cylinder Hirth engine, giving it a top speed of 110 m.p.h. *Baby Bird* was first flown by Harold Nemer on Aug. 4, 1984, at Camarillo, California, USA.

The smallest jet is *Silver Bullet*, which was built by Bob and Mary Ellen Bishop of Aguila, Arizona, USA, in 1976. It is 12 ft. long, has a 17-ft. wingspan, weighs 437 lbs., and can fly at 300 m.p.h.

↑ FASTEST WINGED AIRCRAFT

On Oct. 3, 1967, the US-built rocket plane X-15A-2, piloted by Major William J. "Pete" Knight (USA), achieved an absolute speed record of Mach 6.7 (4,520 m.p.h.) above the Mojave Desert, California, USA. This record stood until it was broken by the Space Shuttle in 1980. Neil Armstrong (USA, left) made seven flights in the plane from Dec. 1960 to July 1962, reaching a speed of Mach 5.74 (3,989 m.p.h.) and a peak altitude of 207,500 ft. The highest altitude ever reached by the X-15A was 354,200 ft.

Spacecraft

BIGGEST ROCKET
The biggest rocket ever built was *Saturn 5*, which was 363 ft. high with the *Apollo* spacecraft on top. It weighed 2,857 tons on the launchpad and had a thrust of 3,392 tons.

SMALLEST ROCKET
The smallest rocket in the world was *Pegasus,* a 49-ft.-2-in.-long three-stage booster that was first launched in 1990. It has now been succeeded by an operational *Pegasus XL* version.

MOST POWERFUL ROCKET
The giant *N1* rocket, designed as a key part of the Soviet programme to land a person on the Moon, had a thrust of 4,546 tons. However, it exploded shortly after takeoff on its first launch in Feb. 1969, and three other launch attempts also failed.

MOST EXPENSIVE ROCKETS
The US rocket *Saturn 5* was built for the *Apollo* Moon-landing programme, which had cost approximately $25 billion by the time of the first flight to the Moon in July 1969. Commercial customers have been charged a total of more than $120 million for launches to orbit communications satellites aboard the US commercial rocket *Titan*. *Titan* is no longer on the market.

CHEAPEST ROCKETS
The cheapest US rocket was *Pegasus*, which was developed with a budget of $45 million and cost approximately $10 million per launch.

Even cheaper rockets have probably been built in China and the former Soviet Union, but precise costings have never been made available.

FASTEST SPACECRAFT
The joint NASA–German *Helios A* and *B* solar probes reach a record speed of approximately 157,000 m.p.h. every time they reach the perihelion of their solar orbits – the point at which they are closest to the Sun.

SMALLEST MANNED SPACECRAFT
The Manned Maneuvering Unit (MMU), used by astronauts working outside the Space Shuttle, is 4 ft. tall, 2 ft. 8 in. wide, 3 ft. 8 in. deep, and weighs just 240 lbs. Powered by nitrogen thrusters, it was first used on shuttle mission STS-41-B in Feb. 1984, when astronaut Bruce McCandless maneuvered up to 328 ft. away from *Challenger*.

MOST RELIABLE LAUNCH SYSTEM
Between April 1981 and Jan. 1998, the US Space Shuttle successfully completed 88 out of 89 launches, giving it a reliability rate of 98.8%.

LEAST RELIABLE LAUNCH SYSTEM
The US satellite launch vehicle *Pegasus* made 14 successful and 12 unsuccessful launches between April 5, 1990, and May 6, 1997, giving it a reliability rate of just 53.85%.

OLDEST ORBITING SATELLITE
The oldest satellite that is still orbiting the Earth is the 3.08-lb. *Vanguard 1* (USA), which was launched in March 1958. It is still in orbit, but no longer operational. By March 20, 2000, it had completed 165,869 orbits of the Earth, a total distance of 5.6 billion miles.

⊙ MOST REMOTE MAN-MADE OBJECT
Voyager 1, which was launched from Cape Canaveral, Florida, USA, in Sept. 1977, is currently the most remote man-made object in the Universe, being at a record distance of 7.1 billion miles from Earth as of Feb. 2000. Now at the very edge of the Solar System, it is expected to enter interstellar space within approximately 10 years.

⊙ LONGEST SHUTTLE FLIGHT
Columbia's 21st mission, STS-80, began on Nov. 19, 1996, and lasted for 17 days, 15 hrs., 53 min., and 26 sec. to main gear shutdown, beating its own previous record. The mission had a crew of five: Ken Cockrell (commander), Tom Jones, Tamara Jernigan, Story Musgrave and Kent Rominger (left to right).

→ MOST EXPENSIVE TELESCOPE

The 30-year Hubble Space Telescope project has a total budget of $7 billion. Development began in 1980 and Hubble was launched on April 25, 1990. It is scheduled to be in orbit until 2010.

FASTEST ESCAPE VELOCITY FROM EARTH

On Oct. 7, 1990, the ESA *Ulysses* spacecraft achieved a record escape velocity of 33,936 m.p.h. from the Earth after deployment from the Space Shuttle *Discovery*. The craft was en route to an orbit around the Sun via a flyby of Jupiter.

MOST POWERFUL ROCKET ENGINE

The *RD–170*, which was built in the former USSR in 1980, has a thrust of 793 tons in open Space and 728 tons at the Earth's surface. It also has a turbopump rated at 190 Mw. The engine powered the four strap-on boosters of the *Energiya* booster, launched in 1987.

FIRST DIRECT LUNAR HIT

On Sept. 14, 1959, the Soviet space probe *Luna II* achieved the first ever direct hit on the Moon, landing at a location near the Sea of Tranquillity.

FLYBY CLOSEST TO A CELESTIAL OBJECT

On July 28, 1999, the spacecraft *Deep Space 1* (*DS1*) passed within 6 miles of the asteroid 9969 Braille. *DS1* moved at a relative speed of nearly 10 miles/sec., more than 50 times faster than the speed of a commercial jet, and twice as fast as the Space Shuttle.

CLOSEST APPROACH TO THE SUN BY A ROCKET

On April 16, 1976, the research spacecraft *Helios B* approached within 27 million miles of the Sun.

BIGGEST SHUTTLE PAYLOAD

Chandra, the 45-ft.-long X-ray telescope launched by the NASA STS-93 mission in July 1999, is the biggest payload ever carried by the Space Shuttle.

LOUDEST LAUNCH

The noise created by the launch of the unmanned *Apollo 4* on Nov. 9, 1967, was so great that the resulting air pressure wave was detected at the Lamont-Doherty Geological Observatory 1,100 miles away.

Buildings & Structures 1

TALLEST BUILDING

The world's tallest free-standing tower (as opposed to guyed mast) is the CN Tower in Toronto, Canada, which has a height of 1,815 ft. Excavation for the erection of the 128,000-ton reinforced, post-tensioned concrete structure began on Feb. 12, 1973, and it was finally "topped out" on April 2, 1975. A 416-seat restaurant revolves in the tower's Sky Pod at 1,151 ft., giving diners views of hills up to 75 miles away.

TALLEST OFFICE BUILDINGS

Petronas Towers in Kuala Lumpur, Malaysia, became the world's tallest office building in March 1996, when 241-ft.-tall stainless steel pinnacles were placed on top of the 88-story towers, bringing their height to 1,482 ft.

The Universal Financial Center in the new Pudong business district of Shanghai, China, will be taller than Petronas Towers when it is completed in 2001. It will be a record 1,490 ft. high, with 95 stories of offices and hotel accommodation above ground and three stories below ground.

TALLEST APARTMENT BLOCKS

The John Hancock Center in Chicago, Illinois, USA, is 1,127 ft. high. Of its 100 stories, only floors 44–92 are residential.

The tallest purely residential apartment block is the 70-story Lake Point Tower in Chicago, Illinois, USA, which is 640 ft. high and contains a total of 879 apartments.

BIGGEST PALACES

The Imperial Palace, located in the center of Beijing, China, covers 178 acres. The outline of the palace survives from the reign of the third Ming Emperor, Yongle (1402–24), but owing to constant reconstruction work most of the intramural buildings (five halls and 17 palaces) date from the 18th century.

The biggest residential palace in the world is Istana Nurul Iman in Bandar Seri Begawan, Brunei, which is owned by the Sultan of Brunei. Completed in Jan. 1984 at a reported cost of $422 million, it has 1,788 rooms, 257 lavatories, and enough garage space to accommodate the Sultan's 153 cars.

⊙ LONGEST CABLE SUSPENSION BRIDGE

The Akashi-Kaikyo Bridge, which joins the islands of Honshu and Awaji, Japan, has a main span of 6,532 ft. The bridge was opened to traffic in April 1998.

MOST EXPENSIVE HOUSE

The most expensive house ever built was the Hearst Ranch at San Simeon, California, USA, which was put up for media tycoon William Randolph Hearst between 1922 and 1939 at a total cost of more than $30 million – the equivalent today of $277 million. The house has more than 100 rooms, a 105-ft.-long heated swimming pool, and a garage with room for 25 limousines.

⊙ BIGGEST SQUARE

Tiananmen Square, the "Gate of Heavenly Peace," in Beijing, China, covers an area of 98 acres. Built in the early part of the 20th century, it was the site of Mao Zedong's proclamation of the People's Republic in 1949, and the massacre of pro-democracy protestors 40 years later.

OLDEST HOTEL

The Hoshi Ryokan in the village of Awazu, Japan, dates back to the year 717 A.D., when Garyo Hoshi built an inn near a hot water spring that was said to have miraculous healing powers. The water is still celebrated for its recuperative effects, and the hotel now has 100 bedrooms.

BIGGEST HOTEL

The MGM Grand Hotel/Casino in Las Vegas, Nevada, USA, consists of four 30-story towers on a site covering 112 acres. The hotel has 5,005 rooms, a 15,200-seat arena, and a 33-acre theme park.

BIGGEST OFFICE

The World Trade Center in New York City, USA, has a total of 12 million ft.^{2} of rentable space available in its seven buildings, including 4.37 million ft.^{2} in each of the twin towers. Around 50,000 people work in some 500 companies and organizations located in the mammoth complex, and a further 70,000 tourists and business people visit it every day.

TALLEST STRUCTURES

The tallest structure ever built was the guyed Warszawa Radio mast at Konstantynow, Poland, which was 2,120 ft. tall prior to its collapse during renovation work on Aug. 10, 1991. The mast, which weighs 541 tons, was completed on July 18, 1974, and put into operation four days later on July 22, 1974. Since 1991 it has been described as "the world's longest tower".

The tallest structure currently standing is a 2,064-ft. stayed television transmitting tower located between Fargo and Blanchard, North Dakota, USA. The tower was built for Channel 11 of KTHI TV in 30 days (Oct. 2 to Nov. 1, 1963) by Hamilton Erection, Inc. of York, South Carolina, USA. It remained the tallest structure in the world until the completion of the guyed radio mast at Konstantynow.

BIGGEST MUD BUILDING

The Grand Mosque Degne in Mali is the largest mud building in the world. Built in 1905 to the design of an 11th-century mosque, it is 328 ft. long and 131 ft. wide.

BIGGEST IGLOO

The Ice Hotel in Jukkasjärvi, Sweden, has a total floor area of a record 32,292 ft.^{2} and can sleep up to 150 hotel guests per night.

BIGGEST PYRAMID

The largest pyramid in the world is the Quetzalcóatl Pyramid at Cholula de Rivadavia, 63 miles to the southeast of Mexico City, Mexico. It stands an imposing 177 ft. tall, with a base that covers an area of nearly 45 acres. Its total volume has been estimated at 4.3 million yds.^{3}

→ TALLEST HOTEL

The sail-shaped Burj Al Arab or Arabian Tower in Dubai, United Arab Emirates, is the tallest hotel in the world, measuring a record 1,053 ft. from ground level to the top of its mast. Built on a man-made island, it boasts 202 suites and a total floor area of 1.2 million ft.^{2} Approximately 3,500 designers, engineers, and building workers were involved in its construction.

Buildings & Structures 2

BIGGEST DOME

The world's largest dome is the Louisiana Superdome in New Orleans, Louisiana, USA, completed in May 1975. It is 273 ft. tall, has a diameter of 680 ft., and can seat up to 97,365 people for conventions and 76,791 for American football games.

TALLEST SCAFFOLDING

The world's tallest scaffolding was erected around the New York City Municipal Building, USA, by the Regional Scaffolding & Hoisting Co., Inc. in 1988. In place until 1992, the scaffolding was 650 ft. high with a volume of 4,800,000 ft.[3]

TALLEST TOTEM POLE

The world's tallest totem pole is the 180.2-ft. Spirit of Lekwammen, which was erected in Aug. 1994 at Victoria, British Columbia, Canada. Masterminded by Richard Krentz (Canada), it took nine months to carve. It was partially dismantled in Aug. 1997, but its base section, which is approximately 49 ft. in height, remains at the site.

LONGEST WALL

The Great Wall of China runs 2,150 miles between Shanhaiguan, on the Gulf of Bohai, and Yumenguan, with an additional 2,194 miles of branches and spurs. Construction of the wall began during the reign of Emperor Qin Shi Huangdi (221–210 B.C.).

BIGGEST WINDOWS

Three matching arch-shaped windows in the Palace of Industry and Technology, Paris, France, each have an extreme width of 715 ft. and a maximum height of 164 ft.

THICKEST WALLS

The city walls of Ur-nammu at Ur (now Muqayyar, Iraq) were 89 ft. thick. They were destroyed by the Elamites in 2006 B.C.

HEAVIEST DOOR

The radiation shield door in the National Institute for Fusion Science at Toki, Japan, weighs a record-breaking 708.6 tons. It is 38.5 ft. high, 37.4 ft. wide, and 6.6 ft. thick. The door was installed in Dec. 1994 by Itoki Co., Ltd.

LONGEST TUNNEL

The longest tunnel of any kind is the New York City–West Delaware water supply tunnel, which runs for 105 miles from the Rondout reservoir into the Hillview reservoir in Yonkers, New York City, USA. The tunnel was built between 1937 and 1944 and has a diameter of 13.5 ft.

LONGEST STAIRWAY

The service stairway for the Niesenbahn funicular railway near Spiez, Switzerland, climbs to a height of 5,476 ft. with 11,674 steps.

LONGEST SPIRAL STAIRCASE

A spiral staircase in the Mapco–White County Coal Mine, Carmi, Illinois, USA, is a record 1,102 ft. deep, with 1,520 steps.

SHORTEST ESCALATOR

The moving walkway at Okadaya More's Shopping Mall, Kawasaki, Japan, has a vertical rise of just 32.8 in.

TALLEST FOUNTAIN

"The Fountain," located in a lake in Fountain Hills, Arizona, USA, emits a column of water with a record-breaking height of 562 ft. when operating at full pressure.

TALLEST CEMETERY

The permanently illuminated Memorial Necrópole Ecumênica in Santos, Brazil, is 10 stories high and covers an area of 4.4 acres. Construction was begun in March 1983 and the first burial took place in July 1984.

⊙ **TALLEST LIGHTHOUSE**

The world's tallest lighthouse is the imposing steel Marine Tower, located at Yamashita Park in Yokohama, Japan. It has a height of 348 ft., power of 600,000 candelas, and a visibility range of 20 miles.

BIGGEST CEMETERY

The world's biggest cemetery is Ohlsdorf Cemetery in Hamburg, Germany, which covers an area of 988 acres. It has been in use since 1877 and had been host

⊙ **LONGEST ESCALATOR RIDE**

The world's longest escalator ride can be had on the four-section outdoor escalator at Ocean Park, Hong Kong, China. The escalator has an overall length of 745 ft. and it boasts a total vertical rise of 377 ft.

to 982,117 burials and 413,589 cremations up to the end of 1996, when it was made into a museum.

BIGGEST COMMUNAL TOMB
A tomb housing 180,000 World War II dead on Okinawa, Japan, was enlarged in 1985 to accommodate another 9,000 bodies thought to be buried on the island.

BIGGEST CREMATORY
The Nikolo-Arkhangelskiy Crematory in Moscow, Russia, is the world's largest, with an area of 519 acres. Completed in March 1972, it has seven British-designed twin cinerators and six "Halls of Farewell" for atheists.

BIGGEST OBELISK
The obelisk of Pharaoh Tuthmosis III was brought from Aswan, Egypt, by Emperor Constantius in 357 A.D. and was repositioned in the Piazza San Giovanni in Rome, Italy, in 1588. Once 118 ft. tall, it now stands at a height of 107.6 ft. and weighs 448 tons.

TALLEST INDOOR WATERFALL
A waterfall in the lobby of the International Center Building, Detroit, Michigan,

← TALLEST MONUMENT
The world's tallest monument is the stainless steel Gateway To The West in St. Louis, Missouri, USA, completed on Oct. 28, 1965, to commemorate westward expansion after the Louisiana Purchase of 1803. A sweeping arch that spans 630 ft. and rises to the same height, it cost $29 million to build. It was designed by Finnish-American architect Eero Saarinen.

USA, is 114 ft. tall, with a backdrop consisting of 9,000 ft.^{2} of marble.

LONGEST JETTY
The longest deep-water jetty in the world is the 5,000-ft. Quai Hermann du Pasquier in Le Havre, France.

BIGGEST TIDAL BARRIER
The Oosterscheldedam, a storm-surge barrier in the southwest Netherlands, is 5.6 miles long, with 65 concrete piers and 62 steel gates.

BIGGEST MAZES
The biggest maze ever constructed was the KIDS Global Forest Maze in Black Jack City Park, St. Charles, Missouri, USA, which was open to the public between Sept. and Oct. 1997. Built of plastic fencing and covered with pictures drawn by children, it had a total area of 333,500 ft.^{2}

The world's biggest permanent maze is the Dole Pineapple Garden Maze at the Dole Plantation, Honolulu, Hawaii, USA. Constructed in 1997, it has a 100,000-ft.^{2} area and 1.7 miles of paths.

TALLEST FLAGPOLE
The world's tallest flagpole is at Panmunjon, North Korea, near the border with South Korea. It is 525 ft. high and flies a flag 98 ft. long.

Travel & Transportation

LONGEST TRAIN ROUTE
The world's longest train journey (without changing tracks) is the 6,347-mile Trans-Siberian trip between Moscow and Vladivostok, Russia. It is scheduled to take 7 days, 20 hours, and 25 minutes.

LONGEST BUS ROUTE
The world's longest regularly scheduled bus trip is operated by Expreso Internacional Ormeño SA of Lima, Peru, and covers the 6,003 miles between Caracas, Venezuela, and Buenos Aires, Argentina, in 214 hours. The journey includes a 12-hour stop in Santiago, Chile, and a 24-hour stop in Lima, Peru.

LONGEST TRAM ROUTE
The world's longest tram journey, from Krefeld St. Tönis to Witten Annen Nord, Germany, is 65.5 miles long. With luck at the eight interconnections, the trip can be completed in five and a half hours.

LONGEST MOTORABLE ROAD
The Pan-American Highway, which runs from Fairbanks, Alaska, USA, to Brasilia, Brazil, is over 15,000 miles in length. There is, however, a small, incomplete section in Panama and Colombia known as the Darién Gap.

LONGEST ORBITAL FREEWAY
The M25 orbital freeway around London, UK, is 121.5 miles long. Work on the six-lane freeway (nicknamed "The Road To Hell") began in 1972, and was completed on Oct. 29, 1986, at an estimated cost of $1.32 billion.

HIGHEST ROADS
The highest motorable road in the world is in Khardungla Pass, Kashmir, at an altitude of 18,641 ft. It was completed in 1976 by the Border Roads Organization, New Delhi, India, and has been open to motor vehicles since 1988.

A military road which is closed to foreign traffic runs at an altitude of 19,225 ft. above the Changlung Valley, Askai, China (administered by China but claimed by India).

LOWEST ROAD
The world's lowest road runs along the Israeli shores of the Dead Sea at an altitude of 1,289 ft. below sea level.

⊙ SUBWAY SYSTEM WITH MOST STATIONS
The MTA New York City Transit in New York City, USA, has 468 stations in a network that covers 230 miles. The subway, the first section of which opened on Oct. 27, 1904, serves an estimated 5.1 million passengers per day, or 1.86 billion per year.

BIGGEST PORT
The Port of New York and New Jersey, USA, is the world's largest, with a navigable waterfront of 755 miles and berthing capacity for 391 ships at any one time.

It has 261 general cargo berths, 130 other piers, and there is a total of 422 acres of warehouse space.

BUSIEST PORTS
The world's busiest port is Rotterdam, in the Netherlands, which covers an area of 39 miles² and handled 310.5 million tons of seagoing cargo in 1998.

The world's busiest container port is Hong Kong, China, which handled 14.6 million Twenty-foot Equivalent Units (TEUs) in 1998.

BIGGEST RAILROAD STATION
The world's largest railroad station is Beijing West Railway Station, Beijing, China. Built between April 1995 and June 1997, it covers an area 132.9 acres.

BUSIEST RAILROAD SYSTEM
In 1998, trains operated by the East Japan Railway Co. made an average of 12,305 journeys per

⊙ BIGGEST AIRPORT TERMINAL
The world's largest airport terminal is the Hong Kong International Airport Passenger Terminal Building, which is 1,422 yds. long and covers an area of 136 acres. Opened in July 1998, it has 48 aircraft parking stands, 1.7 miles of moving walkways, 5,500 doors, 80,000 light fittings, and approximately 28.9 acres of carpeting.

day over a network of 4,684 miles. An estimated 16.4 million passengers used the railroad every weekday.

HIGHEST RAILROAD STATION
Cóndor station on the Rio Mulatos to Potosí line, Bolivia,

⊙ LONGEST CABLE CAR ROUTE
The longest passenger-carrying cable car route is the Teleférico Mérida, which runs from Mérida City, Venezuela (altitude 5,379 ft.), all the way to Pico Espejo (altitude 15,629 ft.). Passengers change cars three times on the 8-mile ascent.

is the world's highest, at an altitude of 15,700 ft.

LONGEST RAIL NETWORK
The USA has the world's longest rail network, with 149,133 miles of track.

LONGEST TRAFFIC JAMS
The longest ever traffic jam occurred on Feb. 16, 1980. It stretched 109 miles northwards from Lyon towards Paris, France.

A traffic jam of 18 million cars was reported crawling bumper-to-bumper over the East–West German border on April 12, 1990.

MOST VISITED COUNTRY
According to the World Tourism Organization, France receives more foreign tourists than any other country, with 70 million in 1998.

HIGHEST-SPENDING TOURISTS
The world's highest-spending tourists are those from the USA, who spent $51.22 billion abroad in 1997.

GREATEST INCOME FROM TOURISM
The USA receives more income from tourism than any other country, with $71.1 billion spent there in 1998.

BIGGEST TRAVEL AGENCY
In terms of branches and staff numbers, the world's largest

travel agency is the Japan Travel Bureau. Established in 1912, JTB currently has 13,300 employees, 315 domestic branches and 69 overseas branches.

LONGEST FOOTPATH
The longest designated footpath in the world is the 2,158-mile-long Appalachian National Scenic Trail in the eastern USA. The trail stretches from Katahdin in central Maine to Springer Mountain in north Georgia.

LONGEST ROAD TUNNEL
The two-lane St. Gotthard road tunnel, which runs from Göschenen to Airolo, Switzerland, is 10.1 miles long and was opened to traffic on Sept. 5, 1980. A total of 19 workers lost their lives during its construction, which began in 1969 and cost $420 million.

LONGEST CANAL
The Belomorsko-Baltiyskiy Canal, which runs from Belomorsk to Povenets, Russia, is 141 miles long and has 19 locks. It was completed in 1933 with the use of forced labour.

BUSIEST AIRPORT
A total of 73.474 billion international and domestic passengers embarked or disembarked at Hartsfield International Airport, Atlanta, Georgia, USA, in 1998.

↑ BUSIEST INTERNATIONAL AIRLINE
In 1998, British Airways flew a record-breaking total of 67.59 billion international passenger miles. United Airlines was a distant second with 46.7 billion miles and Lufthansa placed third with a total of 43.4 billion miles.

BUSIEST INTERCONTINENTAL AIR ROUTE
The busiest intercontinental air route in the world is London, UK, to New York City, USA. More than 3.3 million passengers fly the 3,442 miles between the two cities annually.

MOST EXTENSIVE TRAMWAY SYSTEM
St. Petersburg, Russia, has the most extensive tramway system in the world. A total of 2,402 cars run on 64 different routes over 429 miles of track.

LONGEST MONORAIL
The Osaka Monorail, Japan, runs between Osaka International Airport and Hankyu Railway station, with a second stage running between Hankyu and Keihan Railway Kadomashi station. Opened in Aug. 1997, it has a total operational length of 14 miles.

Science 1

MOST COMMON ELEMENTS

The most common element in existence is hydrogen, which makes up over 90% of the Universe and 70.68% of the Solar System.

On Earth, the most common elements are iron, which accounts for 36% of the Earth's mass, and molecular nitrogen (N_2), which makes up 78.08% of the Earth's atmosphere by volume, or 75.52% by mass.

NEWEST AND HEAVIEST ELEMENT

In Jan. 1999, a team of scientists based at the Lawrence Livermore National Laboratory, California, USA, and the Joint Institute for Nuclear Research, Dubna, Russia, announced the creation of element 114. Ununquadium, as it has been called provisionally, is the newest and heaviest element in the world. Resulting from the bombardment of a neutron-enriched plutonium isotope by a calcium isotope, it contains 114 protons, and is claimed to be much more stable than other superheavy atoms. However, scientists have yet to discover element 113.

SOFTEST MINERAL

Talc is the softest mineral on Earth, with a value of 1.00 on the Mohs' scale, the standard scale used for measuring the hardness of materials. It is so soft that it can be scratched very easily by a fingernail.

SWEETEST SUBSTANCE

Thaumatin, a protein extracted from the fleshy arils that cover the seeds of the katemfe plant (*Thaumatococcus daniellii*), is 6,150 times sweeter than sucrose (table sugar). The plant is found in parts of west Africa.

MOST BITTER SUBSTANCES

The world's most bitter-tasting substances are based on the denatonium cation and are produced commercially as benzoate and saccharide. A dilution made from one part in 500 million can be detected, and one part in 100 million will leave a lingering taste.

MOST TOXIC SUBSTANCES

The most toxic substance on Earth is the radioactive element thorium 228 (Th 228, or radiothorium). Just 1.1×10^{-17} oz./yd.^{3} is enough to kill a person.

The most toxic nonradioactive element is beryllium (Be), which is lethal to humans at a concentration of 9×10^{-8} oz./yd.^{3}

The most toxic man-made substance is the compound 2, 3, 7, 8-tetrachlorodibenzo-*p*-dioxin, or TCDD. Environmental concentrations of TCDD above 50 parts per trillion (p.p.t.) have been said to be hazardous to health.

SMELLIEST SUBSTANCES

Both ethyl mercaptan (C_2H_5SH) and butyl seleno-mercaptan (C_4H_9SeH) could claim to be the most evil of the 17,000 smells classified to date. The smells have been described as a combination of garlic, onions, rotting cabbage, burnt toast and sewer gas.

⊙ HARDEST ELEMENT

Diamond, an allotrope of carbon (C), has a value of 15.00 on the Mohs scale (see "Softest Mineral").

⊙ LONGEST GENETIC SEQUENCE DETERMINED

On Dec. 1, 1999, researchers from the Sanger Centre near Cambridge, England, Keio University, Tokyo, Japan, the University of Oklahoma, Norman, USA, and Washington University, St. Louis, Missouri, USA, announced that they had succeeded in deciphering 97% of the long arm of chromosome 22 (22q). There are 23 pairs of chromosomes in the human genome: 22, the second smallest of these, carries genes linked to congenital heart disease, schizophrenia, learning disabilities, the workings of the immune system and several cancers.

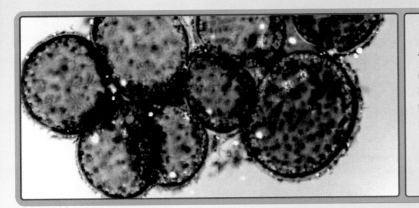

⊙ BIGGEST BACTERIUM

The bacterium *Thiomargarita namibiensis* (sulfur pearl of Namibia) is the largest prokaryotic organism yet known to science. Visible to the naked eye, it can reach a width of 0.029 in. The species was discovered in sediments off the Namibian coast by biologist Heide Schulz from the Max Planck Institute for Marine Microbiology in Bremen, Germany, during a research trip made on the Russian vessel *Petr Kottsov* in 1997.

MOST POWERFUL NERVE GAS

Ethyl S-2-diisopropylamino-ethylmethylphosphonothiolate, or VX, is 300 times more powerful than the nerve gas $COCl_2$ used in World War I. Developed at the Chemical Defence Experimental Establishment at Porton Down, Wiltshire, UK, in 1952, it is so deadly that 0.00001 oz. taken orally will prove lethal.

DEADLIEST BACTERIAL TOXIN

The anaerobic bacterium *Clostridium botulinum*, which causes botulism, is so deadly that only 1 oz. could kill 30 million tons of living matter, while 1 lb. could kill the entire human population. The bacterium is mainly found in improperly canned meat and it grows only in the complete absence of oxygen.

STRONGEST ACID SOLUTION

A 50% solution of antimony pentafluoride in hydrofluoric acid (fluoro-antimonic acid $HF:SbF_5$) is 1,018 times stronger than concentrated sulfuric acid.

BIGGEST PROTEIN

A molecule of titin, or connectin, which is found in muscle cells, can be up to one micron long (0.00004 in.), bigger than some cells. The protein contains 30,000 amino acids.

BIGGEST MICROBES

The biggest known microbes are the extinct calcareous foraminifera (*Foraminiferida*) of the genus *Nummulites*. Specimens up to 6 in. wide have been found in the Middle Eocene rocks of Turkey.

← BIGGEST CLONED ANIMAL

Xiangzhong Yang of the University of Connecticut, USA, and scientists from the Kagoshima Prefectural Cattle Breeding Development Institute, Kyushu, Japan, announced on Jan. 6, 2000, that they had successfully cloned six calves from skin cells taken from a bull's ear. Grown in a laboratory for the first three months, the cells were specially cultured so that scientists were able to make alterations to their DNA. Four of the calves, two of which died, were born in Dec. 1998, and the other two were born in Feb. 1999.

Science 2

HIGHEST TEMPERATURE
The highest man-made temperature on record is 950 million°F – 30 times hotter than the center of the Sun. It was created on May 27, 1994, at the Tokamak Fusion Test Reactor at the Princeton Plasma Physics Laboratory, New Jersey, USA, using a deuterium–tritium plasma mix.

LOWEST TEMPERATURE
The lowest temperature ever was created at the University of Sussex, England, on Sept. 22, 1998, by a team led by Dr. Malcolm Boshier. For about one second, 100,000 rubidium atoms were cooled to a few hundred billionths of a degree above the coldest temperature possible – absolute zero −459.67°F.

MOST POWERFUL ELECTRIC CURRENT
The largest ever electric current was achieved by scientists at Oak Ridge National Laboratory, Oak Ridge, Tennessee, USA, in April 1996. They sent a current of 2 million amperes/cm.^{2} down a superconducting wire. By contrast, household wires carry a current of less than 1,000 amperes/cm.^{2}

SMALLEST ARTIFACT
The tips of probes on scanning tunnelling microscopes (STMs) have been shaped to end in a single atom – the last three layers form the world's smallest human-made pyramid, of seven, three and one atoms. In Jan. 1990, it was announced that scientists at the IBM Almaden Research Center, San Jose, California, USA, had used an STM to move and reposition single atoms of xenon on a nickel surface in order to spell out the initials "IBM." Other laboratories have used similar techniques on single atoms of other elements.

SMALLEST TRANSISTOR
On Nov. 15, 1999, Lucent Technologies of Murray Hill, New Jersey, USA, announced the record-breaking development of a transistor with a length measured at a minuscule 50 nanometers, making it roughly 2,000 times shorter than the width of a single human hair. The component is known as a "vertical" transistor because all its components are built on top of a silicon wafer and its current flows vertically.

⊙ **MOST EXTRACTED COMPOUND**
In 1998 a total of 165 million tons of sodium chloride (salt) was extracted, mostly for culinary use. Here, workers harvest salt at Trapani, Sicily, Italy.

SMALLEST CALCULATOR
A calculator with a diameter of less than 0.00000004 in. was developed by a team of scientists led by James Gimzewski at IBM Research Division's Zürich Research Laboratory, Zürich, Switzerland, in Nov. 1996. The molecular abacus consists of 10 molecules of carbon 60 that can be moved along a microscopic groove on a copper surface with the tip of a scanning tunnelling microscope.

LONGEST-STANDING MATHS PROBLEMS
The longest-standing maths problem ever was Fermat's Last Theorem, which was posed by the French mathematician Pierre de Fermat in 1630. It remained unsolved until 1995, 365 years later, when Andrew Wiles (UK) showed that $x^n + y^n = z^n$ has no solutions in integers for n being equal to or greater than 3. Wiles currently works at Princeton University, New Jersey, USA.

The longest-standing maths problem still to be solved is Goldbach's Conjecture, posed by Christian Goldbach in 1742. It states that every even positive integer greater than three is the sum of two (not necessarily distinct) primes, and has yet to be either proved or disproved.

⊙ **MOST EXTRACTED METALLIC ELEMENT**
In 1998, a total of 705 million tons of iron was extracted. Widely used for structural and engineering purposes, iron also forms the basis of all permanent magnets and electromagnets. Here, a worker at the Man Roland factory in Henbach, Germany, pours liquid iron into a mold during the manufacture of a printing machine.

MOST ACCURATE VERSION OF PI

The most decimal places to which pi (π) has been calculated is 206,158,430,000, by Professor Yasumasa Kanada of the University of Tokyo, Japan. Professor Kanada made two separate calculations using different methods, and compared the results using computer programs written by Daisuke Takahashi. Both the main program and the verification program were run on a Hitachi SR8000/480 supercomputer, the former from Sept. 18–20, 1999, and the latter from June 26–27, 1999.

HIGHEST KNOWN PRIME NUMBER

The highest known prime number is $2^{6,972,593} - 1$, which denotes two, multiplied by itself 6,972,593 times, minus one. The number, which has 2,098,960 digits, was discovered by Nayan Hajraatwala of Plymouth, Michigan, USA, on June 1, 1999.

LARGEST COMPUTATION

SETI@home, which was launched by the University of California at Berkeley, California, USA, on May 17, 1999, had made a total of 10^{20}, or 100 billion billion, computer calculations as of Dec. 1999. SETI@home is a scientific experiment that harnesses the power of hundreds of thousands of internet-linked computers in the search for extraterrestrial intelligence. Participants download and run a free program that analyzes data from radio telescopes.

FINEST BALANCE

The Sartorius Microbalance Model 4108, manufactured in Göttingen, Germany, weighs objects of up to 0.018 oz. to an accuracy of 0.01µg, or 3.5×10^{-10} oz. – equivalent to little more than one-sixtieth of the weight of the ink on this full stop.

⊙ MOST NOBEL PRIZE WINNERS FROM ONE LABORATORY

A record 11 researchers have received Nobel prizes for work carried out while they were employed at Bell Laboratories, Murray Hill, New Jersey, USA. The winners include Arno Penzias (left) and Robert Wilson, who, together with Professor Piotr Kapitsa of the Academy of Sciences, Moscow, USSR (now Russia), received the 1978 Physics prize for their discovery of faint background radiation, the first direct evidence for the Big Bang theory.

Planet Earth

HIGHEST MOUNTAINS

Mount Everest, in the eastern Himalayas on the Tibet–Nepal border, has a record-breaking height of 29,029 ft. It was officially recognized as the world's highest mountain in 1856, following surveys carried out by the Indian government. The mountain was named after Colonel Sir George Everest, Surveyor General of India from 1830 to 1843.

The Andean peak of Chimborazo, which lies 98 miles south of the equator in Ecuador, is 20,561 ft. high. However, since the Earth's radius in Ecuador is longer than its radius at the latitude of Mount Everest, Chimborazo's summit is, in reality, 7,054 ft. further from the Earth's center than Everest's.

Mauna Kea (White Mountain), which lies on the island of Hawaii, USA, is the world's highest marine mountain. When measured from its submarine base in the Hawaiian Trough, it has a height of 33,480 ft., of which a total of 13,796 ft. are above sea level.

BIGGEST MOUNTAIN RANGES

The largest mountain range in the world is the Mid-Ocean Ridge, which lies entirely below sea level. It extends 40,000 miles from the Arctic Ocean to the Atlantic Ocean, around Africa, Asia and Australia, and under the Pacific Ocean to the west coast of North America. The range's highest point lies 13,800 ft. above the ocean floor.

On land, the world's biggest mountain range is the Himalaya-Karakoram, which contains 96 of the world's 109 peaks over 24,000 ft.

The longest mountain range in the world is the Andes of South America, with a length of approximately 4,700 miles.

LONGEST RIVERS

The two longest rivers in the world are the Nile and the Amazon; which is the longer river is really a question of definition. The Amazon has several mouths, so the exact point at which it ends continues to be uncertain. If the Pará estuary (the most distant mouth) is counted, then its length is approximately 4,190 miles. The Nile was once officially recorded as having a length of 4,145 miles, but has since lost a few miles of meanders due to the formation of Lake Nasser behind the Aswan High Dam.

⊙ MOST ACTIVE VOLCANO

Kilauea, on Hawaii, USA, is the world's most active volcano. It has been erupting on a continuous basis since 1983, and discharges lava at a rate of 177 ft.^{3} per second.

DEEPEST LAKE

The world's deepest lake is Lake Baikal in Siberia, Russia. The deepest point of the lake, the Olkhon Crevice, has a record depth of 5,370 ft., of which 3,875 ft. are below sea level.

⊙ BIGGEST DESERT

The Sahara in North Africa is the largest desert in the world, stretching to a maximum length of 3,200 miles from east to west and 1,400 miles from north to south. It covers an area of approximately 3,579,000 miles^2. Small areas of the desert are below sea level, but it is mainly a plateau with a central mountain system.

BIGGEST LAKE

The Caspian Sea, an inland sea which covers parts of Azerbaijan, Russia, Kazakhstan, Turkmenistan, and Iran, is the world's largest lake. It is 760 miles long, with an area of 143,560 miles^2 and an estimated volume of 21,500 miles^3.

BIGGEST OCEAN

The Pacific Ocean covers an area of 64,186,300 miles^2, or 32.6% of the Earth's surface.

SMALLEST OCEAN

The world's smallest ocean is the Arctic Ocean, which has a surface area of 5,105,700 miles^2.

DEEPEST POINT IN THE OCEAN

In 1951, H.M. Survey Ship *Challenger* identified the Marianas Trench in the Pacific Ocean as the deepest point of all the world's oceans. The unmanned Japanese probe *Kaiko*, which descended to the bottom of the trench in 1995, recorded a depth of 35,797 ft.

BIGGEST ISLAND

Discounting Australia, which has an area of 2,966,200 miles^2 but is usually regarded as a continental land mass, the largest island in the world is Greenland, with an area of about 840,000 miles^2.

The largest sand island in the world is Fraser Island, Queensland, Australia, which has an area of 642 miles^2. One sand dune on the island is 75 miles long.

LONGEST REEF

The Great Barrier Reef, situated off the coast of Queensland, Australia, stretches a total distance of 1,260 miles. Between 1962 and 1971 and again between 1979 and 1991, corals on large areas of the central section of the reef were devastated by the

crown-of-thorns starfish (*Acanthaster planci*). In 1995 devastation of the reef started again, and is still going on.

LONGEST FJORD

The longest fjord in the world is the Nordvest Fjord arm of Scoresby Sund in eastern Greenland, which extends 195 miles inland from the sea.

BIGGEST CAVE

The largest cave chamber in the world is the Sarawak Chamber (Lubang Nasib Bagus) in the Gunung Mulu National Park, Sarawak, Malaysia. It is a record-breaking 2,300 ft. long and 230 ft. high, with an average width of 985 ft.

HIGHEST WATERFALL →

The world's highest waterfall is the Salto Angel (Angel Falls) in Venezuela, which lies on a branch of the Carrao River. It has a total drop of 3,212 ft. and a longest single drop of 2,648 ft. The waterfall was named after James Angel, a US adventurer who crash-landed his plane on a nearby mesa (a high, rocky tableland) in 1937.

Human Body

OLDEST PEOPLE

The oldest person for whose age there is irrefutable evidence was Jeanne Louise Calment of France. She was born on Feb. 21, 1875, and died in Arles, France, on Aug. 4, 1997, aged 122. Calment was the last person to have met the artist Vincent Van Gogh.

Shigechiyo Izumi of Isen, Japan, lived longer than any other man, reaching an authenticated age of 120 years, 237 days. Born on June 29, 1865, Izumi was recorded as a six-year-old in Japan's first census of 1871. He worked until he was 105, and took up smoking when he was 70. He attributed his long life to "God, Buddha, and the Sun." He died on Feb. 21, 1986.

The oldest living man is Benjamin Harrison Holcomb, who was born on July 3, 1889, in Robinson, Kansas, USA. He has lived most of his life in Oklahoma, and with his family participated in the Cheyenne–Arapaho land run in Oklahoma Territory when he was two years old. He now lives in the Carnegie Nursing Home, Oklahoma, where three of his five children, Lucile Holcomb, 85, Leona Holcomb, 84, and John Holcomb, 80, help to care for him daily.

LIGHTEST PERSON

Lucia Xarate, a 26.4-in.-tall midget from San Carlos, Mexico, weighed just 4 lbs. 8 oz. at the age of 17. Her weight had increased to 13 lbs. by the time of her 20th birthday in 1883.

HEAVIEST PEOPLE

The heaviest person of all time was Jon Minnoch (USA). In March 1978, Minnoch, who was 6 ft. 1 in. tall, was admitted to the hospital with heart failure, where his weight was calculated to be over 1,400 lbs. After nearly two years on a diet of 1,200 calories per day, he had reduced to 476 lbs., but when he died, on Sept. 10, 1983, he weighed more than 798 lbs.

The heaviest ever woman is Rosalie Bradford (USA), who is said to have registered a weight of 1,198 lbs.in 1987.

HEAVIEST TWINS

The world's heaviest twins were Billy Leon and Benny Loyd McCrary, otherwise known as McGuire, of Hendersonville, North Carolina, USA. Born on Dec. 7, 1946, they were of average size until the age of six. In Nov. 1978, Billy and Benny weighed 743 lbs. and 722 lbs. respectively. Billy died in July 1979.

⊙ OLDEST LIVING PERSON

The oldest living person whose date of birth can be authenticated is Eva Morris of Stone, Staffordshire, England, who was born on Nov. 18, 1885. A widow since the late 1930s, Mrs. Morris attributes her long life to keeping active and drinking a daily cup of tea laced with whiskey.

TALLEST WOMEN

The tallest woman for whose height there is reliable evidence was Zeng Jinlian of Yujiang village in the Bright Moon Commune, Hunan Province, China. She was 8 ft. 1.5 in. tall when she died on Feb. 13, 1982, aged 17.

Sandy Allen of Niagara Falls, Ontario, Canada, is the tallest living woman, with a height of 7 ft. 7 in.

SHORTEST PEOPLE

The shortest ever female was Pauline Musters, who measured 1 ft. at the time of her birth in Ossendrecht, Netherlands, and 1 ft .9.6 in. at the age of nine. A postmortem carried out after her death from pneumonia with meningitis at the age of 19 in New York City, USA, showed her to be 2 ft. tall, although there was evidence of elongation of the body after death.

The world's shortest mature man for whose height there is independent evidence was Gul Mohammed of New Delhi, India. When examined at Ram Manohar Hospital, New Delhi, in 1990, he was found to be just 1 ft. 10.5 in. tall. He died of a heart attack in 1997.

⊙ LONGEST FINGERNAILS

The world's longest fingernails are those of Shridhar Chillal of Poona, India. On July 8, 1998, the nails on his left hand were measured on the television show *Guinness World Records: Primetime* and found to have a total length of 20 ft. 2.25 in. He does not grow the nails on his right hand.

SHORTEST TWINS

The shortest twins in the world record were Matyus and Béla Matina of Hungary (later the USA), who were both 2 ft. 6 in. tall.

The shortest living twins are John and Greg Rice of West Palm Beach, Florida, USA. Both measure 2 ft. 10 in.

LONGEST BEARD

Hans Langseth had a record-breaking 17-ft. 6-in.-long beard at the time of his burial in Kensett, Iowa, USA, in 1927.

LONGEST BEARDS ON WOMEN

Janice Deveree (USA) had a 14-in.-long beard in 1884.

The living woman with the longest beard is Vivian Wheeler of Wood River, Illinois, USA. The beard's longest strand measured 8 in. in 1999.

LONGEST MUSTACHE

The mustache of Kalyan Ramji Sain of Sundargarth, India, grown since 1976, reached a span of 133.4 in. – right side 67.7 in. and left side 65.7 in. – in July 1993.

BIGGEST FEET

Excluding cases of elephantiasis, the biggest feet currently known are those of Matthew McGrory of Pennsylvania, USA, who wears a record size 28.5 shoes.

LONGEST TOENAILS

The world's longest toenails are those of Louise Hollis of Compton, California, USA. They reached a combined length of 7 ft. 3 in. in 1991. Today, each is approximately 6 in. long.

SMALLEST WAIST

The smallest waist of a person of normal height was 13 in., for Ethel Granger (UK). She reduced to this measurement from a natural 22 in. between 1929 and 1939.

⊙ TALLEST MEN

The tallest man in medical history was Robert Wadlow (above) from Alton, Illinois, USA. When measured in June 1940, shortly before his death, he was 8 ft. 11.1 in. tall. The tallest living man is Radhouane Charbib (Tunisia), who measures 7 ft. 8.9 in.

↓ OLDEST SIAMESE TWINS

The oldest living Siamese twins are Masha and Dasha Krivoshlyapovy of Moscow, Russia, who were born on Jan. 4, 1950. Masha and Dasha are dicephales tetrabrachius dipus twins, meaning that, although they have separate torsos, they share a single pair of legs.

Animal World 1

BIGGEST ANIMAL

The biggest animal on Earth is the blue whale (*Balaenoptera musculus*), the largest specimen of which, caught in 1947, weighed in at a record 187 tons. Newborn calves are 20–26 ft. long and weigh up to 2.9 tons, growing on average to 25.6 tons by the age of 12 months.

BIGGEST LAND MAMMAL

The male African bush elephant (*Loxodonta africana africana*) is the biggest of the land mammals. The largest specimen on record is a male shot in Mucusso, Angola, on Nov. 7, 1974. This elephant had an estimated standing height of 13 ft. and is thought to have weighed 12 tons.

TALLEST MAMMAL

The world's tallest mammal is the giraffe (*Giraffa camelopardalis*), which is found in the dry savannah and open woodland areas of sub-Saharan Africa. The tallest giraffe on record was a Masai bull (*Giraffa camelopardalis tippelskirchi*) named George, who arrived at Chester Zoo, UK, from Kenya in Jan. 1959. Standing 19 ft. tall, his "horns" almost grazed the roof of the 20-ft. giraffe house by the time he was nine years old.

SMALLEST MAMMAL

The smallest mammal in the world is the bumblebee or Kitti's hog-nosed bat (*Craseonycteris thonglongyai*), which is confined to about 21 limestone caves on the Kwae Noi River, Kanchanaburi Province, Thailand. As its name suggests, its body is no bigger than that of a large bumblebee, with a head-and-body length of 1.1–1.3 in. and a wingspan of 5.1–5.7 in. It weighs 0.06–0.07 oz.

SLOWEST MAMMAL

The three-toed sloth of tropical South America (*Bradypus tridactylus*) has an average ground speed of 6–8 ft. per minute, or 0.06–0.1 m.p.h. In the trees it can accelerate to 15 ft. per minute, or 0.17 m.p.h.

FASTEST LAND MAMMALS

Over short distances (up to 1,800 ft.), the fastest land mammal is the cheetah (*Acinonyx jubatus*), which has a possible maximum speed of 62 m.p.h.). In Feb. 1999 the cheetah Nyana-Spier, kept at Cheetah Outreach (founded by Annie Beckhelling of Cape Town, South Africa), was officially timed on a track. It ran 109 yds. in a record-breaking 6.08 sec., with an acceleration of 0 to 50 m.p.h. in 3.6 sec. and an average speed of 37 mph.

⊙ **SMALLEST PRIMATE**
The smallest true primate is the pygmy mouse lemur (*Microcebus myoxinus*) of western Madagascar. It has a head-and-body length of 2.4 in., a tail length of 5.4 in., and an average weight of 1.08 oz.

The pronghorn antelope (*Antilocapra americana*) of the western United States, southwestern Canada, and parts of northern Mexico is the fastest land animal over long distances. It can sustain a speed of 35 m.p.h. for 4 miles, 42 m.p.h. for 1 mile, and 55 m.p.h. for 0.5 mile.

LOUDEST ANIMAL SOUNDS

The low-frequency pulses emitted by blue whales (*Balaenoptera musculus*) and fin whales (*Balaenoptera physalus*) when they communicate with each other have been measured at 188 decibels, making them the loudest sounds emitted by any living creature. By contrast, a jumbo jet taking off measures 120 decibels.

The noisiest land animals in the world are the howler monkeys (*Alouatta*) of Central and South America. Their calls, described as a cross between a dog's bark and a donkey's bray, only a

⊙ **HEAVIEST DOGS**
Kell (left), an English mastiff bitch owned by Tom Scott of East Leake, Leicestershire, England, is the heaviest living dog, with a weight of 286 lbs. on Aug. 18, 1999. The heaviest dog on record was Aicama Zorba of La-Susa, an Old English mastiff owned by Chris Eraclides of London, England. "Zorba" weighed in at 343 lbs. at his heaviest, in Nov. 1989.

thousand times louder, can be heard clearly up to 3 miles away.

MOST DISCRIMINATING MAMMALIAN EATER

The koala (*Phascolarctos cinereus*) of eastern Australia feeds almost exclusively on eucalyptus leaves. It browses regularly on just six of the 500 species and selects certain individual trees and leaves in preference to others, sometimes sifting through up to 20 lbs. of leaves a day to find the 1.1 lbs. that it needs.

LONGEST PREGNANCY

The Asiatic elephant (*Elephas maximus*) has an average gestation period of 650 days and can be pregnant for up to 760 days.

⊙ BIGGEST FLYING MAMMALS

The biggest flying mammals in the world are the flying foxes (family *Pteropodidae*), particularly those living in southeast Asia. Several species have a length of 17.7 in, a wingspan of 5 ft. 7 in., and a weight of 3.5 lbs.

BIGGEST KANGAROO →

The male red kangaroo (*Macropus rufus*) of central, southern, and eastern Australia measures up to 5 ft. 11 in. tall when standing, and has a total length (including the tail) of 9 ft. 4 in. It can weigh up to 198 lbs.

BIGGEST RODENT

The capybara or carpincho (*Hydrochoerus hydrochaeris*) of South America has a head-and-body length of 3 ft. 3 in.–4 ft. 3 in. and can weigh up to 174 lbs.

LONGEST RABBIT EARS

Toby II, a sooty-fawn English lop bred and owned by Phil Wheeler of Barnsley, Yorkshire, England, has ears that are 29.3 in. long and 7.4 in. wide.

SMALLEST HORSE

The world's smallest horse is the miniature horse Tara Stables Hope For Tomorrow, known as Hope, owned by Kenneth and Elizabeth Garnett of Vinton, Virginia, USA. In June 1997 Hope measured 21 in. from the ground to the highest point of her withers.

Animal World 2

BIGGEST BIRD
The largest living bird is the North African ostrich (*Struthio camelus camelus*). Males of this flightless sub-species can be 9 ft. in height and weigh 345 lbs.

FASTEST BIRDS
The peregrine falcon (*Falco peregrinus*) is the world's fastest living creature, reaching speeds of at least 124 m.p.h. and possibly as much as 217 m.p.h. when stooping from great heights during territorial displays or when catching prey birds in midair.

The fastest bird on land is the ostrich, which, despite its bulk, can run at speeds of up to 45 m.p.h.

DEEPEST DIVE BY A BIRD
The deepest dive accurately measured for any bird is 1,585 ft., by an emperor penguin (*Aptenodytes forsteri*) in the Ross Sea, Antarctica, in 1990.

LONGEST FLIGHT BY A BIRD
A common tern (*Sterna hirundo*), banded on June 30, 1996, in central Finland, was recaptured alive 16,150 miles away at Rotamah Island, Victoria, Australia at the end of Jan. 1997.

HIGHEST-FLYING BIRDS
The greatest height recorded for a bird is 37,000 ft. A Ruppell's vulture (*Gyps rueppellii*) collided with a commercial aircraft at this height over Abidjan, Côte d'Ivoire (Ivory Coast), on Nov. 29, 1973. The impact killed the bird and damaged one of the aircraft's engines, causing it to shut down, but the plane landed safely without further incident.

On Dec. 9, 1967, an airline pilot spotted about 30 whooper swans (*Cygnus cygnus*) flying over the Outer Hebrides, Highlands & Islands, Scotland, at an altitude of just over 27,000 ft. This height was also confirmed on radar by air traffic control.

MOST PROFICIENT TALKING BIRD
A number of birds are renowned for their ability to reproduce words, but the African gray parrot (*Psittacus erythacus*) excels at it. A female African gray parrot named Prudle, who was owned first by Lyn Logue of London, England, and then by Iris Frost of Seaford, East Sussex, England, won the "Best talking parrot-like bird" title at the British National Cage and Aviary Bird Show for a record 12 consecutive years before retiring in 1976. Prudle had a vocabulary of nearly 800 words.

LONGEST FEATHERS
The Phoenix fowl or Yokohama chicken (a strain of the red junglefowl *Gallus gallus*), which has been bred in Japan for ornamental purposes since the mid-17th century, has the longest feathers of any bird. In 1972 a rooster owned by Masasha Kubota of Kochi, Shikoku, Japan, was reported as having a tail covert 34 ft. 9 in. long.

BIGGEST WINGSPAN
The wandering albatross (*Diomedea exulans*) of the southern oceans has the largest wingspan of any living bird. In 1965, an elderly male with a record-breaking wingspan of 11 ft. 11 in. was caught in the Tasman Sea by members of the Antarctic research ship *USNS Eltanin*.

BIGGEST BIRD'S EGG
The egg of the ostrich (*Struthio camelus*) is normally 6–8 in. long, 4–6 in. in diameter, and weighs 2–4 lbs. It is equal in volume to approximately 24 hens' eggs. Although the shell is only 0.06 in. thick, it can support the weight of an adult human.

⊙ SMALLEST BIRD
Male bee hummingbirds (*Mellisuga helenae*), which live in Cuba and the Isle of Pines, are just 2.2 in. long and weigh 0.056 oz. Females are slightly larger.

⊙ BIGGEST FISH
The world's biggest fish is the rare plankton-feeding whale shark (*Rhincodon typus*), which is found in the warmer parts of the Atlantic, Pacific, and Indian Oceans. The largest specimen on record, captured in 1949, was 41 ft. 6 in. long, measured 23 ft. around the thickest part of the body, and weighed an estimated 14.8–20.7 tons.

The biggest egg on record weighed 5 lbs. 3 oz. and was laid in June 1997 at Datong Xinda ostrich farm, Datong, Shanxi Province, China.

SMALLEST BIRD'S EGG
The vervain hummingbird (*Mellisuga minima*) of the West Indies lays smaller eggs than any other bird. The smallest vervain hummingbird's eggs on record were less than 0.39 in. long and weighed 0.0129 oz. and 0.0132 oz.

An egg laid on Oct. 5, 1998, by a German crested canary owned by M.J. de Rijck of Heijen, Netherlands, was 0.27 in. long, 0.2 in. in diameter, and weighed 0.0009 oz.

BIGGEST BIRD'S NEST
A nest 9 ft. 6 in. wide and 19 ft. 8 in. deep was built by a pair of bald eagles (*Haliaeetus leucocephalus*), and possibly their successors, near St. Petersburg, Florida, USA. It was estimated to weigh more than 1.97 tons when examined in 1963.

LONGEST TIME SPENT UNDERWATER BY A BIRD
In 1969 an emperor penguin (*Aptenodytes forsteri*) made a dive at Cape Crozier, Antarctica, that lasted a record-breaking 18 minutes.

SMALLEST FISH
The shortest marine fish – and the shortest known vertebrate – is the dwarf goby (*Trimmatom nanus*) of the Indo-Pacific region. The average length of the species is just 0.339 in. for males and 0.35 in. for females.

The shortest and lightest freshwater fish is the dwarf pygmy goby (*Pandaka pygmaea*), a colourless and nearly transparent species found in the streams and lakes of Luzon in the Philippines. Males have an average length of 0.343 in. and weigh 0.00014–0.00018 oz.

FASTEST FISH
The cosmopolitan sailfish (*Istiophorus platypterus*) is the fastest species of fish over short distances. In speed trials carried out at the Long Key Fishing Camp, Florida, USA, one sailfish took out 300 ft. of line in 3 seconds, which is equivalent to a velocity of 68 m.p.h. (cf. 60 m.p.h. for the cheetah).

MOST POISONOUS FISH
Although many species of fish are poisonous to eat, the most deadly for humans is the puffer fish (*Tetraodon*) of the Red Sea and Indo-Pacific region. Its ovaries, eggs, blood, liver, intestines and skin all contain the poison tetrodotoxin, less than 0.004 oz. of which will kill an adult in 20 minutes.

MOST FISH EGGS
The ocean sunfish (*Mola mola*) produces up to 30 million eggs at one spawning, each with a diameter of 0.05 in.

OLDEST FISH
A female European eel (*Anguilla anguilla*) named Putte was reported to be 88 years old when it died at Hälsingborg Museum, Sweden, in 1948.

A goldfish named Tish, owned by Hilda and Gordon Hand of Thirsk, N. Yorkshire, England, lived for 43 years after being won at a fairground in 1956.

← SLOWEST FISH
The slowest-moving fish are the sea horses (*Syngnathidas*), of which there are about 30 species. Some of the smaller species, such as the dwarf sea horse (*Hippocampus zosterae*), probably never attain speeds of more than 0.001 m.p.h.

Animal World 3

SMALLEST AMPHIBIAN
The smallest known amphibian is the frog *Eleutherodactylus limbatus*, found in Cuba, which measures just 0.33–0.47 in. from snout to vent.

BIGGEST AMPHIBIAN
The world's biggest amphibian is the Chinese giant salamander (*Andrias davidianus*), which lives in mountain streams in northeastern, central and southern China. The largest specimen on record was 5 ft. 11 in. long and weighed 143 lbs.

SMALLEST SPIDER
Patu marplesi of the family Symphytognathidae from Western Samoa is the world's smallest known spider. A male found in 1965 had an overall length of just 0.017 in. — about the size of one of the full stops on this page.

BIGGEST SPIDER
The world's largest spider is the goliath bird-eating spider (*Theraphosa leblondi*), which lives mainly in the coastal rainforests of Surinam, Guyana, and French Guiana. Two specimens with a

leg-span of 11 in. have been recorded: one found in Venezuela in 1965 and another bred by Robert Bustard of Alyth, Perthshire, Scotland.

BIGGEST SPIDER'S WEB
In Oct. 1998 a cobweb that covered the entire 11.2-acre playing field at Kineton High School, Kineton, Warwickshire, England, was discovered by Ken Thompson, the school's janitor. It had been created by thousands of black money spiders.

BIGGEST CRUSTACEAN
The world's biggest crustacean is the taka-ashi-gani or giant spider crab (*Macrocheira kaempferi*). The largest specimen on record had a claw-span of 12 ft. 2 in. and weighed 41 lbs.

OLDEST CHELONIAN
A Madagascar radiated tortoise (*Astrochelys radiata*) named Tui Malila was presented to the Tongan royal family by Captain James Cook in either 1773 or 1777. It remained in their care until its death in 1965, aged either 188 or 192.

SMALLEST CHELONIAN
The world's smallest chelonian is the speckled cape tortoise or speckled padloper (*Homopus signatus*), which has a shell length of 2.4–3.8 in.

SHORTEST SNAKES
The thread snake (*Leptotyphlops bilineata*) and the Brahminy blindsnake (*Ramphotyphlops braminus*) both have a maximum length of 4.25 in.

LONGEST SNAKE
The reticulated python (*Python reticulatus*) regularly exceeds 20 ft. 6 in. in length. A specimen shot in Celebes, Indonesia, in 1912 was a record 32 ft. 10 in. long.

OLDEST SNAKE
A male common boa (*Boa constrictor constrictor*) named Popeye was a record 40 years and 3 months old when he died at Philadelphia Zoo, Pennsylvania, USA, in April 1977.

SMALLEST LIZARD
Sphaerodactylus parthenopion, a gecko indigenous to Virgin Gorda, British Virgin Islands, is

⊙ FASTEST LAND INSECT
The fastest insects on land are certain large tropical cockroaches of the family Dictyoptera. In an experiment carried out at the University of California at Berkeley, USA, in 1991, a *Periplaneta americana* registered a record speed of 3.36 m.p.h., or 50 body lengths per second.

⊙ LONGEST VENOMOUS SNAKE
The king cobra (*Ophiophagus hannah*), also called the hamadryad, has an average length of 12–15 ft. An 18-ft.-2-in.-long specimen captured near Fort Dickson, Negri Sembilan (now Malaysia), in April 1937, later grew to 18 ft. 9 in. in London Zoo, England. A king cobra is seen here fighting a man in a boxing ring in Bangkok, Thailand.

known from just 15 specimens. The three largest among some pregnant females found in 1964 were 0.7 in. long from snout to vent, with tails of approximately the same length.

SMALLEST CROCODILIAN
The smallest crocodilian in the world is the dwarf caiman (*Paleosuchus palpebrosus*) of northern South America. Females rarely exceed 4 ft. in length, while males are slightly longer at up to 4 ft. 11 in.

BIGGEST REPTILE
The estuarine or saltwater crocodile (*Crocodylus porosus*), which is found throughout the tropical regions of Asia and the Pacific, is the largest reptile in the world. A specimen housed at the Bhitarkanika Wildlife Sanctuary, Orissa State, India, is a record 23 ft. in length.

MOST VENOMOUS JELLYFISH
The Australian sea wasp or box jellyfish (*Chironex fleckeri*) has caused the deaths of at least 70 people over the last 100 years. Without medical aid, its victims can die within four minutes.

SHORTEST ADULT LIFE
Mayflies (*Ephemeroptera*) spend two to three years as nymphs at the bottom of lakes and streams but then live for as little as an hour as winged adults.

MOST FERTILE ANIMAL
With unlimited food and no predators, a single cabbage aphid (*Brevicoryne brassicae*), a species that reproduces asexually, could theoretically create an 809-million ton mass of descendants every year – more than three times the weight of the world's human population.

BIGGEST BUTTERFLY
The biggest butterfly in the world is the Queen Alexandra's birdwing (*Ornithoptera alexandrae*) of Papua New Guinea. Females can have a wingspan exceeding 11 in. and weigh over 0.9 oz.

BIGGEST INSECT EGGS
Eggs laid by the Malaysian stick insect (*Heteropteryx dilitata*) are a record-breaking 0.5 in. long, making them larger than peanuts.

BIGGEST EYES
The Atlantic giant squid (*Architeuthis dux*) has larger eyes than any other animal, either living or extinct. A specimen found in Thimble Tickle Bay, Newfoundland, Canada, in 1878 had eyes with an estimated diameter of 20 in.

MOST DESTRUCTIVE INSECT
The desert locust (*Schistocerca gregaria*), found in the dry and semi-arid regions of Africa, the Middle East and western Asia, is only 1.8–2.4 in. long but can eat its own weight in food every day. In certain weather conditions, vast numbers of desert locusts gather in huge swarms that move throughout the countryside, devouring almost all the vegetation in their path. In a single day, a "small" swarm of about 50 million locusts can eat enough food to sustain 500 people for a year.

← BIGGEST SNAIL
The largest land gastropod is the African giant snail *Achatina achatina*. The biggest specimen on record was 15.5 in. long from snout to tail and weighed exactly 2 lbs. Named Gee Geronimo, it was owned by Christopher Hudson of Hove, E. Sussex, England.

Plant World

TALLEST TREES
An Australian eucalyptus at Watts River, Victoria, Australia, had a height of 435 ft. in 1872. However, it had almost certainly been over 492 ft. tall originally.

The tallest tree standing today is the Mendocino Tree, a coast redwood (*Sequoia sempervirens*) found at Montgomery State Reserve near Ukiah, California, USA. In Sept. 1998 it was 367 ft. 5 in. tall with a diameter of 10 ft. 4 in. It is estimated to be about 1,000 years old.

MOST MASSIVE TREES
The most massive tree ever discovered was Lindsey Creek Tree, a coast redwood (*Sequoia sempervirens*) which grew in the USA. Its trunk had a volume of 90,000 ft.^{3} and its total mass (including foliage, branches and roots) was 3,247 tons. It blew over in a storm in 1905.

The most massive living tree is the giant sequoia (*Sequoiadendron giganteum*) General Sherman, which is found in the Sequoia National Park, California, USA. It is 275 ft. tall with a diameter of 36 ft. 5 in., a circumference of 102 ft. 8 in. and a trunk volume of 52,515 ft.^{3} It has a total weight of approximately 1,968 tons. It has been estimated that the tree contains enough timber to make 5 billion matches.

FASTEST-GROWING TREE
An *Albizzia falcata* planted in Sabah, Malaysia, on June 17, 1974 was found to have grown 35 ft 3 in in 13 months – or about 1.1 in per day.

DEEPEST TREE ROOTS
The roots of a wild fig tree at Echo Caves, near Ohrigstad, Transvaal, South Africa, are known to have penetrated to a record depth of 394 ft.

OLDEST TREE
Eternal God, a 7,000-year-old redwood found in Prairie Creek Redwoods State Park, California, USA, is the oldest living tree on record. It is 238 ft. tall and has a diameter of 19 ft. 7 in.

BIGGEST WEED
The giant hogweed (*Heracleum mantegazzianum*), originally from the Caucasus, can reach a height of 12 ft. and has 35.8-in.-long leaves.

BIGGEST FLOWER
The mottled orange-brown and white parasitic plant *Rafflesia arnoldii* has the largest flower of any plant in the world. Each bloom is 35.8 in. wide and can weigh up to 24.3 lbs., with petals up to 0.75 in. thick.

⊙ LONGEST SEAWEED
The longest species of seaweed is the Pacific giant kelp (*Macrocystis pyrifera*). It can grow up to 197 ft. in length, at a rate of 18 in. per day.

⊙ MOST POISONOUS FUNGUS
The yellowish-olive death cap (*Amanita phalloides*) is responsible for 90% of all fatal poisonings caused by fungi. Less than 1.8 oz. will cause vomiting, delirium, collapse, and then death in humans between 6 and 15 hours after being eaten.

MOST DAMAGING WEED
The virulence of a weed is generally measured by the number of different crops it can affect and the number of countries in which it is known to grow. On this basis, the world's most damaging weed would appear to be the purple nutgrass or nutsedge (*Cyperus rotundus*), a land weed that is native to India but which attacks 52 crops in 92 countries.

FASTEST-GROWING PLANT
Some species of bamboo grow at a rate of up to 3 ft. per day, or 0.00002 m.p.h.

LONGEST PLANT ROOTS
A single winter rye plant (*Secale cereale*) has been shown to produce 387 miles of roots in 1.8 ft.^{3} of earth.

BIGGEST LEAVES
The raffia palm (*Raffia farinifera* or *Raffia ruffia*) of the Mascarene Islands in the Indian Ocean, and

the Amazonian bamboo palm (*Raffia taedigera*) of South America and Africa, have the largest leaves of any plants. Their leaf blades can grow to a length of up to 65 ft. 7 in., with 13-ft. petioles.

BIGGEST SEED

The giant fan palm (*Lodoicea maldivica, Lodoicea callipyge* or *Lodoicea sechellarum*) – the double coconut or coco de mer – grows wild in the Seychelles. The single-seeded fruit produced by the plant weighs up to 44 lbs. and can take 10 years to develop.

SMALLEST SEED

Epiphytic orchids have the smallest seeds of any plant in the world, with 28.13029 billion per oz.

BIGGEST FUNGUS

A single living clonal growth of the underground fungus *Armillaria ostoyae* covers an area of approximately 1,500 acres in the forests of Washington State, USA. It is between 500 and 1,000 years old.

TALLEST CACTUS

The world's tallest cactus is the saguaro (*Cereus giganteus* or *Carnegiea gigantea*). A specimen found in the Maricopa Mountains, Arizona, USA, in 1988 had branches that rose to a record height of 58 ft.

TALLEST DOMESTICALLY GROWN CACTUS

A cactus grown by Dr. A. Kashi of Karnataka, India, was an enormous 45 ft .tall in March 1998.

TALLEST DOMESTICALLY GROWN SUNFLOWER

In 1986, M. Heijms of Oirschot, Netherlands, grew a giant sunflower with a total height of 25 ft. 5 in.

BIGGEST ROSE BUSH

A specimen of the rose bush Lady Banksia (*Rosa banksiae*) at Tombstone, Arizona, USA, has a trunk circumference of 13 ft. 6 in., stands 9 ft. high, and covers an area of 8,000 ft.[2]

SMELLIEST FLOWER

Amorphophallus titanum, known as the corpse flower, is the smelliest flower on Earth. When it blooms, it releases an odor similar to that of rotten flesh, which can be smelled a distance of 880 yds. away.

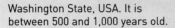

⊙ MOST HEADS ON ONE SUNFLOWER

In Sept. 1998. Grigore Clim of Suceava. Romania. grew a sunflower with a record-breaking 61 heads.

↓ BIGGEST ORCHID FLOWER

The flower of the Jacob's Ladder orchid (*Paphiopedilum sanderianum*) has petals that can grow up to 35.5 in. long in the wild.

Prehistoric World

EARLIEST SCIENTIFIC DESCRIPTION OF A DINOSAUR

The first dinosaur to be described scientifically was *Megalosaurus bucklandi* ("great fossil lizard") in 1824. Remains of this bipedal flesh-eater were found by workmen before 1818 in a quarry at Stonesfield, Oxfordshire, England, and were later placed in the University Museum at Oxford.

EARLIEST DINOSAUR

The world's oldest known dinosaur bones were found in Madagascar in Oct. 1999 by an international team of scientists from the Field Museum, Chicago, Illinois, USA. The fossils date from 230 million years ago (the Triassic period), making them about 3 million years older than those of the previous record-holder, *Eoraptor lunensis*.

BIGGEST DINOSAUR

The largest ever land animals were sauropod dinosaurs, a group of long-necked, long-tailed four-legged plant-eaters that lived in most areas of the world during the Jurassic and Cretaceous periods (about 208-65 million years ago). The brachiosaurid *Brachiosaurus altithorax* ("arm lizard") weighed 44–49 tons, and the diplodocids *Seismosaurus hali* ("earthquake lizard") and *Supersaurus vivanae* both weighed an estimated 49–98 tons. The titanosaurid *Argentinosaurus* is believed to have weighed up to 98 tons, an estimate based on its vast vertebrae.

BIGGEST CARNIVORE

A skeleton of the largest predatory dinosaur was discovered in Neuquén, Argentina, in 1995. Named *Giganotosaurus carolinii*, the dinosaur was 40 ft. long and weighed 7.8 tons. The bones suggest that it was both taller and more heavily built than *Tyrannosaurus rex*. It lived about 110 million years ago.

⊙ SMALLEST-BRAINED DINOSAURS

Stegosaurus ("plated lizard"), which lived about 150 million years ago, had a brain weighing only 2.5 oz. – 0.00002% of its computed body weight of 3.25 tons. This compares with a percentage of 0.0006 for an elephant and 1.88 for a human. It is possible that the brains of some sauropods were proportionately even smaller. The picture is from the movie *The Lost World: Jurassic Park* (USA, 1997).

⊙ OLDEST INTACT MAMMOTH

The oldest intact mammoth on record was found by a group of French scientists in Siberia, Russia, in Oct. 1999. The animal is estimated to be 23,000 years old, and has tusks weighing 143 lbs. each. The objective of the expedition, which was sponsored by the Discovery Channel, was to find DNA from this extinct species to perform cloning experiments.

TALLEST DINOSAUR

The remains of a Sauroposeidon discovered in 1994 in Oklahoma, USA, belong to what is believed to be the tallest creature to have ever walked the Earth. The Sauroposeidon stood 60 ft. tall and weighed 59 tons, with a neck about a third longer than that of the Brachiosaurus, its nearest competitor. It lived approximately 110 million years ago, during the mid-Cretaceous period.

LONGEST DINOSAUR

Based on the evidence of footprints, the brachiosaurid Breviparopus may have attained a length of 157 ft. from the head to the tip of the tail, making it the longest vertebrate on record.

The diplodocid *Seismosaurus halli*, which was discovered in New Mexico, USA, in 1980, was estimated to be 128–170 ft. long. In 1999 the dinosaur's bones were reconstructed at the Wyoming Dinosaur Center, Thermopolis, Wyoming, USA, creating a skeleton with a total length of 135 ft. This was disassembled in Aug. 1999, and taken on tour around the USA.

SMALLEST ADULT DINOSAURS

The chicken-sized Compsognathus ("pretty jaw"), a carnivorous dinosaur that lived in southern Germany and southeast France approximately 145 million years ago, measured 23 in. from the snout to the tip of the tail, weighing about 6 lb. 8 oz. The insect-eating Saltopus and the plant-eating Lesothosaurus, both of which lived about 200 million years ago, were of a similar size.

BIGGEST-BRAINED DINOSAURS

The most intelligent dinosaurs were Troodontids (formerly known as Saurornithoidids). They had the largest brain-to-body size ratio of all non-avian dinosaurs, making them about as intelligent as modern-day birds. Their large brains, huge eyes and grasping hands indicate that they had a predatory life-style similar to that of small wildcats.

FASTEST DINOSAUR

The large-brained, 220-lb. Dromiceiomimus ("emu mimic lizard") of the late Cretaceous period, from Alberta, Canada, could probably outsprint an ostrich, which has a top speed of over 37 m.p.h.

DINOSAUR WITH MOST TEETH

Pelecanimimus, an ornithomimid ("birdlike dinosaur"), had over 220 very sharp teeth.

BIGGEST SKULL

The long-frilled Torosaurus ("bull lizard"), a ceratopsid, had the largest skull of any known land animal. The 25-ft.-long herbivore's skull was up to 9 ft. 10 in. in length (including the fringe) and weighed up to 1.97 tons. The Torosaurus itself weighed up to 7.8 tons. It lived between Montana and Texas, USA.

BIGGEST CLAWS

The therizinosaurids ("scythe lizards"), which lived in Mongolia in the late Cretaceous period, had the largest claws of any known animal. The claws of *Therizinosaurus cheloniformis* were up to 36 in. long along the outer curve. It has been suggested that they were designed for grasping and tearing apart large victims, but as this dinosaur had a feeble skull with very few (or no) teeth, it was more likely to have lived on termites.

OLDEST FOSSIL PLANT

The oldest known fossil plant is the 428-million-year-old Cooksonia, which grew in Ireland during the Silurian period.

EARLIEST BIRDS

The earliest bird is known from two partial skeletons found in Texas, USA, in rocks dating back 220 million years. Named *Protoavis texensis* in 1991, this pheasant-sized creature caused much controversy as it is many millions of years older than the previous record-holder, the more familiar *Archaeopteryx lithographica* (the fossil of which was found in Jurassic sediments in Germany). However, as it is still unclear whether Protoavis will be widely accepted as a true bird, Archaeopteryx, a 153-million-year-old crow-sized flier, remains the earliest officially recognized bird.

Astronomy

MOST LUMINOUS OBJECT
The most luminous object in the sky is the quasar HS1946+7658, which is at least 1.5×10^{15} times more luminous than the Sun.

BIGGEST STRUCTURE IN THE UNIVERSE
The largest structure found in the Universe to date is a cocoon-shaped shell of galaxies about 650 million light years across. Its discovery by a team of French astronomers, led by Georges Paturel, was announced in June 1994.

NEAREST STARS
Excluding our own Sun, the nearest star is the very faint Proxima Centauri, which is 4.23 light years away.

The nearest star visible to the naked eye is the Southern Hemisphere binary Alpha Centauri, which is 4.40 light years distant.

YOUNGEST STARS
The youngest stars in the Universe are believed to be two protostars known collectively as IRAS–4. Buried deep in dust clouds in the nebula NGC1333, 1,100 light years distant, they were discovered in May 1991 by a combined British, German and American team. They will not blaze as fully fledged stars for at least another 100,000 years.

SMALLEST STARS
Neutron stars, which may have a mass up to three times that of the Sun, are 6–18 miles in diameter.

OLDEST STARS
By Jan. 1991, a group of astronomers led by Timothy Beers (USA) had discovered 70 stars that they believe to be the oldest in the Galaxy. The stars, which were detected in the halo high above the disk of the Milky Way, were formed approximately 1 billion years after the Big Bang. The group eventually expect to detect a further 430 such stars.

BIGGEST STAR
The M-class supergiant Betelgeuse (*alpha Orionis*), which is 430 light years away from Earth, has a diameter of 609 million miles – 700 times greater than that of the Sun.

BIGGEST CONSTELLATION
The largest constellation is Hydra (the Sea Serpent). It covers an area of 1,302.844 deg.², or 3.16% of the whole sky, and contains at least 68 stars visible to the naked eye.

SMALLEST CONSTELLATION
The smallest of the 88 constellations is Crux Australis (the Southern Cross), which has an area of 68.477 deg.², or 0.16% of the whole sky.

BRIGHTEST STAR IN THE GALAXY
Pistol, which was discovered by the Hubble Space Telescope in Oct. 1997, is 10 million times brighter than the Sun. However, it cannot be seen with the naked eye from Earth as most of its light is absorbed by space dust. Astronomers calculate that it emits as much energy in six seconds as the Sun does in a year. While this makes it the most powerful star yet identified, it also suggests that it will burn itself out within a short time.

SMALLEST SATELLITE
The smallest satellite of any planet in the Solar System is Deimos, the outer moon of Mars.

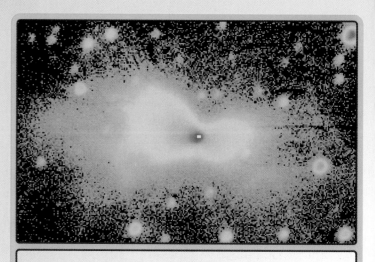

⊙ COLDEST PLACE IN THE UNIVERSE
The Boomerang nebula, a cloud of dust and gases 5,000 light years away from Earth, has a temperature of -454 °F.

⊙ MOST POWERFUL X-RAY TELESCOPE
The Chandra X-Ray Telescope, which was launched in July 1999, has resolving power equivalent to the ability to read the letters on a stop sign at a distance of 12 miles. It orbits the Earth more than 200 times higher than the Hubble Space Telescope, observing X-rays from high-energy regions of the Universe. Chandra's power comes from the size and smoothness of its mirrors.

Irregularly shaped, it has an average diameter of 7.8 miles and a mass of 1.8×10^{15} kg – 40 million times less than that of the Moon.

BIGGEST SATELLITE
The biggest satellite of any planet in the Solar System is Ganymede, orbiting Jupiter. It has a diameter of 3,273 miles and a mass of 1.46×10^{23} tons – 2.017 times that of the Moon.

SMALLEST AND COLDEST PLANET
Pluto has a diameter of 1,442 miles and a mass 0.0022 that of the Earth. Its surface temperature is believed to be similar to that of Neptune's moon Triton, which is –387 °F – the lowest surface temperature

→ MOST DURABLE TV ASTRONOMER
The Sky At Night, which is shown monthly on British television, has been presented by Patrick Moore without a break since April 24, 1957. By Jan. 2000 a total of 553 shows had been broadcast.

observed on a natural body in the Solar System.

BIGGEST PLANET
Jupiter is the largest of the nine major planets, with an equatorial diameter of 88,849 miles and a polar diameter of 83,085 miles. Its mass is 317.8 times, and its volume 1,323.3 times, that of the Earth. It also has the shortest period of rotation of any planet, resulting in a 9-hr. 55-min. 29.69-sec. day.

HOTTEST PLANET
Measurements taken by the *Venera* (USSR) and *Pioneer* (USA) probes indicate Venus' surface temperature to be 867 °F.

BRIGHTEST PLANET
If Jupiter and the Earth were viewed at the same distance, Jupiter would be approximately 164 times brighter.

Viewed from Earth, the very brightest of the five planets normally visible to the naked eye (Jupiter, Mars, Mercury, Saturn, and Venus) is Venus, with a maximum magnitude of –4.4.

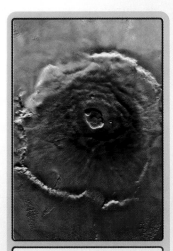

⊙ HIGHEST MOUNTAIN
Olympus Mons is the highest mountain in the Solar System. Its peak is 17 miles above its base, making it nearly three times higher than Mt. Everest. Despite its great height, Olympus Mons has a very gentle slope, being over 20 times wider than it is high.

GREATEST METEOR SHOWER
The greatest meteor shower on record occurred on the night of Nov. 16–17, 1966, when the Leonid meteors, which occur every 33 years, 3 months, were seen between western North America and eastern Russia (then USSR). It was calculated that meteors passed over Arizona, USA, at a rate of 2,300 per minute for 20 minutes on Nov. 17, 1966.

BIGGEST METEORITE
A 9-ft. 10-in. by 8-ft. 10.-in meteorite found at Hoba West, near Grootfontein, Namibia, in 1920, was estimated to weigh 58 tons.

LONGEST ECLIPSE
The longest possible eclipse of the Sun is 7 min. 31 sec. The longest eclipse in recent times took place west of the Philippines on June 20, 1955, lasting for 7 min. 8 sec. An eclipse of 7 min. 29 sec. is expected to occur in the mid-Atlantic Ocean on July 16, 2186.

BIGGEST COMET
Centaur 2060 Chiron, which was discovered in May 1977, has a diameter of 113 miles.

BIGGEST ASTEROID
The first asteroid discovered, 1 Ceres, is the largest, with an average diameter of 585 miles.

SMALLEST ASTEROID
Discovered on May 21, 1993, the asteroid 1993KA2 has a diameter of about 16 ft.

Weather

⊙ HOTTEST PLACE
Temperatures of over 120.2°F were recorded in Death Valley, California, USA, on 43 consecutive days in July and Aug. 1917.

HIGHEST SHADE TEMPERATURE
A shade temperature of 136.4°F was recorded at Al'Aziziyan, Libya, on Sept. 13, 1922.

WINDIEST PLACE
A surface wind speed of 231 m.p.h. was recorded at Mount Washington, New Hampshire, USA, on April 12, 1934.

MOST TORNADOES IN 24 HOURS
A total of 148 tornadoes swept through the southern and midwestern states of the USA from April 3 to 4, 1974.

MOST TORNADOES BY AREA
The United Kingdom has the highest frequency of tornadoes in proportion to its area, with an average of one tornado per 2,856 miles² recorded every year.

FASTEST TORNADO
The highest speed measured to date in a tornado is 280 m.p.h., at Wichita Falls, Texas, USA, on April 2, 1958.

LONGEST STORM-CHASING CAREER
David Hoadley of Falls Church, Virginia, USA, has chased storms since 1956 and has devoted most of his adult life to cataloguing them on film and video. He covered 20,000 miles and waited eight years before he saw his first tornado.

MOST THUNDERY DAYS
Between 1967 and 1976 an average of 251 thundery days per year was recorded in Tororo, Uganda.

GREATEST TEMPERATURE RANGES
The temperature in Verkhoyansk, Siberia, Russia, has been as low as –90.4°F and as high as 98.6°F – a range of 189°C.

Between Jan. 23 and 24, 1916, the temperature in Browning, Montana, USA, fell from 44.6°F to –56.2°F.

On Jan. 22, 1943 the temperature at Spearfish, South Dakota, USA, rose from –4°F at 7.30 a.m. to 44.6°F at 7.32 a.m.

MOST SUNSHINE
Yuma, Arizona, USA, experiences an average of 4,055 hours of sunshine (out of a possible 4,456 hours) per year.

From Feb. 1967 to March 1969 St Petersburg, Florida, USA, recorded 768 consecutive sunny days.

BIGGEST SNOWFLAKE
During a snowstorm at Fort Keogh, Montana, USA, on Jan. 28, 1887, ranch owner Matt Coleman discovered a snowflake that was 15 in wide and 8 in thick, and which he later described as being 'larger than milk pans' in the magazine *Monthly Weather Review*. A mail courier who was caught in the same snowstorm witnessed the fall of these giant flakes over several miles.

HEAVIEST HAILSTONES
Hailstones weighing up to 2.2 lb each are reported to have killed 92 people in Gopalganj, Bangladesh, on April 14, 1986.

GREATEST SNOWFALLS
Snow with a depth of 451 in was recorded at Tamarac, California, USA, in March 1911.

Between Feb. 1971 and Feb. 1972 a record 12,246 in of snow fell at Paradise, Mt Rainier, Washington, USA, a record for a single year.

The most snow produced in a single snowstorm is 189 in, which fell at Mt Shasta Ski Bowl, California, USA, from 13 to 19 Feb. 1959.

The greatest snowfall over a 24-hour period is 76 in, recorded at Silver Lake, Colorado, USA, from April 14 to 15, 1921.

COLDEST PLACES
Polyus Nedostupnosti (Pole of Inaccessibility), Antarctica, has an extrapolated annual mean temperature of –72.4°F.

The coldest measured annual mean temperature is –70.6°F, recorded at Plateau Station, Antarctica.

The coldest permanently inhabited place in the world is the village of Oymyakon in Siberia, Russia, which has a population of 4,000. The temperature there descended to –90.4°F in 1933 and to an unofficial –97.6°F more recently.

MOST RAINY DAYS
Mt Waialeale on Kauai, Hawaii, USA, has up to 350 rainy days per year.

⊙ LOWEST TEMPERATURE
The lowest natural temperature reliably recorded on the Earth's surface was –128.6°F, measured at Vostok, Antarctica, on July 21, 1983.

MOST INTENSE RAINFALL

On Nov. 26, 1970, a record 1.5 in of rain fell in one minute at Basse Terre, Guadeloupe.

HIGHEST RAINFALL

Mawsynram, Meghalaya State, India, has an average annual rainfall of 467 in.

A total of 1,042 in of rain fell at Cherrapunji, India, in the 12-month period between 1 Aug 1860 and July 31, 1861. This included a record monthly rainfall of 366 in. in July 1861.

BIGGEST FLOOD

The world's largest freshwater flood occurred approximately 18,000 years ago, when a 75-mile-long ice-dammed lake in the Altay Mountains, Siberia, Russia, broke, allowing the water to pour out. The main flow of water was estimated to be 1,600 ft deep and to have travelled at a speed of 100 m.p.h.

⊙ DRIEST PLACE

The Atacama Desert in northern Chile experiences virtually no rain. Occasional squalls will strike small areas of the desert several times a century.

⊙ MOST TORNADOES SIGHTED

Gene Moore of San Antonio, Texas, USA, has seen over 263 tornadoes in 30 years of storm-chasing, including eight in one day on 10 April, 1997. His main period of activity is between March and June, when severe weather is most likely to occur.

Diseases & Parasites 1

MOST DANGEROUS ANIMAL

Malarial parasites of the genus *Plasmodium*, which are carried by Anopheles mosquitoes, have probably been responsible for half of all human deaths (excluding wars and accidents) since the Stone Age. According to 1993 World Health Organization estimates, between 1.4 million and 2.8 million people die from malaria each year in sub-Saharan Africa alone.

BIGGEST PARASITE

The broad or fish tapeworm *Diphyllobothrium latum*, which inhabits the small intestine of fish and sometimes humans, is normally 30–40 ft. long but has been known to reach 60 ft. A specimen that lived for 10 years would shed bodily segments 5 miles long and release 2 billion eggs.

BIGGEST PARASITIC NEMATODES

Placentonema gigantissimus, which infects the placenta of sperm whales, is the world's biggest parasitic nematode. It can reach a length of 25 ft.

The largest parasitic nematode found in humans is the Guinea worm *Dracunculus medinensis*, a subcutaneous species whose females can reach 3 ft. 11 in. in length. The adult worms spend their lives travelling through the human body, and eventually emerge through blisters in the skin to shed eggs.

LONGEST-LIVING PARASITE

A lifespan of 27 years has been reliably recorded for the medicinal leech *Hirudo medicinalis*.

MOST BLOODTHIRSTY PARASITES

The indistinguishable eggs of the hookworms *Ancylostoma duodenale* and *Necator americanus* are found in the feces of 1.3 billion people worldwide. In cases of heavy infestation, the lining of the gut is so thickly covered with worms that they look like the pile of a carpet. The bleeding that results from their feeding adds up to 2.6 million gal of blood worldwide every day.

MOST SUCCESSFUL PARASITIC WORM IN HUMANS

The large roundworm *Ascaris lumbricoides*, which can be up to 1 ft. 6 in. in length, parasitizes the small intestine of approximately 25% of the human population. The simultaneous migration of large quantities of Ascaris larvae through the lungs can cause severe haemorrhagic pneumonia.

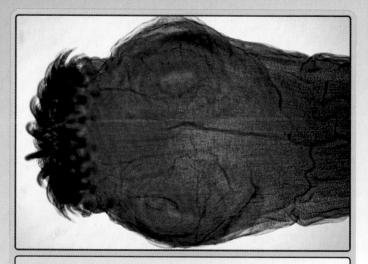

☉ BIGGEST PARASITE SPECIMEN

The beef tapeworm *Taeniarhynchus saginatus* usually grows to a length of around 16 ft. However, the largest specimen on record was over 75 ft. long – 15 ft. longer than the biggest *Diphyllobothrium latum* (see main text).

LONGEST PARASITIC FAST

The soft tick *Ornithodoros turicata*, which spreads the spirochaete that causes relapsing fever, has been known to survive for up to five years without food.

☉ MOST COMMON CONTAGIOUS DISEASE

The most common infectious disease is the cold. Caused by a group of rhinoviruses of which there are at least 180 types, the condition is almost universal, and is only avoided by those living in small isolated communities or in the frozen wastes of Antarctica.

MOST PARASITIZED HOST SPECIES

Stagnicola emarginata, a type of freshwater snail from the Great Lakes of the USA and Canada, transmits parasites that cause "swimmer's itch." This snail is a host for the larvae of at least 35 species of parasitic fluke.

MOST ADAPTABLE FLUKE

Most flukes infect very few different organisms, but the liver fluke *Fasciola hepatica* has been found as an adult in the liver, gallbladder and associated ducts in a range of mammalian species, including sheep, cattle, goats, pigs, horses, rabbits, squirrels, dogs and humans.

MOST USEFUL PARASITE

The medical leech *Hirudo medicinalis*, which was traditionally used by doctors for bloodletting, has made a comeback. In 1991, a team of Canadian surgeons led by Dr. Dean Vistnes took advantage of the anticoagulants in leeches' saliva to drain away blood and prevent it from clotting during an operation to reattach a patient's scalp. The animals used are specially cultured in sterile conditions.

MOST COMMON SKIN INFECTION

Tinea pedis, usually known as "athlete's foot," is the most common skin infection in humans, affecting up to 70% of the population at least once during their lifetime. The symptoms of the condition, which is related to warmth and sweating, include cracked and peeling skin between the toes, intense itching and small blisters that may ooze a clear fluid.

↓ MOST COMMON DISEASES

The world's most common diseases are periodontal conditions such as gingivitis (inflammation of the gums). Across the planet, few people manage to escape their symptoms.

Diseases & Parasites 2

OLDEST DISEASES
Cases of leprosy were described in Egypt as early as 1350 B.C.

Tuberculosis schistosomiasi, an infectious disease of the liver and kidneys, has been found in Egyptian mummies from the 20th dynasty (1250 to 1000 B.C.).

The plague and cholera are both referred to in the Old Testament of the Bible.

MOST COMMON CAUSES OF DEATH
According to the World Health Organization (WHO), 16.71 million, or 31%, of the 53.9 million deaths in 1998 were caused by cardiovascular diseases.

The most common cause of death among children aged 0–4 in the same period was infectious diseases, which accounted for 63% of all fatalities. Infectious diseases also caused a record 48% of all premature deaths – defined by the WHO as deaths before the age of 45.

FASTEST-GROWING DISEASE
According to the UN AIDS report of Dec. 1998, 5.8 million people were infected with HIV in that year. The number of people living with the virus had risen by 10% since 1997, to a total of 33.4 million worldwide.

MOST RESURGENT DISEASE
The deterioration in health services following the breakup of the Soviet Union in 1991 has been a major factor in the spread of diphtheria in the region. The International Red Cross estimates that there were between 150,000 and 200,000 cases of the disease in the countries of the former USSR in 1997. This compares with 2,000 cases in the Soviet Union in 1991.

MOST SUCCESSFUL IMMUNIZATION CAMPAIGN
The WHO declared the world free of smallpox on Jan. 1, 1980. Formerly one of the world's deadliest plagues (causing an estimated 2 million deaths per year in the mid-1960s), it was eradicated by one type of vaccine that was effective against all forms of the disease. The last known death from smallpox was in Aug. 1978, when a medical photographer at Birmingham University, England, was infected with a sample kept for research.

⊙ NEWEST VIRUS
In 1999, the WHO officially recognized the Nipah virus, a paramyxovirus that is clinically similar to Japanese encephalitis. First reported in southeast Asia, Nipah is believed to be transmitted through direct contact with the tissue fluids of infected animals, particularly pigs.

DEADLIEST FLU OUTBREAK
A record 21,640,000 people died worldwide of influenza in 1918 and 1919.

DEADLIEST PANDEMIC
The pneumonic form of plague, also known as the Black Death, killed approximately one quarter of the population of Europe between 1347 and 1351. The disease is caused by the bacterium Yersinia pestis.

DEADLIEST AVIAN FLU OUTBREAK
Avian flu, a strain of influenza previously only known to affect birds, was found to have infected 16 people in Hong Kong, China, in 1997. Four people died from the virus, which is the first to have been passed directly from birds to humans.

DEADLIEST *E.COLI* OUTBREAKS
Twenty people died and 500 became ill after eating meat from a butcher's in Wishaw, Lothian, Scotland, in 1998. It had been contaminated with *Escherichia coli* O157-H7, a dangerous strain of a normally harmless bacterium.

More than 9,500 cases of *E. coli* food poisoning were reported in Japan during an outbreak in summer 1996, with 11 people dying as a result.

⊙ HIGHEST PREVALENCE OF LEPROSY
According to the WHO, at the start of 1999 there were 577,200 registered sufferers of leprosy in India, a figure that had increased by 634,901 to 1,212,101 in July 1999. Brazil had the second largest number of sufferers, with 72,953 in Jan. 1999 and 116,886 by July 1999.

MOST MALARIA EPIDEMICS
According to the WHO, 1991 saw a record 144 epidemics of malaria worldwide. In recent years, the malaria virus has adapted to antimalarial treatments, with new strains showing increasing resistance to previously effective drugs.

MOST DEATHS FROM INFECTIOUS DISEASES
The West African island-republic of São Tomé and Principe has a record 241 deaths a year per 100,000 people from infectious diseases.

FEWEST DEATHS FROM INFECTIOUS DISEASES
Austria has 2.8 deaths per annum per 100,000 people from infectious diseases.

MOST DEATHS FROM RESPIRATORY DISEASES
The Republic of Ireland has 204 deaths a year per 100,000 people from respiratory diseases.

FEWEST DEATHS FROM RESPIRATORY DISEASES
Both Qatar and Malaysia have just 7.5 deaths per annum per 100,000 people from respiratory diseases.

MOST DEATHS FROM CANCER
Guernsey, Channel Islands, has a record 314 deaths a year per 100,000 people from cancer. The sovereign country with the highest rate is Hungary, with 313 deaths per annum per 100,000 people.

FEWEST DEATHS FROM CANCER
The former Yugoslav Republic of Macedonia has just six deaths per annum per 100,000 people from cancer.

MOST SURVIVABLE CANCER
The most survivable cancer is nonmelanoma skin cancer. A total of 97% of patients diagnosed with the disease survive for at least five years.

⊙ MOST URGENT HEALTH PROBLEM
According to the WHO, tobacco-related illness will be the world's leading killer by the year 2020, responsible for more deaths than AIDS, tuberculosis, road accidents, murders, and suicides put together. Populations in developing nations face the greatest risk as 85% of all smokers will come from these countries by the mid-2020s. Here, smokers in South Korea protest against the introduction of new antismoking laws.

↑ DEADLIEST DISEASE
The most deadly disease is rabies encephalitis, a viral infection of the central nervous system that is universally considered to be fatal. However, being bitten by a rabid animal need not necessarily result in death: with immediate treatment the disease can be prevented from entering the central nervous system, and chances of survival are high.

Medical Marvels

BIGGEST PREGNANCY

In 1971, Dr. Gennaro Montanino from Rome, Italy, announced that he had removed 15 fetuses from the uterus of a 35-year-old woman who was four months pregnant. A fertility drug was responsible for this unique incidence of quindecaplets.

BIGGEST MULTIPLE BIRTHS

A record 10 children (two boys and eight girls) are reported to have been born at Bacacai, Brazil, on April 22, 1946. Reports of 10 children in one birth were also received from Spain in 1924 and China in 1936.

The highest fully authenticated number of children produced in one birth is nine (nonuplets), to Geraldine Brodick at the Royal Hospital for Women, Sydney, NSW, Australia, on June 13, 1971. None of the five boys and four girls lived longer than six days.

The record for surviving babies is seven (septuplets), born to Bobbie McCaughey at University Hospital, Iowa, USA, on Nov. 19, 1997, and to Hasna Mohammed Humair at the Abha Obstetric Hospital, Aseer, Saudi Arabia, on Jan. 14, 1998.

MOST CHILDREN

The highest officially recorded number of children born to one mother is 69, to Mrs. Feodor Vassilyev of Shuya, Russia. In a total of 27 confinements between 1725 and 1765, she gave birth to 16 pairs of twins, seven sets of triplets and four sets of quadruplets. Only two of the children died in infancy.

MOST PREMATURE BABY

James Gill, the son of Brenda and James Gill, was born 128 days premature on May 20, 1987, in Ottawa, Ontario, Canada. He weighed 1.5 lbs.

LONGEST SURVIVAL OUTSIDE WOMB

When Jane Ingram of Suffolk, England, became pregnant with triplets, one fertilized egg became an ectopic pregnancy. Six weeks into the pregnancy, her fallopian tube ruptured and the rogue egg attached itself to the exterior wall of her uterus, developing its own placenta. The egg continued to grow, and on Sept. 3, 1999, 29 weeks into the pregnancy, a boy, Ronan, was delivered by Cesarean section, along with his two sisters Olivia and Mary.

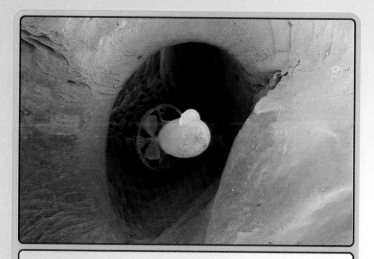

⊙ SMALLEST MEDICAL SUBMARINE

In 1999 German company MicroTEC produced a microsubmarine just 0.16 in. in length, with a diameter of 0.025 in. Made using computer-guided lasers, the submarine will be used to travel to sites of blockage or damage in blood vessels and repair them from within.

LONGEST INTERVAL BETWEEN CHILDREN

The longest interval between the birth of two children to the same mother is 41 years,185 days. Elizabeth Ann Buttle of Cwmann, Carmarthenshire, Wales, gave birth to Belinda on May 19, 1956, and Joseph on Nov. 20, 1997, aged 60.

SHORTEST INTERVAL BETWEEN CHILDREN

The shortest interval between the birth of two children in separate confinements is 209 days. Margaret Blake of Luton, Bedfordshire, England, gave birth to Conor on March 27, 1995, and Bunty on Oct. 23, 1995.

OLDEST MOTHERS

Rosanna Dalla Corta of Viterbo, Italy, is reported to have given birth to a baby boy at the age of 63 in July 1994.

Arceli Keh is also said to have been 63 when she gave birth in 1996 at the University of Southern California, USA.

LONGEST OPERATION

An operation carried out in Chicago, Illinois, USA, to remove

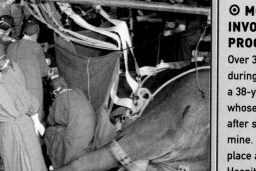

⊙ MOST VETS INVOLVED IN ONE PROCEDURE

Over 30 vets worked together during an operation on Motola, a 38-year-old cow elephant whose left foot was destroyed after she stepped on a land mine. The procedure took place at the Hang Chat Elephant Hospital in Lampang, Thailand, in Aug. 1999. The vets used enough anesthetic to knock out 70 humans.

⊙ YOUNGEST MULTI-ORGAN TRANSPLANT PATIENT

Sarah Marshall from Cobourg, Ontario, Canada, was just 5 months, 24 days old when she was given a new liver, bowel, stomach and pancreas at the Children's Hospital in London, Ontario, on Aug. 7, 1997. Sarah had been born suffering from the rare condition megacystis-microcolon-intestinal hypoperistalsis syndrome.

a cyst from one of the ovaries of patient Gertrude Levandowski lasted for 96 hours from Feb. 4 to 8, 1951. Mrs Levandowski's weight fell from 616 lbs. to 308 lbs. in the course of the operation.

MOST OPERATIONS ENDURED

From July 22, 1954, to the end of 1994, Charles Jensen of Chester, South Dakota, USA, had 970 operations to remove tumors associated with basal cell nevus syndrome.

EARLIEST HEART TRANSPLANT

The first ever heart transplant was performed at the Groote Schuur Hospital, Cape Town, South Africa, on Dec. 3, 1967, by a team headed by Prof. Christiaan Barnard. The patient, 55-year-old Louis Washkansky, survived for 18 days after the operation.

EARLIEST HAND TRANSPLANT

On Sept. 24, 1998, a team of eight surgeons in Lyon, France, performed the world's first hand transplant. They stitched the hand of a dead man to the wrist of 48-year-old Clint Hallam (Australia), who had lost his hand in a chainsaw accident nine years previously. The 14-hour operation involved attaching bones in the new hand to exposed bones in Hallam's wrist, fixing them using a metal plate with screws, and then connecting the arteries, veins, nerves, muscles and tendons.

BIGGEST GALLBLADDER REMOVED

On March 15, 1989, Prof. Bimal C. Ghosh of the National Naval Medical Center, Bethesda, Maryland, USA, removed a gallbladder weighing 23 lb. from a 69-year-old woman. The patient made a full recovery.

MOST ORGANS TRANSPLANTED

Daniel Canal of Miami, Florida, USA, received his third set of four new organs in June 1998. He was given a new stomach, liver, pancreas and small intestine at Jackson Children's Hospital, Miami, three times in a little over a month, when the first two sets were rejected. The surgeon was Dr. Andreas Tzakis.

YOUNGEST PATIENT TO UNDERGO A TRANSPLANT

On Nov. 8, 1996, one-hour-old Cheyenne Pyle became the youngest transplant patient ever when she received a heart at Jackson Children's Hospital, Miami, Florida, USA.

↓ FIRST ARTIFICIAL EYE

On Jan. 17, 2000, it was announced that a patient, known only as "Jerry," who lost his sight 36 years ago, can see again thanks to an artificial eye developed by US eye specialist William Dobelle. Dobelle has created a pair of glasses attached to a miniature camera and an ultrasonic range finder, which feed signals to a computer worn on Jerry's waistband. This computer then processes the video and distance data and sends it to another computer, which in turn transmits it to 68 platinum electrodes implanted in Jerry's brain, on the surface of his visual cortex. Jerry "sees" a simple display of dots defining the outline of an object.

Environment & Ecology 1

MOST CHEMICALLY POLLUTED TOWN
The Russian town of Dzerzhinsk, which has a population of 285,000, is home to dozens of factories that produce chlorine, pesticides and, in the past, chemical weapons. The Kaprolaktam plant in particular emits 590 tons of vinyl chlorine, a carcinogenic gas, every year. Greenpeace has declared Dzerzhinsk the site of the worst chemical pollution in Russia and its lake the most poisonous in the world. Average life expectancy in the town is just 42 for men and 47 for women.

MOST POLLUTED MAJOR CITY
Mexico City, Mexico, has levels of sulfur dioxide, carbon monoxide, ozone and suspended atmospheric particulate matter more than double those deemed acceptable by the World Health Organization (WHO). The city also has high levels of lead and nitrogen dioxide pollution.

LOWEST OZONE LEVELS
The world's lowest ozone levels within the ozone layer were recorded between Oct. 9 and 14, 1993, over the South Pole,

⊙ WORST LAND POLLUTION
From Feb. to Oct. 1994, thousands of tons of crude oil flowed across the Arctic tundra of the Komi Republic, Russia. An estimated 98,400 tons of oil leaked in a spillage that was 11.2 miles long.

Antarctica, when a reading of 91 Dobson units (DU) was obtained. A figure of at least 300 DU is needed to shield the Earth from solar ultraviolet radiation and to sustain biological systems as we know them.

HIGHEST CO2 EMISSIONS
The USA has the highest carbon dioxide emissions of any country in the world. In 1995 (the most recent year for which figures are available), 5.4 billion tons of the gas were emitted, which is equivalent to about 20.2 tons per capita.

The biggest emitter of carbon dioxide in relation to population is the United Arab Emirates. A total of 29.6 tons per capita was emitted in 1995.

WORST MARINE POLLUTION
Between 1953 and 1967, a fertilizer factory in Minamata Bay, Kyushu, Japan, managed by Shin Nippon Chisso Co., Ltd., deposited methyl mercury compound into the sea. Up to 4,500 people were seriously harmed and 800 died as a result of the factory's actions.

WORST RIVER POLLUTION
In Nov. 1986, firefighters fighting a blaze at the Sandoz chemical works in Basel, Switzerland, flushed a total of 29.5 tons of agricultural chemicals into the river Rhine, killing 500,000 fish.

WORST OIL TANKER DISASTER
When the *Atlantic Empress* collided with the *Aegean Captain* off the coast of Tobago on July 19, 1979, a record 275,520 tons of oil were spilled into the Caribbean Sea.

⊙ MOST MINING DAMAGE TO AN ISLAND
The 8-mile² Pacific island-state of Nauru is covered by beds of phosphate, derived from rich deposits of guano. The whole of the center of the island has been mined, producing a "lunar landscape," with only a narrow strip of coast still under vegetation. The deposits will be worked out by around 2010.

WORST NUCLEAR REACTOR DISASTER

The world's worst ever nuclear reactor disaster took place at Chernobyl No 4 in the USSR (now Ukraine) on April 28, 1986. Contamination was experienced over an area of 10,900 miles^2 and about 1.7 million people were exposed to varying amounts of radiation. The official death toll in the immediate aftermath of the disaster was 31, but no systematic records have been kept of fatalities since then.

MOST LETHAL SMOG

From Dec. 4-9, 1952, between 3,500 and 4,000 people, mainly children and the elderly, died in London, England, from acute bronchitis caused by inhaling thick smog.

MOST DEVASTATING AIR POLLUTION

More than 6,300 people have died from the effects of a poisonous cloud of methyl isocyanate that escaped from Union Carbide's pesticide plant near Bhopal, India, on Dec. 3, 1984,. The company made a settlement of $391 million to compensate victims and their relatives.

BIGGEST TOXIC CLOUD

In Sept. 1990, a fire at a factory handling beryllium in Ust Kamenogorsk, USSR (now Kazakhstan), released a toxic cloud that extended at least as far as the Chinese border, more than 186 miles away.

BIGGEST LAKE SHRINKAGE

The lake that has shrunk the most in recent times is the Aral Sea, which lies on the border between Uzbekistan and Kazakhstan. It decreased in size from 26,300 miles^2 in 1950 to 25,500 miles^2 in 1960, 13,500 miles^2 in 1990 and 10,500 miles^2 in 1994, by which time it had divided into two smaller bodies of water. The lake's shrinkage is almost entirely due to the extraction of water from the major rivers that feed it, for irrigation purposes.

MOST ACIDIC RAIN

A pH reading of 2.83 was recorded over the Great Lakes in the USA and Canada in 1982. By contrast, most rainwater has a pH of 5.6. A neutral reading is pH 7.0.

↓ BIGGEST CONSUMER OF ENERGY

The USA is the world's largest consumer of both fossil fuels (coal, oil, and natural gas) and of commercial energy (these plus nuclear and hydro power). In 1998 it consumed a total of 1.937 billion tons of oil equivalent (Mtoe) of fossil fuels and 2.147 Mtoe of commercial energy.

Environment & Ecology 2

MOST PAPER RECYCLED
In Germany, between 70 and 80% of paper and cardboard is recycled after use.

MOST ORGANICALLY FARMED LAND
An estimated 10% of the land in Austria is farmed organically.

HIGHEST SOLAR ENERGY USE PER CAPITA
In relation to its population, Switzerland uses more solar energy than any other country in the world, with 1.82 W per capita used in 1999. It is followed by Germany, with 0.71 W per capita, and Japan, with 0.65 W per capita.

MOST SOLAR-POWERED WATER HEATERS PER CAPITA
More than 80% of Israeli buildings contain solar-powered water heaters, amounting to one solar-powered water heater for every 10 people.

MOST ECO-FRIENDLY CAR RENTAL FIRM
Kobe-Eco-Car, which was established on Jan. 30, 1998, in Kobe, Japan, is the world's first company dedicated to the rental of environmentally friendly vehicles. The firm currently has a total of 53 vehicles for hire, comprising electric vehicles, compressed natural gas vehicles and hybrid cars.

BEST-SELLING HYBRID CAR
To date, over 30,000 Toyota Prius hybrid cars have been sold in Japan. The Prius, which was launched on Oct. 14, 1997, is a hybrid-powertrain vehicle combining a 1.5-liter gasoline engine with a generator that halves emissions, cuts smog chemicals by up to 90%, and goes twice as far as a standard car on 0.3 gal. of fuel. During one Japanese test cycle, the car achieved a fuel consumption of 77 m.p.g.

MOST ECO-FRIENDLY GAS-POWERED CAR
The SULEV-rated (Super Ultra-Low Emission Vehicle) Accord EX Sedan, developed by Honda, has the lowest emission levels of any gas-powered car. A SULEV engine emits only 2.3 lbs. of ozone-forming hydrocarbons per 100,000 miles of driving, or 86% less than a Low Emission Vehicle (LEV).

⊙ HIGHEST GLASS RECYCLING RATE
Switzerland leads the world in recycling glass, with an estimated 91% of all glass products sold in the country being recycled after use. It is closely followed by Austria and the Netherlands, both of which recycle over 80% of all disposable glass.

RAREST LIVING CREATURE
The world's rarest living creature is the Abingdon Island giant tortoise (*Geochelone elephantopus abingdoni*), which is represented by just one specimen, an aged male named Lonesome George. As there is virtually no hope of discovering another specimen, this particular subspecies is now effectively extinct.

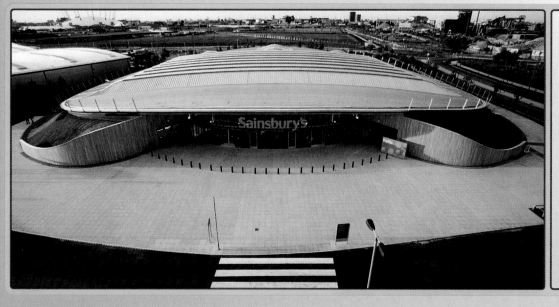

⊙ MOST ENERGY-EFFICIENT SUPERMARKET
A 35,000 ft.² supermarket in Greenwich, London, England, operated by J. Sainsbury plc., has heating and electricity bills that are 50% lower than those of a normal supermarket of equivalent size. The store has a number of energy-saving features, including an on-site combined heat and power plant, wind turbines, and photovoltaic cells.

RAREST LAND MAMMAL

The Javan rhinoceros (*Rhinoceros sondaicus*) is the world's rarest land mammal. The species has been decimated by the use of its horns in traditional Oriental medicines and, to a lesser extent, by the destruction of its habitats. There are now an estimated 60 specimens remaining in Indonesia and Vietnam.

RAREST MARINE MAMMAL

The baiji or Yangtze river dolphin (*Lipotes vexillifer*), which lives mainly in the middle reaches of the Yangtze River, China, has an estimated population of just 150.

⊙ BIGGEST LANDSCAPE RESTORATION PROJECT

The current $8-billion project to restore as much as possible of the Everglades wetlands, Florida, USA, is the biggest ecological restoration project in history. The Everglades are the largest remaining subtropical wilderness in the USA.

← RAREST BIRD OF PREY

Only 61 Californian condors (*Gymnogyps californianus*), most of which were bred in captivity, exist in the wild, with about 99 in captivity as of April 2000.

Natural Disasters

MOST PEOPLE KILLED IN AN EARTHQUAKE

An earthquake that struck the Shaanxi, Shanxi, and Henan Provinces of China on Feb. 2, 1556, is believed to have killed approximately 830,000 people.

The highest death toll in modern times was caused by a quake that hit Tangshan, China, on July 28, 1976. The official figure of 655,237 deaths was adjusted to 750,000 and then to 242,000.

MOST DAMAGE CAUSED BY AN EARTHQUAKE

An earthquake that hit the Kanto Plain, Japan, on Sept. 1, 1923, destroyed an estimated 575,000 dwellings in Tokyo and Yokohama. The official total of people killed and missing in the quake and its resultant fires was 142,807.

MOST PEOPLE MADE HOMELESS BY AN EARTHQUAKE

More than 1 million people in a 3,400-mile^2 area of Guatemala were made homeless Feb. 4, 1976, by an earthquake along the Montagua Fault, the boundary between the Caribbean and North American plates.

MOST PEOPLE KILLED BY A HURRICANE

A hurricane that hit the Ganges Delta Islands, Bangladesh, between Nov. 12 and 13, 1970, killed an estimated 1 million people in the area.

MOST DAMAGE CAUSED BY A HURRICANE

Hurricane Andrew, which hit Homestead, Florida, USA, between Aug. 23 and 26, 1992, caused an estimated $15.5 billion worth of damage.

MOST PEOPLE KILLED BY A FLOOD

An estimated 900,000 people were killed when the Huang He (Yellow River), Huayan Kou, China, burst its banks in Oct. 1887.

MOST DAMAGE CAUSED BY A FLOOD

According to official figures, 890,000 dwellings were destroyed when the Hwai and Yangtze Rivers in eastern China flooded in Aug. 1950. In addition, 3.5 million acres of land in the area were left untillable for the entire planting season, causing further hardship.

⊙ MOST DAMAGE CAUSED BY A HAILSTORM

A hailstorm that struck Munich, Germany, in July 1984, caused an estimated $1 billion worth of damage to trees, buildings, and motor vehicles.

MOST PEOPLE MADE HOMELESS BY A FLOOD

Monsoon rains in India's West Bengal State in Sept. 1978, caused extensive river flooding which rendered 15 million people homeless.

⊙ MOST TREES DESTROYED IN A STORM

A total of 270 million trees were felled or split by a storm that hit France on Dec. 26 and 27, 1999. The storm lasted for 30 hours, causing 87 deaths and an estimated $8 billion worth of damage. In Paris, the Bois de Boulogne and the Bois de Vincennes lost a total of 140,000 trees between them, while around 10,000 trees were felled in the Versailles palace grounds.

MOST PEOPLE KILLED IN A TYPHOON

Approximately 10,000 people were killed when a violent typhoon with winds of up to 100 m.p.h. struck Hong Kong on Sept. 18, 1906.

MOST PEOPLE MADE HOMELESS BY A TYPHOON

An estimated 1.12 million people lost their homes when Typhoon Ike struck the Philippines on Sept. 2, 1984, killing 1,363 and injuring a further 300.

MOST PEOPLE KILLED BY A TSUNAMI

Approximately 27,000 people were drowned when a tsunami hit the west coast of Japan in 1896.

MOST PEOPLE KILLED BY A CYCLONE

Between 300,000 and 500,000 people were estimated to have died when a cyclone hit East Pakistan (now Bangladesh) on Nov. 12, 1970. Winds of up to

⊙ MOST DEVASTATING MONSOONS

Monsoons that swept through Thailand between Sept. and Dec. 1983. killed around 10,000 people and caused more than $400 million worth of damage. Up to 100,000 people contracted waterborne diseases and 15,000 people were evacuated from their homes.

MOST PEOPLE KILLED BY A VOLCANIC ERUPTION

A total of 92,000 people were killed when the Tambora volcano in Sumbawa, Indonesia (then Dutch East Indies), erupted in April 1815.

MOST PEOPLE KILLED IN A FAMINE

Between 1959 and 1961, approximately 40 million people died of starvation in northern China.

150 m.p.h. and a 50-ft.-high tidal wave lashed the coast, the Ganges Delta, and the islands of Bhola, Hatia, Kukri Mukri, Manpura, and Rangabali.

MOST PEOPLE KILLED BY A GEYSER

In Aug. 1903, four people were killed when Waimangu geyser in New Zealand erupted. The victims, standing 89 ft. away, were blown distances of up to 2,625 ft.

MOST DAMAGING ICE STORM

From Jan. 6 to 14, 1998, an ice storm wreaked havoc across eastern Canada and adjoining parts of the USA, shutting down airports and train stations, blocking roads and cutting off power to 3 million people. Tens of thousands of pylons were toppled and the entire commercial and business center of Montreal was blacked out. The total cost of the damage was estimated at $650 million.

MOST PEOPLE KILLED IN A LANDSLIDE

On May 31, 1970, more than 18,000 people were killed by a landslide on the slopes of Mt. Huascarán in the Yungay region of Peru, making it the most devastating landslide on record.

MOST DAMAGE CAUSED BY A LANDSLIDE

A series of landslides in California, USA, in Jan. 1969, resulted in damage worth $138 million.

MOST PEOPLE KILLED BY DROUGHT

An estimated 500,000 people died of starvation in the Sahel, Sub-Saharan Africa, following droughts in the region during 1984 and 1985.

COSTLIEST NATURAL DISASTER

The earthquake that struck Kobe, Japan, in Jan. 1995, caused record losses of $100 billion.

⊙ MOST PEOPLE MADE HOMELESS BY A HURRICANE

Hurricane Mitch, which struck Central America between Oct. 26, and Nov. 4, 1998, caused 9,745 deaths and destroyed 93,690 dwellings, leaving approximately 2.5 million people dependent on international aid efforts. The hurricane, which reached a maximum speed of 180 m.p.h., gathered strength over the Caribbean Sea before hitting the coast of Honduras and moving slowly inland, touching the El Salvador–Honduras border before heading into Guatemala. It was finally downgraded to a tropical storm after entering the southern Gulf of Mexico.

Soccer 1

MOST GAMES PLAYED

Peter Shilton (England) made a record 1,390 senior appearances in the course of his career. These included 1,005 appearances in the English League: 286 for Leicester City (1966–74); 110 for Stoke City (1974–77); 202 for Nottingham Forest (1977–82); 188 for Southampton (1982–87); 175 for Derby County (1987–92); 34 for Plymouth Argyle (1992–94); one for Bolton Wanderers (1995); and nine for Leyton Orient (1996–97). He also played in one League play-off, 86 FA Cup games, 102 League Cup games, 125 full internationals, 13 Under-23 games, four Football League XI games, and 53 various European and other club competitions.

MOST GOALS IN A CAREER

The most goals scored in a specified period is 1,279, by Pelé (Edson Arantes do Nascimento) in 1,363 games for Brazil, Santos, and the New York Cosmos from Sept. 7, 1956, to Oct. 1, 1977. His best year was 1959, when he scored 126 goals, and the *Milesimo* (1,000th) came during his 909th first-class game on Nov. 19, 1969, when he scored a penalty for his club Santos at the Maracanã Stadium, Rio de Janeiro, Brazil. After retirement he scored two further goals in special appearances.

MOST GOALS IN A GAME

The highest score in a first-class game is 36, a record set when Arbroath beat Bon Accord 36–0 in a Scottish Cup game on Sept. 5, 1885. Seven further goals were disallowed for offside.

The most goals scored by one player in a first-class game is 16, by Stephan Stanis for Racing Club de Lens v. Aubry-Asturies in a wartime French Cup game in Lens, France, on Dec. 13, 1942.

LONGEST CLEAN SHEET

The longest period that any goalkeeper has prevented goals being scored past him in top-class competition is 1,275 min., by Abel Resino of Atlético Madrid, Spain, to March 17, 1991.

MOST GOALS SCORED BY A GOALKEEPER

José Luis Chilavert (Paraguay and Vélez Sarsfield of Argentina) scored a record 49 official and international goals between July 1992 and March 2000.

⊙ HEAVIEST PLAYER

The biggest player in representative soccer was the England international goalkeeper Willie Henry "Fatty" Foulke (1874–1916), who was 6 ft. 3 in. tall and weighed up to 364 lbs. He once stopped a game by snapping the goalpost.

MOST CONSECUTIVE HAT TRICKS

The most consecutive top division games in which a player has scored hat tricks is four. Masashi Nakayama, who plays for Jubilo Iwata in the Japanese League, scored five goals v. Cerezo Osaka at Nagai Stadium on April 15, 1998; four goals v. Sanfrecce Hiroshima at Jubilo Iwata Stadium on April 18, 1998; four goals v. Avispa Fukuoka at Kumamoto City Stadium on April 25, 1998; and three goals v. Consadole Sapporo at Jubilo Iwata Stadium on April 29, 1998.

FASTEST GOAL

Ricardo Olivera scored just 2.8 seconds after the start of play for Río Negro against Soriano at José Enrique Rodó, Soriano, Uruguay, on Dec. 26, 1998 – the fastest goal in first-class soccer.

MOST WORLD CLUB CHAMPIONSHIPS

The record for wins in the World Club Championship, contested between the winners of the European Cup and the Copa Libertadores, is three, held jointly by Peñarol of Uruguay (1961, 1966, 1982); Nacional of Uruguay (1971, 1980, 1988); and AC Milan of Italy (1969, 1989, 1990).

⊙ HIGHEST-SCORING TIE

On Aug. 7, 1999, Racing Genk tied 6–6 with Westerlo in the Belgian league. Genk's Branko Strupar (in blue) scored three penalties and Westerlo's Toni Brogno claimed four goals, two of them from the spot. The record was equalled on March 19, 2000, when Gimnasia y Esgrima de la Plata played Colón de Santa Fe in the Argentine league.

MOST EUROPEAN CUPS

The European Cup, contested since 1956 by the winners of the European leagues, has been won a record eight times by Real Madrid of Spain (1956–60, 1966, 1998, 2000).

MOST COPA LIBERTADORES WINS

The Copa Libertadores, contested since 1960 by the winners of the South American leagues, has been won seven times by Club Atlético Independiente of Argentina (1964–65, 1972–75, 1984).

⊙ MOST VALUABLE SOCCER CLUB

Manchester United, in the English Premier League, has a market capitalization value of $1.48 billion. The club won 14 major trophies in the 1990s, thanks to players such as David Beckham (above), Eric Cantona, and Peter Schmeichel.

MOST CUP-WINNERS CUPS

The Cup-Winners Cup, contested until 1999 by the winners of the national cups in Europe, was won a record four times by Barcelona (1979, 1982, 1989, 1997).

MOST CUP OF CHAMPION CLUBS WINS

The Cup of Champion Clubs, contested since 1964 by the winners of the African leagues, has been won four times by Zamalek of Egypt (1984, 1986, 1993, 1996).

← MOST EXPENSIVE PLAYER

The highest transfer fee quoted for a player is a reported $45 million for striker Christian Vieri (Italy), who moved between the Italian clubs Lazio and Internazionale in June 1999. Vieri, who grew up in Australia, has also played for Atlético Madrid (Spain) and Juventus.

MOST EXPENSIVE DEFENDER

In May 1998, defender Jaap Stam was sold by PSV Eindhoven (Netherlands) to Manchester United (England) for a record $18 million. The seven-year deal was worth $18.3 million to the Dutch international, then 26 years old.

MOST VALUABLE SUBSTITUTES BENCH

For a game against Celta Vigo on Jan. 9, 2000, FC Barcelona coach Louis Van Gaal named Pep Guardiola, Sergi Barjuan, Ruud Hesp, Frederic Dehu, Frank and Ronald de Boer, and Rivaldo as substitutes, creating a sub's bench laden with over $160 million worth of talent. Of the players named, only Rivaldo played.

Soccer 2

MOST GOALS IN AN INTERNATIONAL

The most goals scored in a senior men's international is 20, when Kuwait beat Bhutan 20-0 in Kuwait on Feb. 14, 2000.

The most goals scored by one player in an international game is 10, by Sofus Nielsen for Denmark v. France (17–1) in the 1908 Olympics; and by Gottfried Fuchs for Germany v. Russia (16–0) in the 1912 Olympics.

The highest score in a women's international is 21–0, by Japan v. Guam at Guangzhou, China, on Dec. 5, 1997; by Canada v. Puerto Rico at Toronto, Canada, on Aug. 28, 1998; by Australia v. American Samoa at Auckland, New Zealand, on Oct. 9, 1998; and by New Zealand v Samoa, also at Auckland, New Zealand, on Oct. 9, 1998.

⊙ MOST WOMEN'S WORLD CUP WINS

The USA has won two of the three women's World Cup tournaments held since 1991, in 1991 and 1999. The most recent final ended with a penalty shootout, with Brandi Chastain (above) scoring the decisive goal.

LONGEST INTERNATIONAL CLEAN SHEET

The longest period that a goalkeeper has prevented goals from being scored in international games is 1,142 min., by Dino Zoff (Italy) from Sept. 1972 to June 1974.

MOST WORLD CUP WINS

Brazil have won four of the 16 World Cup tournaments held so far (1958, 1962, 1970, and1994).

Edson Arantes do Nascimento, known as Pelé (Brazil), is the only player to have been in three World Cup-winning teams, in 1958, 1962 and 1970.

HIGHEST SCORE IN A WORLD CUP GAME

The highest score in a game during the finals stages of the World Cup is 10, by Hungary v. El Salvador (10–1) at Elche, Spain, on June 15, 1982.

The highest combined score in the finals tournament is 12, a record set when Austria beat Switzerland 7–5 at Lausanne, Switzerland, on June 26, 1954.

The highest score in any World Cup game is 17–0, when Iran beat The Maldives in a qualifying game played in Damascus, Syria, on June 2, 1997.

MOST WORLD CUP FINALS APPEARANCES

The record for appearances in finals tournaments is five, held by Antonio Carbajal (Mexico) – 1950, 1954, 1958, 1962 ,and 1966 – and Lothar Matthäus (Germany) – 1982, 1986, 1990, 1994, and 1998. Matthäus played in a record 25 games.

YOUNGEST AND OLDEST WORLD CUP PLAYERS

The youngest player ever in a finals game is Norman Whiteside, who was 17 years, 41 days old when he played for Northern Ireland against Yugoslavia on June 17, 1982.

The youngest scorer in a finals game is Pelé, who was 17 years, 239 days old when he scored for Brazil against Wales at Gothenburg, Sweden, on June 19, 1958.

The oldest participant in the World Cup is Roger Milla, who was 42 years, 39 days old when he played for Cameroon against Russia on June 28, 1994. During this game, he scored his team's only goal, also making him the oldest ever scorer in the finals.

⊙ MOST CAPS

The greatest number of appearances for a national team, as recognized by FIFA, is 144, by Lothar Matthäus (Germany) from 1980 to 2000.

BIGGEST WORLD CUP ATTENDANCES

The greatest recorded crowd at a World Cup game (and the largest at any soccer game) was 199,854, for Brazil v. Uruguay at the Maracanã Municipal Stadium, Rio de Janeiro, Brazil, on July 16, 1950. Uruguay won this, the deciding game of the tournament, 2–1.

The greatest combined number of spectators for a tournament is 3,587,538, for the 52 games in the 1994 World Cup in the USA.

MOST OLYMPIC GAMES WINS

The record for wins in Olympic soccer tournaments is three, held by Great Britain (1900, 1908, and 1912) and Hungary (1952, 1964, and 1968).

MOST SOUTH AMERICAN CHAMPIONSHIPS

Argentina have won the South American Championships (Copa América since 1975) a record 15 times (1910, 1921, 1925, 1927, 1929, 1937, 1941, 1945–47, 1955, 1957, 1958, 1991, and 1993).

MOST EUROPEAN CHAMPIONSHIPS

Germany have won the European Championships a record three times, in 1972, 1980 and 1996 (the first two as West Germany).

MOST CONCACAF CHAMPIONSHIPS

Costa Rica have won the CONCACAF Championships (CONCACAF Gold Cup since 1991) 10 times (1941, 1946, 1948, 1953, 1955, 1960, 1961, 1963, 1969,and 1989).

MOST ASIAN CUP WINS

The record for Asian Cup wins is three, held by Iran (1968, 1972, 1976) and Saudi Arabia (1984, 1988, 1996).

MOST AFRICAN CUP OF NATIONS WINS

The record for wins in the African Cup Of Nations is four, held by Ghana (1963, 1965, 1978, 1982) and Egypt (1957, 1959, 1986, 1998).

◉ WORLD CUP WITH MOST ENTRANTS

A record 198 national soccer federations, out of a total of 203, registered to play in qualifiers for the 17th World Cup, which will be hosted jointly by South Korea and Japan in 2002. It will be the first time the tournament has been staged in Asia.

→ MOST PENALTIES MISSED IN AN INTERNATIONAL

Martín Palermo (Argentina) missed three penalties during his team's defeat by Colombia in the 1999 Copa América in Paraguay. His first shot hit the goalpost, the second landed in the stands, and the third one was saved.

Basketball

HIGHEST SCORE IN AN NBA GAME

The highest combined score in an NBA game is 370, a record set when the Detroit Pistons beat the Denver Nuggets 186–184 at Denver, Colorado, USA, on Dec. 13, 1983. Overtime was played after a 145–145 tie in regulation time.

The highest combined score in regulation time is 320. This occurred when the Golden State Warriors beat Denver 162–158 on Nov. 2, 1990.

TALLEST NBA PLAYER

Romanian-born Gheorghe Muresan of the New Jersey Nets, who made his professional debut in 1994, is 7 ft. 7 in. tall.

BIGGEST NBA WINNING MARGIN

The Cleveland Cavaliers beat the Miami Heat 148–80 on Dec. 17, 1991 – a record 68-point margin.

MOST POINTS IN AN NBA QUARTER

The most points scored in a quarter is 58, by Buffalo at Boston, Massachusetts, USA, on Oct. 20, 1972.

MOST POINTS IN AN NBA HALF

The Phoenix Suns scored a record 107 points in the first half of a game against Denver on Nov. 11, 1990.

YOUNGEST NBA PLAYER

Jermaine O'Neal was 18 years, 53 days old when he made his

⊙ MOST WOMEN'S OLYMPIC TITLES

The record for the most women's Olympic titles is held jointly by the USA and the USSR, with three each. The USA won in 1984, 1988, and 1996, and the USSR won in 1976, 1980, and 1992 (taking the last title as the Unified team of the former USSR). Kim (left) of South Korea is seen with McRae of the USA in a game played during the 1996 Olympics.

⊙ MOST POINTS IN AN NBA GAME

Wilt "The Stilt" Chamberlain scored 100 points for Philadelphia against New York at Hershey, Pennsylvania, USA, on March 2, 1962. This included a record 36 field goals and 28 free throws, as well as a record 59 points in a half. Chamberlain died on Oct. 12, 1999.

professional debut for the Portland Trail Blazers, playing against the Denver Nuggets on Dec. 5, 1996.

MOST POINTS IN AN NBA SEASON

In the 1961/62 season Wilt Chamberlain scored a record 4,029 points for Philadelphia. He also set season records for the highest scoring average (50.4 per game) and for field goals (1,597).

MOST POINTS IN AN NBA CAREER

Kareem Abdul-Jabbar (originally Lew Alcindor), who played for the Milwaukee Bucks from 1969 to 1975 and the Los Angeles Lakers from 1975 to 1989, scored a record 38,387 points during his career – an average of 24.6 points per game. This

included 15,837 field goals in regular season games and 5,762 points and 2,356 field goals in play-off games.

HIGHEST NBA CAREER AVERAGE

The highest career average for players exceeding 10,000 points is 31.5, by Michael Jordan, who scored 29,277 points in 930 games for the Chicago Bulls between 1984 and 1998. Jordan also holds the record for the highest career average in play-off games, at 33.4 (5,987 points scored in 179 games from 1984 to 1998).

MOST NBA TITLES

The Boston Celtics have won a record-breaking 16 NBA titles: in 1957, from 1959 to 1966, and in 1968, 1969, 1974, 1976, 1981, 1984, and 1986.

LONGEST NBA CAREER (MINUTES)

Kareem Abdul-Jabbar played for a total of 57,446 minutes in the course of his career. He also took part in the most play-off games – a record 237.

MOST NBA GAMES PLAYED IN A SEASON

The record for the greatest number of complete games played in one season is 79, by Wilt Chamberlain for Philadelphia in 1961/62. During this period he was on court for a record 3,882 minutes.

MOST WINS IN AN NBA SEASON

The Chicago Bulls had a record 72 wins in the 1995/96 season.

MOST CONSECUTIVE NBA WINS

The Los Angeles Lakers won 33 games in succession from Nov. 5, 1971, through to Jan. 7, 1972.

MOST LOSSES IN AN NBA SEASON

In the 1972/73 season the Philadelphia 76ers lost a record 73 out of 82 games. This total included a 20-game losing streak.

LONGEST GAME

The longest game of basketball lasted for a record-breaking 24 hours and was played by the Suncoast Clippers at Maroochydore Eagles Basketball Stadium, Queensland, Australia, from Nov. 21 to 22, 1998.

HIGHEST SLAM DUNK

Michael "Wild Thing" Wilson of the Harlem Globetrotters slam dunked a regulation basketball through a goal set at a height of 12 ft. at Conseco Fieldhouse, Indiana, USA, on April 1, 2000.

MOST FREE THROWS

Jim Connolly (USA) holds the records for the most successful free throws in both one minute (35) and in 10 minutes (280). The records were set at St. Peter's School, Pacifica, California, USA, on Oct. 10 and Oct.12, 1998, respectively.

MOST BALLS DRIBBLED

Joseph Odhiambo of Mesa, Arizona, USA, has the unique ability to dribble five basketballs at the same time.

LONGEST DRIBBLE

Over a 24-hour period in May 1998, Jamie Borges (USA) dribbled a basketball a distance of 96.89 miles without "travelling" (carrying the ball without dribbling). The record was set at Barrington High School, Rhode Island, USA.

MOST BALLS SPUN

Michael Kettman of St. Augustine, Florida, USA, simultaneously spun 28 regulation basketballs on a specially designed frame for five seconds on May 25, 1999.

BIGGEST CROWD

A record 80,000 spectators turned out to watch the final of the European Cup Winners' Cup between AEK Athens and Slavia Prague at the Olympic Stadium, Athens, Greece, on April 4, 1968.

MOST WORLD TITLES

Yugoslavia have won four men's World Championship titles: in 1970, 1978, 1990, and 1998.

The most women's World Championship titles won is six, by the USSR (in 1959, 1964, 1967, 1971, 1975, and 1983); and by the USA (in 1953, 1957, 1979, 1986, 1990, and 1998).

MOST MEN'S OLYMPIC TITLES

The USA have won a record 11 men's Olympic titles since basketball was introduced to the Games in 1936. To date, they have lost just two of their Olympic games, both of them to the USSR.

← MOST GAMES IN AN NBA CAREER

Robert Parish played a record 1,611 NBA regular season games over 21 seasons for the Golden State Warriors (1976–80), the Boston Celtics (1980–94), the Charlotte Hornets (1994–96), and the Chicago Bulls (1996–97).

Rugby

RUGBY UNION
MOST CAREER POINTS
William "Dusty" Hare scored 7,337 points in first-class games from 1971 to 1989. Of these, 4,427 points were for Leicester, 1,800 were for Nottingham, 240 were for England, 88 were for the British Isles, and 782 were scored in other representative games.

MOST CAREER TRIES
Alan Morley (UK) scored a total of 473 tries in senior rugby games between 1968 and 1986. This included 378 tries for Bristol, a record for one club.

MOST POINTS IN INTERNATIONAL GAMES
Between 1991 and 2000, Neil Jenkins scored 984 points in a total of 80 games for Wales and the British Lions.

MOST TRIES IN INTERNATIONAL GAMES
David Campese (Australia) scored a record 64 tries in 101 international games between 1982 and 1996.

MOST POINTS IN ONE MATCH
Jannie van der Westhuizen (South Africa) scored 94 points (14 tries, nine conversions, one dropped goal, and one penalty goal) for Carnarvon when they played Williston at North West Cape, South Africa, on March 11, 1972.

MOST WORLD CUP POINTS SCORED
The leading scorer in World Cup games is Gavin Hastings, who scored a total of 227 points in 13 games for Scotland between 1987 and 1995.

MOST CLUB APPEARANCES
Roy Evans (UK) played in a record 1,193 club games in the course of his career, always in the position of tight head prop. This total includes 1,007 games played for Osterley between Sept. 1950 and April 1989.

Allan Robertshaw (UK) played in a total of 1,075 games for York.

MOST WORLD CUP APPEARANCES
Sean Fitzpatrick (New Zealand) played in 17 World Cup games between 1987 and 1995.

HIGHEST SCORE IN A GAME
The highest score in any game was 194–0, a record set when

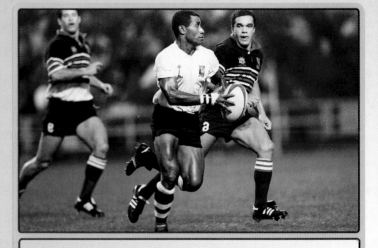

⊙ MOST HONG KONG SEVENS WINS
Fiji have won the Hong Kong Sevens a record nine times, in 1977, 1978, 1980, 1984, 1990–92, 1998, and 1999. The 1997 event was replaced by the World Cup Sevens, which Fiji also won. Waisale Serevi of Fiji (center) is seen in action against Vaughn Going (left) and Rob Santos of Hong Kong during a World Cup Sevens game.

Comet beat fellow Danish team Lindo on Nov. 17, 1973.

HIGHEST WORLD CUP SCORE
The highest score in a World Cup game occurred when New Zealand beat Japan 145–17 at Bloemfontein, South Africa, on June 4, 1995.

BIGGEST CROWD
A record 107,069 spectators turned out to watch Australia's 28–7 victory over New Zealand at Stadium Australia, Sydney, NSW, Australia, on Aug. 28, 1999.

RUGBY LEAGUE
MOST CAREER POINTS
Neil Fox scored a record 6,220 points (2,575 goals, including four drop goals and 358 tries) in a senior Rugby League career that lasted from April 1956 to Aug. 1979. Of these, 4,488 were for Wakefield Trinity, 1,089 were for five other clubs, 228 were for Great Britain, 147 were for Yorkshire, and 268 were scored in other representative games.

MOST CAREER TRIES
Brian Bevan (Australia) scored a total of 796 tries in 18 seasons between 1945 and 1964. Of

⊙ MOST POINTS IN A SEASON (LEAGUE)
During the 1994/95 season, Wigan scored 1,735 points in league and cup games. The club also holds the record for the most consecutive league games wins, with 31 from Feb. 1970 to Feb. 1971. Shaun Edwards, who played for the club between 1983 and 1997, is seen here scoring a try against Oldham in March 1995.

these, 740 were for Warrington, 17 were for Blackpool (both UK), and 39 were scored in other representative games.

MOST POINTS SCORED IN ONE GAME
George Henry "Tich" West (UK) scored 53 points (10 goals and a record 11 tries) for Hull Kingston Rovers in a Challenge Cup tie against Brookland Rovers on March 4, 1905.

MOST POINTS SCORED IN AN INTERNATIONAL
The most points scored in an international is 32, by Andrew Johns for Australia against Fiji at Newcastle, NSW, Australia, on July 12, 1996; and by Bobby Goulding for Great Britain against Fiji at Nadi, Fiji, on Oct. 5, 1996.

⊙ MOST INTERNATIONAL APPEARANCES (UNION)
Philippe Sella (France) played in a total of 111 international games between 1982 and 1995, during which he scored 30 tries.

← MOST WORLD CUP WINS (UNION)
Since the Rugby Union World Cup was first contested in 1987, Australia has had a record two wins, in 1991 and 1999. Here, Tim Horan lifts the 1999 trophy following Australia's 35–12 defeat of France.

HIGHEST TRANSFER FEES
A reported $1.2 million was paid by Rugby Union club Newcastle to Wigan (both UK) for Va'aiga Tuiagamala (Western Samoa) in Feb. 1997.

The costliest cash-only transfer was $777,260, paid by Wigan to Widnes for Martin Offiah (UK) in Jan. 1992.

MOST WORLD CUP WINS
Australia have won the World Cup seven times, in 1957, 1968, 1970, 1977, 1988, 1992, and 1995. They also won the International Championship of 1975.

HIGHEST SCORE IN AN INTERNATIONAL GAME
The highest score in an international game is 86–6, a record set when Australia defeated South Africa at Gateshead, Tyne and Wear, England, on Oct. 10, 1995.

FASTEST TRIES
Lee Jackson (UK) scored a try nine seconds after kickoff for Hull against Sheffield Eagles in a Yorkshire Cup semifinal played at Sheffield, S. Yorkshire, England, on Oct. 6, 1992.

The fastest try in an international game was scored 15 seconds after kickoff by Bobby Fulton for Australia against France at Bradford, W. Yorkshire, England, on Nov. 1, 1970.

Football

MOST SUPER BOWL WINS
The Super Bowl was first held in 1967 between the winners of the NFL and the AFL. The greatest number of wins is five, by the San Francisco 49ers (1982, 1985, 1989, 1990, and 1995); and by the Dallas Cowboys (1972, 1978, 1993, 1994, and 1996).

The player who has played on the most Super Bowl-winning teams is Charles Hayley, with a total of five. He played twice with the San Francisco 49ers (1989 and 1990) and three times with the Dallas Cowboys (1993, 1994, and 1996).

HIGHEST SUPER BOWL SCORES
The records for the highest team score and the highest victory margin were set when the San Francisco 49ers beat the Denver Broncos 55–10 in New Orleans, Louisiana, on Jan. 28, 1990.

The record for the highest combined score was set in 1995, when the San Francisco 49ers beat the San Diego Chargers 49–26.

MOST SUPER BOWL MVPs
Joe Montana, quarterback with the San Francisco 49ers, was voted Most Valuable Player (MVP) in three Super Bowls: 1982, 1985, and 1990.

MOST NFL TITLES
The Green Bay Packers have won a record 13 NFL titles: 1929–31, 1936, 1939, 1944, 1961, 1962, 1965–67, 1996, and 1997.

MOST GAMES PLAYED
George Blanda played in a record 340 NFL games in 26 seasons: for the Chicago Bears (1949–58); the Baltimore Colts (1950); the Houston Oilers (1960–66), and the Oakland Raiders (1967–75).

The most consecutive games played is 282, by Jim Marshall (Cleveland Browns, 1960, and Minnesota Vikings, 1961–79).

MOST POINTS
George Blanda scored a record 2,002 points for the Chicago Bears, Baltimore Colts, Houston Oilers, and Oakland Raiders between 1949 and 1975.

The most points scored in a season is 176, by Paul Hornung (Green Bay Packers) in 1960.

The record for one game is 40, by Ernie Nevers for the Chicago Cardinals v. the Chicago Bears on Nov. 28, 1929.

HIGHEST SCORES
On Oct. 7, 1916, Georgia Tech of Atlanta scored 222 points, including a record 32 touchdowns, against Cumberland University of Lebanon, Tennessee, who failed to score.

The highest score in an NFL game is 73, by the Chicago Bears v. the Washington Redskins (0) in the 1940 NFL Championship game in Washington, D.C., on Dec. 8, 1940. The highest score in a regular season game is 72, by the Washington Redskins v. the New York Giants (41) in Washington on Nov. 27, 1966. The combined score of 113 is also a record.

MOST CONSECUTIVE WINS
The Chicago Bears have recorded the most consecutive NFL victories, with 17 in 1933/34.

The most consecutive NFL games played without defeat is 25, by the Canton Bulldogs. They achieved 22 wins and 3 ties from 1921 to 1923.

LONGEST PASS COMPLETION
A pass completion of 99 yds. has been achieved on eight occasions and has always

⊙ MOST TOUCHDOWNS
Jerry Rice (San Francisco 49ers) made 180 touchdowns in NFL games between 1985 and 1999. He also holds the Super Bowl career records for touchdowns (seven), yards gained receiving (512), and pass receptions (28).

⊙ MOST VALUABLE NFL FRANCHISES
According to *Forbes* magazine, the most valuable NFL franchise is that of the Dallas Cowboys (above), which was worth $663 million in Sept. 1999. However, in May 2000, the Washington Redskins' franchise was sold for $800 million.

⊙ MOST PASSES COMPLETED

Dan Marino (Miami Dolphins) completed a total of 4,967 passes between 1983 and his retirement in 2000. He holds many other records, including most yards gained passing in both a career (61,631) and a season (5,084 in 1984).

MOST GRAY CUP WINS
The Toronto Argonauts won a record 14 Gray Cups between 1914 and 1997.

MOST CFL GAMES PLAYED
Lui Passaglia played in a record 390 CFL games for the BC Lions between 1976 and 1999.

MOST CFL POINTS SCORED
Lui Passaglia scored 3,811 points for the BC Lions between 1976 and 1999.

Lance Chomyc scored 236 points for the Toronto Argonauts in the 1991 season.

resulted in a touchdown. The most recent was a Brett Favre pass to Robert Brooks (Green Bay Packers), against the Chicago Bears on Sept. 11, 1995.

LONGEST RUN FROM SCRIMMAGE
Tony Dorsett scored on a touchdown run of 99 yds. for the Dallas Cowboys v. the Minnesota Vikings on Jan. 3, 1983.

HIGHEST ATTENDANCES
The most spectators at any game is 103,985, for Super Bowl XIV (Pittsburgh Steelers v. L.A. Rams), at the Rose Bowl, Pasadena, California, on Jan. 20, 1980.

The largest crowd for a regular season game is 102,368, for the L.A. Rams v. the San Francisco 49ers at the Los Angeles Coliseum, California, on Nov. 10, 1957.

BIGGEST TV AUDIENCE
The biggest TV audience for a game was 128.5 million, for the NBC transmission of Super Bowl XXX between Dallas and Pittsburgh on Jan. 28, 1996.

← MOST YARDS GAINED PASSING
Kurt Warner threw 414 yds. for the St. Louis Rams in Super Bowl XXXIV in Atlanta, Georgia, on Jan. 30, 2000.

Golf

LOWEST SCORE OVER 18 HOLES

Five players have played a course of over 6,500 yds. with a score of 58. The most recent was Shigeki Maruyama (Japan), in a qualifying event for the US Open, at Woodmont Country Club, Rockville, Maryland, (par 71, 6,539 yd) on June 5, 2000.

The US PGA tournament record for 18 holes is 59, by Al Geiberger (USA) in the Danny Thomas Classic, on the 7,249-yd., 72-par Colonial GC course, Memphis, Tennessee, USA, on June 10, 1977; by Chip Beck (USA) in the Las Vegas Invitational, on the 6,979-yd., 72-par Sunrise GC course, Las Vegas, Nevada, USA, on Oct. 11, 1991; and by David Duval (USA) in the Bob Hope Chrysler Classic, La Quinta, California, USA, on Jan. 24, 1999.

Other golfers who have scored 59 over 18 holes in major non-PGA tournaments include: Sam Snead (USA) in the third round of the Sam Snead Festival at White Sulphur Springs, West Virginia, USA, on May 16, 1959; Gary Player (South Africa) in the second round of the Brazilian Open in Rio de Janeiro, Brazil, on Nov. 29, 1974; David Jagger (UK) in a Pro-Am tournament prior to the 1973 Nigerian Open at Ikoyi GC, Lagos, Nigeria; and Miguel Martin (Spain) in the Argentine Southern Championship at Mar de Plata, Argentina, on Feb. 27, 1987.

The lowest recorded score by a woman on a 5,600-yd.,18-hole course is 61, by Se Ri Pak (South Korea) at the Jamie Farr Kroger Classic, Sylvania, Ohio, USA, on July 10, 1998.

⊙ HIGHEST SEASON'S EARNINGS

In 1999, Karrie Webb (Australia, above) earned a total of $1,591,959 in prize money on the US LPGA tour – a women's record. The men's record is $6,616,585, by Tiger Woods (USA), also in 1999.

⊙ MOST INDIVIDUAL RYDER CUP WINS

Nick Faldo (GB) holds the record for the most match wins by an individual in the Ryder Cup, with 23 from 46 played. He has also scored the most points, with 25, having halved four other matches. Faldo participated in the competition a record 11 times between 1977 and 1997.

MOST US OPEN WINS

The US Open has been won four times by: Willie Anderson (1901 and 1903–05); Bobby Jones Jr. (1923, 1926, 1929, and 1930); Ben Hogan (1948, 1950, 1951, and 1953); and Jack Nicklaus (1962, 1967, 1972, and 1980).

LOWEST US OPEN SCORES

The lowest score in a round of the US Open is 63, by Johnny Miller on the 6,920-yd., 71-par course at the Oakmont Country Club, Pennsylvania, on June 17, 1973; and by Jack Nicklaus and Tom Weiskopf (both USA) at Baltusrol Country Club (a 7,015-yd. course), New Jersey, both on June 12, 1980.

The lowest score over four rounds is 272, by Jack Nicklaus (63, 71, 70, 68) in June 1980; and by Lee Janzen (USA) (67, 67, 69, 69) in June 1993, both at Baltusrol.

LOWEST BRITISH OPEN SCORES

The lowest score in a round at the British Open is 63, by Mark Hayes (USA) at Turnberry, S. Ayrshire, Scotland, in 1977; Isao Aoki (Japan) at Muirfield, E. Lothian, Scotland, in 1980; Greg Norman (Australia) at Turnberry in 1986; Paul Broadhurst (GB) at St. Andrews, Fife, Scotland, in 1990; Jodie Mudd (USA) at Royal Birkdale, Merseyside, England, in 1991; and Nick Faldo (GB) and the late Payne Stewart (USA), both at Royal St. Georges, Sandwich, England, in 1993.

MOST RYDER CUP TEAM WINS

The USA has won the biennial Ryder Cup, played between the USA and Europe, 24 times to Europe's seven (with two draws) to 1999.

MOST SOLHEIM CUP WINS

The Solheim Cup, contested between the top female professionals of Europe and the USA, was first held in 1990. The USA has had four wins: in 1990, 1994, 1996, and 1998. Europe won in 1992.

The most wins by a player is 12, by Laura Davies (GB) from 19 matches (1990–98); and by Dottie Pepper (USA) from 17 matches (1990–98). The most points scored is 12.5, by both players.

MOST WORLD CUP WINS

The World Cup has been won most often by the USA, with 22 wins from 1955 to 1999. The only men to have been on six winning teams are Arnold Palmer (USA): 1960, 1962–64, 1966, and 1967; and Jack Nicklaus: 1963, 1964, 1966, 1967, 1971, and 1973. Nicklaus won the individual title three times, in 1963, 1964, and 1971.

LOWEST WORLD CUP TEAM SCORE

Fred Couples and Davis Love III (both USA) scored 536 for 144 holes at Dorado, Puerto Rico, from Nov. 10 to 13, 1994.

HIGHEST CAREER EARNINGS

By May 1, 2000, Tiger Woods had won $14,730,860 in prize money on the PGA tour. Woods turned professional in Aug. 1996.

Betsy King (USA) holds the women's record, with $6,583,199 earned between 1977 and May 2000.

YOUNGEST AND OLDEST NATIONAL CHAMPIONS

Thuashni Selvaratnam (Sri Lanka) was only 12 years, 324 days old when she won the Sri Lankan Ladies' Amateur Open Golf Championship on April 29, 1989.

Pamela Fernando (Sri Lanka) was 54 years, 282 days old when she won the Sri Lankan Women's Championship on July 17, 1981.

↓ BIGGEST MARGIN OF VICTORY

Tiger Woods (USA) won the US Open in June 2000 by 15 strokes, a record for a major tournament. He finished with a total of 272, 12 under par.

Tennis

⊙ HIGHEST-EARNING SISTERS IN TENNIS

The most successful tennis-playing sisters are Venus and Serena Williams (USA), who have each won over $7.5 million in prize money to date. Venus (behind in the picture) turned professional in 1994, aged 14, with Serena following in 1997, aged 16. In 1999, they became the only sisters to have met in a WTA final – the Lipton Championships – which Venus won 6–1, 4–6, 6–4. They have also played doubles together, and in 1999 won both the French and US Open titles.

MOST GRAND SLAM WINS

Margaret Court (Australia) holds the record for the most singles titles won in Grand Slam tournaments, with a total of 24 (11 Australian, five US, five French, and three Wimbledon) between 1960 and 1973.

The record for men's singles Grand Slam titles is 12, held jointly by Roy Emerson of Australia (six Australian, two French, two US, and two Wimbledon between 1961 and 1967); and Pete Sampras of the USA (two Australian, six Wimbledon, and four US between 1990 and 1999).

The most Grand Slam tournament wins by a doubles partnership is 20, by Althea Brough and Margaret Du Pont (both USA): three French, 12 US, and five Wimbledon from 1942 to 1957; and by Martina Navrátilová and Pam Shriver (both USA): seven Australian, four French, four US, and five Wimbledon from 1981 to 1989.

John Newcombe and Tony Roche (both Australia) won 12 men's doubles Grand Slam titles (four Australian, two French, one US, and five Wimbledon) between 1965 and 1976.

MOST WIMBLEDON WINS

Billie-Jean King (USA) won a record 20 titles between 1961 and 1979: six singles, 10 women's doubles, and four mixed doubles.

Elizabeth Ryan (USA) won 19 doubles titles (12 women's and seven mixed) from 1914 to 1934.

Martina Navrátilová has won nine women's singles titles: in 1978, 1979, 1982–87, and 1990.

The most titles won in the men's championships is 13, by Hugh Doherty (GB), with five singles titles (1902–06) and eight men's doubles titles (1897–1901 and 1903–05).

YOUNGEST AND OLDEST WIMBLEDON CHAMPIONS

Martina Hingis (Switzerland) was 15 years, 282 days old when she won the women's doubles with Helena Sukova (Czech Republic) in 1996.

Margaret Du Pont (USA) was 44 years, 125 days old when she won the mixed doubles with Neale Fraser (Australia) in 1962.

MOST APPEARANCES AT WIMBLEDON

Arthur Gore (GB) made a record 36 appearances at Wimbledon between 1888 and 1927.

Jean Borotra (France) participated in the men's singles competition 35 times between 1922 and 1964. He then went on to play in the veterans' doubles until 1977, when he was 78.

MOST US OPEN WINS

Margaret Du Pont won 25 titles between 1941 and 1960: 13 women's doubles (12 with Althea Brough), nine mixed doubles, and three singles.

The men's record is 16, by Bill Tilden (USA), including seven men's singles titles (1920–25 and 1929). The singles record is shared with Richard Sears (USA): 1881–87; and William Larned (USA): 1901, 1902, and 1907–11.

The most women's singles titles is eight, by Molla Mallory (USA): 1915–18, 1920–22, and 1926.

YOUNGEST AND OLDEST US OPEN WINNERS

Vincent Richards (USA) was 15 years, 139 days old when he won the men's doubles with Bill Tilden (USA) in 1918.

The youngest men's singles champion was Pete Sampras (USA), who won the title in 1990, aged 19 years, 28 days.

The youngest women's champion was Tracy Austin (USA), who won the 1979 women's singles aged 16 years, 271 days.

The oldest singles champion was William Larned (USA), who was 38 years, 242 days old when he won the 1911 men's singles.

The oldest women's champion was Margaret Du Pont (USA), who was 42 years, 166 days old when she won the 1960 mixed doubles.

MOST FRENCH OPEN WINS

Margaret Court won a record 13 titles from 1962 to 1973: five singles, four women's doubles, and four mixed doubles.

The women's singles record is seven, achieved by Chris Evert of the USA (1974, 1975, 1979, 1980, 1983, 1985, and 1986).

⊙ MOST WIMBLEDON MEN'S SINGLES WINS

Pete Sampras (USA) holds the record for the most Wimbledon men's singles titles, with a total of six (1993–95 and 1997–99). He also holds the career earnings record for men, having made $38,808,561 to the end of 1999.

↓ FASTEST SERVICE

Greg Rusedski (GB) achieved a record serve of 149 m.p.h. during the ATP Champions' Cup at Indian Wells, California, USA, on March 14, 1998. The fastest server in the women's game is Venus Williams (USA), who recorded a serve of 127.4 m.p.h. during the European Indoor Championships at Zürich, Switzerland, on Oct. 16, 1998.

Henri Cochet (France) won nine titles (four singles, three men's doubles, and two mixed doubles) between 1926 and 1930.

MOST AUSTRALIAN OPEN WINS

Margaret Court won a record 23 titles: 11 women's singles (1960–66, 1969–71, and 1973), eight women's doubles (1961–63, 1965, 1969–71, and 1973), and four mixed doubles (1963–65 and 1969).

Roy Emerson (Australia) won a record six men's singles titles: in 1961 and from 1963 to 1967.

MOST ATP TOUR WORLD CHAMPIONSHIP WINS

Ivan Lendl (Czechoslovakia) won five titles: in 1982, 1983, 1986 (two), and 1987, appearing in nine successive finals between 1980 and 1988.

John McEnroe and Peter Fleming (both USA) won a record seven doubles titles between 1978 and 1984.

Baseball

⊙ MOST WORLD SERIES WINS
Played annually between the winners of the National League (NL) and the American League (AL), the World Series was first staged unofficially in 1903, and was held officially from 1905. The New York Yankees (AL) hold the record of 25 wins, achieved between 1923 and 1999. Yankees pitcher Roger Clemens is pictured above.

MOST GAMES PLAYED
Pete Rose played in 3,562 games and was at bat 14,053 times for the Cincinnati Reds (NL, 1963–78 and 1984–86), the Philadelphia Phillies (NL, 1979–83), and the Montreal Expos (NL, 1984).

Cal Ripken Jr. played 2,632 consecutive games for the Baltimore Orioles (AL) from May 30, 1982, to Sept. 19, 1998.

In 1962, Maury Wills played 165 games for the Los Angeles Dodgers (NL) in one season.

MOST HOME RUNS
Hank Aaron holds the major league career record with 755 home runs: 733 for the Milwaukee Braves (NL, 1954–65) and Atlanta Braves (NL, 1966–74), and 22 for the Milwaukee Brewers (AL) in 1975 and 1976.

George Herman "Babe" Ruth hit 714 home runs in 8,399 times at bat – a record rate of 8.5%.

Mark McGwire hit 70 home runs in 162 games for the St. Louis Cardinals (NL) in the 1998 season.

Sammy Sosa of the Chicago Cubs (NL) holds the record for the most home runs in one month, hitting 20 in June 1998.

The most home runs in a week is 10, by Frank Howard of the Washington Senators (AL), from May 12 to 18, 1968.

The most consecutive games hitting home runs is eight, by Dale Long for the Pittsburgh Pirates (NL) in May 1956; Don Mattingly for the New York Yankees (AL) in July 1987; and Ken Griffey Jr. for the Seattle Mariners (AL) in July 1993.

MOST AT BATS IN A SEASON
The record for the most at bats in a season is 705, achieved by Willie Wilson of the Kansas City Royals (AL), in 1980.

ONLY 40/40 CLUB MEMBERS
Three players have hit 40 home runs and stolen 40 bases in a season: Jose Canseco (Oakland Athletics, AL) in 1988, Barry Bonds (San Francisco Giants, NL) in 1996, and Alex Rodriguez (Seattle Mariners, AL) in 1998.

MOST GAMES PITCHED
By April 27, 2000, Jesse Orosco had pitched 1,093 games for the New York Mets (NL), L.A. Dodgers (NL), Cleveland Indians (AL), Milwaukee Brewers (AL), Baltimore Orioles (AL), and St. Louis Cardinals (NL).

MOST GAMES WON BY A PITCHER
The most games won by a pitcher is 511, by Cy Young, who also played 749 complete games in his career: for Cleveland (NL, 1890–98), St. Louis (NL, 1899–1900), Boston (AL, 1901–08), Cleveland (AL, 1909–11), and Boston (NL, 1911). He pitched a record total of 7,356 innings.

Carl Hubbell pitched the New York Giants (AL) to a record 24 consecutive wins: 16 in 1936 and eight in 1937.

MOST CONSECUTIVE SCORELESS INNINGS
Orel Hershiser of the L.A. Dodgers (NL) pitched 59 consecutive scoreless innings from Aug. 30 to Sept. 28, 1988.

MOST VALUABLE WORLD SERIES PLAYERS
Three men have won the Most Valuable Player award twice: Sandy Koufax (Los Angeles Dodgers, NL, 1963, 1965); Bob Gibson (St. Louis Cardinals, NL, 1964, 1967); and Reggie Jackson (Oakland Athletics, AL, 1973, and New York Yankees, AL, 1977).

YOUNGEST PLAYERS
Joseph Henry Nuxhall played one game for the Cincinatti Reds (NL), aged 15 years, 314 days, in June 1944. He did not play again in the National League until 1952.

⊙ LONGEST HOME RUN
The record for the longest measured home run in a major league game is 634 ft. It was achieved by Mickey Mantle for the New York Yankees (AL) against the Detroit Tigers (AL) at Briggs Stadium, Detroit, Michigan, USA, on Sept. 10, 1960.

The youngest player in a World Series was Fred Lindstrom, who was 18 years, 339 days old when he played for the New York Giants (NL) on Oct. 24, 1924.

OLDEST PLAYERS
Leroy "Satchel" Paige pitched for the Kansas City Athletics (AL) aged 59 years, 80 days on Sept. 25, 1965.

The oldest World Series player was Jack Quinn of the Philadelphia Athletics. He was 47 years, 91 days old when he played on Oct. 4, 1930.

MOST NATIONAL LEAGUE TITLES
The record for the most National League titles is 18, held by the L.A. Dodgers (formerly the Brooklyn Robins and the Brooklyn Dodgers).

LONGEST GAMES
The Brooklyn Dodgers (NL) and the Boston Braves (NL) played to a 1–1 tie after 26 innings on May 1, 1920.

The Chicago White Sox (AL) played the longest game in elapsed time – 8 hr. 6 min. –

before beating the Milwaukee Brewers 7–6 in the 25th inning on May 9, 1984.

MOST SPECTATORS
An estimated 114,000 spectators watched a demonstration game between Australia and a US Services team during the Olympic Games in Melbourne, Australia, on Dec. 1, 1956.

The record World Series attendance is 420,784, for the six games between Oct. 1 and 8, 1959, when the L.A. Dodgers beat the Chicago White Sox 4–2.

The US single-game attendance record is 92,706, for the fifth game of this series, played at the Memorial Coliseum, Los Angeles, California, USA, on Oct. 6 1959.

A record total of 4,483,350 people attended the home games of the Colorado Rockies (NL) in the course of the 1993 season.

The record for the highest ever season attendance for all major league baseball games is 70,372,221, set in 1998.

↓ MOST OLYMPIC WINS
Baseball became a full Olympic sport in 1992, and the gold medals in both 1992 and 1996 were taken by Cuba. Cuba has also won the World Cup a record 22 times, between 1939 and 1998.

Cricket

BEST TEST ALL-ROUNDERS
The best all-round record is that of Kapil Dev (India), who scored 5,248 runs (averaging 31.05), took 434 wickets (averaging 29.64), and held 64 catches in 131 matches between 1978 and 1994.

Ian Botham (England) is the only player to have scored 100 and taken eight wickets in one Test innings, with 108 and 8–34 for England v. Pakistan at Lord's, England, from June 15 to 19, 1978. He also scored 114 and took 13 wickets (6–58 and 7–48) for England v. India at Bombay, India, from Feb. 15 to 19, 1980.

Imran Khan scored 117 (6–98 and 5–82) for Pakistan v. India at Faisalabad, Pakistan, from Jan. 3 to 8, 1983.

LONGEST TEST MATCH
The longest recorded cricket match was the "timeless" Test between England and South Africa, played at Durban, South Africa, from March 3 to 14, 1939. It was abandoned after 10 days (one was rained off) because the ship taking the visitors home was due to leave. The total playing time was 43 hrs. 16 min., and a record Test match aggregate of 1,981 runs was scored.

HIGHEST TEST INNINGS
Sri Lanka scored 952–6 v. India at Colombo, Sri Lanka, from Aug. 4 to 6, 1997.

Brian Lara scored 375, a record for a Test batsman, in 12 hrs. 48 min. for West Indies v. England at Recreation Ground, St. John's, Antigua, from April 16 to 18, 1994.

MOST WICKETS IN A TEST INNINGS
Two bowlers have taken all 10 wickets in a Test match innings. Jim Laker took 10–53 in his second innings for England v. Australia at the Old Trafford stadium, Manchester, England, on July 31, 1956; and Anil Kumble (India) took 10–74 for India v. Pakistan at Ferozeshah Kolta Stadium, New Delhi, India, on Feb. 7, 1999. Laker had taken 9–37 in his first innings, giving him a first-class record of 19 wickets in a match.

HIGHEST ODI SCORES
The highest innings score in a one-day international is 398–5, by Sri Lanka v. Kenya in a World Cup match in Kandy, Sri Lanka, on March 6, 1996.

The highest innings score between Test-playing nations is 376–2, by India v. New Zealand at Hyderabad, India, on Nov. 8, 1999.

The biggest victory margin is 232, by Australia v. Sri Lanka (323–2 to 91) in Australia, on Jan. 28, 1985.

⊙ MOST ODI WICKETS
The most wickets taken in one-day internationals is 423 (an average of 23.64), by Wasim Akram (Pakistan) in 303 matches between 1985 and 2000.

LOWEST ODI SCORE
The lowest completed innings total on record is 43, scored by Pakistan v. West Indies in Cape Town, South Africa, on Feb. 25, 1993.

HIGHEST ODI PARTNERSHIP
The highest-scoring batting partnership in a one-day international is 331, by Sachin Tendulkar (186 not out) and Rahul Dravid (153) for India v. New Zealand at Hyderabad, India, on Nov. 8, 1999.

⊙ 150S AGAINST MOST NATIONS
On March 26, 2000, during the second Test against New Zealand, Australian captain Steve Waugh became the first cricketer to have scored 150 runs in an innings against all eight Test-playing nations.

HIGHEST INNINGS

Brian Lara scored 501 not out in 7 hrs. 54 min. for Warwickshire v. Durham at Edgbaston, England, in June 1994.

LONGEST INDIVIDUAL INNINGS

Rajiv Nayyar (India) batted for 16 hrs. 55 min. when scoring 271 for Himachal Pradesh v. Jammu and Kashmir at Chamba, India, from Nov. 1 to 3, 1999.

The longest innings without scoring is 101 minutes, by Geoff Allott for New Zealand v. South Africa at Auckland on March 2, 1999. Allott faced 77 deliveries.

MOST RUNS OFF AN OVER

The first batsman to score 36 runs off a six-ball over was Gary Sobers, off the bowling of Malcolm Nash, for Nottinghamshire v. Glamorgan at Swansea, Wales, on Aug. 31, 1968. His record was equaled by Ravi Shastri for Bombay v. Baroda at Bombay, India, on Jan. 10, 1985, off Tilak Raj Sharma.

HIGHEST INNINGS IN THE WORLD CUP FOR THE BLIND

The highest individual score in the inaugural World Cup for the Blind was 262 not out, by Mansood Jan for Pakistan v. South Africa at Roshanara Club, New Delhi, India, on Nov. 19, 1998.

BEST BOWLING IN THE WORLD CUP FOR THE BLIND

The best bowling analysis was 3–12, by Bhalaji Damor for India v. Sri Lanka at Roshanara Club on Nov. 18, 1998.

MOST INTERNATIONAL APPEARANCES BY A WOMAN

The most international appearances by a female cricketer is 126 (19 Tests and 107 one-day internationals), by Deborah Hockley (New Zealand) between 1979 and 2000.

FASTEST BOWLER

The highest electronically measured speed for a ball bowled is 99.7 m.p.h., by Jeff Thomson for Australia v. West Indies in Dec. 1975.

YOUNGEST PLAYERS

The youngest first-class player is reputed to be Esmail Ahmed Baporia (India), who played for Gujarat v. Baroda at Ahmedabad, India, on Jan. 10, 1951, aged 11 years, 261 days.

The youngest Test player is Mushtaq Mohammad, who was 15 years, 124 days old when he played for Pakistan v. West Indies at Lahore, Pakistan, on March 26, 1959.

The youngest Test captain was the Nawab of Pataudi, who was 21 years, 77 days old when he led India v. West Indies at Bridgetown, Barbados, on March 23, 1962.

OLDEST PLAYERS

The oldest player in first-class cricket was Raja Maharaj Singh, one of the governors of Bombay, India. He was 72 years, 192 days old when he batted (scoring 4) for his own XI against a Commonwealth XI on the opening day of a match played at Bombay from Nov. 25 to 27, 1950.

The oldest player to represent a country recognized by the International Cricket Council is Wally Glynn, who was 65 years, 269 days old when he played for Malta v. Greece during the European Cricket Federation Nations' Championship at Zuoz, Switzerland, on Aug. 21, 1997.

OLDEST UMPIRE

Joe Filliston (UK), who died in 1964, applied to become an umpire at the age of 82, and was still umpiring at the age of 100.

HIGHEST ATTENDANCES

The greatest attendance for one day of a cricket match is 90,800, for the second day of the Test between Australia and the West Indies at Melbourne, Australia, on Feb. 11, 1961.

The biggest crowd for one match is an estimated 394,000 over five days, for the Test between India and England at Calcutta, India, from Jan. 1 to 6, 1982.

The record for a Test series is 933,513, for Australia v. England (five matches) in 1936/37.

The record for a limited-overs game is an estimated 90,450 at Calcutta, India, on Nov. 10, 1991, to see India play South Africa on the latter's return to official international cricket.

→ MOST TEST WICKETS

Courtney Walsh (West Indies) claimed his 435th victim in 114 Tests on March 27, 2000, during the second Test against Zimbabwe at his home ground, Sabina Park, Kingston, Jamaica. The batsman was Henry Olonga, caught by Wavell Hinds.

Ball Sports 1

MOST VOLLEYBALL WORLD CHAMPIONSHIPS

The USSR has won six men's titles: 1949, 1952, 1960, 1962, 1978, and 1982.

The record number of women's titles is five, by the USSR: 1952, 1956, 1960, 1970, and 1990.

MOST OLYMPIC VOLLEYBALL WINS

The USSR has won a record four women's titles (1968, 1972, 1980, and 1988); and three men's titles (1964, 1968, and 1980).

MOST OLYMPIC VOLLEYBALL MEDALS

The only player to have won four Olympic medals is Inna Ryskal (USSR), who took silver in 1964 and 1976, and gold in 1968 and 1972.

The men's record is three, held by Yuriy Poyarkov of the USSR (gold in 1964 and 1968 and bronze in 1972); Katsutoshi Nekoda of Japan (gold in 1972, silver in 1968 ,and bronze in 1964); and Steve Timmons of the USA (gold in 1984 and 1988, and bronze in 1992).

MOST AVP BEACH VOLLEYBALL TITLES

Karch Kiraly (USA) had won a record 141 AVP (Association of Volleyball Professionals) tour titles to the end of the 1999 season, with record AVP tour earnings of $2,844,065 by April 2000.

⊙ MOST WORLD HANDBALL CHAMPIONSHIPS

The most men's indoor titles is four, by Sweden (1954, 1958, 1990, and 1999); and by Romania (1961, 1964, 1970, and 1974). The outdoor title has been won five times, by West Germany between 1938 and 1966. Here, a member of the Swedish team (left) is pictured in Sweden's 1999 final against Croatia.

⊙ MOST NETBALL WORLD CHAMPIONSHIPS

Australia has won the World Championships a record eight times: in 1963, 1971, 1975, 1979, 1983, 1991, 1995, and 1999. Liz Ellis (Australia, left) is seen here with Alex Astle (England) during the 1999 semifinals.

MOST INTERNATIONAL NETBALL APPEARANCES

Kendra Slawinski (GB) made a record 128 international appearances between 1981 and 1995.

MOST WOMEN'S WORLD HANDBALL CHAMPIONSHIPS

A record three women's titles have been won by: Romania (outdoor in 1956 and 1960, and indoor in 1962); East Germany (indoor in 1971, 1975, and 1978); and the USSR (indoor in 1982, 1986, and 1990).

MOST OLYMPIC HANDBALL TITLES

The USSR has won the men's title a record three times: in 1976, 1988, and 1992 (the last as the CIS).

The most women's titles is two, by the USSR (1976 and 1980); and South Korea (1988 and 1992).

HIGHEST INTERNATIONAL HANDBALL SCORE

The record for the highest score in an international match was set in Aug. 1981, when the USSR beat Afghanistan 86–2 in the "Friendly Army Tournament" in Miskolc, Hungary.

MOST WORLD KORFBALL CHAMPIONSHIPS

The most wins in the World Championships is five, by the Netherlands: 1978, 1984, 1987, 1995, and 1999.

HIGHEST KORFBALL SCORE

The highest score by a team in the finals of the World Championships is 23, by the Netherlands v. Belgium (who scored 11) in 1999.

BIGGEST KORFBALL TOURNAMENT

On June 12, 1999, a record 1,796 players took part in the Kom Keukens/Ten Donck International Youth Korfball Tournament in Ridderkerk, Netherlands.

MOST AFL LEAGUE PREMIERSHIPS

The greatest number of AFL League Premierships is 16, by Carlton between 1906 and 1995.

MOST GOALS IN AN AFL SEASON

The highest number of goals scored in an AFL season is 150, by Bob Pratt (South Melbourne) in 1934; and Peter Hudson (Hawthorn) in 1971.

MOST AFL GAMES
The record for the most AFL games played is held by Michael Tuck (Hawthorn), with 426 between 1972 and 1991.

MOST TENPIN BOWLING WORLD CUPS
The World Cup, which was instituted in 1965, is contested annually by the national champions of the Fédération Internationale des Quilleurs (FIQ). The highest number of wins is four, by Paeng Nepomuceno (Philippines): 1976, 1980, 1992, and 1996.

MOST PROFESSIONAL BOWLING ASSOCIATION TITLES
Earl Anthony (USA) won a record 41 PBA titles in the course of his career.

LONGEST BOWLING MARATHON
Thomas Becker (USA) bowled for a record 24 hrs. 41 min. at the Brunswick Superbowl Lanes, Littleton, Colorado, USA, from Feb. 28 to March 1, 1999.

MOST OUTDOOR BOWLS WORLD CHAMPIONSHIPS
The Leonard Trophy has been won four times by Scotland: 1972, 1984, 1992, and 1996.

David Bryant (GB) has won a record six World Championship gold medals: three singles titles (1966, 1980, and 1988), one triples title (1980), and the Leonard Trophy in 1980 and 1988.

Margaret Johnston (Ireland) has won a record five women's titles: the singles in 1992 and 2000, and the pairs in 1988, 1992, and 1996. Elsie Wilke (New Zealand) has also won two women's singles titles, in 1969 and 1974.

David Bryant and Tony Allcock have won the pairs six times: in 1986, 1987, and from 1989 to 1992.

HIGHEST BOWLS SCORES
The highest score in a fours match (21 ends) is 67–5, by Sorrento Bowling Club v. Sportsmans (both Australia) at Duncraig, Western Australia, on March 14, 1998.

The highest score in an international match is 63–1, a record set when Swaziland beat Japan in a World Championships match in Melbourne, Australia, on Jan. 16, 1980.

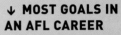

↓ MOST GOALS IN AN AFL CAREER
Tony Lockett (right) scored a record 1,357 AFL career goals between 1983 and his retirement in 1999. He is seen here with Nathan Burke, playing for Sydney against St. Kilda in the 11th round of the 1999 season.

Ball Sports 2

⊙ FASTEST BALL SPEED

The fastest speed reached by a ball in any ball game is approximately 188 m.p.h. in pelota. This compares with a recorded speed of 170 m.p.h. for a golf ball driven off a tee.

MOST PELOTA
WORLD CHAMPIONSHIPS

The Federación Internacional de Pelota Vasca has held World Championships every four years since 1952. The most wins is seven, by Juan Labat (Argentina) between 1952 and 1966; and by Riccardo Bizzozero (Argentina) between 1970 and 1982.

The most successful pair are Juan Labat and Roberto Elías (Argentina), who won the Trinquete Share four times: in 1952, 1958, 1962, and 1966.

The most wins in the long court game, Cesta Punta, is three, by José Hamuy of Mexico (with two different partners): in 1958, 1962, and 1966.

MOST SQUASH
WORLD CHAMPIONSHIPS

Jahangir Khan (Pakistan) has won six World Open titles: from 1981 to 1985, and in 1988. He has also won the International Squash Rackets Federation world individual title three times: in 1979, 1983, and 1985.

Susan Devoy (New Zealand) has won a record four women's World Open titles: in 1985, 1987, 1990, and 1992.

The most men's world team titles won is six, by Australia (1967, 1969, 1971, 1973, 1989 and 1991); and by Pakistan (1977, 1981, 1983, 1985, 1987, and 1993).

The most women's world team titles won is also six, by Australia: in 1981, 1983, 1992, 1994, 1996, and 1998.

SHORTEST CHAMPIONSHIP
SQUASH MATCH

In a British Open match played at Lamb's Squash Club, London, England, on April 9, 1992, Philip Kenyon (GB) beat Salah Nadi (Egypt) in just 6 min. 37 sec. The score was 9–0, 9–0, 9–0.

LONGEST CHAMPIONSHIP
SQUASH MATCH

The longest ever championship match lasted for 2 hrs. 45 min., a record set when Jahangir Khan (Pakistan) beat Gamal Awad (Egypt) 9–10, 9–5, 9–7, 9–2 in the final of the Patrick International Festival at Chichester, W. Sussex, England, on March 30, 1983. The first set alone lasted for a record 1 hr. 11 min.

FASTEST SQUASH BALL SPEED

In Jan. 1988, Roy Buckland (GB) served a squash ball at a speed of 144.6 m.p.h. during tests at the Wimbledon Squash and Badminton Club, London, England. The ball's initial speed at the racket was 150.8 m.p.h.

MOST TABLE TENNIS
WORLD CHAMPIONSHIPS

The greatest number of women's team titles (the Marcel Corbillon Cup) is 13, by China: in 1965, 1975, 1977, 1979, 1981, 1983, 1985, 1987, 1989, 1993, 1995, 1997, and 2000.

The most men's team titles (the Swaythling Cup) is 12, by Hungary (1926, 1928–31, 1933 – two titles – 1935, 1938, 1949, 1952, and 1979); and by China (1961, 1963, 1965, 1971, 1975, 1977, 1981, 1983, 1985, 1987, 1995, and 1997).

MOST WORLD RACKETBALL
CHAMPIONSHIPS

The World Racketball Championships, which are based around the US version of the game, racquetball, were instituted in 1981 and have been held biennially since 1984. The USA has won a record nine team titles: in 1981, 1984, 1986 (jointly with Canada), 1988, 1990, 1992, 1994, 1996, and 1998.

MOST INTERNATIONAL FIELD
HOCKEY APPEARANCES

By Jan. 2000, Jaques Brinkman had represented the Netherlands in a record 316 international games.

HIGHEST FIELD HOCKEY
SCORES

The record for the highest score by a team in a men's international game is held by India, who defeated the USA 24–1 during the 1932 Olympic Games in Los Angeles, California, USA.

The record by a women's team was set in London, England, on Feb. 3, 1923, when England beat France 23–0.

MOST INTERNATIONAL
CAREER FIELD HOCKEY
GOALS

Paul Litjens (Netherlands) has scored a record 267 goals in 177 international games.

MOST ROLLER HOCKEY
WORLD CHAMPIONSHIPS

Portugal won a record 14 roller hockey world titles between 1947 and 1993.

⊙ MOST SQUASH
WORLD OPEN TITLES

Jansher Khan (Pakistan) has won a record eight World Open titles: in 1987, 1989 and 1990, and from 1992 to 1996.

HIGHEST LACROSSE SCORES
The record for the highest team score in an international game is by the Great Britain and Ireland women's team, who defeated US team Long Island 40–0 during their 1967 tour of the USA.

The record for the highest team score in a men's World Cup game was set on July 25, 1994, when Scotland beat Germany 34–3 in Greater Manchester, England.

The record score for a lacrosse team in the World Cup Premier Division is the USA's 33–2 win over Japan in Greater Manchester, England, on July 21, 1994.

⊙ MOST LACROSSE INTERNATIONALS
Vivien Jones played in 99 international games between 1977 and 1999: 87 for Wales, nine for the Celts, and three for Great Britain.

MOST POOL WORLD TITLES
Ralph Greenleaf (USA) won the world professional pool title a record 19 times between 1919 and 1937.

FASTEST POOL TABLE CLEARANCES
The shortest time in which anyone has potted all 15 balls is 26.5 seconds, by Dave Pearson (GB) at Pepper's Bar and Grill, Windsor, Ontario, Canada, on April 4, 1997.

The women's record is 37.07 seconds, by Susan Thompson (GB) at the Phoenix Pool & Snooker Club, Wallasey, England, on Dec. 1, 1996.

HIGHEST SNOOKER BREAKS
Tony Drago (Malta) made a break of 149 in a witnessed practice frame at West Norwood, London, England, on Feb. 1, 1995. Eddie Manning (GB) did this too at the Willie Thorne Snooker Centre, Leicester, England, on May 19, 1997. Both breaks involved a free ball, which created an "extra" red with all 15 reds still on the table.

The only "16 red" clearance in a tournament was completed by Steve James (UK), who made 135 against Alex Higgins (UK) in the World Professional Championships at Sheffield, S. Yorkshire, England, on April 14, 1990.

← MOST OLYMPIC TABLE TENNIS GOLDS
Deng Yaping (China) has won a record four Olympic titles: the women's singles and doubles (with Qiao Hang) in both 1992 and 1996. The men's record is two, by Lui Guoliang (China): the singles and doubles (with Kong Linhui) in 1996.

Track-and-field 1

MOST OLYMPIC GOLDS
The most Olympic gold medals won by a man is 10, by Raymond Ewry (USA): in the standing high, long, and triple jumps in 1900, 1904, 1906, and 1908.

The most gold medals won by a woman is four, by Fanny Blankers-Koen (Netherlands): the 100 m., 200 m. 80-m. hurdles, and 4 x 100-m. relay in 1948; Betty Cuthbert (Australia): the 100 m., 200 m., and 4 x 100-m. relay in 1956, and the 400 m. in 1964; Bärbel Wöckel (GDR): the 200 m. and 4 x 100-m. relay in both 1976 and 1980; and Evelyn Ashford (USA): the 100 m. in 1984, and the 4 x 100-m. relay in 1984, 1988, and 1992.

MOST WINS AT ONE OLYMPICS
The highest number of gold medals won at a single Olympics is five, achieved by Paavo Nurmi (Finland): the 1,500 m., 5,000 m., 10,000-m. cross-country individual, and team events, and the 3,000-m. team event in 1924.

The most medals won in individual events is four, by Alvin Kraenzlein (USA): the 60 m., 110-m. hurdles, 200-m. hurdles, and long jump in 1900.

MOST WORLD CHAMPIONSHIP MEDALS
Merlene Ottey (Jamaica) has won a record 14 medals in the World Athletics Championships, with three gold, four silver, and seven bronze from 1983 to 1997.

The most medals won by a man is 10, by Carl Lewis (USA). He took a record eight golds (100 m., long jump, and 4 x 100-m. relay in 1983; 100 m., long jump, and 4 x 100-m. relay in 1987; 100 m. and 4 x 100-m. relay in 1991), a silver in the long jump in 1991, and a bronze in the 200 m. in 1993.

MOST RECORDS SET IN A DAY
Jesse Owens (USA) set six world records in 45 minutes at Ann Arbor, Michigan, USA, on May 25, 1935. He ran 100 yds. in 9.4 sec. at 3:15 p.m., made a 26-ft. 8-in.

⊙ FASTEST 200 M. AND 400 M.
The records for the 200 m. (19.32 sec., set in Atlanta, Georgia, USA, on Aug. 1, 1996) and both the indoor and outdoor 400 m. (44.63 sec. in Atlanta on March 4, 1995, and 43.18 sec. in Seville, Spain, on Aug. 26, 1999 respectively) are all held by Michael Johnson (USA).

long jump at 3:25 p.m., ran 220 yds. (and 200 m.) in 20.3 sec. at 3:45 p.m., then covered the 220-yd. (and 200-m.) low hurdles at 4 p.m.

LONGEST WINNING SEQUENCE
The record at a track event is 122, by Ed Moses (USA) at the 400-m. hurdles between Aug. 1977 and June 1987.

FASTEST MASS RELAYS
The fastest time for a 100 x 100-m. relay is 19 min. 14.19 sec., set by a team from Antwerp at Merksem, Belgium, on Sept. 23, 1989.

The fastest time for a 100 x 1-mile relay is 7 hrs. 35 min. 55.4 sec., by the Canadian Milers Athletic Club at York

⊙ LONGEST DISTANCE COVERED IN ONE HOUR
Tegla Loroupe (Kenya) covered a distance of 18,340 m. (11 miles 697.4 yds.) in one hour at Bergholzhausen, Germany, on Aug. 7, 1998. The men's record is 21,101 m. (13 miles 197 yds.), set by Artur Barrios (Mexico, now USA) at La Flèche, France, on March 30, 1991.

University, Toronto, Canada, on Dec. 20, 1998.

The record for a team of 211 runners running the standard marathon distance (210 x 200 m., 1 x 195 m.) is 1 hr. 38 min. 50.97 sec., by the Kanagawa Prefecture High School Sport Federation at Hiratsuka Stadium, Japan, on May 5, 1998.

FASTEST WOMEN'S MARATHON
The women's official world marathon record is 2 hrs. 20 min. 43 sec., achieved by Tegla Loroupe (Kenya) in Berlin, Germany, on Sept. 26, 1999.

OLDEST MARATHON
The Boston Marathon, the world's longest-running major marathon, was first held on April 19, 1897, when it was run over a distance of 24 miles 1,232 yds. John A. Kelley (USA) finished the marathon 61 times between 1928 and 1992, winning in 1933 and 1945.

HIGHEST MARATHON
The biennial Everest Marathon, first run on Nov. 27, 1987, is the highest marathon in the world. It begins at an altitude of 17,100 ft. at Gorak Shep and ends at Namche Bazar (both Nepal), at an altitude of 11,300 ft. The fastest times to complete this race are 3 hrs. 56 min. 10 sec., by Hari Roka (Nepal) in 1999; and 5 hrs. 16 min. 3 sec., by Anne Stentiford (UK) in 1997.

MOST MARATHON COMPETITORS
The record number of confirmed finishers in a marathon is 38,706, at the centennial race in Boston, Massachusetts, USA, on April 15, 1996.

A record 105 men ran the London Marathon, England, in under 2 hrs. 20 min., and 46 in under 2 hrs. 15 min., on April 21, 1991; and a record 11 men ran the Boston Marathon, USA, in under 2 hrs. 10 min. on April 18, 1994.

On Aug. 5, 1984, a record nine women ran the first women's Olympic marathon, held in Los Angeles, California, USA, in under 2 hrs. 30 min.

→ FASTEST MARATHON
Khalid Khannouchi (Morocco) ran the Chicago Marathon, Illinois, USA, in a record 2 hrs. 5 min. 42 sec. on Oct. 24, 1999. He took 23 seconds off the previous record, set by Ronaldo da Costa (Brazil) on Sept. 20, 1998.

MOST MARATHONS COMPLETED
Horst Preisler (Germany) completed 949 marathons between 1974 and March 2000.

FASTEST INTERCONTINENTAL MARATHON COMPLETION
Tim Rogers (GB) completed a marathon on each of the seven continents in 99 days between Feb. 13 and May 23, 1999. He began with the Antarctica Marathon on King Jorge Island, and followed with marathons in the USA (North and Central America), South Africa (Africa), France (Europe), Brazil (South America), and Hong Kong (Asia), before finishing with a marathon at Huntly, New Zealand (Oceania).

Kimi Puntillo (USA) completed a marathon on each of the seven continents in 700 days between Nov. 3, 1996, and Oct. 4, 1998. She began with the New York Marathon (North and Central America) and also ran marathons in Antarctica, London (Europe), Nepal (Asia), Tanzania (Africa), and Sydney (Oceania), before finishing with a marathon in Argentina (South America).

FASTEST HALF-MARATHONS
The world's best time for a half-marathon on a properly measured course is 59 min. 5 sec., by Paul Tergat (Kenya) in Lisbon, Portugal, on March 26, 2000.

The women's official half-marathon record is 66 min. 43 sec., by Masako Chika (Japan) at Tokyo, Japan, on April 19, 1997.

Track-and-field 2

OLDEST OLYMPIC TRACK-AND-FIELD MEDALISTS

The oldest winner of an event was Patrick "Babe" Macdonald (USA). He was 42 years, 26 days old when he won the 56-lb. weight throw in Belgium in 1920.

The oldest medalist was Tebbs Lloyd Johnson (GB). He was 48 years, 115 days old when he won a bronze medal in the 50,000-m. walk in London, England, in 1948.

The oldest female medalist was Dana Zátopková (Czechoslovakia), who was 37 years, 348 days old when she took silver in the javelin in Rome, Italy, in 1960.

YOUNGEST OLYMPIC TRACK-AND-FIELD CHAMPIONS

The youngest gold medalist in a track-and-field event was Barbara Jones (USA). She was 15 years, 123 days old when she ran in the winning 4 x 100-m. relay team at Helsinki, Finland, in July 1952.

The youngest men's champion was Bob Mathias (USA), in the decathlon in London, England, in 1948, aged 17 years 263 days.

YOUNGEST AND OLDEST TRACK-AND-FIELD RECORD-BREAKERS

Wang Yan (China) was 14 years, 334 days old when she set an individual women's 5,000-m. walk record of 21 min. 33.8 sec. in China on March 9, 1986.

The youngest man to break an individual record was Thomas Ray (GB). He pole-vaulted 11 ft. 2.5 in. aged 17 years, 198 days on Sept. 19, 1879.

Marina Styepanova (USSR) set a 400-m. hurdle record at Tashkent, USSR (now Uzbekistan) on Sept. 17, 1986, aged 36 years, 139 days.

Gerhard Weidner (West Germany) set a 20-mile walk record aged 41 years, 71 days at Hamburg, Germany, on May 24, 1974.

⊙ MOST DECATHLON POINTS

Tomas Dvorak (Czech Republic) scored a record 8,994 points in the decathlon in Prague, Czech Republic, on July 3–4, 1999. He is seen here taking part in the shot event, where he recorded a distance of 54 ft. 11.8 in.

⊙ LONGEST JAVELIN THROWS

The longest javelin throw by a woman is 220 ft. 1 in., by Mirela Manjani-Tzelili (Greece) at Seville, Spain, on August 28, 1999. The men's record is 323 ft. 1 in., by Jan Zelezny (Czech Republic) at Jena, Germany, on May 25, 1996.

MOST WORLD TRIATHLON CHAMPIONSHIPS

The World Triathlon Championship has been won four times by Simon Lessing (GB): in 1992, 1995, 1996, and 1998.

The most wins in the women's event is two, by Michelle Jones of Australia (1992 and 1993); Karen Smyers of the USA (1990 and 1995); and Emma Carney of Australia (1995 and 1997).

An unofficial World Championship has been held annually in Nice, France, since 1982. The race is made up of a 4,000-m. swim (3,200 m. prior to 1988), a 120-km. bicycle ride, and a 32-km. run. Mark Allen (USA) has won a record 10 times: from 1982 to 1986 and from 1989 to 1993.

Paula Newby-Fraser (Zimbabwe) has had a record four women's wins: from 1989 to 1992.

BEST WORLD TRIATHLON CHAMPIONSHIP TIMES

The best men's World Championship time is 1 hr. 39 min. 50 sec., by Simon Lessing (GB) in Cleveland, Ohio, USA, in 1996.

The fastest time by a woman is 1 hr. 50 min. 52 sec., by Jackie Gallagher (Australia) in Cleveland, Ohio, USA, in 1996.

The record times in the unofficial championship are: 5 hrs. 46 min. 10 sec., by Mark Allen (USA) in 1986; and 6 hrs. 27 min. 6 sec., by Erin Baker (New Zealand) in 1988.

LONGEST TRIATHLON
In 17 days 22 hrs. 50 min. between March 21 and April 8, 1998, David Holleran (Australia) completed a triathlon of 1,578 miles. It consisted of a 42-km. swim, a 2,000-km. bicycle ride, and a 500-km. run.

MOST INDOOR PENTATHLON POINTS
The most points is 4,991, by Irina Belova (CIS) in Berlin, Germany, on Feb. 14–15, 1992. Her results were: 60-m. hurdles, 8.22 sec.; high jump, 1.93 m. (6 ft. 4 in.); shot, 13.25 m. (43 ft. 5.5 in.); long jump, 6,67 m. (21 ft. 10.5 in.); and 800 m., 2 min. 10.26 sec.

MOST POINTS IN A HEPTATHLON
The record in the heptathlon is 7,291 points, by Jackie Joyner-Kersee (USA) on Sept. 23–24, 1988, at the Olympics in Seoul, South Korea. Her results were: 100-m. hurdles, 12.69 sec.; high jump, 1.86 m. (6 ft. 1 in.); shot, 15.80 m. (51 ft. 10 in.); 200 m., 22.56 sec.; long jump, 7.27 m. (23 ft. 10 in.); javelin, 45.66 m. (149 ft. 10 in.); and 800 m., 2 min. 8.51 sec.

The men's record is 6,476 points, by Dan O'Brien (USA) at Toronto, Canada, on March 13–14, 1993. His results were: 60 m., 6.67 sec.; long jump, 7.84 m. (25 ft. 8.5 in.); shot, 16.02 m. (52 ft. 6.5 in.); high jump, 2.13 m. (6 ft. 11.75 in.); 60-m. hurdles, 7.85 sec.; pole vault, 5.20 m. (17 ft. 0.75 in.); and 1,000 m., 2 min. 57.96 sec.

HIGHEST POLE VAULTS
The highest indoor pole vault is 6.15 m. (20 ft. 2 in.), by Sergey Bubka (Ukraine) at Donetsk, Ukraine, on Feb. 21, 1993. Bubka also holds the record for the outdoor event, with a vault of 6.14 m. (20 ft. 1.75 in.) at Setriere, Italy, on July 31, 1994.

Stacey Dragila (USA) holds both the women's records, with an indoor vault of 4.62 m. (15 ft. 1.75 in.) at Atlanta, Georgia, USA, on March 3, 2000; and an outdoor vault of 4.60 m. (15 ft. 1 in.) at Seville, Spain, on Aug. 21, 1999.

LONGEST HAMMER THROWS
The longest hammer throw on record is 86.74 m. (284 ft. 7 in.), by Yuriy Sedykh (USSR) at Stuttgart, Germany, on Aug. 30, 1986.

The women's record is 76.07 m. (249 ft. 7 in.), by Mihaela Melinte (Romania) at Rudlingen, Germany, on Aug. 29, 1999.

BEST STANDING HIGH JUMPS
The best high jump from a standing position is 1.9 m. (6 ft. 2.75 in.), by Rune Almen (Sweden) at Karlstad, Sweden, on May 3, 1980.

The women's best is 1.52 m. (4 ft. 11.75 in.), by Grete Bjødalsbakka (Norway) in 1984.

BEST STANDING LONG JUMPS
The best standing long jump is 3.71 m. (12 ft. 2 in.), by Arne Tvervaag (Norway) in 1968.

The women's record is 2.92 m. (9 ft. 7 in.), by Annelin Mannes (Norway) on March 7, 1981.

← **LONGEST INDOOR TRIPLE JUMPS**
Ashia Hansen (GB) set a women's record of 15.16 m. (49 ft. 8.75 in.) in Valencia, Spain, on Feb. 28, 1998. The men's record is 17.83 m. (58 ft. 6 in.), by Alliacer Urrutia (Cuba).

Gymnastics & Weight Lifting

MOST OLYMPIC WEIGHT LIFTING MEDALS

Norbert Schemansky (USA) has won a record four Olympic medals: gold in the middle-heavyweight class in 1952; silver in the heavyweight class in 1948; and bronze in the heavyweight class in both 1960 and 1964.

Naim Suleymanoglü (Turkey) has won a record three golds: in 1988 and 1992 at 60 kg.; and in 1996 at 64 kg.

MOST OLYMPIC WEIGHT LIFTING EVENTS

Between 1960 and 1976, Imre Földi (Hungary) participated in a record five Games in the 56-kg. class, winning gold in 1972.

MOST WEIGHT LIFTING RECORDS BROKEN

Between Jan. 24, 1970, and Nov. 1, 1977, Vasiliy Alekseyev (USSR) broke 80 official world weight lifting records. He won two Olympic gold medals in this period: in 1972 and 1976.

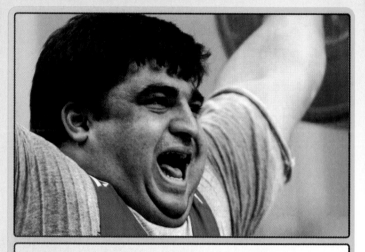

⊙ WORLD SNATCH RECORD

Hossein Rezazadeh (Iran) snatched 206 kg. in the +105-kg. class in Athens, Greece, on Nov. 28, 1999. The 21-year-old is only the fourth Iranian to have set a senior weight lifting world record.

⊙ RECORD 56-KG. CLASS LIFT

On Nov. 22, 1999, Halil Mutlu (Turkey) lifted a total of 302.5 kg., a new record for the 56-kg. class, in Athens, Greece. He also holds the 56-kg. class records for snatch (187.5 kg., also set at Athens) and for the clean and jerk (166.5 kg., set at Sofia, Bulgaria, on April 25, 2000).

MOST MEN'S WEIGHT LIFTING MEDALS

Naim Suleymanoglü has won a record 10 world titles (including Olympic titles): in 1985, 1986, 1988, 1989, and 1991–96. Born to a Turkish family in Bulgaria, he was forced to take a Bulgarian version of his last name, and competed for Bulgaria as Suleimanov until he defected to Turkey in 1986. He was banned from international competitions for a year after his defection, but subsequently competed for Turkey before retiring in 1997.

MOST WOMEN'S WEIGHT LIFTING MEDALS

Li Hongyun (China) won a record total of 13 medals in the 60/64-kg. class between 1992 and 1996.

YOUNGEST WEIGHT LIFTING RECORD BREAKER

Naim Suleimanov (Bulgaria) was just 16 years, 62 days old when he set records for clean and jerk (160 kg.) and total

(285 kg.) in the 56-kg. class, at Allentown, New Jersey, USA, on March 26, 1983.

OLDEST WEIGHT LIFTING RECORD BREAKER

Norbert Schemansky (USA) was 37 years, 333 days old when he snatched a record 362 lbs. in the then unlimited heavyweight class, in Detroit, Michigan, USA, in 1962.

MOST POWER LIFTING WORLD CHAMPIONSHIPS

The most men's world titles is 17, by Hideaki Inaba (Japan) in the 52-kg. class from 1974 to 1983 and from 1985 to 1991.

The most women's world titles is seven, by Natalya Rumyantseva (Russia) at 82.5 kg. from 1993 to 1999.

MOST OLYMPIC GYMNASTICS MEDALS

Larisa Latynina (USSR) won a total of 18 medals (nine gold, five silver, and four bronze) between 1956 and 1964 – a record for any Olympic discipline.

The men's record is 15 (seven gold, five silver, and three bronze), by Nikolay Andrianov (USSR) between 1972 and 1980.

Aleksandr Dityatin (USSR) won a record eight medals (three gold, four silver, and one bronze) at one Games, in Moscow, USSR (now Russia), in 1980.

The most individual gold medals won by a woman is seven, by Vera Caslavska-Odlozil (Czechoslovakia): three in Tokyo, Japan, in 1964, and four (one shared) in Mexico in 1968.

MOST WORLD CUP GYMNASTICS TITLES
Nikolay Andrianov, Aleksandr Dityatin, Maria Yevgenyevna (all USSR), and Li Ning (China) have each won two World Cup overall titles.

MOST RHYTHMIC GYMNASTICS INDIVIDUAL WORLD TITLES
The most overall individual world titles in rhythmic gymnastics is three, by Maria Gigova (Bulgaria): 1969, 1971, and 1973 (shared); and Maria Petrova (Bulgaria): 1993, 1994, and 1995 (shared).

In 1997, Bianka Panova (Bulgaria) won all four apparatus gold medals, all with maximum scores, and a team gold.

Marina Lobach (USSR) won the rhythmic gymnastics title with perfect scores in all six disciplines at the 1988 Olympic Games.

→ MOST RHYTHMIC GYMNASTICS TEAM WORLD TITLES
Bulgaria has won a record nine team titles: in 1969, 1971, 1981, 1983, 1985, 1987, 1989 (shared), 1993, and 1995. Maria Petrova (right) was a member of both the 1993 and 1995 teams.

YOUNGEST WORLD GYMNASTICS CHAMPIONS
Aurelia Dobre (Romania) won the women's overall world title aged 14 years, 352 days at Rotterdam, Netherlands, on Oct. 23, 1987.

In 1990, Daniela Silivas (Romania) revealed that she had been born on May 9, 1971, a year later than she had previously claimed, which meant that she was 14 years, 185 days old when she won the gold medal for balance beam on Nov. 10, 1985.

The youngest male world champion was Dmitriy Bilozerchev (USSR), who was 16 years, 315 days old when he won at Budapest, Hungary, on Oct. 28, 1983.

YOUNGEST INTERNATIONAL GYMNAST
Pasakevi Voula Kouna (Greece) was just 9 years, 299 days old at the start of the Balkan Games held at Serres, Greece, in 1981.

MOST WORLD TRAMPOLINING TITLES
The World Championships, instituted in 1964, have been held biennially since 1968. The most men's titles is five, by Aleksandr Moskalenko (Russia): three individual titles from 1990 to 1994 and two pairs, in 1992 and 1994. Brett Austine (Australia) has also won three individual titles: at double mini from 1982 to 1986.

The women's record is nine titles, achieved by Judy Wills (USA): five individual titles between 1964 and 1969, two pairs, in 1966 and 1967, and two tumbling, in 1965 and 1966.

YOUNGEST TRAMPOLINING COMPETITOR
The youngest competitor in an international trampolining event was Andrea Holmes (GB), who was 12 years, 131 days old when she took part in the World Championships in Montana, USA, on May 13, 1982.

Water Sports

⊙ LONGEST YACHT RACE

The Vendée Globe Challenge, which starts and finishes at Les Sables d'Olonne, France, is a record 22,500 nautical miles long (25,882 miles). The fastest time in which it has been completed is 105 days 20 hrs. 31 min. by Christophe Auguin (France, right) in the sloop *Geodis* in 1997.

Royal Naval Sailing Association in Aug. 1973. The race always starts in England, but the specific course, the number of legs, and the location of the stops vary every time.

CLOSEST AMERICA'S CUP RACE

The closest ever finish in an America's Cup race took place on Oct. 4, 1901, when *Shamrock II* (GB) finished two seconds ahead of *Columbia* (USA).

MOST INDIVIDUAL AMERICA'S CUP APPEARANCES

Dennis Conner (USA) competed in a record six America's Cups between 1974 and 1995.

LOWEST SCORE AT AN OLYMPIC YACHTING REGATTA

The lowest score by the winner of an Olympic regatta is three penalty points (five wins, one second place, and one disqualification from seven starts) by *Superdocious* in the Flying Dutchman class at Acapulco Bay, Mexico, in Oct. 1968. The yacht was crewed by Rodney Pattisson and Iain Macdonald-Smith (both GB).

MOST OLYMPIC YACHTING GOLDS

The most individual yachting gold medals won is four, by Paul Elvstrøm (Denmark) in the Firefly class in 1948 and in the Finn class in 1952, 1956, and 1960.

Elvstrøm also holds the record for being the first person to win individual titles at four successive Olympic Games.

OLDEST YACHT RACE

The oldest round-the-world sailing competition on record is the quadrennial Whitbread Round the World race, which was inaugurated by the UK's

MOST AMERICA'S CUP WINS AS SKIPPER

Three skippers have steered their yachts to three America's Cup title wins: Charlie Barr of the USA (1899, 1901, and 1903); Harold Vanderbilt of the USA (1930, 1934, and 1937); and Dennis Conner of the USA (1980, 1987, and 1989).

⊙ FASTEST MALE BACKSTROKE SWIMMER

Lenny Krayzelburg (USA) currently holds five backstroke world records. At the Pan Pacific swimming championships in Sydney, NSW, Australia, in Aug. 1999, he took the long-course records for the 50-m. (24.99 sec.), the 100-m. (53.60 sec.), and the 200-m. (1 min. 55.87 sec). He then went on to capture the short-course 100-m. and 200-m. records in Feb. 2000, with times of 51.28 sec. and 1 min. 52.43 sec. respectively.

MOST WORLD WATER POLO CHAMPIONSHIP WINS

The most men's World Championship wins is two, by: the USSR (1975 and 1982); Italy (1978 and 1994); and Yugoslavia (1986 and 1991).

MOST WATER POLO GOALS IN AN INTERNATIONAL CONTEST

The greatest number of goals scored in an international contest is 13, by Debbie Handley for Australia in their 16–10 win over Canada at the World Championship in Guayaquil, Ecuador, in 1982.

MOST OLYMPIC WATER POLO TITLES

Hungary has won a record six men's team titles: in 1932, 1936, 1952, 1956, 1964, and 1976.

Five men have won three Olympic gold medals: George Wilkinson (GB), in 1900, 1908, and 1912; Paul Radmilovic (GB), in 1908, 1912, and 1920; Charles Sidney Smith (GB), in 1908, 1912, and 1920; Deszö Gyarmati (Hungary), in 1952, 1956, and 1964; and György Kárpáti (Hungary), in 1952, 1956, and 1964.

MOST WORLD SWIMMING CHAMPIONSHIP MEDALS

The most World Championship medals won is 13, by Michael Gross (West Germany): five gold, five silver, and three bronze between 1982 and 1990.

The most medals won by a woman is 10, by Kornelia Ender (GDR): eight gold and two silver from 1973 to 1975.

The most gold medals won by a man is six, by James Montgomery (USA): two individual and four relay from 1973 to 1975.

The most medals won at a single World Championship is seven, by Matthew Biondi (USA): three gold, one silver, and three bronze in 1986.

MOST SWIMMING WORLD RECORDS

The most swimming world records set by a woman is 42, by Ragnhild Hveger (Denmark) between 1936 and 1942.

The most records set by a man is 32, by Arne Borg (Sweden) between 1921 and 1929.

The most records set in events that are currently recognized is 26, by Mark Spitz (USA) between 1967 and 1972. The women's record is 23, by Kornelia Ender (GDR) from 1973 to 1976.

MOST OLYMPIC SWIMMING TITLES

The greatest number of individual gold medals won is five, by Krisztina Egerszegi (Hungary): in the 100-m. backstroke in 1992, the 200-m. backstroke in 1988, 1992, and 1996, and the 400-m. medley in 1992.

The most individual gold medals won by a man is four, by: Charles Daniels of the USA (in the 100-m. freestyle in 1906 and 1908, the 220-yd. freestyle in 1904, and the 440-yd. freestyle in 1904); Roland Matthes of the GDR (in the 100-m. backstroke and the 200-m. backstroke in 1968 and 1972); Tamás Daryni of Hungary (in the 200-m. medley and the 400-m. medley in 1988 and 1992); Aleksandr Popov of Russia (in the 50-m. freestyle and the 100-m. freestyle in 1992 and 1996); and Mark Spitz of the USA (see below).

The most golds won by a swimmer is nine, by Mark Spitz: in the 4 x 100-m. freestyle and the 4 x 200-m. freestyle in 1968, and in the 100-m. freestyle, the 200-m. freestyle, the 100-m. butterfly, the 200-m. butterfly, the 4 x 100-m. freestyle, the 4 x 200-m. freestyle, and the 4 x 100-m medley in 1972.

The most golds won by a woman is six, by Kristin Otto (GDR): in the 50-m. freestyle, the 100-m. freestyle, the 100-m. backstroke, the 100-m. butterfly, the 4 x 100-m. freestyle, and the 4 x 100-m. medley in 1988.

The most Olympic medals won is 11, by Mark Spitz (nine gold, one silver, and one bronze in 1968 and 1972); and Matt Biondi of the USA (eight gold, two silver, and one bronze between 1984 and 1992).

MOST WORLD DIVING CHAMPIONSHIP WINS

Greg Louganis (USA) has won a record five world titles: the highboard in 1978, and both the springboard and high board in 1982 and 1986.

MOST OLYMPIC DIVING MEDALS

The most medals won is five, by Klaus Dibiasi of Italy (three gold and two silver from 1964 to 1976); and Greg Louganis of the USA (four gold and one silver in 1976, 1984, and 1988).

GREATEST DISTANCES SWUM IN 24 HOURS

Anders Forvass (Sweden) swam a record distance of 63.3 miles in the 25-meter Linköping public swimming pool, Sweden, on Oct. 28–29, 1989.

The record in a 50-meter pool is a distance of 62.8 miles, by Grant Robinson (Australia) at Mingara Leisure Centre, Tumbi Umbi, NSW, Australia, on June 28–29, 1997.

Hockey

MOST NHL GAMES PLAYED

Gordie Howe took part in a record 1,767 regular season games and 157 play-off games over a record 26 seasons. He played for the Detroit Red Wings from 1946 to 1971, and for the Hartford Whalers in the 1979/80 season. He also played in 419 regular season games and 78 play-off games for the Houston Aeros and the New England Whalers in the World Hockey Association (WHA) from 1973 to 1979, giving him a career total of 2,421 major league games.

MOST NHL CAREER POINTS

Wayne Gretzky (the Edmonton Oilers, the Los Angeles Kings, the St. Louis Blues and the New York Rangers) has scored a record 2,857 points from 1,487 NHL regular season and play-off games, a total that is made up of 894 goals and 1,963 assists.

HIGHEST-SCORING GAMES

The highest combined score in a World Championship game

is 58–0, a record set when Australia beat New Zealand in Perth, Western Australia, on March, 1987.

The highest combined score in an NHL game is 21, a record which occurred when the Montréal Canadiens beat the Toronto St. Patricks 14–7

on Jan. 10, 1920; and when the Edmonton Oilers beat the Chicago Black Hawks 12–9 on Dec. 11, 1985.

The most goals scored by one team is 16, a record set when the Montréal Canadiens beat the Québec Bulldogs (3) on Nov. 3, 1920.

⊙ **LONGEST NHL PICKUP GAME**

The 2000 NHL All-Star Game squad No. 5 played for a record 18 hrs. 55 min. 41 sec. during the Labatt Blue NHL pickup marathon on Feb. 2–3, 2000. The event raised money for the charity Hockey Fights Cancer.

The most points scored in a US major league game is 10, by Jim Harrison (three goals and seven assists) for Alberta, later the Edmonton Oilers, in a WHA match at Edmonton on Jan. 30, 1973. Darryl Sittler also scored 10 (six goals and four assists), for the Toronto Maple Leafs v. the Boston

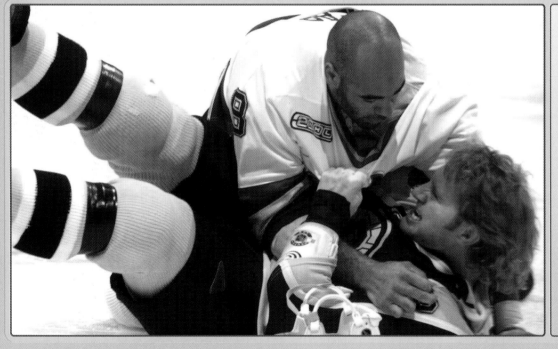

⊙ **LONGEST BAN FOR AN ON-ICE INFRACTION**

In Feb. 2000, Marty McSorley of the Boston Bruins (bottom) was suspended for 23 games following an incident during an NHL game in which he hit Donald Brashear of the Vancouver Canucks (top) on the head with his stick. They are seen here fighting earlier in the game, which took place at Vancouver, British Columbia, Canada, on Feb. 21, 2000.

Bruins in an NHL game in Toronto, Canada, on Feb. 7, 1976.

The most goals in a game is seven, by Joe Malone in the Québec Bulldogs' 10–6 win over the Toronto St. Patricks in Québec City, Canada, on Jan. 31, 1920.

The most assists in a game is seven, by Billy Taylor for Detroit v. Chicago on March 16, 1947; and three times by Wayne Gretzky for Edmonton: against Washington on Feb. 15, 1980, against Chicago on Dec. 11, 1985, and against Québec on Feb. 14, 1986.

MOST TEAM GOALS IN AN NHL SEASON

The most team goals scored in a season is 446, by the Edmonton Oilers in 1983/84, when they also achieved a record 1,182 points.

MOST SUCCESSFUL TEAMS

The Detroit Red Wings won a record 62 games in 1995/96.

The highest percentage of wins in a season is 87.5%, achieved by the Boston Bruins in 1929/30 with 38 wins in 44 games.

The longest unbeaten run during a season is 35 games (25 wins and 10 ties), by the Philadelphia Flyers from Oct. 14, 1979, to Jan. 6, 1980.

FASTEST NHL GOAL

The shortest time taken to score after the opening whistle is five seconds, by Doug Smail for the Winnipeg Jets on Dec. 20, 1981. His record was equaled by Bryan Trottier for the New York Islanders on March 22, 1984; and by Alexander Mogilny for the Buffalo Sabres on Dec. 21, 1991.

MOST NHL GOALTENDING WINS

Terry Sawchuk played a record 971 games as goaltender for Detroit, Boston, Toronto, Los Angeles, and the New York Rangers from 1949 to 1970. In this time, he achieved a record 447 wins (to 330 losses, 172 ties, and 22 no-decisions) and had a record 103 career shutouts. Jacques Plante, who had 434 NHL wins, surpassed Sawchuk's overall figure by adding 15 wins in his one season in the WHA, giving him a senior league total of 449 wins from 868 games.

Bernie Parent achieved a record 47 wins, with 13 losses and 12 ties, for Philadelphia in the 1973/74 season.

Gerry Cheevers went a record 32 successive games without defeat for the Boston Bruins in 1971/72.

MOST STANLEY CUP WINS

The Montréal Canadiens have had a record 24 wins from 32 finals: in 1916, 1924, 1930, 1931, 1944, 1946, 1953, 1956–60, 1965, 1966, 1968, 1969, 1971, 1973, 1976–9, 1986, and 1993. Joseph Henri Richard played on a record 11 cup-winning teams between 1956 and 1973.

MOST STANLEY CUP POINTS

Wayne Gretzky has scored 382 Stanley Cup points (122 goals and 260 assists) in his career. He also holds the record for the most Stanley Cup points in a season, with 47 in 1985.

→ MOST POINTS IN AN NHL SEASON

The most points in a season is 215, by Wayne Gretzky for the Edmonton Oilers in 1985/86, including a record 163 assists. Gretzky also holds the record for the most goals in a season, with 92 in 1981/82.

Winter Sports 1

MOST MEDALS IN SUMMER AND WINTER OLYMPICS
The only person to have won a gold medal at both the Summer and the Winter Games is Edward Eagan (USA). He took the light-heavyweight boxing title in 1920, and was a member of the winning four-man bobsled team in 1932.

The first woman to win a medal at both Games was Christa Luding (West Germany). She took three medals for speed skating – golds in the 500-m. in 1984 and the 1,000-m. in 1988, and silver in the 500-m. in 1988 – and silver in the bicycling sprint in 1988.

MOST WORLD SKIBOB TITLES
The most individual combined skibob titles is four, by Petra Tschach-Wlezcek (Austria) from 1988 to 1991.

The most men's titles is three, by Walter Kronseil (Austria) from 1988 to 1990.

HIGHEST SKIBOB SPEED
The highest speed ever attained in a skibob is 108 m.p.h., by Romuald Bonvin (Switzerland) at Les Arcs, France, on May 2, 1999.

MOST WORLD CHAMPIONSHIP SPEED-SKATING TITLES
The most world titles won in women's speed-skating events is eight, by Gunda Niemann-Stirnemann (Germany): 1991–93 and 1995–99.

The greatest number of men's overall titles is five, by Oscar Mathisen of Norway (1908, 1909, and 1912–14); and by Clas Thunberg of Finland (1923, 1925, 1928, 1929, and 1931).

BEST WORLD CHAMPIONSHIP SPEED-SKATING SCORES
The lowest score with which the men's overall speed-skating title has been won is 152.651 points, by Rintje Ritsma (Netherlands) at Hamar, Norway, on Feb. 6–7, 1999.

The lowest score for the women's title is 161.479 points, by Gunda Niemann-Stirnemann (Germany) at Hamar on Feb. 6–7, 1999.

MOST OLYMPIC SPEED-SKATING TITLES
The most Olympic speed-skating titles won is six, by Lidiya Pavlovna Skoblikova (USSR): two in 1960 and four in 1964.

The most Olympic golds won by a man is five, by Clas Thunberg of Finland (1924 and 1928, including one tied); and by Eric Heiden of the USA, at the 1980 Games at Lake Placid, New York, USA.

MOST OLYMPIC SPEED-SKATING MEDALS
The most medals won is eight, by Karin Kania (GDR): three golds, four silvers, and one bronze from 1980 to 1988.

The most men's medals won is seven, by Clas Thunberg (Finland): five golds, one silver, and one tied bronze from 1924 to 1928; and by Ivar Ballangrud (Norway): four golds, two silvers, and one bronze from 1928 to 1936.

GREATEST DISTANCE SKATED IN 24 HOURS
Martinus Kuiper (Netherlands) skated a record 339 miles 1,200 yds. in 24 hours from Dec. 12 to 13, 1988, at Alkmaar, Netherlands.

LONGEST ICE-SKATING RACE
The world's longest ice-skating race is the *Elfstedentocht* ("Tour of the Eleven Towns"), which was first held in the Netherlands in 1909. Covering a distance of 124 miles 489 yds. (200 km.), it currently takes place at a number of sites, including Lake Vesijärvi in Finland, the Ottawa River in Canada, and Lake Weissensee in Austria. The men's record is 5 hrs. 40 min. 37 sec., by Dries van Wijhe (Netherlands); and

the women's record is 5 hrs. 48 min. 8 sec., by Alida Pasveer (Netherlands), both at Lake Weissensee, Austria, on Feb. 11, 1989.

MOST WORLD FIGURE-SKATING TITLES
The most men's individual world figure-skating titles is 10, by Ulrich Salchow (Sweden): 1901–05 and 1907–11.

The women's record is also 10, by Sonja Henie (Norway) from 1927 to 1936.

⊙ HIGHEST SOLO FIGURE-SKATING MARKS
Midori Ito of Japan (above), achieved a record seven sixes in the World Women's Championships in Paris, France, in 1989. She matched the record set by Donald Jackson (Canada) in the World Men's Championships in Prague, Czechoslovakia (now Czech Republic), in 1962.

⊙ MOST WORLD CURLING CHAMPIONSHIPS
Canada holds the record for both the most women's (11) and the most men's (26) World Championship titles. Pictured above is Canadian skipper Kelly Law, curling her stone down the sheet in the World Curling Championships match against France in Glasgow, Scotland, on April 1, 2000.

MOST FIGURE-SKATING GRAND SLAMS

Three skaters have achieved the figure-skating "Grand Slam" – the World, Olympic, and European titles in the same year – twice. They are: Karl Schäfer of Austria (1932 and 1936); Sonja Henie of Norway (also 1932 and 1936); and Katarina Witt of West Germany (1984 and 1988).

MOST OLYMPIC FIGURE-SKATING TITLES

The most Olympic gold medals won by a figure-skater is three, by Gillis Grafström of Sweden (1920, 1924, and 1928); by Sonja Henie of Norway (1928, 1932, and 1936); and by Irina Rodnina of the USSR. Rodnina won her medals in the pairs, with two different partners – Aleksey Ulanov in 1972, and her husband Aleksandr Zaitsev in 1976 and 1980.

HIGHEST FIGURE-SKATING MARKS

The most sixes awarded in an international championship is 29, to Jayne Torvill and Christopher Dean (both GB) at the World Ice Dance Championships in Ottawa, Canada, in March 1984. This total was made up of seven in the compulsory dances, a perfect set of nine for presentation in the set pattern dance, and 13 in the free dance.

MOST LUGEING TITLES

The most world lugeing titles (including Olympic titles) is six, by Georg Hackl (Germany), who won the single-seater in 1989, 1990, 1992, 1994, 1997, and 1998.

Margit Schumann (West Germany) has won five women's world titles: 1973–75, 1976, (Olympic) and 1977.

Stefan Krausse and Jan Behrendt (both Germany) have won a record six two-seater titles: 1989, 1991–93, 1995, and 1998.

MOST WORLD BOBSLED TITLES

Eugenio Monti (Italy) won 11 titles – eight two-man and three four-man – from 1957 to 1968.

MOST OLYMPIC INDIVIDUAL BOBSLED MEDALS

The most medals won in individual bobsled events is seven, by Bogdan Musiol (GDR, later Germany): one gold, four silver, and one bronze between 1980 and 1988 (GDR); and one silver in 1992 (Germany).

The most Olympic gold medals won is three, by Meinhard Nehmer and Bernhard Germeshausen (both West Germany): the 1976 two-man, and the 1976 and 1980 four-man.

HIGHEST LUGEING SPEED

The highest photo-timed lugeing speed is 85.4 m.p.h., by Asle Strand (Norway) at Tandådalens Linbana, Sälen, Sweden, on May 1, 1982.

FASTEST CRESTA RUN TIMES

The Cresta Run course at St. Moritz, Switzerland, is 3,976 ft. long with a drop of 515 ft. The fastest time recorded there is 50.09 sec., by James Sunley (GB) on Feb. 13, 1999. His average speed was 54.13 m.p.h.

MOST CRESTA RUN WINS

The most wins in the Cresta Run Grand National is eight, by Nino Bibbia of Italy (1960–64, 1966, 1968, and 1973); and by Franco Gansser of Switzerland (1981, 1983–86, 1988, 1989, and 1991).

← **FASTEST SPEED-SKATER**
Jeremy Wotherspoon (Canada) holds the record for both the 500-m. (34.63 sec.) and the 1,000-m. (1 min. 8.49 sec.) speed-skating events, both of which he set in Calgary, Canada, in Jan. 2000.

Winter Sports 2

MOST WORLD ALPINE CHAMPIONSHIP TITLES

The World Alpine Championships were inaugurated at Mürren, Switzerland, in 1931. The most titles won by a man is seven, by Toni Sailer (Austria). He won all four Alpine events (giant slalom, slalom, downhill, and non-Olympic Alpine combination) in 1956, and downhill, giant slalom, and combined in 1958.

The record for the greatest number of titles won by a woman is held by Christl Cranz (Germany). She won seven individual titles – four slalom (1934 and 1937–39) and three downhill (1935, 1937, and 1939) – and five combined (1934, 1935, and 1937–39). She also won the gold medal for the combined at the 1936 Olympics.

MOST WORLD CUP SNOWBOARDING TITLES

Karine Ruby of France has won a record 11 women's titles: overall from 1996 to 1998, slalom from 1996 to 1998, giant slalom from 1995 to 1998, and snowboard cross in 1997.

LONGEST ALL-DOWNHILL SKI RUN

The longest all-downhill ski run is the Weissfluhjoch-Küblis Parsenn course near Davos, Switzerland, which is 7.59 miles in length.

MOST SUCCESSIVE OLYMPIC SKIING TITLES

Ulrich Wehling (West Germany) is the only skier to have won the same event at three successive Games, with golds in the Nordic combined in 1972, 1976, and 1980.

MOST WORLD NORDIC CHAMPIONSHIP TITLES

The greatest number of titles won (including Olympic titles) is 18, by Bjørn Dæhlie (Norway): 12 individual and six relay titles between 1991 and 1998. Dæhlie won a record total of 29 World Nordic Championship medals between 1991 and 1999.

The most women's titles is 17, by Yelena Välbe (Russia): 10 individual and seven relay titles between 1989 and 1998.

The most medals won is 23, by Raisa Smetanina (USSR, later CIS) between 1974 and 1992. This total includes seven gold medals.

LONGEST RACE

The world's longest Nordic ski race is the 55.3-mile Vasaloppet in Sweden. There were a record 10,934 starters in March 1977, and a record 10,650 finishers in March 1979. The shortest time taken to complete the race is 3 hrs. 38 min. 57 sec., by Peter Göransson (Sweden) on March 1, 1998.

MOST SKI JUMPING MEDALS

Birger Ruud (Norway) won a record five medals: in 1931, 1932, and 1935–37. He is the only person to have won Olympic events in both the Alpine and Nordic disciplines, taking the ski jumping and the Alpine downhill titles in 1936.

LONGEST SKI JUMPS

The longest ski jump recorded in a World Cup event is 703.3 ft., by Martin Schmitt (Germany) at Planica, Slovenia, on March 19, 1999. This distance was achieved in the second of Schmitt's two jumps in the competition. His first jump had been measured at 718.5 ft., but he fell and so the distance was not officially recognized.

The women's record is 367.5 ft., by Eva Ganster (Austria) at Bischofshofen, Austria, on Jan. 7, 1994.

MOST WORLD CHAMPIONSHIP SKI ORIENTEERING TITLES

Finland has won the women's ski orienteering relay title seven times: in 1975, 1977, 1980, 1988, 1990, 1998, and 2000.

Sweden has won the men's relay title six times: in 1977, 1980, 1982, 1984, 1990, and 1996.

Annika Zell (Sweden) has won a record 14 medals, including six golds.

BIGGEST SKI RACE

The Finlandia Ski Race runs 46.6 miles from Hämeenlinna to Lahti, Finland. On Feb. 26, 1984, it had a record 13,226 starters and 12,909 finishers.

The record for the most women's individual ski orienteering titles is four, by Ragnhild Bratberg (Norway): the Classic in 1986 and 1990, and the Sprint in 1988 and 1990.

The men's world record for the most individual titles is also four, by Nicolo Corradini (Italy): the Classic in 1994 and 1996, and the Sprint in 1994 and 2000.

MOST VERTICAL FEET SKIED
On April 29, 1998, Edi Podivinsky, Luke Sauder, Chris Kent (all Canada), and Dominique Perret (Switzerland) skied a record total of 353,600 ft. in 14 hrs. 30 min. The record was achieved on a slope at Blue River, British Columbia, Canada.

Jennifer Hughes (USA) skied a total of 305,525 ft. at Atlin, British Columbia, Canada, on April 20, 1998.

GREATEST DISTANCE SKIED
Seppo-Juhani Savolainen (Finland) covered a world record total distance of 258.2 miles at Saariselkä, Finland, in 24 hours from April 8 to 9, 1988.

The women's 24-hour record is 205 miles, set by Sisko Kainulaisen (Finland) at Jyväskylä, Finland, from March 23 to 24, 1985.

MOST SNOWBOARDING WORLD CHAMPIONSHIP TITLES
The most titles won (including Olympic titles) is three, by Karine Ruby (France). She won the giant slalom in 1996, the Olympic title in 1998, and the snowboard cross in 1997. No man has won more than one title.

→ MOST NATIONS' CUP WINS
Alexandra Meissnitzer (Austria) is shown on her way to winning the women's World Cup downhill in Veysonnaz, Switzerland, on Dec. 19, 1998. Austria has won the Nations' Cup, awarded on the combined results of individual performances in the World Cup, a record 20 times.

Combat Sports 1

MOST GRECO-ROMAN WORLD WRESTLING TITLES
Aleksandr Karelin (Russia) won a record 12 world titles in the Under 130-kg. class between 1988 and 1999.

MOST OLYMPIC WRESTLING MEDALS
Wilfried Dietrich (Germany) has won a record five medals: gold in 1960 (freestyle), silver in 1956 and 1960 (both Greco-Roman), and bronze in 1964 (Greco-Roman) and 1968 (freestyle).

MOST OLYMPIC WRESTLING TITLES
Three Olympic titles have been won by: Carl Westergren of Sweden (1920, 1924, and 1932); Ivar Johansson of Sweden (two in 1932, and 1936); Aleksandr Medved of the USSR (1964, 1968, and 1972); and Aleksandr Karelin of Russia (1988, 1992, and 1996).

LONGEST WRESTLING BOUT
The longest recorded bout lasted 11 hrs. 40 min., when Martin Klein (Estonia, representing Russia) beat Alfred Asikáinen (Finland) at the Greco-Roman 75-kg. "A" event at the 1912 Olympic Games.

MOST WORLD CHAMPIONSHIP FENCING TITLES
The most individual world titles is five, by Aleksandr Romankov (USSR), all at foil, in 1974, 1977, 1979, 1982, and 1983.

Christian d'Oriola (France) won four world foil titles (1947, 1949, 1953, and 1954), as well as two individual Olympic titles (1952 and 1956).

Four women foilists have won three world titles: Helene Mayer of Germany (1929, 1931, and 1937); Ilona Schacherer-Elek of Hungary (1934, 1935, and 1951); Ellen Müller-Preis of Austria (1947, 1949, and 1950); and Cornelia Hanisch of West Germany (1979, 1981, and 1985). Ilona Schacherer-Elek also won two individual Olympic titles, in 1936 and 1948.

MOST OLYMPIC FENCING TITLES
Aladár Gerevich (Hungary) won a record seven golds – one individual and six team – between 1932 and 1960.

The women's record is four, by Yelena Novikova (USSR): one individual and three team between 1968 and 1976.

Three individual Olympic titles have been won by: Ramón Fonst of Cuba (1900 and two in 1904); and Nedo Nadi of Italy (1912 and two in 1920). Nadi also won three team golds in 1920, giving him a record five fencing golds at one Games.

MOST OLYMPIC FENCING MEDALS
Edoardo Mangiarotti (Italy) won a record 13 Olympic medals between 1936 and 1960: six gold, five silver, and two bronze.

The women's record is seven, by Ildikó Sági of Hungary: two gold, three silver, and two bronze between 1960 and 1976.

MOST BOXING TITLES RECAPTURED
The only boxer to have won a world title five times at one weight is "Sugar" Ray Robinson (USA). He set this record at the Chicago Stadium, Illinois, USA, on March 25, 1958, when he beat Carmen Basilio (USA) to regain the world middleweight title for the fourth time.

MOST BOXING TITLE BOUTS
The record number of title bouts in a career is 37 – 18 of which ended in "no decision" – by

⊙ MOST WOMEN'S OLYMPIC TEAM FENCING GOLDS
The USSR have won a record four gold medals (all at foil): in 1960, 1968, 1972, and 1976. When the épée was introduced in 1996, the French team, which included Valérie Barlois (left), took the title.

⊙ MOST HEAVYWEIGHT TITLES RECAPTURED
Two boxers have regained the world heavyweight championship twice: Muhammad Ali and Evander Holyfield (both USA). Here, Holyfield is seen at the weigh-in for his unified heavyweight championship bout against Lennox Lewis (GB) at Madison Square Garden, New York City, USA, on March 11, 1999.

the three-time world welterweight champion Jack Britton (USA) between 1915 and 1922.

The record for bouts without "no decision" outcomes is 34, including a record 31 wins, by Julio César Chávez (Mexico) between 1984 and 1996.

SHORTEST AND LONGEST REIGNS AS BOXING WORLD CHAMPION
Tony Canzoneri (USA) was world light-welterweight champion for just 33 days, from May 21 to June 23, 1933.

Joe Louis (USA) was world heavyweight champion for 11 years, 252 days, from 1937 until his retirement in 1949.

YOUNGEST HEAVYWEIGHT BOXING CHAMPION
Mike Tyson (USA) was 20 years, 144 days old when he beat Trevor

Berbick (USA) to win the WBC championship at Las Vegas, Nevada, USA, on Nov. 22, 1986.

LONGEST BOXING MATCHES
The longest recorded fight with gloves took place between Andy Bowen and Jack Burke (both USA) at New Orleans, Louisiana, USA, on April 6–7, 1893. It lasted for 7 hrs. 19 min. (110 rounds), and was declared a no contest (later changed to a draw).

The longest world title fight under Queensberry Rules took place between lightweights Joe Gans (USA) and Oscar Nelson (Denmark) at Goldfield, Nevada, USA, on Sept. 3, 1906. Gans won in the 42nd round on a foul.

BOXING MATCH WITH MOST ROUNDS
A fight between Jack Jones and Patsy Tunney (both UK) in Cheshire, England, in 1825 had a record 276 rounds. It lasted for 4 hrs. 30 min.

MOST KNOCKDOWNS IN A BOXING TITLE FIGHT
Vic Toweel (South Africa) knocked down Danny O'Sullivan (GB) 14 times in 10 rounds, before the latter retired, in their world bantamweight fight in Johannesburg, South Africa, on Dec. 2, 1950.

MOST CONSECUTIVE BOXING KNOCKOUTS
The record for consecutive knockouts is 44, by Lamar Clark (USA) from 1958 to 1960. On the night of Dec. 1, 1958, he knocked out six opponents (five of them in the first round) at Bingham, Utah, USA.

MOST BOXING KNOCKOUTS IN A CAREER
The greatest number of finishes classed as knockouts in a career is 145 (129 in professional bouts), by Archie Moore (USA) between 1936 and 1963.

→ OLDEST COMPETITION
The world's oldest continuously sanctioned sporting competition is the Kirkpinar Wrestling Festival, Turkey, which has been held since 1460. The event is staged on the Sarayici Peninsula, near Edirne.

Combat Sports 2

MOST SUCCESSFUL SUMO WRESTLERS

Yokozuna (grand champion) Sadji Akiyoshi, alias Futabayama, had a record 69 consecutive wins between 1937 and 1939.

Yokozuna Koki Naya, alias Taiho, had won the Emperor's Cup 32 times by the time he retired in 1971.

Ozeki (second highest rank) Tameemon Torokichi, alias Raiden, won 254 bouts and lost only 10 in 21 years, giving him a record winning rate of 96.2%.

HEAVIEST SUMO WRESTLER

The heaviest *rikishi* (professional sumo wrestler) on record is Samoan-American Salevaa Atisanoe, alias Konishiki, of Hawaii, USA. He weighed in at 589 lbs. at Tokyo's Ryogoku Kokugikan (National Arena) on Jan. 3, 1994.

MOST SUMO BOUTS

Hawaiian-born Jesse Kuhaulua, alias Takamiyama, fought a record 1,231 consecutive *Makunouchi* (top-division) bouts in July 1972. In Sept. 1981, he became the first non-Japanese to win an official *Makunouchi* tournament.

The most bouts in all divisions is 1,631, by Yukio Shoji, alias Aobajo, between 1964 and 1986.

The greatest number of bouts in a career is 1,891, by Kenji Hatano, alias Oshio, between 1962 and 1988.

MOST SUMO BOUT SUCCESSES

Yokozuna Mitsugu Akimoto, alias Chiyonofuji, won the Kyushu *Basho* (one of the six annual sumo tournaments) for eight successive years (1981–1988). He also holds the records for the most career wins (1,045) and the most *Makunouchi* (top-division) wins (807).

⊙ MOST MEN'S JUDO WORLD TITLES

David Douillet (France, left) has won five world and Olympic titles: in the Over 95-kg. class in 1993, 1995, and 1997, in the Open in 1995, and in the Olympic Over 95-kg. class in 1996. Yasuhiro Yamashita (Japan) has also won five world and Olympic titles: three in the Over 95-kg. class, and one each in the Open and the Olympic Over 95-kg. class.

⊙ MOST WOMEN'S JUDO WORLD TITLES

Belgian Ingrid Berghmans (bottom) has won a record six women's world titles: in the Open in 1980, 1982, 1984, and 1986, and in the Under 72-kg. class in 1984 and 1989. In 1988, when women's judo was introduced as an Olympic demonstration sport, Berghmans won the 72-kg. event.

In 1978 Toshimitsu Ogata, alias Kitanoumi, won a record 82 of the 90 bouts that top *rikishi* fight annually. He is also the youngest sumo wrestler to have attained the rank of *yokozuna*, setting this record in July 1974, aged 21 years, 61 days.

MOST SUCCESSFUL SUMO BROTHERS

After winning the *Natsu* (summer) *Basho* in 1998, *Ozeki* Wakanohana was promoted to the rank of *yokozuna*, a rank that his younger brother Takanohana had held since 1994. This was the first time in the 1,500-year history of the sport that two brothers had attained this rank. Wakanohana retired in March 2000.

MOST TAE KWON DO WORLD CHAMPIONSHIP TITLES

The most men's world titles is four, by Chung Kook-hyun (South Korea): in the light-middleweight class in 1982 and 1983, and in the welterweight class in 1985 and 1987.

The most women's world titles is two, by: Lee Eun-young of South Korea (in the lightweight class in 1987 and 1989); Lynette Love of the USA (in the heavyweight class in 1987 and 1991); Lee Seung-min of South Korea (in the featherweight class in 1993 and 1995); and Jung Myung-suk of South Korea (in the heavyweight class in 1993 and 1995).

MOST TAE KWON DO OLYMPIC TITLES

The most gold medals won in the men's event is two, by Ha Tae-kyung (South Korea): in the flyweight class in 1988, and in the welterweight class in 1992.

The most golds won in the women's event is two, by Chen Yi-an (Taiwan): in the bantamweight class in 1988, and in the lightweight class in 1992.

MOST KARATE WORLD CHAMPIONSHIP TITLES

Great Britain has won a record six world titles in the men's Kumite team event (inaugurated in 1970): in 1975, 1982, 1984, 1986, 1988, and 1990.

The women's team event was inaugurated in 1992. Great Britain has had a record two wins: in 1992 and 1996.

The most individual women's Kumite titles is four, by Guus van Mourik (Netherlands): in the Over 60-kg. class in 1982, 1984, 1986, and 1988.

The most Kumite titles won by a man is three, by José Manuel Egea (Spain): in the Open in 1988, and in the Under 80-kg. class in 1990 and 1992; and by Wayne Otto (GB): in the Open in 1990, and in the Under 75-kg. class in 1992 and 1996.

The most individual women's Kata titles is four, by Yuki Mimura (Japan): in 1988, 1990, 1992, and 1996.

The most individual men's Kata titles is three, by Tsuguo Sakumoto (Japan): in 1984, 1986, and 1988.

A Kata team event was introduced at the 1986 World Championships. Since then, Japan has failed to win just two World Championship titles: the men's in 1990, which was won by Italy; and the women's in 1986, which was won by Taiwan.

MOST JUDO OLYMPIC TITLES

The most gold medals won in the men's event is two, by: Wilhelm Ruska of the Netherlands (in the Over 93-kg. class and the Open in 1972); Peter Seisenbacher of Austria (in the 86-kg. class in 1984 and 1988); Hitoshi Saito of Japan (in the Over 95-kg. class in 1984 and 1988); and Waldemar Legien of Poland (in the 78-kg. class in 1988, and in the 86-kg. class in 1992). No woman has won more than one gold medal.

→ BIGGEST SUMO GRAND CHAMPION

Hawaiian-born Chad Rowan, alias Akebono, is the tallest and heaviest *yokozuna* (grand champion) in sumo history. He is 6 ft. 8 in. tall and weighs 507 lbs. In Jan. 1993, Akebono became the first foreign *rikishi* to be promoted to the rank of *yokozuna*.

Extreme Sports 1

⊙ BEST-ATTENDED EXTREME SPORTS EVENT

The 1999 ESPN Summer X-Games, held in San Francisco, California, USA, were attended by a record 268,390 spectators over 10 days. The X-Games were inaugurated in 1994, and have grown to become the largest extreme sports showcase in the world, in terms of both audience (live and televised) and prize money. Clifford Adoptante (USA) is seen here in action during the Freestyle Motocross event.

FASTEST STREET SKIER

The highest speed ever achieved downhill on a public road by a street skier is 63 m.p.h., by Douglas Lucht (USA) on Golden Eagle Boulevard, Fountain Hills, Arizona, USA, on March 7, 1998. To meet street skiing guidelines, Lucht had to wear ski bindings and boots attached to in-line wheeled frames that did not exceed 42 in. in length.

FASTEST SKATEBOARDERS

The highest speed ever recorded by a skateboarder is 78.37 m.p.h., by Roger Hickey (USA) on a course near Los Angeles, California, USA, on March 15, 1990. Hickey was riding in a prone position.

The standing position record is 62.55 m.p.h., by Gary Hardwick (USA) at Fountain Hills, Arizona, USA, on Sept. 26, 1998.

LONGEST SKATEBOARD JUMP

On Oct. 12, 1999, Andy Macdonald (USA) set a long jump record of 52 ft. 10 in., clearing four cars, in East Lansing, Michigan, USA.

HIGHEST AIR

Danny Way (USA) stuck a 16-ft. 6-in. air (method air) jump from a halfpipe at Brown Field, San Diego, California, USA, on Aug. 3, 1998.

LONGEST DISTANCE SKATEBOARDED

On Nov. 4–5, 1993, Eleftherios Argiropoulos (Greece) covered 271.3 miles in 36 hrs. 33 min. 17 sec. at Ekali, Greece.

FASTEST BUTT BOARDER

Darren Lott (USA) achieved a speed of 65 m.p.h. on a butt board at Fountain Hills, Arizona, USA, on Sept. 26, 1998.

FASTEST IN-LINE SKATERS

Graham Wilkie and Jeff Hamilton (both USA) each achieved a speed of 64.02 m.p.h. in Arizona, USA, on Sept. 26, 1998.

FASTEST SAND BOARDERS

Erik Johnson (USA) achieved a speed of 51 m.p.h. during the Sand Master Jam at Dumont Dunes, California, USA, on April 12, 1999.

The fastest female sand boarder is Nancy Sutton (USA), who achieved a speed of 44.7 m.p.h. at Sand Mountain, Nevada, USA, on Sept. 19, 1998.

⊙ MOST ROTATIONS IN AIR OFF A HALFPIPE

During the 1999 X-Games, held in San Francisco, California, USA, Tony Hawk (USA) completed the first ever midair 900° skateboarding trick.

MOST MOUNTAIN BOARDING WORLD TITLES

Jason T. Lee (USA) has won two World Championship titles: in 1997 and 1998.

FASTEST GRAVITY SPEED BIKER

Alternative International Sports, the sanctioning body for gravity speed biking, recognizes Dwight Garland (USA) as the world's fastest rider after he achieved a record speed of 64.02 m.p.h. on Sept. 26, 1998. A gravity speed bike has a tubular steel chassis, front and rear brakes, and a fairing to increase aerodynamic efficiency. It runs on pneumatic racing slicks.

FASTEST BICYCLIST ON A GLACIER

The fastest speed ever attained bicycling down a glacier is 131.82 m.p.h., by Christian Taillefer (France) on a Peugeot Cycle at the Speed Ski Slope in Vars, France, in March 1998.

MOST X-GAMES SNOW MOUNTAIN BIKING MEDALS

The most medals won for snow mountain biking is three, by Cheri Elliott (USA): the 1997 gold speed medal and the 1998 silver speed and silver difficulty medals.

MOST X-GAMES SNOWBOARDING MEDALS

The most X-Games snowboarding medals won by a woman is six, by Barrett Christy (USA) in 1998 and 1999.

The men's record is three, by Shaun Palmer (USA): gold medals in the Boarder X discipline in 1997, 1998, and 1999.

MOST X-GAMES SKI BOARDING MEDALS

Mike Nick (USA) won a gold medal in the 1998 X-Games Slopestyle event and a silver medal in the 1999 Triple Air discipline.

MOST X-GAMES ICE CLIMBING GOLD MEDALS

Will Gadd (USA) has won a record three X-Games gold medals for ice climbing: the difficulty medal in 1998 and 1999, and the speed medal in 1998.

The women's record is also three, by Kim Csizmazia (USA): the difficulty medal in 1998 and 1999, and the speed medal in 1998.

BIGGEST SKATE PARK

The Vans Skatepark at Potomac Mills Mall, Prince William, Virginia, USA, covers an area of 61,640 ft². The park was opened to the public on April 15, 2000.

SKATING GLOSSARY

aciddrop: Skating off an object with an ollie or touching the board with your hands.

air: Riding with all four wheels off the ground; short for "aerial."

fat: Also "phat." High or far, denoting a board trick performed over a great distance or height. *"Now that was a* fat *jump!"*

grind: Scraping one or both axles on a curb, rail, or other object. There are many variations of this trick.

halfpipe: A U-shaped ramp, usually with a flat section in the middle.

impossible: A trick that involves spinning the board around either foot while in the air.

ollie: A jump performed by tapping the tail (rear) of the board on the ground.

shoveit: Turning the board without turning your body; shoving the board around so that it spins under your feet.

sick: Good. Used in the same way as "wicked" or "rad." *"That trick she pulled was* sick*!"*

stoked: A feeling of having done something well. *"You must be pretty* stoked *after pulling off that trick!"*

← HIGHEST OLLIE

On Feb. 6, 2000, Danny Wainwright (UK) popped a record-breaking ollie of 44.48 in. off flat ground to win the Reese Forbes Ollie Challenge at the ASR Show, Long Beach, California, USA.

Extreme Sports 2

LONGEST SWIM UNDER ICE WITHOUT EQUIPMENT
Wim Hof (Netherlands) swam a record distance of 187 ft. under ice in a lake near the Finnish village of Kolari on March 16, 2000. He did not use any special equipment, but wore only swimming trunks and a pair of goggles.

LONGEST UNDERWATER SWIMS WITH EQUIPMENT
In a 24-hour period from Feb. 21 to 22, 1985, Paul Cryne (UK) and Samir Sawan al Awami (Qatar) swam 49.04 miles from Doha to Umm Said, both Qatar, and back again, using subaqua equipment. They were underwater for 95.5% of the time.

On Oct. 17–18, 1987, a relay team of six people swam underwater for a total distance of 94.44 miles, using subaqua equipment. They were in a swimming pool in Olomouc, Czechoslovakia.

HIGHEST-EARNING SURFERS
Kelly Slater (USA) earned a record $708,230 in the course of his surfing career. Slater retired at the end of the 1998 season.

The women's career earnings record is $296,875, by Pam Burridge (Australia).

MOST WORLD PROFESSIONAL SERIES SURFING TITLES
The World Professional series was inaugurated in 1975. The men's title has been won a record six times by Kelly Slater (USA): in 1992 and from 1994 to 1998.

The women's professional title has been won a record four times by: Frieda Zamba of the USA (1984–1986 and 1988); Wendy Botha of Australia, formerly South Africa (1987, 1989, 1991, and 1992); and Lisa Andersen of Australia (1994–97).

⊙ OLDEST SNOWBOARDER
The oldest person to snowboard regularly is 80-year-old Wong Yui Hoi, who was born in China in Jan. 1920 and now lives in Canada. He took up snowboarding in 1995.

⊙ LONGEST SAND-BOARDING BACK FLIP
On May 20, 2000, Josh Tenge from Incline Village, Nevada, USA, performed a back flip measuring a record 44 ft. 10 in. The record was set at the X-West Huck Fest, Sand Mountain, Nevada.

MOST WORLD AMATEUR SURFING CHAMPIONSHIP TITLES
The World Amateur Surfing Championships were inaugurated in May 1964. The most wins is three, by Michael Novakov (Australia): in the Kneeboard event in 1982, 1984, and 1986.

MOST BODY-BOARDING CHAMPIONSHIPS
Mike Stewart (USA) has won nine World Championships, eight national tour titles, and 11 pipeline championships.

MOST KNEE-BOARDING WORLD CHAMPIONSHIP TITLES
Mario Fossa (Venezuela), known to his fans as the "King Of Dizzy," won five consecutive Pro Tour titles from 1987 to 1991. Knee boarders perform tricks while kneeling on a short, squat board.

HIGHEST-LATITUDE WINDSURF
On July 14, 1985, Gerard-Jan Goekoop (Netherlands), the doctor on the Dutch expedition ship *Plancius*, windsurfed alongside the pack ice of the North Pole at a latitude of 80° N.

MOST WHITE-WATER FREESTYLE KAYAKING TITLES
Germany has won a record two white-water freestyle kayaking world titles: in 1991 and 1995.

HIGHEST BUNGEE JUMP FROM A BUILDING
On Oct. 5, 1998, A.J. Hackett (New Zealand) made a 590-ft. 10-in. bungee jump off the Sky Tower Casino, the tallest building in Auckland, New Zealand. He attached himself to two steel cables to avoid hitting the tower.

BIGGEST MASS BUNGEE JUMP
On Sept. 6, 1998, a record 25 people made a bungee jump from a 171-ft. platform suspended in front of the Deutsche Bank headquarters in Frankfurt, Germany. The jump was part of a "skyscraper festival" organized by Frankfurt City Council.

MOST PARACHUTE DESCENTS

Don Kellner (USA) holds the record for the most parachute descents, having made a total of 29,000 by March 7, 2000.

Cheryl Stearns (USA) holds the women's record, with 13,500 descents, mainly over the USA, made to June 2000.

The most descents in 24 hours, in accordance with the rules of the United States Parachute Association (USPA), is 476, by Jay Stokes (USA) at Yuma, Arizona, USA, from Nov. 12 to 13, 1999.

BIGGEST MASS PARACHUTE JUMP FROM A BALLOON

On April 22, 2000, a record 20 skydivers from the Paraclub Flevo in Lelystad, Netherlands, jumped from a Cameron A–415 PH–AGT balloon over Harfsen, Netherlands. Twelve of the skydivers jumped at the same time, thereby setting an additional record – the biggest simultaneous parachute jump from a balloon.

MOST FOUR-MAN TEAM FORMATIONS IN A SKYDIVE

On Sept. 23, 1999, four members of the Arizona Airspeed Team, USA – Daniel Brodsky-Chenfeld, Jack Jeffries, Mark Kirkby, and Kirk Verners – arranged themselves into 39 formations while skydiving during the 1999 US Formation Skydiving Championships, Sebastian, Florida, USA.

BIGGEST FORMATION FREEFALL

On Dec. 16, 1999, 282 skydivers, members of the World Team '99 (USA), came together for 7.11 seconds in the sky above Ubon Ratchathani, Thailand, to make the largest freefall formation.

BIGGEST MASS FREEFALL

On April 18, 2000, a record total of 588 parachutists exited at 12,000 ft. from seven aircraft flying in formation over Rio de Janeiro, Brazil.

← MOST JET SKIING TITLES

Marc Sickerling (Germany), who competes in the freestyle discipline, was crowned International Jet Ski Boating Association (IJSBA) European Champion five times (1991–1994 and 1998), Pro World Champion twice (1995 and 1996) and Expert World Champion in 1994. He was also crowned Union Internationale Motonautique (UIM) European and World Champion in 1997 and European Champion in 1998.

Auto Sports

YOUNGEST WORLD RALLY CHAMPIONSHIP WINNER
Colin McRae (GB) was 27 years, 89 days old when he won the 1995 World Rally Championship title.

MOST WORLD DRIVERS' CHAMPIONSHIP WINS
The World Drivers' Championship has been won a record four times by two drivers: Juha Kankkunen of Finland (1986, 1987, 1991, and 1993); and Tommi Makinen, also of Finland (1996, 1997, 1998, and 1999).

MOST CONSECUTIVE WORLD RALLY CHAMPIONSHIPS
Tommi Makinen and his co-driver Risto Mannisenmaki (both Finland) have won a record four consecutive World Rally Championship titles: in 1996, 1997, 1998, and 1999.

MOST MANUFACTURERS' WORLD CHAMPIONSHIP WINS
Lancia won a record 11 Manufacturers' World Championships from 1972 to 1992.

MOST MONTE CARLO RALLY WINS
The Monte Carlo Rally has been won four times by: Sandro Munari of Italy (1972, 1975, 1976, and 1977); and by Walter Röhrl and his co-driver Christian Geistdorfer, both of West Germany (1980 and 1982–84).

LONGEST RALLY
The longest rally on record was the 1977 Singapore Airlines London–Sydney Rally, which covered 19,330 miles from Covent Garden, London, England, to Sydney Opera House, NSW, Australia. It was won by Andrew Cowan, Colin Malkin, and Michael Broad (all GB) in a Mercedes 280E.

FASTEST LAPS AT LE MANS
The fastest ever lap in the Le Mans 24-hour race is 3 min. 21.27 sec., by Alain Ferté (France) in a Jaguar XJR-9LM, on June 10, 1989. His average speed over the 8-mile 724-yd. course was 150.429 m.p.h.

Hans Stück (West Germany) set the fastest practice-lap speed record – 156.381 m.p.h. – on June 14, 1985.

MOST LE MANS WINS
The most Le Mans wins by a manufacturer is 16, by Porsche: 1970, 1971, 1976, 1977, 1979, 1981–87, 1993, and 1996–98.

The most wins by an individual is six, by Jacky Ickx (Belgium): 1969, 1975–77, 1981, and 1982.

GREATEST DISTANCE COVERED IN A LE MANS RACE
Dr. Helmut Marko (Austria) and Gijs van Lennep (Netherlands) covered a distance of 3,315 miles 517 yds. in a 4,907-cc flat-12

⊙ YOUNGEST WINNER OF A WORLD DRIVERS' CHAMPIONSHIP POINT
On March 26, 2000, Jensen Button (GB) became the youngest driver to claim a Formula One World Drivers' Championship point, at the age of 20 years, 67 days. Button, who was driving with the Williams team in his first season of Formula One, had finished sixth in the Brazilian Grand Prix at Interlagos, São Paulo.

⊙ FASTEST FUNNY CAR DRAG RACER
John Force (USA) reached a record speed of 324.059 m.p.h. from a 440-yd. standing start in a '99 Ford Mustang at Gainsville, Florida, USA, on March 21, 1999.

Porsche 917K Group 5 sports car on June 12–13, 1971.

The greatest distance covered on the current circuit is 3,313 miles 423 yds., by Jan Lammers (Netherlands), Johnny Dumfries (GB), and Andy Wallace (GB) in a Jaguar XJR-9LM on June 11–12, 1988. Their average speed was 138.047 m.p.h.

MOST SUCCESSFUL INDIANAPOLIS 500 DRIVERS
Three drivers have each won the Indianapolis 500-mile race four times: A.J. Foyt Jr. of the USA (1961, 1964, 1967, and 1977); Al Unser Sr. of the USA

(1970, 1971, 1978, and 1987); and Rick Mears of the USA (1979, 1984, 1988, and 1991).

BEST INDIANAPOLIS 500 STARTING STATISTICS
A.J. Foyt Jr. (USA) started a record 35 consecutive Indianapolis 500 races between 1958 and 1992.

FASTEST INDIANAPOLIS 500 RACE
Arie Luyendyk (Netherlands) won in a record 2 hrs. 41 min. 18.404 sec. on May 27, 1990, driving a Lola-Chevrolet. His average speed was 185.986 m.p.h.

FASTEST INDIANAPOLIS 500 QUALIFYING LAPS
The highest average speed over the four qualifying laps is 236.992 m.p.h.,

including a one-lap record of 237.505 m.p.h., by Arie Luyendyk (Netherlands) in a Reynard-Ford-Cosworth on May 12, 1996.

MOST SUCCESSFUL GRAND PRIX MANUFACTURERS
The greatest number of Grand Prix championships won by a manufacturer is nine, by Williams (1980, 1981, 1986, 1987, 1992–94, 1996, and 1997); and by Ferrari (1961, 1964, 1975–77, 1979, 1982, 1983, and 1999).

The McLaren team won 15 of the 16 Grand Prix races in the 1988 season: Ayrton Senna

(Brazil) won eight and Alain Prost (France) won seven. The McLaren Formula One cars, powered by Honda engines. amassed more than three times the points of their nearest rivals, Ferrari.

MOST GRAND PRIX VICTORIES
Alain Prost (France) had a record 51 wins from 199 Grand Prix races between 1980 and 1993. In the course of his career, he gained a record 798.5 Grand Prix points.

↓ MOST WORLD CHAMPIONSHIP WINS
Juha Kankkunen of Finland (right) won a record 23 World Championship races between 1989 and 1999. He is seen below in his Subaru Impreza, during the Argentinian rally in May 2000.

Bike Sports

MOST WORLD CHAMPIONSHIP CYCLING TITLES
Koichi Nakano (Japan) won 10 consecutive professional sprint titles (1977–86).

The most wins in a men's amateur event is seven, by Daniel Morelon (France) for sprint in 1966, 1967, 1969–71, 1973, and 1975; and by Leon Meredith (GB) for the 100-km. motor paced in 1904, 1905, 1907–09, 1911, and 1913.

The most women's titles is 11, by Jeannie Longo-Ciprelli (France): for pursuit in 1986, 1988, and 1989; for road in 1985–87, 1989, and 1995; for points in 1989; and for time trial in 1995 and 1996.

MOST OLYMPIC CYCLING MEDALS
The most titles won at a single Games is three, by: Paul Masson (France) in 1896; Francisco Verri (Italy) in 1906; and Robert Charpentier (France) in 1936.

Daniel Morelon (France) won two gold medals in 1968 and a third in 1972; he also won a silver in 1976 and a bronze in 1964. Marcus Hurley (USA) won four events in the "unofficial" 1904 cycling program.

BEST-ATTENDED SPORTING EVENT
An estimated 10 million people turn out to watch the annual Tour de France cycle race, which takes place over three weeks.

MOST TOUR DE FRANCE WINS
The greatest number of wins in the Tour de France is five, by: Jacques Anquetil of France (1957 and 1961–64); Eddy Merckx of Belgium (1969–72 and 1974); Bernard Hinault of France (1978, 1979, 1981, 1982, and 1985); and Miguel Induráin of Spain (1991–95).

FASTEST TOUR DE FRANCE SPEED
The fastest average speed in the Tour de France is 25.027 m.p.h., by Lance Armstrong (USA) in 1999.

CLOSEST TOUR DE FRANCE
The closest Tour de France race on record took place in 1989, when Greg LeMond (USA) beat Laurent Fignon (France) by just eight seconds. LeMond's time was 87 hrs. 38 min. 35 sec.

MOST TOUR OF SPAIN WINS
The record for the most wins in the Tour of Spain is three, by Tony Rominger (Switzerland) from 1992 to 1994.

MOST TOUR OF ITALY WINS
The greatest number of wins in the Tour of Italy is five, by: Alfredo Binda of Italy (1925, 1927–29, and 1933); Fausto Coppi of Italy (1940, 1947, 1949, 1952, and 1953); and Eddy Merckx of Belgium (1968, 1970, and 1972–74).

MOST TOUR OF BRITAIN WINS
Four riders have won the Tour of Britain twice: Bill Bradley of the UK (1959 and 1960); Leslie West of the UK (1965 and 1967); Fedor den Hertog of the Netherlands (1969 and 1971); and Yuriy Kashurin of the USSR (1979 and 1982).

LONGEST ONE-DAY CYCLE RACE
The longest single-day "massed start" road race is the 342 to 385-mile race from Bordeaux to Paris, France. The highest average speed achieved in the event is 29.32 m.p.h., by Herman van Springel (Belgium) in 1981. He covered 363.2 miles in 13 hrs. 35 min. 18 sec.

MOST WORLD MOTORCYCLE CHAMPIONSHIP TITLES
The most World Championship titles won is 15, by Giacomo Agostini (Italy): seven at 350 cc from 1968 to 1974, and eight at

⊙ **FASTEST OLYMPIC 1 KM.**
On July 24, 1996, Florian Rousseau (France) set an Olympic cycling record of 1 min. 2.712 sec. for the men's 1-km. unpaced standing start in Atlanta, Georgia, USA.

"Peel" (St. John's) course on the Isle of Man in 1907, the series has been run on the island's "Mountain" circuit, which has 264 curves, since 1911. The race speed record, which stands at 1 hr. 51 min. 59.6 sec., was established by Steve Hislop (GB) on June 12, 1992, when he won the Senior TT on a Norton motorcycle. His average speed was 121.28 m.p.h.

MOST ISLE OF MAN TT EVENTS WON

Joey Dunlop (Ireland) had a record 23 victories in the Isle of Man TT races between 1977 and 1998.

The record for the most events won in one year is four, by Phillip McCallen (Ireland): the Formula One, Junior, Senior, and Production events in 1996.

MOST MOTOCROSS WINS

Joël Robert (Belgium) has won six 250 cc Motocross World Championship titles: in 1964 and from 1968 to 1972. Between April 25, 1964, and June 18, 1972, he also won a record 50 250 cc Grand Prix titles.

MOST WORLD SPEEDWAY CHAMPIONSHIP WINS

The World Speedway Championship was inaugurated at Wembley, London, England, on Sept. 10, 1936. The most wins is six, by Ivan Mauger (New Zealand): in 1968–70, 1972, 1977, and 1979.

500 cc (1966–1972 and 1975). Agostini also holds the record for the only man to have won two world titles in five consecutive years.

Angel Roldan Nieto (Spain) has won a record seven 125 cc titles: in 1971, 1972, 1979, and 1981–84. He has also won a record six 50 cc titles: in 1969, 1970, 1972, and 1975–77.

Phil Read (GB) won a record four 250 cc titles: in 1964, 1965, 1968, and 1971.

Rolf Biland (Switzerland) has won seven world sidecar titles: in 1978, 1979, 1981, 1983, and 1992–94.

The most wins in a single class in one season is 12, by Michael Doohan (Australia) in the 500 cc class in 1997.

The world's most successful manufacturer is Honda (Japan), whose machines won 48 World Championships between 1961 and 1999.

OLDEST MOTORCYCLE RACE

The oldest annually contested motorcycle race in the world is the Auto-Cycle Union Tourist Trophy (TT) series. First held on the 15.81-mile

← **FASTEST TOUR DE FRANCE STAGE**

On July 7, 1999, Mario Cipollini (Italy) won the Tour de France's fourth regular stage, which runs for 120 miles between Laval and Blois, with an average speed of 31.29 m.p.h.

The former World Team Cup was won a record nine times, by England/Great Britain (Great Britain in 1968 and 1971–73; and England in 1974, 1975, 1977, 1980, and 1989); and by Denmark in 1978, 1981, 1983–88, and 1991.

Barry Briggs (NZ) reached the finals a record 18 times: from 1954 to 1970 and in 1972. He won the world title in 1957, 1958, 1964, and 1966, and scored a record 201 points from 87 races.

The World Pairs Championships have been held unofficially since 1968 and officially since 1970. Renamed the World Team Championships in 1994, they have been won a record nine times by Denmark: in 1979, 1985–91, and 1995.

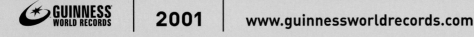
Horse Sports

MOST SUCCESSFUL RACEHORSES

The racehorse with the best win-loss record was Kincsem, a Hungarian mare foaled in 1874. It was unbeaten in 54 races throughout Europe from 1876 to 1879.

Camarero, foaled in 1951, was unbeaten in 56 races in Puerto Rico from April 19, 1953, to its first defeat on Aug. 17, 1955.

Chorisbar, foaled in 1935, won 197 of its 324 races in Puerto Rico between 1937 and 1947.

Lenoxbar, foaled in 1935, won 46 races from 56 starts in one year, in Puerto Rico in 1940.

Doctor Syntax, foaled in 1811, holds the record for the most wins in one race, having won the Preston Gold Cup seven times (1815–1821).

MOST CONSECUTIVE LOSSES

On Sept. 6, 1999, Zippy Chippy, a nine-year-old gelding owned and trained by Felix Monserrate (USA), recorded his 86th consecutive loss when he came in third in a field of six at a county fair in Northampton, Massachusetts, USA.

MOST SUCCESSFUL TRAINERS

Jack Van Berg (USA) has had the greatest number of wins in one year, with 496 in 1976.

The career record is 8,100 wins, by Dale Baird (USA) between 1962 and May 2000.

The most money won in a year is a record $17.8 million, by Darrell Lukas (USA) in 1988.

He also holds the career record, with $177 million won to date.

MOST SUCCESSFUL JOCKEYS

Bill Shoemaker (USA) rode a record total of 8,833 winners from 40,350 mounts over a career which stretched from March 1949 to his retirement in Feb. 1990. Shoemaker's racing weight was 97 lbs. and he is 4 ft. 11 in. tall.

⊙ HIGHEST-EARNING RACEHORSES

The career earnings record for a racehorse is $10 million, by US champion Cigar (left, foaled in 1990) from 1993 to 1996. This includes a single-year record of $4.9 million in 1996. The top-earning filly or mare is Hokuto Vega (foaled in 1990), who had winnings of $8.3 million in Japan between 1993 and 1997.

The most races won by a jockey in one year is 598 from 2,312 mounts, by Kent Desormeaux (USA) in 1989.

Christopher McCarron (USA) had record career earnings of $236 million between 1974 and April 2000.

The most money won by a jockey in one year is $28.4 million, by Yutaka Take (Japan) in Japan in 1993.

MOST SUCCESSFUL OWNERS

The most lifetime wins by an owner is 4,775, by Marion Van Berg (USA) over 35 years in North America.

The most wins in a year is 494, by Dan Lasater (USA) in 1974.

The most money won in one year is $9.09 million, by Allen Paulson (USA) in North America and Dubai in 1996.

FASTEST RACEHORSES

The highest race speed recorded by a racehorse is 43.26 m.p.h. – 440 yds. in 20.8 seconds – by Big Racket in Mexico City, Mexico, on

⊙ BIGGEST PRIZE FOR ONE RACE

The 2000 Dubai World Cup, held at Nad Al Sheba, Dubai, United Arab Emirates, on March 25, 2000, had a total prize fund of $6 million, with the winner receiving 3.6 million. The race was won by Godolphin stable's Dubai Millennium, ridden by Frankie Dettori. His time was 2 minutes, giving him a record winning rate of $30,000 per second.

Feb. 5, 1945; and by Onion Roll in Thistledown, Cleveland, Ohio, USA, on Sept. 27, 1993.

The highest speed over a 1.5-mile course is 37.82 m.p.h., by three-year-old Hawkster at Santa Anita Park, Arcadia, California, USA, on Oct. 14, 1989. Carrying 121 lbs., its time was 2 min. 22.8 sec.

MOST RUNNERS IN A RACE
A record 66 horses took part in the Grand National at Aintree, Merseyside, England, on March 22, 1929.

MOST SHOW-JUMPING WORLD CHAMPIONSHIPS
The most men's World Championship titles is two, by Hans Günter Winkler of West Germany (1954 and 1955); and Raimondo d'Inzeo of Italy (1956 and 1960).

The greatest number of women's titles is also two, by Jane "Janou" Tissot (France) on Rocket in 1970 and 1974. The women's competition was only held between 1965 and 1974. The most wins in the team competition, which was inaugurated in 1978, is three, by France (1982, 1986, and 1990).

MOST OLYMPIC SHOW-JUMPING MEDALS
The most Olympic show-jumping gold medals won is five, by Hans Günter Winkler (West Germany): four team medals in 1956, 1960, 1964, and 1972, and the individual Grand Prix in 1956. Winkler also won a team silver in 1976 and a team bronze in 1968, giving him a record overall total of seven Olympic medals.

The most team wins is seven, by Germany (as West Germany in 1972 and 1988) in 1936, 1956, 1960, 1964, and 1996.

BEST OLYMPIC SHOW-JUMPING SCORE
The lowest score obtained by a winner is no faults by: Frantisek Ventura (Czechoslovakia) on Eliot in 1928; Alwin Schockemöhle (West Germany) on Warwick Rex in 1976; and Ludger Beerbaum (Germany) on Classic Touch in 1992.

→ **MOST SHOW-JUMPING WORLD CUPS**
The most wins in the World Cup is three, by Hugo Simon (Austria): on Gladstone in 1979, and on ET FRH in 1996 and 1997.

Sports Reference

SPEED & SKILL

TRACK-AND-FIELD

MEN'S OUTDOOR RECORDS

100 m.
9.79, Maurice Greene (USA), Athens, Greece, June 16, 1999

200 m.
19.32, Michael Johnson (USA), Atlanta, Georgia, USA, Aug. 1, 1996

400 m.
43.18, Michael Johnson (USA), Seville, Spain, Aug. 26, 1999

800 m.
1:41.11, Wilson Kipketer (Denmark), Cologne, Germany, Aug. 24, 1997

1,000 m.
2:11.96, Noah Ngeny (Kenya), Rieti, Italy, Sept. 5, 1999

1,500 m.
3:26.00, Hicham El Guerrouj (Morocco), Rome, Italy, July 14, 1998

1 mile
3:43.13, Hicham El Guerrouj (Morocco), Rome, Italy, July 7, 1999

2,000 m.
4:44.79, Hicham El Guerrouj (Morocco), Berlin, Germany, Sept. 7, 1999

3,000 m.
7:20.67, Daniel Komen (Kenya), Rieti, Italy, Sept. 1, 1996

5,000 m.
12:39.36, Haile Gebrselassie (Ethiopia), Helsinki, Finland, June 13, 1998

10,000 m.
26:22.75, Haile Gebrselassie (Ethiopia), Hengelo, Netherlands, June 1, 1998

20,000 m.
56:55.6, Arturo Barrios (Mexico, now USA), La Flèche, France, March 30, 1991

25,000 m.
1:13:55.8, Toshihiko Seko (Japan), Christchurch, New Zealand, March 22, 1981

30,000 m.
1:29:18.8, Toshihiko Seko (Japan), Christchurch, New Zealand, March 22, 1981

1 hour
21,101 m., Arturo Barrios (Mexico, now USA), La Flèche, France, March 30, 1991

110-m. hurdles
12.91, Colin Jackson (GB), Stuttgart, Germany, Aug. 20, 1993

400-m. hurdles
46.78, Kevin Young (USA), Barcelona, Spain, Aug. 6, 1992

3,000-m. steeplechase
7:55.72, Bernard Barmasai (Kenya), Cologne, Germany, Aug. 24, 1997

4 x 100-m. relay
37.40, USA (Michael Marsh, Leroy Burrell, Dennis A. Mitchell, Carl Lewis), Barcelona, Spain, Aug. 8, 1992; USA (John A. Drummond Jr., Andre Cason, Dennis A. Mitchell, Leroy Burrell), Stuttgart, Germany, Aug. 21, 1993

4 x 200-m. relay
1:18.68, Santa Monica Track Club (USA) (Michael Marsh, Leroy Burrell, Floyd Wayne Heard, Carl Lewis), Walnut, California, USA, 17 April 1994

4 x 400-m. relay
2:54.20, USA (Jerome Young, Antonio Pettigrew, Tyree Washington, Michael Johnson), New York, USA, July 23, 1998

4 x 800-m. relay
7:03.89, Great Britain (Peter Elliott, Garry Cook, Steve Cram, Sebastian Coe), Crystal Palace, London, England, Aug. 30, 1982

4 x 1,500-m. relay
14:38.8, West Germany (Thomas Wessinghage, Harald Hudak, Michael Lederer, Karl Fleschen), Cologne, Germany, Aug. 17, 1977

High Jump
2.45 m. (8 ft. 0.5 in.), Javier Sotomayor (Cuba), Salamanca, Spain, July 27, 1993

Pole Vault
6.14 m. (20 ft. 1 in.), Sergey Bubka (Ukraine), Setriere, Italy, July 31, 1994

Long Jump
8.95 m. (29 ft. 4.5 in.), Mike Powell (USA), Tokyo, Japan, Aug. 30, 1991

Triple Jump
18.29 m. (60 ft. 0.25 in.), Jonathan Edwards (GB), Gothenburg, Sweden, Aug. 7, 1995

Shot Put
23.12 m. (75 ft. 10.25 in.), Randy Barnes (USA), Los Angeles, California, USA, May 20, 1990

Discus
74.08 m. (243 ft.), Jürgen Schult (GDR), Neubrandenburg, Germany, June 6, 1986

Hammer Throw
86.7 m. (284 ft. 7 in.), Yuriy Sedykh (USSR, now Russia), Stuttgart, Germany, Aug. 30, 1986

Javelin
98.48 m. (323 ft. 1 in.), Jan Zelezny (Czech Republic), Jena, Germany, May 25, 1996

Decathlon
8,994 points, Tomas Dvorak (Czech Republic), Prague, Czech Republic, July 3–4, 1999
Day 1: 100 m.: 10.54; Long Jump: 7.9 m. (25 ft. 11 in.); Shot Put: 16.76 m. (54 ft. 11.75 in.); High Jump: 2.04 m. (6 ft. 9.5 in.); 400 m.: 48.08
Day 2: 110-m. hurdles: 13.73; Discus: 8.33 m. (158 ft. 6.75 in.); Pole Vault: 4.90 m. (16 ft. 0.75 in.); Javelin: 72.32 m. (237 ft. 3 in.); 1,500 m.: 4:37.20

WOMEN'S OUTDOOR RECORDS

100 m.
10.49, Florence "Flo Jo" Griffith-Joyner (USA), Indianapolis, Indiana, USA, July 16, 1988

200 m.
21.34, Florence "Flo Jo" Griffith-Joyner (USA), Seoul, South Korea, Sept. 29, 1988

400 m.
47.60, Marita Koch (GDR), Canberra, Australia, Oct. 6, 1985

800 m.
1:53.28, Jarmila Kratochvílová (Czechoslovakia), Munich, Germany, July 26, 1983

1,000 m.
2:28.98, Svetlana Masterkova (Russia), Brussels, Belgium, Aug. 23, 1996

1,500 m.
3:50.46, Qu Yunxia (China), Beijing, China, Sept. 11, 1993

1 mile
4:12.56, Svetlana Masterkova (Russia), Zürich, Switzerland, Aug. 14, 1996

2,000 m.
5:25.36, Sonia O'Sullivan (Ireland), Edinburgh, Scotland, July 8, 1994

3,000 m.
8:06.11, Wang Junxia (China), Beijing, China, Sept. 13, 1993

5,000 m.
14:28.09, Jiang Bo (China), Beijing, China, Oct. 23, 1997

10,000 m.
29:31.78, Wang Junxia (China), Beijing, China, Sept. 8, 1993

20,000 m.
1:06:48.8, Isumi Maki (Japan), Amagasaki, Japan, Sept. 20, 1993

25,000 m.
1:29:29.2, Karolina Szabó (Hungary), Budapest, Hungary, April 23, 1988

30,000 m.
1:47:05.6, Karolina Szabó (Hungary), Budapest, Hungary, April 23, 1988

1 hour
18,340 m., Tegla Loroupe (Kenya), Borgholzhausen, Germany, Aug. 7, 1998

100-m. hurdles
12.21, Yordanka Donkova (Bulgaria), Stara Zagora, Bulgaria, Aug. 20, 1988

400-m. hurdles
52.61, Kim Batten (USA), Gothenburg, Sweden, Aug. 11, 1995

4 x 100-m. relay
41.37, GDR (Silke Gladisch, Sabine Rieger, Ingrid Auerswald, Marlies Gohr), Canberra, Australia, Oct. 6, 1985

4 x 200-m. relay
1:28.15, GDR (Marlies Göhr, Romy Muller, Bärbel Wöckel, Marita Koch), Jena, Germany, Aug. 9, 1980

4 x 400-m. relay
3:15.17, USSR (Tatyana Ledovskaya, Olga Nazarova, Maria Pinigina, Olga Bryzgina), Seoul, South Korea, Oct. 1, 1988

4 x 800-m. relay
7:50.17, USSR (Nadezhda Olizarenko, Lyubov Gurina, Lyudmila Borisova, Irina Podyalovskaya), Moscow, Russia, Aug. 5, 1984

High Jump
2.09 m. (6 ft. 10.25 in.), Stefka Kostadinova (Bulgaria), Rome, Italy, Aug. 30, 1987

Pole Vault
4.62 m. (15 ft. 2 in.), Stacey Draglia (USA), Phoenix, Arizona, USA, May 28, 2000

Long Jump
7.52 m. (24 ft. 8 in.), Galina Chistyakova (USSR), Leningrad, USSR, June 11, 1988

Triple Jump
15.5 m. (50 ft. 10.25 in.), Inessa Kravets (Ukraine), Gothenburg, Sweden, Aug. 10, 1995

Shot Put
22.63 m. (74 ft. 3 in.), Natalya Lisovskaya (USSR), Moscow, Russia, June 7, 1987

Discus
76.80 m. (252 ft.), Gabriele Reinsch (GDR), Neubrandenburg, Germany, July 9, 1988

Javelin
67.09 m. (220 ft. 1 in.), Mirela Manjani-Tzelili (Greece), Seville, Spain, Aug. 28, 1999

Hammer Throw
76.07 m. (249 ft. 6 in.), Mihaela Melinte (Romania), Rudlingen, Germany, Aug. 29, 1999

3,000-m. steeplechase
9:48.88, Yelena Motalova (Russia), Tula, Russia, July 31, 1999

Heptathlon
7,291 points, Jackie Joyner-Kersee (USA), Seoul, South Korea, Sept. 23–24, 1988
100-m. hurdles: 12.69; High Jump: 1.86 m. (6 ft. 1.25 in.); Shot Put: 15.8 m. (51 ft. 10 in.); 200 m.: 22.56; Long Jump: 7.27 m. (23 ft. 10.25 in.); Javelin: 45.66 m. (149 ft. 10 in.); 800 m.: 2:08.51

MEN'S INDOOR RECORDS

50 m.
5.56, Donovan Bailey (Canada), Reno, Nevada, USA, Feb. 9, 1996; Maurice Greene (USA), Los Angeles, California, USA, Feb. 13, 1999

60 m.
6.39, Maurice Greene (USA), Madrid, Spain, Feb. 3, 1998

200 m.
19.92, Frank Fredericks (Namibia), Liévin, France, Feb. 18, 1996

400 m.
44.63, Michael Johnson (USA), Atlanta, Georgia, USA, March 4, 1995

800 m.
1:42.67, Wilson Kipketer (Denmark), Paris, France, March 9, 1997

1,000 m.
2:14.96, Wilson Kipketer (Denmark), Birmingham, England, Feb. 20, 2000

1,500 m.
3:31.18, Hicham El Guerrouj (Morocco), Stuttgart, Germany, Feb. 2, 1997

1 mile
3:48.45, Hicham El Guerrouj (Morocco), Ghent, Belgium, Feb. 12, 1997

3,000 m.
7:24.90, Daniel Komen (Kenya), Budapest, Hungary, Feb. 6, 1998

5,000 m.
12:50.38, Haile Gebrselassie (Ethiopia), Birmingham, England, Feb. 14, 1999

50-m. hurdles
6.25, Mark McKoy (Canada), Kobe, Japan, March 5, 1986

60-m. hurdles
7.30, Colin Jackson (GB), Sindelfingen, Germany, March 6, 1994

4 x 200-m. relay
1:22.11, Great Britain (Linford Christie, Darren Braithwaite, Ade Mafe, John Regis), Glasgow, Scotland, March 3, 1991

4 x 400-m. relay
3:02.83, USA (Andre Morris, Dameon Johnson, Deon Minor, Milton Campbell), Maebashi, Japan, March 7, 1999

5,000-m. walk
18:07.08, Mikhail Shchennikov (Russia), Moscow, Russia, Feb. 14, 1995

High Jump
2.43 m. (7 ft. 11.5 in.), Javier Sotomayor (Cuba), Budapest, Hungary, March 4, 1989

Pole Vault
6.15 m. (20 ft. 2 in.), Sergey Bubka (Ukraine), Donetsk, Ukraine, Feb. 21, 1993

Long Jump
8.79 m. (28 ft. 10 in.), Carl Lewis (USA), New York, USA, Jan. 27, 1984

Triple Jump
17.83 m. (58 ft. 6 in.), Alliacer Urrutia (Cuba), Sindelfingen, Germany, March 1, 1997

Shot Put
22.66 m. (74 ft. 4 in.), Randy Barnes (USA), Los Angeles, California, USA, Jan. 20, 1989

Heptathlon
6,476 points, Dan Dion O'Brien (USA), Toronto, Canada, March 13–14, 1993. 60 m.: 6.67; Long Jump: 7.84 m. (25 ft. 8.5 in.); Shot Put: 16.02 m. (52 ft. 6.5 in.); High Jump: 2.13 m. (6 ft. 11.75 in.); 60-m. hurdles: 7.85; Pole Vault: 5.20 m. (17 ft. 0.75 in.); 1,000 m.: 2:57.96

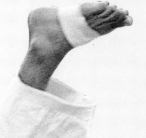

1 mile
4:17.14, Doina Melinte (Romania), East Rutherford, NJ, USA, Feb. 9, 1990

3,000 m.
8:33.82, Elly van Hulst (Netherlands), Budapest, Hungary, March 4, 1989

5,000 m.
14:47.36, Gabriela Szabo (Romania), Dortmund, Germany, Feb. 13, 1999

50-m. hurdles
6.58, Cornelia Oschkenat (GDR), Berlin, Germany, Feb. 20, 1988

60-m. hurdles
7.69, Lyudmila Narozhilenko (Russia), Chelyabinsk, Russia, Feb. 4, 1993

4 x 200-m. relay
1:32.55, SC Eintracht Hamm (West Germany) (Helga Arendt, Silke-Beate Knoll, Mechthild Kluth, Gisela Kinzel), Dortmund, Germany, Feb. 19, 1988; LG Olympia Dortmund

WOMEN'S INDOOR RECORDS

50 m.
5.96, Irina Privalova (Russia), Madrid, Spain, Feb. 9, 1995

60 m.
6.92, Irina Privalova (Russia), Madrid, Spain, Feb. 11, 1993, and Feb. 9, 1995

200 m.
21.87, Merlene Ottey (Jamaica), Liévin, France, Feb. 13, 1993

400 m.
49.59, Jarmila Kratochvílová (Czechoslovakia), Milan, Italy, March 7, 1982

800 m.
1:56.40, Christine Wachtel (GDR), Vienna, Austria, Feb. 13, 1988

1,000 m.
2:30.94, Maria Mutola (Mozambique), Stockholm, Sweden, Feb. 25, 1999

1,500 m.
4:00.27, Doina Melinte (Romania), East Rutherford, NJ, USA, Feb. 9, 1990

(Germany) (Esther Moller, Gabi Rockmeier, Birgit Rockmeier, Andrea Phillip), Karlsruhe, Germany, Feb. 21, 1999

4 x 400-m. relay
3:24.25, Russia (Tatyana Chebykina, Svetlana Goncharenko, Olga Kotlyarova, Natalya Nazarova), Maebashi, Japan, March 7, 1999

3,000-m. walk
11:40.33, Claudia Iovan (Romania), Bucharest, Romania, Jan. 30, 1999

High Jump
2.07 m. (6 ft. 9.5 in.), Heike Henkel (Germany), Karlsruhe, Germany, Feb. 9, 1992

Pole Vault
4.62 m. (15 ft. 2 in.), Stacey Dragila (USA), Atlanta, Georgia, USA, March 3, 2000

Long Jump
7.37 m. (24 ft. 2 in.), Heike Drechsler (GDR), Vienna, Austria, Feb. 13, 1988

Triple Jump
15.16 m. (49 ft. 8.75 in.), Ashia Hansen (GB), Valencia, Spain, Feb. 28, 1998

Shot Put
22.50 m. (73 ft. 10 in.), Helena Fibingerová (Czechoslovakia), Jablonec, Czechoslovakia, Feb. 19, 1977

Pentathlon
4,991 points, Irina Belova (Russia), Berlin, Germany, Feb. 14–15, 1992. 60-m. hurdles: 8.22; High Jump: 1.93 m. (6 ft. 4 in.); Shot Put: 13.25 m. (43 ft. 5.5 in.); Long Jump: 6.67 m. (21 ft. 10.5 in.); 800 m.: 2:10.26

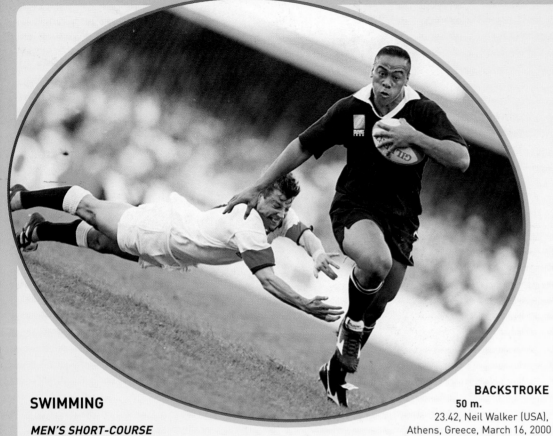

SWIMMING

MEN'S SHORT-COURSE RECORDS

FREESTYLE
50 m.
21.21, Anthony Ervin (USA),
Minneapolis, USA, March 23, 2000

100 m.
46.74, Aleksandr Popov (Russia),
Gelsenkirchen, Germany,
March 19, 1994

200 m.
1:41.10, Ian Thorpe (Australia),
Berlin, Germany, Feb. 5, 2000

400 m.
3:35.01, Grant Hackett (Australia),
Hong Kong, China, April 2, 1999

800 m.
7:34.90, Kieren Perkins (Australia),
Sydney, Australia, July 25, 1993

1,500 m.
14:19.55, Grant Hackett (Australia),
Sydney, Australia, Sept. 27, 1998

4 x 50-m. relay
1:26.99, Netherlands (Mark Veens,
Johan Kenkhuis, Atefan Aartsen,
Pieter van de Hoogenband),
Sheffield, S. Yorkshire, England,
Dec. 12, 1998

4 x 100-m. relay
3:09.57, Sweden (Johan Nystrom,
Lars Frolander, Mattias Ohlin,
Stefan Nystrand), Athens,
Greece, March 16, 2000

4 x 200-m. relay
7:01.33, USA (Josh Davis,
Neil Walker, Scott
Tucker, Chad Carvin),
Athens, Greece,
March 17, 2000

BACKSTROKE
50 m.
23.42, Neil Walker (USA),
Athens, Greece, March 16, 2000

100 m.
50.75, Neil Walker (USA), Athens,
Greece, March 19, 2000

200 m.
1:52.43, Lenny Krayzelburg (USA),
Berlin, Germany, Feb. 6, 2000

BREASTSTROKE
50 m.
26.70, Mark Warnecke (Germany),
Sheffield, S. Yorkshire, England,
Dec. 11, 1998

100 m.
57.66, Ed Moses (USA),
Minneapolis, USA,
March 24, 2000

200 m.
2:06.40, Ed Moses (USA),
Minneapolis, USA, March 25, 2000

BUTTERFLY
50 m.
23.19, Lars Frolander (Sweden),
Athens, Greece, March 19, 2000

100 m.
50.44, Lars Frolander (Sweden),
Athens, Greece, March 17, 2000

200 m.
1:51.76, James Hickman (GB),
Paris, France, March 28, 1998

MEDLEY
100 m.
52.79, Neil Walker (USA), Athens,
Greece, March 18, 2000

200 m.
1:54.65, Jani Sievinen (Finland),
Kuopio, Finland, Jan. 21, 1994;
Atilla Czene (Hungary),
Minneapolis, USA, March 23, 2000

400 m.
4:04.24, Matthew Dunn (Australia),
Perth, Australia, Sept. 24, 1998

4 x 50-m. relay
1:35.51, Germany (Thomas
Rupprath, Mark Warnecke,
Alexander Luderitz, Stephan
Kunzelmann); Sweden (Daniel
Carlsson, Patrick Isaksson, Jonas
Akesson, Lars Frolander), Sheffield,
S. Yorkshire, England, Dec. 13, 1998

4 x 100-m. relay
3:28.88, Australia (Matt Welsh, Phil
Rogers, Michael Klim, Chris Fydler),
Hong Kong, China, April 4, 1999

WOMEN'S SHORT-COURSE RECORDS

FREESTYLE
50 m.
23.59, Therese Alshammar
(Sweden), Athens, Greece,
March 18, 2000

100 m.
52.17, Therese
Alshammar
(Sweden),

Athens, Greece, March 17, 2000

200 m.
1:54.17, Claudia Poll (Costa Rica), Gothenburg, Sweden, April 18, 1997

400 m.
4:00.03, Claudia Poll (Costa Rica), Gothenburg, Sweden, April 19, 1997

800 m.
8:15.34, Astrid Strauss (GDR), Bonn, Germany, Feb. 6, 1987

1,500 m.
15:43.31, Petra Schneider (GDR), Gainesville, Florida, USA, Jan. 10, 1982

4 x 50-m. relay
1:38.45, Sweden (Johann Sjoberg, Anna-Karin

Kammerling, Therese Alshammar, Malin Svahnstrom), Lisbon, Portugal, Dec. 10, 1999

4 x 100-m. relay
3:34.55, China (Le Jingyi, Na Chao, Shan Ying, Nian Yin), Gothenburg, Sweden, April 19, 1997

4 x 200-m. relay
7:49.11, Great Britain (Claire Huddart, Nicola Jackson, Karen Legg, Karen Pickering), Athens, Greece, March 16, 2000

BACKSTROKE
50 m.
27.27, Sandra Voelker (Germany), Sheffield, S. Yorkshire, England, Dec. 13, 1998

100 m.
58.50, Angel Martino (USA), Palma de Mallorca, Spain, Dec. 3, 1993

200 m.
2:06.09, He Cihong (China), Palma de Mallorca, Spain, Dec. 5, 1993

BREASTSTROKE
50 m.
30.77, Han Xue (China), Gelsenkirchen, Germany, Feb. 2, 1997

100 m.
1:05.57, Penny Heyns (South Africa), Johannesburg, South Africa, Sept. 5, 1999

200 m.
2:20.22, Masami Tanaka (Japan), Hong Kong, China, April 2, 1999

BUTTERFLY
50 m.
26.00, Jenny Thompson (USA), College Park, Maryland, USA, Nov. 18, 1999

100 m.
56.56, Jenny Thompson (USA), Athens, Greece, March 18, 2000

200 m.
2:04.16, Susan O'Neill (Australia), Sydney, Australia, Jan. 18, 2000

MEDLEY
100 m.
59.30, Jenny Thompson (USA), Hong Kong, China, April 2, 1999

200 m.
2:07.79, Allison Wagner (USA), Palma de Mallorca, Spain, Dec. 5, 1993

400 m.
4:29.00, Dai Gouhong (China), Palma de Mallorca, Spain, Dec. 2, 1993

4 x 50-m. relay
1:49.47, Sweden (Johann Sjoberg, Anna-Karin Kammerling, Therese Alshammar, Emma Igelstrom), Lisbon, Portugal, Dec. 12, 1999

4 x 100-m. relay
3:57.46, University of Georgia, USA (Courtney Shealy, Kristy Kowal, Keegan Walkley, Maritza Correia), Minneapolis, USA, March 16, 2000

MEN'S LONG-COURSE RECORDS

FREESTYLE
50 m.
21.64, Aleksandr Popov (Russia), Moscow, Russia, June 16, 2000

100 m.
48.21, Aleksandr Popov (Russia), Monte Carlo, Monaco, June 18, 1994

200 m.
1:45.51, Ian Thorpe (Australia), Sydney, Australia, May 15, 2000

400 m.
3:41.33, Ian Thorpe (Australia), Sydney, Australia, May 13, 2000

800 m.
7:46.00, Kieren Perkins (Australia), Victoria, Canada, Aug. 24, 1994

1,500 m.
14:41.66, Kieren Perkins (Australia), Victoria, Canada, Aug. 24, 1994

4 x 100-m. relay
3:15.11 USA (David Fox, Joe Hudepohl, Jon Olsen, Gary Hall), Atlanta, Georgia, USA, Aug. 12 1995

4 x 200-m. relay
7:08.79, Australia (Ian Thorpe, William Kirby, Grant Hackett, Michael Klim), Sydney, Australia, Aug. 25, 1999

BACKSTROKE
50 m.
24.99, Lenny Krayzelburg (USA), Sydney, Australia, Aug. 28, 1999

100 m.
53.60, Lenny Krayzelburg (USA), Sydney, Australia, Aug. 24, 1999

200 m.
1:55.87, Lenny Krayzelburg (USA), Sydney, Australia, Aug. 27, 1999

BREASTSTROKE
50 m.
27.61, Alexander Dzhaburiya (Ukraine), Kharkov, Ukraine, April 27, 1996

100 m.
1:00.36, Roman Sloudnov (Russia), Moscow, Russia, June 15, 2000

200 m.
2:10.16, Mike Barrowman (USA), Barcelona, Spain, July 29, 1992

BUTTERFLY
50 m.
23.60, Geoffrey Huegill (Australia), Sydney, Australia, May 14, 2000

100 m.
51.81, Michael Klim (Australia), Canberra, Australia, Dec. 12, 1999

200 m.
1:55.18, Tom Malchow (USA), Charlotte, North Carolina, USA, June 18, 2000

MEDLEY
200 m.
1:58.16, Jani Sievinen (Finland), Rome, Italy, Sept. 11, 1994

400 m.
4:12.30, Tom Dolan (USA), Rome, Italy, Sept. 6, 1994

4 x 100-m. relay
3:34.84, USA (Jeff Rouse, Jeremy Linn, Mark Henderson, Gary Hall Jr.), Atlanta, Georgia, USA, July 26, 1996

WOMEN'S LONG-COURSE RECORDS

FREESTYLE
50 m.
24.39, Inge de Bruijn (Netherlands), Rio de Janeiro, Brazil, June 11, 2000

100 m.
53.80, Inge de Bruijn (Netherlands), Sheffield, S. Yorkshire, England, May 28, 2000

200 m.
1:56.78, Franziska van Almsick (Germany), Rome, Italy, Sept. 6, 1994

400 m.
4:03.85, Janet Evans (USA), Seoul, South Korea, Sept. 22, 1988

800 m.
8:16.22, Janet Evans (USA), Tokyo, Japan, Aug. 20, 1989

1,500 m.
15:52.10, Janet Evans (USA), Orlando, Florida, USA, March 26, 1988

4 x 100-m. relay
3:37.91, China (Le Jingyi, Shan Ying, Le Ying, Lu Bin), Rome, Italy, Sept. 7, 1994

4 x 200-m. relay
7:55.47, GDR (Manuela Stellmach, Astrid Strauss, Anke Möhring, Heike Friedrich), Strasbourg, France, Aug. 18, 1987

BACKSTROKE
50 m.
28.25, Sandra Voelker (Germany), Berlin, Germany, June 17, 2000

100 m.
1:00.16, He Cihong (China), Rome, Italy, Sept. 10, 1994

200 m.
2:06.62, Krisztina Egerszegi (Hungary), Athens, Greece, Aug. 25, 1991

BREASTSTROKE
50 m.
30.83, Penny Heyns (South Africa), Sydney, Australia, Aug. 28, 1999

100 m.
1:06.52, Penny Heyns (South Africa), Sydney, Australia, Aug. 23, 1999

200 m.
2:23.64, Penny Heyns (South Africa), Sydney, Australia, Aug. 27, 1999

BUTTERFLY

50 m. 25.64, Inge de Bruijn (Netherlands), Sheffield, S. Yorkshire, England, May 26, 2000

100 m. 56.69, Inge de Bruijn (Netherlands), Sheffield, S. Yorkshire, England, May 27, 2000

200 m.
2:05.81, Susan O'Neill (Australia), Sydney, Australia, May 17, 2000

MEDLEY
200 m.
2:09.72, Wu Yanyan (China), Shanghai, China, Oct. 17, 1997

400 m.
4:34.79, Chen Yan (China), Shanghai, China, Oct. 17, 1997

4 x 100-m. relay
4:01.67, China (He Cihong, Dai Guohong, Liu Limin, Le Jingyi), Rome, Italy, Sept. 10, 1994

CYCLING

MEN'S WORLD RECORDS

These records are recognized by the Union Cycliste Internationale (UCI). As of Jan. 1, 1993, their list no longer distinguishes between records set by professionals and amateurs, indoor and outdoor records, or records set at altitude and sea level.

UNPACED STANDING START
1 km. 1:00.613, Shane Kelly (Australia), Bogotá, Colombia, Sept. 26, 1995

4 km. 4:11.114, Chris Boardman (GB), Manchester, England, Aug. 29, 1996

4-km. team 4:00.958, Italy (Adler Capelli, Cristiano Citton, Andrea Collinelli, Mauro Trentini), Manchester, England, Aug. 31. 1996

1 hour 56.376 km., Chris Boardman (GB), Manchester, England, Sept. 6, 1996

UNPACED FLYING START
200 m. 9.865, Curtis Harnett (Canada), Bogotá, Colombia, Sept. 28, 1995

500 m. 26.649, Aleksandr Kiritchenko (USSR), Moscow, USSR, Oct. 29, 1988

WOMEN'S WORLD RECORDS

UNPACED STANDING START
500 m. 34.017, Felicia Ballanger (France), Bogotá, Colombia, Sept. 29, 1995

3 km. 3:30.974, Marion Clignet (France), Manchester, England, Aug. 31, 1996

1 hour 48.159 km., Jeanie Longo-Ciprelli (France), Mexico City, Mexico, Oct. 26, 1996

UNPACED FLYING START
200 m. 10.831, Olga Slyusareva (Russia), Moscow, Russia, April 25, 1993

500 m. 29.655, Erika Salumäe (USSR), Moscow, USSR, Aug. 6, 1987

MEN'S OLYMPIC RECORDS

UNPACED STANDING START

1 km. 1:02.712, Florian Rousseau (France), Atlanta, Georgia, USA, July 24, 1996

4 km. 4:19.699, Andrea Collinelli (Italy), Atlanta, Georgia, USA, July 24, 1996

4-km. team 4:05.930, France (Christophe Capelle, Philippe Ermenault, Jean-Michel Monin, Francis Moreau), Atlanta, Georgia, USA, July 27, 1996

UNPACED FLYING START

200 m. 10.129, Gary Neiwand (Australia), Atlanta, Georgia, USA, July 24, 1996

WOMEN'S OLYMPIC RECORDS

UNPACED STANDING START

3 km. 3:32.371, Antonella Bellutti (Italy), Atlanta, Georgia, USA, July 24, 1996

UNPACED FLYING START

200 m. 11.212, Michelle Ferris (Australia), Atlanta, Georgia, USA, July 26, 1996

SPEED SKATING

MEN'S RECORDS

500 m.
34.63, Jeremy Wotherspoon (Canada), Calgary, Alberta, Canada, March 18, 2000

1,000 m.
1:08.35, Jeremy Wotherspoon (Canada), Calgary, Alberta, Canada, March 18, 2000

1,500 m.
1:45.56, Jakko Jan Leeuwangh (Netherlands), Calgary, Alberta, Canada, Jan. 29, 2000

3,000 m.
3:43.76, Steven Elm (Canada), Calgary, Alberta, Canada, March 17, 2000

5,000 m.
6:18.72, Gianni Romme (Netherlands), Calgary, Alberta, Canada, Jan. 30, 2000

10,000 m.
13:08.71, Gianni Romme (Netherlands), Calgary, Alberta, Canada, March 29, 1998

WOMEN'S RECORDS

500 m.
37.55, Catriona Le May Doan (Canada), Calgary, Alberta, Canada, Dec. 29, 1997

1,000 m.
1:14.61, Monique Garbrecht (Germany), Calgary, Alberta, Canada, Feb. 21, 1999

1,500 m.
1:55.50, Annamarie Thomas (Netherlands), Calgary, Alberta, Canada, March 20, 1999

3,000 m.
4:00.51, Gunda Niemann-Stirnemann (Germany), Calgary, Alberta, Canada, Jan. 30, 2000

5,000 m.
6:56.84, Gunda Niemann-Stirnemann (Germany), Hamar, Norway, Jan. 16, 2000

HORSE RACING

EPSOM DERBY
(UK, first run 1780)
Fastest time: 2:32.31
Lammtarra, 1995
Most wins (Jockey): 9
Lester Piggott 1954–83
Most wins (Trainer): 7
Robert Robson 1793–1823
John Porter 1868–99
Fred Darling 1922–41
Most wins (Owner): 5
3rd Earl of Egremont 1782–1826
HH Aga Khan III 1930–52

PRIX DE L'ARC DE TRIOMPHE
(France, first run 1920)
Fastest time: 2:24.6
Peintre Célèbre, 1997
Most wins (Jockey): 4
Jacques Doyasbère 1942–51
Frédéric Head 1966–79
Yves Saint Martin 1970–84
Pat Eddery 1980–87
Most wins (Trainer): 4
Charles Semblat 1942–49
Alec Head 1952–81
François Mathet 1950–82
Most wins (Owner): 6
Marcel Boussac 1936–49

VRC MELBOURNE CUP
(Australia, first run 1861)
Fastest time: 3:16.3
Kingston Rule, 1990
Most wins (Jockey): 4
Bobby Lewis 1902–27
Harry White 1974–79
Most wins (Trainer): 11
Bart Cummings 1965–99
Most wins (Owner): 4
Etienne de Mestre 1861–78

KENTUCKY DERBY
(USA, first run 1875)
Fastest time: 1:59.4
Secretariat, 1973
Most wins (Jockey): 5
Eddie Arcaro 1938–52
Bill Hartack 1957–69
Most wins (Trainer): 6
Ben Jones 1938–52
Most wins (Owner): 8
Calumet Farm
1941–68

GRAND NATIONAL
(UK, first run 1839)
Fastest time: 8:47.8
Mr. Frisk, 1990
Most wins (Jockey): 5
George Stevens 1856–70
Most wins (Trainer): 4
Fred Rimell 1956–76
Most wins (Owner): 3
James Machell 1873–76
Sir Charles Assheton-Smith
1893–1913
Noel Le Mare 1973–77

JAPAN CUP
(Japan, first run 1981)
Fastest time: 2:22.2
Horlicks, 1989
Most wins (Jockey): 2
Yukio Okabe 1985–92

BALL SPORTS

BASEBALL

AL – American League
NL – National League

WORLD SERIES
Most series played in: 14,
Yogi Berra (New York, AL),
1947–63
**Most series played in by a
pitcher:** 11, Whitey Ford (New
York, AL), 1950–64
Most home runs in a game: 3
Babe Ruth (New York, AL),
Oct. 6, 1926 and Oct. 9, 1928;
Reggie Jackson (New York, AL),
Oct. 18, 1977
Runs batted in in a game: 6
Bobby Richardson (New
York, AL), Oct. 8, 1960
**Strikeouts in a
game:** 17, Robert
Gibson (St. Louis,
NL), Oct. 2, 1968
**Perfect game (9
innings):**
Don Larsen
(New York, AL)
v. Brooklyn,
Oct. 8, 1956

MAJOR LEAGUE BATTING RECORDS

AVERAGE
Career: .367, Ty Cobb
(Detroit, AL; Philadelphia,
AL), 1905–28
Season: .438, Hugh Duffy
(Boston, NL), 1894

RUNS SCORED
Career: 2,245, Ty Cobb, 1905–28
Season: 196, Billy Hamilton
(Philadelphia, NL), 1894

HOME RUNS
Career: 755, Hank Aaron
(Milwaukee, NL; Atlanta, NL;
Milwaukee, AL), 1954–76
Season: 70, Mark McGwire
(St. Louis, NL), 1998

RUNS BATTED IN
Career: 2,297, Hank Aaron,
1954–76
Season: 191, Hack Wilson
(Chicago, NL), 1930
Game: 12, Jim Bottomley
(St. Louis, NL), Sept. 16, 1924;
Mark Whiten (St. Louis, NL),
Sept. 7, 1993

BASE HITS
Career: 4,256, Pete Rose
(Cincinnati, NL; Philadelphia, NL;
Montreal, NL; Cincinnati, NL),
1963–86

Season: 257, George Sisler
(St. Louis, AL), 1920
Consecutive hits: 12
Pinky Higgins (Boston, AL),
June 19–21, 1938
Moose Dropo (Detroit, AL),
July 14–15, 1952
**Consecutive games batted in
safely:** 56, Joe DiMaggio (New
York, AL), May 15–July 16, 1941

TOTAL BASES
Career: 6,856, Hank Aaron,
1954–76
Season: 457, Babe Ruth, 1921

STOLEN BASES
Career: 1,344, Rickey Henderson
(Oakland, AL; New York, AL;
Oakland, AL; Toronto, AL; Oakland,
AL; San Diego, NL; Anaheim, AL;
Oakland, AL; New York, AL;
Seattle, AL), 1979–2000
Season: 130, Rickey Henderson
(Oakland, AL), 1982

CONSECUTIVE GAMES PLAYED:
2,632, Cal Ripken Jr.
(Baltimore, AL),
May 30, 1982–Sept. 19, 1998

Sports Reference

MAJOR LEAGUE PITCHING RECORDS

GAMES WON
Career: 511, Cy Young (Cleveland, NL; St. Louis, NL; Boston, AL; Cleveland, AL; Boston, NL), 1890–1911
Season: 60, Hoss Radbourn (Providence, NL), 1884
Consecutive games won: 24, Carl Hubbell (New York, NL), 1936–37

SHUTOUTS
Career: 110, Walter Johnson (Washington, AL), 1907–27
Season: 16
George Bradley (St. Louis, NL), 1876
Grover Alexander (Philadelphia, NL), 1916

STRIKEOUTS
Career: 5,714, Nolan Ryan (New York, NL; California, AL; Houston, NL; Texas, AL), 1966–93
Season: 383, Nolan Ryan (California, AL), 1973 (513, Matthew Kilroy (Baltimore, AA), 1886)
Game (9 innings): 20
Roger Clemens (Boston, AL) v. Seattle, April 29, 1986; and v. Detroit, Sept. 18, 1996

Kerry Wood (Chicago, NL) v. Houston, May 6, 1998

NO-HIT GAMES
Career: 7, Nolan Ryan, 1973–91

EARNED RUN AVERAGE
Season: 0.90, Ferdinand Schupp (140 innings) (New York, NL), 1916; 0.96, Dutch Leonard (222 innings) (Boston, AL), 1914; 1.12, Robert Gibson (305 innings) (St. Louis, NL), 1968

FOOTBALL

SUPER BOWL GAME AND CAREER RECORDS

MOST POINTS
Game: 18
Roger Craig (San Francisco 49ers), 1985
Jerry Rice (San Francisco 49ers), 1990, 1995
Ricky Watters (San Francisco 49ers), 1995
Terrell Davis (Denver Broncos), 1998
Career: 42, Jerry Rice, 1989–90, 1995

MOST TOUCHDOWNS
Game: 3
Roger Craig, 1985
Jerry Rice, 1990, 1995
Ricky Watters, 1995
Terrell Davis, 1998
Career: 7, Jerry Rice, 1989–90, 1995

MOST TOUCHDOWN PASSES
Game: 6, Steve Young (San Francisco 49ers), 1995
Career: 11, Joe Montana (San Francisco 49ers), 1982, 1985, 1989–90

MOST YARDS GAINED PASSING
Game: 414, Kurt Warner (St. Louis Rams), 2000
Career: 1,142, Joe Montana, 1982, 1985, 1989–90

MOST YARDS GAINED RUSHING
Game: 204, Timmy Smith (Washington Redskins), 1988
Career: 354, Franco Harris (Pittsburgh Steelers), 1975–76, 1979–80

MOST YARDS GAINED RECEIVING
Game: 215, Jerry Rice, 1989
Career: 512, Jerry Rice, 1989–90, 1995

MOST PASSES COMPLETED
Game: 31, Jim Kelly (Buffalo Bills), 1994
Career: 83, Joe Montana, 1982, 1985, 1989–90

PASS RECEPTIONS
Game: 11
Dan Ross (Cincinnati Bengals), 1982
Jerry Rice, 1989
Career: 28, Jerry Rice, 1989–90, 1995

FIELD GOALS
Game: 4
Don Chandler (Green Bay Packers), 1968
Ray Wersching (San Francisco 49ers), 1982

Career: 5, Ray Wersching, 1982, 1985

MOST VALUABLE PLAYER
Joe Montana, 1982, 1985, 1990

NFL RECORDS

MOST POINTS
Career: 2,002, George Blanda (Chicago Bears, Baltimore Colts, Houston Oilers, Oakland Raiders), 1949–75
Season: 176, Paul Hornung (Green Bay Packers), 1960
Game: 40, Ernie Nevers (Chicago Cardinals) v. Chicago Bears, Nov. 28, 1929

MOST TOUCHDOWNS
Career: 180, Jerry Rice (San Francisco 49ers), 1985–99
Season: 25, Emmitt Smith (Dallas Cowboys), 1995
Game: 6
Ernie Nevers (Chicago Cardinals) v. Chicago Bears, Nov. 28, 1929
William Jones (Cleveland Browns) v. Chicago Bears, Nov. 25, 1951
Gale Sayers (Chicago Bears) v. San Francisco 49ers, Dec. 12, 1965

MOST YARDS GAINED RUSHING
Career: 16,726, Walter Payton (Chicago Bears), 1975–87
Season: 2,105, Eric Dickerson (Los Angeles Rams), 1984
Game: 275, Walter Payton (Chicago Bears) v. Minnesota Vikings, Nov. 20, 1977

MOST YARDS GAINED RECEIVING
Career: 18,883, Jerry Rice, 1985–99
Season: 1,848, Jerry Rice, 1995
Game: 336, Willie Anderson (Los Angeles Rams) v. New Orleans Saints, Nov. 26, 1989

MOST COMBINED NET YARDS GAINED
Career: 21,803, Walter Payton (Chicago Bears), 1975–87
Season: 2,535, Lionel James (San Diego Chargers), 1985

Game: 404, Glyn Milburn (Denver Broncos) v. Seattle Seahawks, Dec. 10, 1996

MOST YARDS GAINED PASSING
Career: 61,631, Dan Marino (Miami Dolphins), 1983–99
Season: 5,084, Dan Marino, 1984
Game: 554, Norm Van Brocklin (Los Angeles Rams) v. New York Yanks, Sept. 28, 1951

MOST PASSES COMPLETED
Career: 4,967, Dan Marino, 1983–99
Season: 404, Warren Moon (Houston Oilers), 1991
Game: 45, Drew Bledsoe (New England Patriots) v. Minnesota Vikings, Nov. 13, 1994

PASS RECEPTIONS
Career: 1,206, Jerry Rice, 1985–99
Season: 123, Herman Moore, (Detroit Lions), 1995
Game: 18, Tom Fears (Los Angeles Rams) v. Green Bay Packers, Dec. 3, 1950

MOST TOUCHDOWN PASSES
Career: 420, Dan Marino, 1983–99
Season: 48, Dan Marino, 1984
Game: 7
Sid Luckman (Chicago Bears) v. New York Giants, Nov. 14, 1943
Adrian Burk (Philadelphia Eagles) v. Washington Redskins, Oct. 17, 1954
George Blanda (Houston Oilers) v. New York Titans, Nov. 19, 1961
Y.A. Tittle (New York Giants) v. Washington Redskins, Oct. 28, 1962
Joe Kapp (Minnesota Vikings) v. Baltimore Colts, Sept. 28, 1969

FIELD GOALS
Career: 439, Gary Anderson (Pittsburgh Steelers, 1982–94; Philadelphia Eagles, 1995–96; San Francisco 49ers, 1997; Minnesota Vikings, 1999)
Season: 39, Olindo Mare (Miami Dolphins), 1999
Game: 7
Jim Bakken (St. Louis Cardinals) v. Pittsburgh Steelers, Sept. 24, 1967

Sports Reference

Rich Karlis (Minnesota Vikings) v. Los Angeles Rams, Nov. 5, 1989 Chris Boniol (Dallas Cowboys) v. Green Bay Packers, Nov. 18, 1996 **Longest:** 63 yds. (57.6 m.) Tom Dempsey (New Orleans Saints) v. Detroit Lions, Nov. 8, 1970; Jason Elam (Denver Broncos) v. Jacksonville Jaguars, Oct. 25, 1998

CRICKET

FIRST-CLASS (FC) AND TEST CAREER

BATTING
MOST RUNS
FC: 61,237, Sir Jack Hobbs (avg. 50.65), Surrey/England, 1905–34
Test: 11,174, Allan Border (avg. 50.56), Australia (156 Tests), 1978–94

MOST CENTURIES
FC: 197, Sir Jack Hobbs (in 1,315 innings), Surrey/England, 1905–34
Test: 34, Sunil Gavaskar (in 214 innings), India, 1971–87

HIGHEST AVERAGE
FC: 95.14, Sir Don Bradman, NSW/South Australia/Australia, 1927–49 (28,067 runs in 338 innings, including 43 not outs)
Test: 99.94, Sir Don Bradman (6,996 runs in 80 innings), Australia (52 Tests), 1928–48

BOWLING
MOST WICKETS
FC: 4,187, Wilf Rhodes (avg. 16.71), Yorkshire/England, 1898–1930
Test: 439, Courtney Walsh (avg. 25.11), West Indies, 1984–2000

LOWEST AVERAGE
Test: 10.75, George Lohmann (112 wickets), England (18 Tests), 1886–96 (minimum 25 wickets)

WICKET-KEEPING
MOST DISMISSALS
FC: 1,649, Bob Taylor, Derbyshire/England, 1960–88

Test: 381, Ian Healy, Australia (111 Tests), 1988–99

MOST CATCHES
FC: 1,473, Bob Taylor, Derbyshire/England, 1960–88
Test: 353, Ian Healy, Australia (111 Tests), 1988–99

MOST STUMPINGS
FC: 418, Leslie Ames, Kent/England, 1926–51
Test: 52, William Oldfield, Australia (54 Tests), 1920–37

FIELDING
MOST CATCHES
FC: 1,018, Frank Woolley, Kent/England, 1906–38
Test: 157, Mark Taylor, Australia (104 Tests), 1989–99

GOLF

MOST MAJOR GOLF TITLES
British Open: 6
Harry Vardon 1896, 98, 99, 1903, 11, 14
British Amateur: 8
John Ball 1888, 90, 92, 94, 99, 1907, 10, 12
US Open: 4
Willie Anderson 1901, 03–05
Bobby Jones Jr. 1923, 26, 29, 30
Ben Hogan 1948, 50, 51, 53

Jack Nicklaus 1962, 67, 72, 80
US Amateur: 5
Bobby Jones Jr. 1924, 25, 27, 28, 30
US PGA: 5
Walter Hagan 1921, 24–27
Jack Nicklaus 1963, 71, 73, 75, 80
US Masters: 6
Jack Nicklaus 1963, 65, 66, 72, 75, 86
US Women's Open: 4
Betsy Earle-Rawls 1951, 53, 57, 60
Mickey Wright 1958, 59, 61, 64
US Women's Amateur: 6
Glenna Vare 1922, 25, 28–30, 35
British Women's Amateur: 4
Charlotte Pitcairn Leitch 1914, 20, 21, 26
Joyce Wethered 1922, 24, 25, 29

Jack Nicklaus is the only golfer to have won five different major titles (the British Open, US Open, US Masters, US PGA, and US Amateur titles) twice, and a record 20 all told (1959–86).

In 1930 Bobby Jones achieved a unique "Grand Slam" of the US and British Open and Amateur titles.

TARGET SPORTS

SHOOTING

MEN'S RECORDS

Rifle 50 m. 3 x 40 shots
1,287.9 (1,186 + 101.9)
Rajmond Debevec (Slovenia), Munich, Germany, Aug. 29, 1992

Rifle 50 m. 60 shots prone
704.8 (600 + 104.8)

Christian Klees (Germany), Atlanta, Georgia, USA, July 25, 1996

Air rifle 10 m. 60 shots
700.6 (598 + 102.6)
Jason Parker (USA), Munich, Germany, May 23, 1998

Double trap 150 targets
194 (146 + 48)
Daniele Di Spigno (Italy), Tampere, Finland, July 7, 1999

Pistol 50 m. 60 shots
676.2 (577 + 99.2)
William Demarest (USA), Milan, Italy, June 4, 2000

Rapid-fire pistol 25 m. 60 shots
699.7 (596 + 103.7)
Ralf Schumann (Germany), Barcelona, Spain, June 8, 1994

Air pistol 10 m. 60 shots
695.1 (593 + 102.1)
Sergey Pyzhyanov (USSR), Munich, Germany, Oct. 13, 1989

Running target 10 m. 30/30 shots
687.9 (586 + 101.9)
Ling Yang (China), Milan, Italy, June 6, 1996

Trap 125 targets
150 (125 + 25)
Marcello Tittarelli (Italy), Suhl, Germany, June, 11, 1996

Skeet 125 targets
150 (125 + 25) Jan Heinrich (Germany), Lonato, Italy, June 5, 1996
Andrea Benelli (Italy), Suhl, Germany, June 11, 1996
Ennio Falco (Italy), Lonato, Italy, April 19, 1997
Harald Jensen (Norway), Kumamoto City, Japan, June 1, 1999
Franck Durbesson (France), Sydney, Australia, March 31, 2000

WOMEN'S RECORDS

Rifle 50 m. 3 x 20 shots
689.7 (592 + 97.7)
Vessela Letcheva (Bulgaria), Munich, Germany,

June 15, 1995
689.7 (591 + 98.7)
Wang Xian (China), Milan, Italy, May 29, 1998

Air rifle 10 m. 40 shots
503.5 (398 + 105.5)
Gaby Buehlmann (Switzerland), Munich, Germany, May 24, 1998

Pistol 25 m. 60 shots
696.2 (594 + 102.2)
Diana Jorgova (Bulgaria), Milan, Italy, May 31, 1994

Air pistol 10 m. 40 shots
493.5 (390 + 103.5)
Ren Jie (China), Munich, Germany, May 22, 1998

Trap 100 targets
95 (71 + 24)
Satu Pusila (Finland), Nicosia, Cyprus, June 13, 1998
95 (71 + 24)
Delphine Racinet (France), Sydney, Australia, March 26, 2000

Double trap 120 targets
149 (113 + 36)
Deborah Gelisio (Italy), Nicosia, Cyprus, June 19, 1995
149 (110 + 39)
Xiang Xu (China), Munich, Germany, Sept. 3, 1995
149 (111 + 38)
Deborah Gelisio (Italy), Munich, Germany, Sept. 3, 1995

Skeet 100 targets
99 (75 + 24)
Svetlana Demina (Russia), Kumamoto City, Japan, June 1, 1999

ARCHERY

MEN (SINGLE FITA ROUNDS)
FITA: 1,368 of 1,440 points
Oh Kyo-moon (South Korea), 1995
90 m.: 331 of 360 points
Chang Yong-ho (South Korea), 1999
70 m.: 345 of 360 points
Jackson Fear (Australia), 1997
50 m.: 351 of 360 points
Kim Kyung-ho (South Korea), 1997
30 m.: 360 of 360 points
Han Seuong-hoon (South Korea), 1994
Team: 4,053 of 4,320 points
South Korea (Oh Kyo-moon, Lee Kyung-chul, Kim Jae-pak), 1995

WOMEN (SINGLE FITA ROUNDS)

FITA: 1,380 of 1,440 points
Chung Chang-sook (South Korea), 1999
70 m.: 343 of 360 points
Chung Chang-sook (South Korea), 1999
60 m.: 350 of 360 points
Kim Jo-soon (South Korea), 1998
50 m.: 345 of 360 points
Kim Moon-sun (South Korea), 1996
30 m.: 360 of 360 points
Ha Na-young (South Korea), 1998

Team: 4,094 of 4,320 points
South Korea (Kim Soo-nyung, Lee Eun-kyung, Cho Yuon-jeong), 1992

INDOOR (18M.)

Men: 596 of 600 points
Magnus Pettersson (Sweden), 1995
Women: 591 of 600 points
Lina Herasymenko (Ukraine), 1996

INDOOR (25M.)

Men: 593 of 600 points
Magnus Pettersson (Sweden), 1993
Women: 592 of 600 points
Petra Ericsson (Sweden), 1991

STRENGTH

WEIGHT LIFTING

IWF WORLD RECORDS

MEN'S RECORDS

On Jan. 1, 1998, the International Weightlifting Federation (IWF) introduced modified bodyweight categories, thereby making all the then-world records redundant.

This is the current list, which features world standards where a record has yet to be set. Results achieved at IWF-approved competitions that exceed the world standards by 0.5 kg. for snatch or clean and jerk, or by 2.5 kg. for the total, will be recognized as world records.

56 kg. bodyweight
Snatch: 137.5 kg.
Halil Mutulu (Turkey), Athens, Greece, Nov. 22, 1999
Clean & Jerk: 166.5 kg.
Halil Mutulu (Turkey), Sofia, Bulgaria, April 25, 2000
Total: 302.5 kg.
Halil Mutulu (Turkey), Athens, Greece, Nov. 22, 1999

62 kg. bodyweight
Snatch: 152.5 kg.
Shi Zhiyong (China), Osaka, Japan, May 3, 2000
Clean & Jerk: 180.5 kg.
Le Maosheng (China), Athens, Greece, Nov. 23, 1999
Total: 325 kg. World Standard

69 kg. bodyweight
Snatch: 162.5 kg.
Galabin Boevski (Bulgaria), Athens, Greece, Nov. 24, 1999
Clean & Jerk: 196 kg.
Galabin Boevski (Bulgaria), Athens, Greece, Nov. 24, 1999

Total: 357.5 kg.
Galabin Boevski (Bulgaria), Athens, Greece, Nov. 24, 1999

77 kg. bodyweight
Snatch: 170.5 kg.
Khach Kyapanaktsyan (Armenia), Athens, Greece, Nov. 25, 1999
Clean & Jerk: 207.5 kg.
Zlatan Vaner (Bulgaria), Sofia, Bulgaria, April 28, 2000
Total: 372.5 kg. World Standard

85 kg. bodyweight
Snatch: 181 kg.
Georgi Asanidze (Georgia), Sofia, Bulgaria, April 29, 2000
Clean & Jerk: 218 kg.
Zhang Yong (China), Tel Aviv, Israel, April 25, 1998
Total: 395 kg. World Standard

94 kg. bodyweight
Snatch: 188 kg.
Akakios Kakiashvilis (Greece),
Athens, Greece, Nov. 27, 1999
Clean & Jerk: 232.5 kg.
Szymon Kolecki (Poland),
Sofia, Bulgaria, April 29, 2000
Total: 417.5 kg. World Standard

105 kg. bodyweight
Snatch: 197.5 kg. World Standard
Clean & Jerk: 242.5 kg.
World Standard
Total: 440 kg. World Standard

+105 kg. bodyweight
Snatch: 206 kg.
Hossein Rezazadeh (Iran),
Athens, Greece, Nov. 28, 1999
Clean & Jerk: 262.5 kg.
World Standard
Total: 465 kg.
Ronny Weller (Germany),
Riesa, Germany, May 3, 1998

IWF WORLD RECORDS

WOMEN'S RECORDS

48 kg. bodyweight
Snatch: 85 kg.
Donka Mincheva (Bulgaria),
Sofia, Bulgaria, April 25, 2000
Clean & Jerk: 113.5 kg.
Donka Mincheva (Bulgaria),
Athens, Greece, Nov. 21, 1999

Total: 195 kg.
Li Zhou (China),
Wuhan, China,
Aug. 29, 1999

53 kg. bodyweight
Snatch: 97.5 kg.
Meng Xianjuan (China), Chiba,
Japan, May 1, 1999
Clean & Jerk: 121.5 kg.
Li Feng-Ying

(Taiwan), Athens, Greece,
Nov. 21, 1999
Total: 217.5 kg.
Meng Xianjuan (China),
Chiba, Japan, May 1, 1999

58 kg. bodyweight
Snatch: 105 kg.
Chen Yanqing (China),
Athens, Greece, Nov. 22, 1999
Clean & Jerk: 131.5 kg.
Ri Song-hui (North Korea),
Osaka, Japan, May 3, 2000
Total: 235 kg.
Chen Yanqing (China),
Athens, Greece, Nov. 22, 1999

63 kg. bodyweight
Snatch: 110 kg.
Lei Li (China), Chiba, Japan,
May 2, 1999
Clean & Jerk: 132.5 kg.
Xiong Meiyin (China),
Athens, Greece, Nov. 23, 1999
Total: 240 kg.
Chen Yui-Lien (Taiwan),
Athens, Greece, Nov. 23, 1999

69 kg. bodyweight
Snatch: 111 kg.
Sun Tianni (China),
Bangkok, Thailand, Dec. 11, 1998
Clean & Jerk: 143 kg.
Sun Tianni (China), Athens, Greece,
Nov. 24, 1999
Total: 255 kg.
Lin Weining (China), Wuhan, China,
Sept. 3, 1999

75 kg. bodyweight
Snatch: 116 kg.
Tang Weifang (China),
Wuhan, China, Sept. 4, 1999
Clean & Jerk: 142.5 kg.
Sun Tianni (China), Osaka, Japan,
May 6, 2000
Total: 252.5 kg.
Tang Weifang (China),
Wuhan, China, Sept. 4, 1999

+75 kg. bodyweight
Snatch: 127.5 kg.
Agata Wrobel (Poland),
Athens, Greece, Nov. 27, 1999
Clean & Jerk: 160.5 kg.
Ding Meiyuan (China),
Osaka, Japan, May 6, 2000
Total: 285 kg.
Ding Meiyuan (China),
Athens, Greece,
Nov. 27, 1999

So You Want To Set A Record...?

⊙ A RUBBER BAND RECORD
John Bain of Wilmington, Delaware, USA, is pictured with his record-breaking rubber band ball, which weighs 2,000 lbs. Do you think you could do better?

Guinness World Records 2001 features many people who have accomplished extraordinary feats. Do you think you have what it takes to become one of those people? If you would like to break, or establish, a record, read on.

"I CAN DO THAT!"
You might not be able to run as fast as Michael Johnson, or sell as many records as Madonna, but everyone can set a record, either as an individual or as part of a team. Why not start a collection? It needn't be expensive: our database has records for collections of buttons, bus tickets, and bottle caps. Or you could get together with friends and try to break the record for the longest paper clip chain or the biggest group hug. Why not set a brand new record?

Every day brings suggestions for new record categories and we try to find ways of accepting as many of these as possible. What we are looking for in a new category is a challenge that is interesting, requires skill, is safe and, most importantly, is likely to attract challenges from other people.

All record-breakers receive a certificate acknowledging that they have become members of an exclusive body – official Guinness World Record holders. To receive this certificate, you don't just have to break a record – you need to prove that you have broken it.

DOCUMENTATION
Any potential record-breaker must allow his or her attempt to be scrutinized. A requirement for all record challenges is a clearly labeled VHS videotape (with the official clock in view where appropriate). Good-quality color photographs or transparencies should also be submitted with the claim. It's a good idea to get your local newspaper or radio or TV station interested in your record challenge and persuade a reporter to be present. Any newspaper cuttings or recordings of the attempt will be useful.

Every record claim must be accompanied by detailed documentation. At least two independent witness statements are needed, and your witnesses should be people of some standing in the community: doctors, lawyers, councillors, police officers, or officials of a professional or sporting body, for example. Some records may also require an expert, such as a surveyor or a public health official, to be present. Witnesses must not be related to you. Witnesses should be able to confirm that they have seen the successful progress and completion of the record attempt, and that the guidelines have been followed.

GUIDELINES
For most human endeavor categories, Guinness World Records has specific guidelines to ensure that all contestants are attempting a record under exactly the same conditions. Only in this way will we be able to compare your achievements.

APPLY EARLY
Whatever record category you decide to attempt, it's important to contact us early. If your proposal is accepted as a new category, we may have to draw up new guidelines with the assistance of experts. So please allow both us and you plenty of time for preparation. You should also check with us shortly before the attempt in order to make sure that the record hasn't recently been broken.

GETTING IN TOUCH
To contact Guinness World Records, call: 0891 517607 (++ 44 891 517607 if calling from outside the UK). Calls currently cost no more than 50p per minute if dialing from within the UK. You can also e-mail us at: infouk@guinnessrecords.com fax us on: 020 7891 4504 (++ 44 20 7891 4504 if dialing from outside the UK) or write to us at: GUINNESS WORLD RECORDS LTD, 338 EUSTON ROAD, LONDON NW1 3BD, UNITED KINGDOM.

WILL MY RECORD BE IN THE BOOK?
Not all new records appear in the book. With tens of thousands of records on the Guinness World Records database, we only have space to include a small fraction of the current records in any one year. The book you are reading now is a selection of the subjects and categories that we believe will be of the most interest to our readers. Also, some long-standing records are left out to give newer record holders a chance of inclusion. The same principle applies to our website, www.guinnessworldrecords.com and to the *Guinness World Records* TV shows.

However, as long as you have an official certificate from Guinness World Records, you are entitled to call yourself a Guinness World Record holder.

TAKING CARE
Safety precautions are an important factor in record guidelines. All record attempts are undertaken at the sole risk of the competitor. Guinness World Records Ltd. cannot be held responsible for any (potential) liability whatever arising out of any such attempt, whether to the claimant or any third party.

Guinness World Records: Primetime

⊙ **LOWEST ROLLER SKATE LIMBO SPLITS**
Xue Wang of Beijing, China, performed the splits under a bar set at 5.75 in. on Sept. 23, 1999.

The second series of *Guinness World Records: Primetime,* hosted by Mark Thompson, was shown on the Fox network. Here are the amazing people featured on it.

HEAVIEST GROIN BREAK
Cliff Flenoy (USA) had two 8-in. x 8-in. x 16-in. concrete blocks smashed on his groin with a 14-lb. sledgehammer.

COCKROACH COFFIN
John Lamedica (USA) was placed in a Plexiglas coffin, and 20,050 cockroaches were poured on him.

HEAVIEST MODEL
Gina Gershwin-Varney (USA) displayed her 821-lb. frame in specialist videos in 1997. She now weighs about 425 lbs.

HIGHEST SLACK LINE WALK
Darrin Carter (USA) walked 100 ft. on a 1-in. wide line, 2,900 ft. above the ground at Yosemite National Park, California, USA.

SMALLEST CORSETED WAIST ON A LIVING PERSON
Cathie Jung (USA) has a waist measuring 15 in.

FASTEST TIME TO ENTER A LOCKED STRAITJACKET
Daniel Smith (USA) entered a locked straitjacket in 2 min. 8 sec.

STEEPEST TIGHTROPE WALK
Javier Gomez (USA), completed a 61.5-ft. tightrope walk ranging between 24° and 44° without a balancing pole.

MOST PIERCED MAN
Luis Antonio Aguero (Cuba) has 230 piercings on his body and head.

MOST DEVELOPED THIRD FOOT
Jose Lopez (USA) had a third foot, consisting of an ankle and four toes, growing from the ankle of his left leg.

MOST SWORDS SWALLOWED AND TWISTED
Brad Byers (USA) swallowed 10 27-in. swords, and rotated them through 180° in his esophagus.

MOST HEAD BOARDS BROKEN
Kevin Shelley (USA) broke 31 1-in.-thick pine boards on his forehead in 30 sec.

FASTEST HUMAN CALCULATOR
Scott Flansburg (USA) added a two-digit number (54) to itself, 35 times in 15 seconds, beating an accountant using a calculator by seven computations.

LONGEST BUBBLE
Alan McKay (New Zealand) created a bubble 105 ft. long. He made it with a bubble wand, dishwashing liquid, glycerol, and water.

LONGEST ZORB BALL JOURNEY
Rich Eley (UK) travelled 1,060 ft. in a Zorb ball in a single roll.

SNAKE SITTING IN A BATHTUB
Jackie Bibby and Rosie Reynolds (both USA) sat in tubs with 75 rattlesnakes.

MOST WEIGHT ON BODY
Kahled Dahdouh (USA) sustained 3,045 lbs. (made up of cinder blocks and three bodybuilders) on his chest for 5 seconds.

FASTEST SPEED ON TITANIUM BOOTS
The fastest speed achieved when pulled by a motorcycle on titanium-soled boots is 156.3 m.p.h. by Gary Rothwell (UK).

MARSHMALLOW NOSE BLOW
Scott Jeckel launched a marshmallow from his nose into the mouth of Ray Perisin, 16 ft. 3.5 in. away.

MOST DOWNLOADED WOMAN
In 1995, Cindy Margolis was filmed by a TV crew, after which 70,000 people downloaded her image in 24 hours. Another TV appearance resulted in her image being downloaded once every 10 seconds for 48 hours.

FIRST SUCCESSFUL CRANIOPAGUS SEPARATION
Vilija and Vatalija Tamulevicius were born in 1987 in Lithuania, joined at the head. Drs. Alexander Konovalov and Kenneth E. Salyer operated to separate the twins and rebuild their skulls.

BEARDED WOMAN
Vivian Wheeler (USA), has a beard measuring 8 in.

HEAVIEST EAR LIFT
Li Jian Hua (China) lifted 110.1 lbs. with his ear for 9.3 seconds.

LONGEST UNDERWATER CAVE
Nohoch Na Chich cave system, Mexico, has over 230,000 ft. of mapped passages.

TARANTULA BUBBLE BLOWING
Ray Macaraeg (USA) blew 117 soap bubbles in 30 seconds with a live tarantula nestled inside his mouth.

FASTEST HOT WATER BOTTLE BLOW-UP
Paul Pumphrey (USA) blew up a standard hot water bottle in 59.3 sec.

UNICYCLE BOWL STACK
Nancy Huey (USA) stacked a record 31 aluminum bowls while on a 7-ft. 6-in.-high unicycle.

HELICOPTER SKY SURFING
Chris Gauge (UK) made 64 spins in the sky surfing position in 20 seconds.

OLDEST UNDISCOVERED TWIN
Hisham Ragab (Egypt) lived for 16 years with the fetus of his twin brother inside his abdomen.

⊙ MOST COBRAS KISSED
Gordon Cates, of Alachua, Florida, USA, kissed 10 monocle cobras and a 15-ft. king cobra consecutively on Sept. 25, 1999.

⊙ HIGHEST SHALLOW DIVE
Danny Higginbottom, of Metairie, Louisiana, USA, dived from a height of 29 ft. into 12.5 in. of water on Aug. 23, 1999. He dedicated his dive to his late father.

HUMAN SPEED BUMP
Tom Owen (USA) was run over by seven consecutive trucks (six pickup trucks and a van) with a combined weight of approximately 12,000 lbs.

HUMAN MILKSHAKE
Gary Bashaw Jr. (USA) mixed milk and chocolate powder in his mouth, and dispensed 1.82 oz. of the mixture through his nose into a beaker.

LONGEST PUMPKIN SHOOT
A pumpkin was "shot" a distance of 4,491 ft. by the Aludium Q-36 Pumpkin Modulator, built and manned by Matt Parker, Chuck Heerde, Rod Litwiller, Steve Young, and James Knepp.

LONGEST DELAYED PARACHUTE DROP
USAF Capt. Joe Kittinger jumped out of an open-air gondola from a helium balloon 102,800 ft. above the earth. He fell for 4 min. 37 sec., reaching a maximum speed of 714 m.p.h. before his parachute was automatically deployed.

LONGEST TRAILER RAMP JUMP
Ray Baumann (Australia) jumped 157 ft. 6 in. in a car with a trailer attached to the back.

MOST RHINESTONES ON BODY
Tina-Marie Stoker (USA) put 26,310 rhinestones on model Morisa Kaplan.

MOST METAL EATEN
Michel Lotito (France) known as M. Mangetout, has eaten 2 lbs. of metal a day since 1959.

MOST FOOT JUGGLES
Ali Bandbaz juggled his brother Massoud Bandbaz 21 times in 30 sec.

HEAVIEST LIVING ATHLETE
Amateur sumo wrestler Manny Yarborough (USA) is 6 ft. 8 in. tall and weighs 704 lbs.

LONGEST TIME SUSPENDED BETWEEN TWO BIPLANES
Yves Rossy (Switzerland) was suspended between two Boeing Sterman PT17s for 9.4 seconds.

FASTEST KETCHUP DRINKER
Dustin Phillips (USA) drank 91% of a 14-oz. bottle of Heinz tomato ketchup through a straw in 33 seconds.

STRETCHIEST SKIN
Gary Turner (UK) stretched the skin of his stomach 6.25 in. He has a rare skin condition called Ehlers-Danlos syndrome (EDS).

DEEPEST TWO-BREATH DIVE
Francisco Ferraras dived 511 ft. at Grand Cayman.

LONGEST EAR SLINGSHOT
Monte Pierce (USA) fired a dime 10 ft. 10.5 in. with his earlobe.

FIRST HAND TRANSPLANT
Clint Hallam (Australia) underwent the world's first successful hand transplant on Sept. 23, 1998.

HIGHEST SPEED MOTORCYCLE CRASH
Ron Cook (USA) survived a crash at 200 m.p.h. when he crashed at El Mirage Dry Lake, California, in July 1998.

BIGGEST JET FIGHTER COLLECTION
Michel Pont (France) has 110 jet fighters.

TALLEST HUMAN CHAIR STACK
The Peking Acrobats (China) created a chair stack 21-ft. high, with six people stacked onto seven chairs.

TIGHTEST FRYING PAN ROLL
Craig Pumphrey (USA) rolled an aluminum frying pan (diameter 12 in.) to a circumference of 9.25 in. in 30 sec.

GLOBE OF DEATH
A team of five motorcyclists led by Robin Tabak (USA) rode inside a steel sphere (diameter 14 ft. 3 in.) around a central person.

LONGEST CANOE WATERFALL DROP
Tao Berman (USA) descended 98.4 ft. in 2.4 seconds in a canoe at the Upper Johnstone Canyon Falls, Alberta, Canada.

MOST UNICYCLE ROPE JUMPS
Unicyclist Peter Rosendahl (Sweden) jumped a record 166 times over a rope in a minute.

180° PARALLEL PARK
Russ Swift (UK) parked a Mini in a space that was only 13 in. longer than the car.

BOW-AND-ARROW FEET
Hang Thu Thi Ngyuen (Vietnam) used her feet to fire an arrow into a target 16 ft. 5 in. away.

THROAT PULL
Tabare Soria Gonzalez (Uruguay) pulled a 3,175-lb. truck a distance of 321 ft.

SKEET HEAD
John Cloherty (USA) shot 15 skeets in a tunnel while walking toward them.

LONGEST RAMP TO TRUCK MOTORCYCLE JUMP
Roger Wells, a.k.a. Johnny Airtime (USA), jumped 135 ft. into a truck travelling at 60 m.p.h. .

MOST EGGS CRUSHED WITH WRIST
Nathan Withers (USA) crushed four eggs with his wrist.

www.guinnessworldrecords.com

You've read the book and seen the TV show... now, coming live to your homes this fall, is **guinnessworldrecords.com**, the interactive media-offering that gives you daily record-breaking news, videos and stories that are guaranteed to **wow** you.

check it out and see for yourself

WHAT YOU CAN DO...

Here are just some of the amazing features

- Check out the **DAILY WOW!**
- Read breaking news!
- Download a video!
- Browse the records!
- Chat with record holders!

⊙ **WANT TO JOIN THE EXCITEMENT AT THE WORLD'S BIGGEST CARNIVAL ?**
Guinnessworldrecords.com webcams will allow you to see the action as it happens. You'll also get to see an amazing range of pictures and records.

⊙ **DO YOU THINK YOU COULD BREAK A RECORD LIKE THIS ?**
At guinnessworldrecords.com you can access rules and guidelines for record attempts, like the world's strongest beard (pictured on the left), or, if you want to try for a brand new record, let us know...

- Send e-cards to friends!
- Attempt a record!
- Suggest a new record!

EVERY DAY, ALL OVER THE WORLD, AMAZING RECORDS ARE BEING BROKEN. CHECK OUT THE DETAILS ON...

guinnessworldrecords.com

⊙ DO YOU THINK YOU CAN DREAM UP A RECORD STRANGER THAN THIS ONE?

Records on the site range from the conventional to the bizarre — pictured here is the world's fastest furniture. You'll be able get hot tips from record holders, find out what it's like to break a record or, if you prefer, just chat.

Stop Press!

Records are being broken all the time, and our meticulous verification process means that we cannot always include all the latest details in the main body of the book. Here are some of the records that had just been confirmed as we went to press. For more details see guinnessworldrecords.com and *Guinness World Records 2002*.

FASTEST PUMPKIN CARVER
On Oct 16, 1999, Jerry Ayers (USA) carved 2,015 lbs. of pumpkins in 7 hrs. 11 min. at Klickman Farms Inc., Elmore, Ohio, USA.

HIGHEST CANINE FREESTYLE JUMP
The highest freestyle jump by a dog is 63 in. by Wolf, a Russian Wolfhound, during the Superdog Show at Klondike Days, Edmonton, Alberta, Canada, on July 28, 1999. Wolf is owned and trained by Seanna O'Neill of Edmonton.

MOST SIBLING PENSIONERS
Of the 10 children (five brothers, five sisters) born into the Feerick family in Ireland between 1910 and 1921, seven were aged between 70 and 90 on May 15, 2000.

BOWLING MARATHON
Thomas Becker (USA) rolled 221 games when bowling for a record 30 hrs. 48 min., in Albuquerque, New Mexico, USA, on Feb. 11–12, 2000. The record attempt raised money for Spinal Muscular Atrophy (SMA) research.

100-M. BREASTSTROKE
Roman Sloudnov (Russia) set a new world record when he swam the 100-m. breaststroke in 1 min. 0.36 sec. in Moscow, Russia, on June 15, 2000.

MOST STAIRS CLIMBED ON A BICYCLE
Javier Zapata (Colombia) broke his own world record on May 20, 2000 by hopping up 943 steps on a bike, without touching the ground. It took him 43 min. 26 sec.

SMALLEST CRYSTAL BOWL
A crystal bowl made by Jim Irish of Rathculliheen, Waterford, Ireland, a former master cutter at Waterford Crystal, was 0.34 in. wide, 0.18 in. high and 0.08 in. thick. It was made with 208 cuts.

FASTEST GOAL IN A SOCCER CUP FINAL
Based on video evidence, the fastest scorer in a cup final is Owen Price, who scored 4.7 seconds after the whistle for Ernest Bevin School against Barking Abbey in the final of the Under-14 Heinz Ketchup Cup at Highbury, London, England, on May 18, 2000.

OLDEST PERSON TO COMPLETE A MARATHON ON EACH CONTINENT
Walter William Galbrecht (USA), known as "Bill," has completed two or more marathons on each of the seven continents. His latest marathons on each of the continents were run when he was 69, in 1997, and when he was 71, in 1999. Bill has run 56 marathons in total.

OLDEST MALE PARACHUTIST – TANDEM JUMP
Bjarne Mæland (Norway) (b. 1899) made his first tandem parachute jump at the age of 100 years, 21 days. He jumped from a height of 10,499 ft. above Stavanger Airport, Sola, Norway, on Sept. 8, 1999.

FASTEST FURNITURE
Edd China and David Davenport's customized sofa car, *The Casual Lofa*, has a top speed of 87 m.p.h.

MOST DIAMOND WEDDINGS IN ONE FAMILY
Thomas and Molly Frey (USA) had 17 children, three of whom celebrated diamond wedding anniversaries. Henry Sebade and Anna Sebade (Frey) were married 69 years; Harvey Frey and Della Frey (Kai) were married 64 years; and Erwin Gralheer and Mary Gralheer (Frey)'s marriage was 70 years.

BIGGEST BOTTLE TOP MURAL
As a joint venture between Interbrew, Total Sports, Internet Sports Network, Webpersonals.com, and Core Audience Entertainment, beer.com was launched on Oct 12, 1999. A mural of the company's logo and website address was created using bottle tops in Toronto's Sky Dome, Canada. It was 240 ft. long and 30 ft. high, and the total area covered with bottle tops measured 383,404 in.[2]

MOST CHILIES EATEN
Eriberto N. Gonzales Jr. consumed 350 chilies in three minutes at the annual Magayon Festival chili-eating contest, held at Peñaranda Park, Legazpi, Albay, Philippines, on May 27, 1999.

MOST SKI FLIPS IN 10 MINUTES
Tommy Waltner (USA) completed 23 front inverted aerial jumps within 10 minutes on April 25, 2000. The event took place on Aspen Mountain, Colorado, USA, in order to raise money for Waltner's "Loops for Lupus" campaign.

HEAVIEST WEIGHT LIFTED WITH A HUMAN BEARD
On March 4, 2000, Antanas Kontrimas (Lithuania) lifted a girl weighing 122.8 lbs. off the ground with his beard.

TEENAGE FEMALE SOLO ARTIST WITH MOST NO. 1 HITS
The teenage female solo performers with the most No. 1 hits are Britney Spears (USA), who was 18 years, 5 months, 3 days old when her single "Oops! I Did It Again" became her third release to reach the

top spot in the UK charts on May 7, 2000; and Billie Piper (UK), who was 17 years, 7 months, 23 days old when her single "Day & Night" became her third No. 1 hit, entering the UK charts on May 21, 2000.

LOUDEST FINGER SNAP
Bob Hatch of Pasadena, California, USA, snapped his fingers with a decibel meter reading of 108, on May 17, 2000.

LONGEST GRAPE SPIT
Robert Bonwell of Aston Tirrold, Oxfordshire, England, spat a grape a record distance of 22.38 ft. at the Aston Tirrold Fête on May 21, 2000.

BIGGEST WOK
The world's largest wok, made by Tony Hancock (UK), is 9 ft. 7 in. in diameter and 2 ft. deep. Hancock used it to stir-fry 882 lbs. of vegetables at the Wing Yip Chinese restaurant and supermarket, Croydon, Surrey, England, on March 16, 2000.

BIGGEST TIP
Gwen Butler, a 29-year-old US barmaid, was given a $2-million tip by Swiss banker Erich Sager after he ate at the Federalist restaurant and cocktail lounge in Boston, Massachusetts, USA, in Feb. 2000.

FASTEST-SELLING POP ALBUM
The record for the greatest first-week´s sales of an album is held by pop group *NSYNC (USA). They sold 2.41 million copies of *No Strings Attached* after it was released on March 21, 2000.

MOST TEMPLES CONSECRATED BY ONE PERSON
His Holiness Pramukh Swami Maharaj, the spiritual master of the Swaminarayan Hindu Mission (BAPS), consecrated 355 temples in 11 countries between April 17, 1971, and May 6, 2000. The highest rate of consecrations was 14 in a month, or one every 2.2 days, in India in Jan. 2000.

MOST BLANK PAGES IN A BOOK
University lecturer Anne Lydiat (UK) published a book with no words on Sept. 9, 1999. The 52 pages of *lost for words...* are blank and represent "a feminine place where there is silence," according to the author.

HIGHEST CLIFFS IN THE SOLAR SYSTEM
NASA's *Voyager 2* probe encountered the planet Uranus and its collection of moons in 1986. Its moon Miranda, which is 293 miles in diameter, has a surface made up of a jumble of bizarre geological features. One of the most prominent is an enormous cliff with a vertical relief of about 12 miles. This cliff, named Verona Rupes, is 3 miles higher than the walls of the Grand Canyon, USA, on Earth. Its height is even more remarkable in comparison with the size of Miranda itself.

BIGGEST MASS WEDDING CEREMONY IN A PRISON
A record 120 inmates of Carandiru Prison, São Paulo, Brazil, married their fiancées in a mass ceremony held on June 14, 2000.

MOST DANCERS
A total of 4,446 children danced "The Time Warp", and 4,506 children disco danced, at an event organized by Mardi Gras Promotions Ltd. at the National Exhibition Centre, Birmingham, England, on June 18, 2000.

FURTHEST RESTING PLACE
On July 31, 1999, NASA's *Lunar Prospector* spacecraft crashed into the lunar surface after 18 months of successful mission operations. Incorporated into this orbiter was a 1.5-in. polycarbonate container holding 1 oz. of the remains of Dr. Eugene Shoemaker. Wrapped around this container was a piece of brass foil inscribed with some of the images of

Shoemaker's pioneering work in planetary science.

SMALLEST AIR GUN
Derek Earp of Northampton, England, built a miniature pre-charged pneumatic air pistol measuring 3 in., in 1999.

BIGGEST MEXICAN WAVE
The largest ever Mexican wave was performed by 3,222 people standing in a single line on the South Downs, Sussex, England, on June 24, 2000. The wave began at Chantry Point and stretched for approximately 3 miles. The event was organized by some of the county's young people as a way of celebrating the millennium, and raised funds for the participants' chosen charities.

Index 1

A

Academy Awards, 61, 64, 94, 112
accidents, 34–35
acid, strongest, 153
acid rain, 181
actors, 108, 112
  highest earning, 98
  highest grossing, 90
  shortest, 92
adventures, 30–33
advertisements, TV, 59, 97
advertising, 59
  biggest agency, 58
aerobics, biggest display, 28
airplanes, 142, 143
  oldest passenger, 10
airplane sickbags,
  biggest collection, 80
AFL, 204, 205
African music, 105
AGM, biggest attendance, 56
air, worst disasters, 34
air force, biggest, 50
aircraft, 142–143
  military, 132, 133
airliners, fastest, 142
albums, best-selling, 100
alcohol, strongest, 72
Alpine skiing, 220
altar boy, oldest, 49
altitude, greatest, 38
ambulances, biggest, 136
American football, 194–195, 246–248
America's Cup, 214
amphibian, biggest, 164
  smallest, 164
amusement parks, 86–87
angels, biggest collection, 81
animals, 19, 160-165
  biggest, 160, 169
  most dangerous, 174
  most expensive, 70
  rarest, 182, 183
animated films, 94
animation, 94, 95

Antarctic, 31, 33
antiwar rally, biggest, 46
apartment block, tallest, 146
applause, loudest, 29
arcade machine, dance marathon, 23
archery, 249
Arctic, 30, 33
army, biggest, 50
  most multinational, 51
arrest, biggest mass, 53
arrests, most, 53
artifact, smallest, 154
asteroid, biggest, 171
  smallest, 171
astronomy, 170–171
athlete, oldest, 10
athletics, 208–211, 236–239
Atlantic, fastest crossing, 31
atlas, most valuable, 65
atomic bombs, 132
  most people killed, 50
ATP tour (tennis), 199
attic, longest time in, 24
auctions, 62–67
audience, biggest, 99, 100, 106
Australian Open (tennis), 199
Australian rules football, 204, 205
authors, 111
  most filmed, 93
  youngest, 9
auto sports, 230–231
automobiles, 134–135
Avian flu, worst outbreak, 176
awards, 112–113

B

bacterium, deadliest, 153
bagel, biggest, 72
baked beans, most eaten, 75
balance, finest, 155
balancing, 18
ball sports, 204–207
ballooning, circumnavigation, 30

worst disaster, 34
balloonist, oldest, 10
band, highest-paid, 55
  richest, 54
bank, biggest, 58
bar, longest, 75
barbecue, biggest, 75
Barbie dolls, biggest collection, 80
barrel jump, longest, 20
baseball, 200–201, 245–246
  most valuable, 66
  most valuable glove, 66
basketball, 190–191
bathtub, longest journey, 24
  longest push, 24
  most rattlesnakes in, 22
bathtub racer, fastest, 16
beans, most eaten, 75
beards, longest, 159
bed maker, fastest, 17
beer, strongest, 72
beer glass pushing, 18
beer mats, biggest collection, 80
  catching, 18
  flipping, 18
bequest, biggest, 60
bhangra music, 104, 105
bicycles, 138–139, 232–233
  most valuable, 66
bicycling, 33, 232–233, 243–244
  down a glacier, 227
big beat music, 102
big business, 56–59
billionaire, youngest, 55
bikes, 138–139, 232–233
bikini, most valuable, 67
bingo, biggest game, 77
bird of prey, rarest, 183
birds, biggest, 162
  biggest egg, 162
  deepest dive, 162
  earliest, 169
  fastest, 162
  highest-flying, 162
  largest wingspan, 162
  longest feathers, 162
  smallest, 162

talking, 162
birth, most premature, 178
birthday party, biggest, 83
birth rates, highest and lowest, 40
bitterest substances, 152
board games, 78
  most played, 77
boats, 214
bobsled, 219
body, human, 158–159
body piercings, 114, 115
body boarding,
  most championships, 228
bodybuilding, 114, 115
bombs, 132, 133
books, 110, 111, 113
  most expensive, 70
  most valuable, 64
Booker Prize, 113
book of signatures, biggest, 47
bookstore, biggest, 69
botijos, biggest collection, 81
bottle openers, biggest collection, 80
bouncy castle, biggest, 87
bowling, 205
bowls, 205
box office, highest gross, 90, 92, 93
boxer, highest-paid, 55
boxing, 222, 223
  most valuable memorabilia, 67
bowling ball stacking, 18
bra, most expensive, 89
breakfast, biggest, 74
breastfeeding, most babies, 29
brick, longest-distance carrying, 24
bride, oldest, 11
bridegroom, oldest, 10
bridge, most hands, 77
  most world titles, 77
Brit awards, 113
bubble gum, biggest collection, 81
bubbles, most people blowing, 26
bucket chain, longest, 26
Buddhist temple, biggest, 48
building, tallest, 146
buildings, 146-149
bungee jumping,
  highest, 228
  most people, 228
bunny hop, biggest, 27
bus tickets, biggest collection, 80
burgers, most stuffed in mouth, 21
burn, longest full-body, 116

buses, 136-137
businessmen, richest, 55
butt boarding, 226
butterfly, biggest, 165

C

cable suspension bridge, longest, 146
cactus, tallest, 167
cake, most candles, 73
calculator, smallest, 154
camcorders, smallest, 130
camera, fastest, 128
  most valuable, 65
  smallest, 128
campaigns, 46–47
Canadian football, 195
cancer, fewest deaths, 177
  most deaths, 177
  most survivable, 177
candles, biggest, 12
  most on a cake, 73
cannon, heaviest, 132
Cape Town-to-Cairo, running, 31
car crash, youngest survivor, 36
car journey, longest, 32
car, longest push, 25
carbon dioxide, highest emissions, 180
card throwing, 20
cards, house of, 20
  most in a fan, 20
carpet, most valuable, 62
cars, 134–135, 230-231
  eco-friendly, 134, 182
cartoons, 94–95
cat, most expensive, 71
cave, biggest, 157
cell phones, 128, 129
  biggest company, 58
  most expensive, 70
cello, most valuable, 63
CEO, highest paid, 56
  lowest paid, 57
Césars, 113
CFL, 195
chairs, most valuable, 62
champagne fountain,
  biggest, 75
chamber pots, biggest collection, 80
charitable foundation, biggest, 60

charities, 60–61
checkers, most opponents, 76
  most world titles, 77
chelonian, oldest, 164
  smallest, 164
chess, highest ratings, 77
chess computer, 119
chewing gum, biggest collection, 81
chicken dance, biggest, 28
Chief Executive Officer, highest paid, 56
  lowest paid, 57
children, most, 178
children's party, biggest, 83
Chinese dumpling, biggest, 73
chorus line, oldest, 109
chromosomes, 152
churches, 48, 49
cigarette lighters, biggest collection, 80
cinema, 90-93, 112, 113
circumnavigation, 30, 31, 32
circus, 108
cities, cheapest, 42
  most expensive, 42
civil-disobedience march, biggest, 46
classical music, 106–107
claws, biggest, 169
clock, most valuable, 62
cloning, 153
clothes, 88–89
clothespin clipping, 18
clothing brand, best-selling, 68
clothing tags, biggest collection, 80
clubbing, 82–83
clubs, 84, 85
CN Tower, fastest pogo stick up, 16
coconut tree, fastest climber, 17
coffee morning, biggest, 27
coin, balancing, 18
  most valuable, 62
coldest places, 172
collecting litter, most people, 26
collectors, 80–81
cologne, most expensive, 70
combat jet, fastest, 142
combat sports, 222–225
comedies, highest grossing, 92
comet, biggest, 171
comic, most valuable, 65
comic strips, 94, 95
commercials, TV, 59, 97
company, biggest, 58
composers, 106
compound, most extracted, 154

computation, biggest, 155
computer games, 120–121
computers, 118–119
concert, biggest on-line, 124
conga, longest, 28
conservation organization, biggest, 47
consoles, games, 120
constellation, biggest, 170
  smallest, 170
contracts, TV, 99
cosmetics company, biggest, 59
cosmetics tycoons, richest, 54
costumes, most in a movie, 91
countries, 40–43
country line dance, biggest, 28
country music, 104, 105
couples to have kissed, 27
couturier, oldest, 11
crawls, longest, 24
credit cards, most, 69
Cresta Run, 219
cricket, 202–203, 248
  most valuable memorabilia, 66
cricket spitting, 20
crime, 52–53
criminal trial, longest, 52
crocodilian, smallest, 165
cross-country running, 208
crosswords, 110
crustacean, biggest, 164
curling,
  most World Championships, 218
currency, least valuable, 43
custard pies, most thrown, 29
cyberpet, most downloaded, 124
cyberstar, most variations, 124
cyclones, 184

D

daisy chain, 26
dance music, 102–103
dance party, longest 82
dancing, 28
  longest marathon, 23
dancing dragon, longest, 29
death, commonest causes, 176
death rates, highest and lowest, 40, 41
decathlon, 210, 237
demolition, fastest bare-handed, 29

demonstration, biggest, 46
dental associations, biggest, 84
department store, biggest, 68
desert, biggest, 156
designer, oldest, 11
  youngest, 9
designer label, fastest growing, 88
diamond, most valuable, 62
diary, best-selling, 111
Dinky toy, most valuable, 62
dinosaurs, 168–169
director, youngest, 9
disasters, 34–35, 184–185
disco ball, biggest, 12
discus, 237, 238
diseases, 174–177
  commonest, 175
  deadliest, 177
  fastest-growing, 176
  most resurgent, 176
  oldest, 176
diving, 215
  youngest world champion, 9
divorce rates, highest and lowest, 41
divorcing couple, oldest, 11
DJ, marathon, 23
  youngest, 8
doctor, youngest, 8
doctors, fewest and most, 41
documentaries, TV, 96
dog, heaviest, 160
  most lives saved, 3
domain names, 122, 125
dome, biggest, 148
domino stacking, 18
dominoes, most toppled, 76
donation, biggest, 60
drag racing, 230
drama, TV, 96
dramatist, oldest, 11
dress, most valuable, 66
driest place, 173
drink, 72–75
driver, oldest, 10
driving simulator, best selling, 120
droughts, 185
drum, biggest, 12
drum 'n' bass, 103

E

E Coli, deadliest outbreak, 176
earrings, biggest collection, 81
earthmover, biggest, 136
earthquakes, 184, 185
  longest feline survival, 37
Easter egg hunt, 27
eating, 72–75
eclipse, longest, 171
ecology, 180–183
e-commerce, 122, 123
economics, 40–43
electrical current, most powerful, 154
electronics, biggest retailers, 69
elements, commonest, 152
  hardest, 152
  heaviest, 152
  newest, 152
e-mail, 119, 123, 125
Emmys, 113
Empire State Building,
  fastest run up, 17
employer, biggest, 58
endangered species, 182, 183
endurance, 22–25
energy, 134, 135, 182
environment, 180–183
environmental campaign, longest-
  running, 47
equestrianism, 234–235
escalator, longest, 148
  longest journey, 24
  shortest, 148
escape velocity, fastest, 145
evacuations, biggest, 50
execution, 53
explosion, worst disaster, 34
extra, TV, most appearances, 99
extreme sports, 226-229
eye, first artificial, 179
eyes, biggest, 165

F

facial hair, 159
fake paintings, biggest collection, 80
falls, 36
family business, oldest, 56

famine, 185
fan clubs, 84, 85
fashion, 88–89
  biggest retail chain, 68
fashion designer, highest-earning, 54
  most at one show, 88
fax machine, smallest, 129
feet, biggest, 159
fencing, 222
ferryboat, worst disaster, 34
festivals, 82–83
field hockey, 206
figure-skating, 218, 219
films, 90–93, 112, 113
  most watched, 22
film costume, most valuable, 64
film poster, most valuable, 64
film producer, highest-earning, 54
film prop, most valuable, 64
fingernails, longest, 158
fire, worst disasters, 34, 35
firearms, 133
fireworks, worst disaster, 35
fish, biggest, 162
  fastest, 163
  most eggs, 163
  most poisonous, 163
  oldest, 163
  slowest, 163
  smallest, 163
fish and chips, biggest portion, 75
fjord, longest, 157
flamenco dancer, fastest, 17
flea market, biggest, 68
flight simulator, best-selling, 121
floods, 173, 184
flotation, biggest, 56
flower, biggest, 166
  smelliest, 167
flu, deadliest outbreak, 176
fluke, most adaptable, 175
flying doctor service,
  most successful, 37
food, 72–75
food fight, biggest annual 82
foot, longest time on one, 24
football,
  American, 194–195, 246–248
  Australian rules, 204, 205
  Canadian, 195
forklift trucks, biggest, 136
Formula One, 230, 231
fragrance,

most expensive, 70
freefalls, biggest, 229
Freemasons, 84
French knitting, longest, 20
French Open (tennis), 199
friendship circle, biggest, 27
fruit stickers, biggest collection, 80
fuel efficiency, 134
funeral, first Space, 38
fungus, biggest, 167
  most poisonous, 166

G

gadgets, 128–131
gambling, 76
games, 76–77, 78, 79
  computer, 120–121
game shows, TV, 97
garlic festival, biggest, 83
gay festivals, biggest, 83
gay rights march, biggest, 46
genetics, 152
geysers, 185
GI Joe, most valuable, 67
gifts 60–61
Giga Pet, oldest, 121
glass pushing, 18
glasses, lightest, 128
gnomes and pixies,
  biggest collection, 80
GNP, 43
goal, fastest (soccer), 186
gold, biggest reserves, 42
golden handshake, biggest, 56
golf, 196–197, 248
  biggest on-line tournament, 124
  youngest hole in one, 9
golf balls, balancing, 18
  biggest collection, 80
golf tee, biggest, 13
golfers,
  highest-earning, 196, 197
graduates, youngest, 8
Grammys, 112
Grand Prix, 230, 231
Grand Slam (tennis), 198
gravity speed biking, 227
Grey Cup, 195
groom, oldest, 10

gross national product, 43
guerrillas, youngest leaders, 51
guitar, most valuable, 63
gum, biggest collection, 81
gunging, most people, 27
guns, 132, 133
gymnastics, 212–213

H

hail, 172, 184
hailstones, heaviest, 172
hailstorms, 184
hair, most valuable, 62
haircutting (most scissors), 18
hairsplitting, 18
half-marathon,
  fastest pushing a baby buggy, 16
hamburgers, most stuffed in mouth, 21
hammer throw, 211, 237, 238
hand-signing, biggest, 29
hand transplant, first, 179
handball, 204
hardware, 118–119
hat, most expensive designer, 88
heads of state, oldest, 44
  shortest, 44
  youngest, 44
headwear, most valuable, 66
health expenditure, highest, 42
  lowest, 42
heart transplant, earliest, 179
heaviest person, 158
  twins, 158
  woman, 158
helicopters, 142
  worst disaster, 34
helmet, most valuable, 66
heptathlon, 211, 238
high jump, 236, 237, 238, 239
Hindu temples, biggest, 48
hip-hop, 102
hockey, field, 206
  ice, 216-217
hole in one, youngest, 9
home pages, 123
hopscotch, biggest grid, 76
  most games, 22
horror movies, 93
horse-drawn trailer, 33

horse racing, 234–235
  gambling, 77
horses, 234–235, 244–245
  smallest, 161
hospitals, 43
hot-air balloonist, oldest, 10
hotel, biggest, 147
  tallest, 147
house, most expensive, 146
house of cards, most stories, 20
hovercraft, 140
  longest journey, 31
hug, biggest, 28
hula hoop spinning, 19
human body, 158–159
human centipede, longest, 27
human chain, longest, 46
human conveyor belt, longest, 27
human logo, biggest, 26
human mobile, biggest, 109
human rainbow, biggest, 27
human rights organization, biggest, 47
  oldest, 85
hurdles, 208, 210, 236, 237, 238, 239
hurricanes, 184, 185

I

ice climbing, 227
ice-cream sundae, biggest, 73
ice hockey, 216–217
ice-skating, 218, 219
  longest race, 219
ice storms, 185
illuminated manuscript,
  most valuable, 65
illustrated manuscript,
  most valuable, 67
immunization, most successful
  campaign, 176
income tax, 42
Indianapolis 500 race, 230, 231
industrialization, 43
infectious disease, commonest, 174
inflatable castle, biggest, 87
inflation, 42
influenza, deadliest outbreak, 176
in-line skating, 226
insect, biggest eggs, 165
  fastest, 164

most destructive, 165
  most expensive, 71
insurance company, biggest, 58
internet, 122–125
investment consultant, highest fees, 56
investor, richest, 56
island, biggest, 157
IT, 118–119

J

jackpots, biggest, 77
javelin, 210, 237, 238
jazz, 106–107
jazz-funk music, 103
jeans, most valuable, 66
jellyfish, most venomous, 165
Jenga, fastest-built tower, 76
jet skiing, most championships, 229
jewel theft, biggest, 52
jewelry, most valuable, 62
jewelry box, most valuable, 62
jigsaw puzzles, 78
jockeys, 234
joss sticks, worst disaster, 35
journeys, 30–33
judge, youngest, 8
judo, 224, 225
jumble sale, biggest, 69

K

kaleidoscope, most valuable, 67
kangaroo, biggest, 161
karate, 225
kayaking, most titles, 228
key rings, biggest collection, 80
keyboard, smallest computer, 118
king, youngest, 44
kiss, longest, 23
kites, 79
  fastest, 17
  longest flight, 25
knee boarding,
  most championships, 228
knitting, French, 20
knot tier, fastest, 16

Koran, 49
korfball, 204

L

lacrosse, 207
lake, biggest, 157
  deepest, 156
land speed, highest, 134
landslides, 185
Latin music, 104
launch, loudest, 145
launch system, least reliable, 144
  most reliable, 144
law and order, 52–53
law firm, biggest, 58
lawn mower, longest journey, 30
leaders, 44–45
leap frog, 24
leaves, biggest, 167
lecturing, highest fees, 57
Lego, biggest structures, 79
legs, most valuable, 114
Le Mans 24-hour race, 230
leprosy, highest prevalence, 176
letters, most valuable, 64
  to newspapers, 110
life expectancy, highest and lowest, 40
lifeguard, oldest, 37
lifesavers, 36–37
life expectancy, highest and lowest, 40
lifesaving society, oldest, 85
lighters, biggest collection, 80
lightest person, 158
lighthouse, tallest, 148
lightning strike, most survived, 36
  most survivors, 36
line dance, biggest, 28
Lite-Brite, biggest picture, 79
litter, most people collecting, 27
live entertainment company,
  biggest, 59
lizard, smallest, 164
lollipop, biggest, 73
long jump, 208, 211, 236, 237, 238, 239
lottery, most wins by a town, 76
  biggest jackpot, 77
loudspeakers, most expensive, 70
lugeing, 219
lunar hit, first, 145

luxury goods tycoon, richest, 54
lyrics, most valuable, 65

M

M&M's flipping, 20
machine guns, 133
magazines, 110, 111
  most expensive, 70
magic societies, 84
majority, biggest, 45
malaria, most epidemics, 177
mall, biggest, 68
mammals, biggest land, 160
  fastest, 160
  flying, 161
  rarest, 183
  slowest, 160
  smallest, 160
  tallest, 160
mammoths, 168
man-made object, most remote, 144
marathons, 209
marine pollution, worst, 180
market capitalization, biggest, 57
markets, biggest, 68
marriage rates, highest and lowest, 41
married couple, oldest, 11
  youngest, 9
martial arts, 224–225
Masonic lodge, oldest, 84
matchstick balancing, 18
math problem, longest standing, 154
meal, most expensive, 74
media, 110–111
media tycoon, richest, 54
medicine, 178–179
memory, 20
men, biggest shortage, 40
metallic element, most extracted, 154
meteor shower, greatest, 171
meteorite, biggest, 171
Mickey Mouse toy, most valuable, 67
microbes, biggest, 153
microlight, circumnavigation, 31
midair collison, worst, 34
milk squirting, 20
milking, cows, 20
  snakes, 20
millennium parties, 82

mineral, softest, 152
Mini, most expensive, 71
Mini Disc players, 130
miniseries, TV, 96
ministers, most female, 45
missiles, 132
modeling, longest career with
  one company, 88
monarchs, heaviest, 45
  youngest, 44
Monopoly, most valuable, 78
monsoons, 185
monster trucks, 116
Moon, first people on, 38
Mormon temple, biggest, 48
mortars, 132
mosque, biggest, 48
mosquito killing, 19
most travelled man, 32
mothers, oldest, 178
motorcycles, 138-139, 232-233
  circumnavigation, 32
  jumps, 116
  pyramid, 27
motorcycling, 232-233
Mount Everest, fastest ascent, 32
mountain biking, 227
mountaineer, most successful, 31
mountaineering, longest fall
  survived, 36
  worst disaster, 34
mountains, biggest ranges, 156
  highest, 156, 171
mustache, longest, 159
movies, 90–93, 112, 113
  movie marathon, longest, 22
MP3, 125
  best-selling player, 130
mugging, 52
mug, biggest, 13
mugs, biggest collection, 81
multiple births, biggest, 178
murderers, 52–53
music, 100–107
music awards, 112, 113
  charts, 100, 101
  chairs, biggest game, 26
  manuscripts, most valuable, 107
  producer, richest, 55
  video, 96, 97
music box, most valuable, 65

N

nail clippers, biggest collection, 80
National Football League, 194–195
National Hockey League, 216–217
navy, biggest, 50
nerve gas, 153
netball, 204
news broadcaster, highest-earning, 98
news organization, biggest, 85
newscaster, virtual, 125
newspapers, 110
NFL, 194–195
  most valuable franchise, 194
NHL, 216–217
nightclubs, 103
  biggest, 82,
  smallest, 83
Nobel prize, most from one lab, 155
  youngest winner, 9
noodle, longest, 75
Nordic skiing, 220
North Pole, 30, 33
North Pole skier, oldest, 10
novels, 111
nuclear bomb, heaviest, 132
nuclear reactor, worst disaster, 181
numbers, most memorized, 20
nurses, most per capita, 41

O

observation wheel, biggest, 87
ocean, biggest, 157
  deepest point, 157
  smallest, 157
office, biggest, 147
office building, tallest, 146
oil and energy company, biggest, 58
old age, 10-11, 158
oldest living man, 158
  living person, 158
oldest man, 158
  person, 158
Olympics, 189, 190, 191, 201, 207, 210,
  212, 213, 214, 215, 218, 219, 220, 221,
  222, 225, 232, 235
  oldest gold medalist, 10
  youngest medalists, 8

one-day internationals
  (cricket), 202, 203
opera, 106, 107
opera singer, youngest, 9
operation, longest, 178
  most, 179
operations, most, 179
optical fibers, narrowest, 129
orbit, longest time in, 38
orchestra, biggest, 107
  oldest, 106
orchid, biggest, 167
organic farming, 182
organizations, 84–85
Orthodox cathedral, biggest, 48
Oscars, 61, 64, 112
  most consecutive nominations, 94
ozone levels, lowest, 180

P

Pacific, fastest crossing, 31
  fastest solar-powered crossing, 33
painting, most valuable, 64
pandemic, deadliest, 176
pantomime horse, fastest, 17
paper airplane, longest flight, 79
paper chain, longest, 26
paper clip chain, longest, 26
paperweight, most valuable, 63
parachute, 229
parachute escapes, 36
parachutists, oldest, 10
parasites, 174–175
  biggest, 174
  longest-living, 174
  most bloodthirsty, 174
parasitic nematode, biggest, 174
parking meters, biggest collection, 80
parties, 82–83
pass-the-parcel, biggest game, 76
peanut throwing, 20
pelota, 206
pen, most expensive, 71
  most valuable, 62
pen and ink drawing, most valuable, 64
pentathlon, 211
performance, 108–109
perfume, most expensive, 70
petitions, 46, 47

Pez dispensers, most valuable, 66
pharmaceutical company, biggest, 58
philately, biggest organization, 84
phones, smallest, 128, 129
photograph, most valuable, 65
physician, youngest, 8
pi, most accurate version, 155
piano, most valuable, 63
piercings, body, 114, 115
pilot, oldest, 10
pinball machine, most expensive, 70
pizza, biggest, 72
  longest delivery route, 75
planes, 142,143
planet, biggest, 171
  brightest, 171
  coldest, 171
  hottest, 171
plants, 166–167
play, longest , 109
  shortest, 109
playing card throwing, 20
playing cards, most in a fan, 20
  biggest, 78
playwright, oldest, 11
polar expeditions, 30, 31, 33
pole climbing, fastest, 16
pole vault, 210, 211, 236, 237, 238, 239
politics, 44–47
pollution, 180–181
pool, 207
pop music, 100–101
pop stars, 100–101
poster, most valuable, 64
pram pushing, fastest, 16
pregnancy, longest, 161
premier, highest-paid, 45
  oldest, 44
  youngest, 44
presidents, oldest, 44
  youngest, 44
primate, smallest, 160
prime minister, highest-paid, 45
  oldest, 44
  youngest, 44
print, most valuable, 64
print runs, biggest, 111
prison, most secure, 53
  most transfers, 52
prisoner of conscience, youngest, 46
  longest held, 47
private housing, 43
prizes, 112–113

producers, TV, 99
professor, youngest, 9
programs, TV, 96–99
protein, 153
pseudonyms, 101
psychologists, biggest organization, 84
pub, biggest, 75
public relations company, biggest, 58
publishing, 110–111, 113
  biggest company, 59
publishing company, biggest, 59
pumpkin shooting, 21
Pulitzer Prizes, 113

Q

Qawaali music, 104
queen, youngest, 44
quizzes, TV, 97

R

R&B, 103
rabbit, longest ears, 161
racehorses, 234, 235
racial-equality rally,
  biggest, 46
racing (horse), 234
racing driver, oldest, 11
  youngest, 11
racketball, 206
raffle, most Rolls-Royces, 77
raï music, 105
railw
railroads, 136-137
rain, 172, 173
  most acidic, 181
rally driving, 230
rap music, 102
rattlesnakes,
  most in bathtub, 22
record company, biggest, 56
recycling, 182
reef, longest, 157
refrigerator magnets, biggest
  collection, 80
reggae, 104

reign, longest, 44
relay races, 208, 210
religion, 48–49
rented housing, 43
reptile, biggest, 165
rescues, 36–37
restaurant, biggest, 74
  most visited, 74
rhythmic gymnastics, 213
rice, fastest eater, 75
richest people, 54–55
rides, 86–87
rifles, 133
ring-o'roses, biggest, 26
rivers, longest, 156
road tunnel, worst disaster, 34
robbery, 52
robots, 126–127
rock festival, biggest, 82
rock music, 100–101
rocket, biggest, 144
  cheapest, 144
  most expensive, 144
  most powerful, 144
  most powerful engine, 145
  smallest, 144
rodent, biggest, 161
roller coasters, 86, 87
roller hockey, 206
Rolls-Royces, most raffled, 77
roots, deepest, 166
  longest, 166
rosebush, biggest, 167
Rotary club, oldest, 84
royal, richest, 54
rubber band shooting, 20
Rubik Cube, fastest, 20
rugby, 192–193
running, 208–209, 236, 237, 238, 239
  backward, 24
Ryder Cup, 196

S

sack racer, fastest, 16
safety belt, most lives saved, 37
salsa music, 104, 105
sampling, 103
sancocho, biggest, 74
sand boarding, longest back flip, 228

satellite, biggest, 171
  oldest, 144
  smallest, 170
sausage, longest, 72
salty snacks company, biggest, 59
scaffolding, tallest, 148
scanner, biggest, 118
school, biggest, 84
science, 152–155
scooter, most expensive, 139
Scottish country dance, biggest, 28
Scrabble, highest scores, 76
scream, loudest, 29
sculpture, most valuable, 64
search engines, 123
seat belt, most lives saved, 37
seaweed, longest, 166
seed, biggest, 167
  smallest, 167
sentences, longest, 53
serial killer, most prolific, 52
sex discrimination,
  biggest settlement, 46
Shakespeare, longest play, 109
shares, biggest price change, 56
shaving, most heads, 29
  most people, 18
shawls, most expensive, 88
sheepshearing, 18
ships, 140–141
shipwreck, most valuable, 141
shoes, most expensive, 88
  most shined, 29
shooting, 248–249
shopping, 68–71
shopping center, biggest, 68
shortest man, 158
  twins, 159
  woman, 158
shot glasses, biggest collection, 81
shot put, 237, 238, 239
show jumping, 235
Shuttle, Space, 39
  biggest payload, 145
  longest flight, 144
Siamese twins, oldest, 159
sickbags, biggest collection, 80
signed books, biggest collection, 81
Sikhs, biggest gathering, 49
single, biggest-selling, 100
sitarist, longest career, 104
sitting, longest time, 22
skate shoes, best-selling, 89

skateboarding, 226, 227
  glossary, 227
skating (ice), 218, 219, 244
skiboarding, 227
skibob, 218
skiing, 220–221
ski jumping, 221
ski lift, worst disaster, 34
skill, 18–21
skin infection, commonest, 17
skittles, highest scores, 76
skull, biggest, 169
  most valuable, 62
slot machine, biggest jackpot, 77
smelliest substance, 152
smog, most lethal, 181
snail, biggest, 165
snake, longest, 164
  oldest, 164
  smallest, 164
snake milking, 20
snooker, 207
snow, 172
snowboarder, oldest, 228
snowboarding, 220, 221, 227
snowflake, biggest, 172
snowmobile, longest journey, 31
soaps and cosmetics company,
  biggest, 59
society, 40–43
software, 118–119
soccer, 186–189
  most valuable programme, 66
  most valuable shirt, 66
solar energy, 182
soldiers, youngest, 9
solitaire, fastest game, 76
songwriters, 100
South Pole, 31, 33
Space, 38–39, 144–145
  worst disaster, 34
spacecraft, 144–145
  fastest, 144
  smallest, 144
space walk, 39
spaghetti firing, 21
speakers, most expensive, 70
special effects, 116–117
spectacles, lightest, 128
speed, greatest attained by humans, 38
speed skating, 218, 219, 244
spice, most expensive, 72
spider, biggest, 164

biggest web, 164
 smallest, 164
spike driver, fastest, 16
spinning top, longest spin, 20
spiral staircase, longest, 148
spirit, most expensive, 72
spitting, 20
sponsored swims, most successful, 61
sport, worst disasters, 35
sporting event, most money raised, 60
sportswear, biggest brand, 69
squash, 206
Stanley Cup, 217
St. Bernard, most lives saved, 37
stage, biggest , 108
stamps, most licked, 20
stamp collectors,
 biggest organization, 84
standing, longest, 22
star, biggest, 170
 brightest, 170
 nearest, 170
 oldest, 170
 smallest, 170
 youngest, 170
steeplechase, 236, 238
stilt walker, fastest, 16
Stock Exchange, oldest, 56
storms, 172, 173, 184
storm chasing, 172, 173
structures, 146-149
 tallest, 147
studio, biggest, 90
stuffed toy, longest, 79
stunts, 116-117
submarines, 141
 worst disaster, 34
suicide, worst mass, 35
suicide rates, highest and lowest, 41
suitcase, biggest, 13
sumo, 224, 225
sundae, biggest, 73
sunflower, most heads, 167
 tallest, 167
sunshine, 172
Super Bowl, 194, 195
Supercross, 232
supermarket, youngest consultant, 8
supermodels, richest, 114
surfboard passing, 27
surfer, highest-earning, 228
surfing, most championships, 228
surf wear, best-selling, 89

survivors, 36–37
sushi roll, longest, 72
Swatch, most expensive, 70
swear words, most in an
 animated movie, 95
sweetest substance, 152
sweets, longest line, 75
swimming, 214, 215, 240–243
 longest ocean, 25
 underwater, 228
Swiss army knife, most expensive, 70
synagogue, biggest, 48

T

table tennis, 206
tae kwon do, 224, 225
talk show host, highest earning, 98
talker, fastest, 17
tallest man, 159
 UK, 75
 woman, 158
tanker disaster, worst, 180
tanks, 132
tap dance, biggest, 28
 fastest, 16
 longest, 28
tap dancer, fastest, 16
tattoos, 114
taxation, 42
teamwork, 26–29
teddy bear, biggest, 79
 most valuable, 65
 smallest, 78
teddy bears' picnic, biggest, 83
teeth, most cleaned, 29
telecommunications company,
 biggest, 58
telegram, most valuable, 64
telephones, smallest, 128, 129
telescope, most expensive, 145
telethon, most money raised, 61
television, 96–99
 awards, 113
temperature, highest, 154, 172
 lowest, 154, 172
temples, 48, 49
tennis, 198–199
 most valuable racket, 66
tenpin bowling, 205

tequila slam, biggest, 75
terrorism, worst attack, 51
Test matches (cricket), 202, 203
theater, 108–109
theatrical production,
 highest-grossing, 109
 most expensive, 108
theft, 52
theme parks, 86–87
thermometers, biggest collection, 81
thimble, most valuable, 63
thunder, 172
tiara, most expensive, 88
tiddledywinks, highest and
 longest jumps, 76
tightrope, longest time on, 22
tightrope walker, oldest, 11
toast, biggest, 74
tobacco company, biggest, 59
toenails, longest, 159
tooth, most valuable, 62
tornadoes, 172
torpedoes, 133
Tour de France, 232, 233
tourism, 151
tourists, highest-spending, 151
toxic cloud, biggest, 181
toxicity, 152
toys, 78–79
toy retailer, biggest, 69
track-and-field, 208–211,
 236-239
trade unions, 84
trains, 136–137
 worst disasters, 34
trampolining, 213
trams, oldest, 137
transfer fee, highest (soccer), 187
transistor, smallest, 154
transplant, most organs, 179
 youngest patient, 179
tree, deepest roots, 166
 fastest-growing, 166
 oldest, 166
 most massive, 166
 tallest, 166
treetopper, fastest, 16
trees, deepest roots, 166
 fastest-growing, 166
 longest time in, 22
 most expensive, 71
 most massive, 166
 most planted, 26

oldest, 166
tallest, 166
triathlon, 210
triple jump, 237, 238, 239
trucks, 136
tsunamis, 184
tuba player, oldest, 11
tunnel, longest, 148
TV, 96–99
  awards, 113
TV commercials, most starring
  company founder, 59
TV sets, 130
TV show, most convulsions
  caused by, 95
twins, 159
  biggest gathering, 29
Twister, biggest sheet, 78
typewriter, most valuable, 62
typhoons, 184
typing, longest marathon, 25

U

UN ambassador, youngest, 8
UN speech, longest, 45
underground train, worst disaster, 34
underwear, best-selling, 89
unicycle, longest ride, 24
unions, 84
US Open (tennis), 198, 199

V

vacuum cleaner, most advanced, 126
valuables, 62–67
vehicles, 136–137
vets, most in one procedure, 178
video, 96, 97
video camera, smallest, 130
video retailer, biggest, 97
virus, computer, 119
  newest, 176
vocal note, highest, 107
  lowest, 107
volcanos, 185
  most active, 156
volleyball, 204

W

walking, 210, 239
  backward, 24
  on hands, 24
wall, longest time sitting against, 22
wall of death, longest ride, 116
  oldest rider, 116
wallet, most expensive, 70
war, 50–51, 132–133
watch, most expensive, 70
water polo, 215
water sports, 214–215
waterfall, highest, 157
wax doll, most valuable, 67
wealth, 54–55
weapons, 132–133
weather, 172–173
websites, 122, 123
wedding dress, most expensive, 88
weed, biggest, 166
  most damaging, 166
weight lifting, 212–213, 250–251
western, highest grossing, 92
wheelchair journey, longest, 32
wheeled trash can, fastest, 16
whiskey, most expensive, 72
white-water kayaking, most titles, 228
wholesale market, biggest, 68
Wimbledon (tennis), 198, 199
wind, fastest, 172
window cleaner, fastest, 16
windows, biggest, 148
windsurfing, highest latitude, 228
wine, most expensive, 72
winter sports, 216–221
World Cup (soccer), 188, 189
World Cup (rugby), 192
World Series (baseball), 200, 201
worship, 48–49
wool, most expensive, 70
world music, 104–105
world wide web, 122–125
worms, charming, 19
  computer, 119
  eating, 21
wrestling, 222
  sumo, 224, 225
  Turkish, 223
wristwatch, most valuable, 63
writers, TV, 98

X

X-Games, 226, 227

Y

yachting, 214
YMCA, biggest dance, 28
yodeler, fastest, 17
yo-yo, biggest, 79
  most tricks, 21

Z

Zippo lighter, most valuable, 66
Zorb ball, longest journey, 21

Index 2

To help you find the records that interest you the most, we've provided a set of communities of interest, tying together all the records that share certain characteristics.

You can look for the icons throughout the book, or scan the lists here.

Achievement

Academy Awards, 61, 64, 94, 112
adventures, 30–33
Atlantic, fastest crossing, 31
awards, 112–113
bequest, biggest, 60
ballooning, circumnavigation, 30
Booker Prize, 113
Brit awards, 113
Cape Town-to-Cairo, running, 31
CEO, highest paid, 56
Césars, 113
charitable foundation, biggest, 60
Chief Executive Officer, highest paid, 56
dog, most lives saved, 37
donation, biggest, 60
Emmys, 113
endurance, 22–25
flying doctor service,
  most successful, 37
golden handshake, biggest, 56
Grammys, 112
hand transplant, first, 179
lifeguard, oldest, 37
lifesavers, 36–37
most travelled man, 32
Moon, first people on, 38
Nobel prize, most from one lab, 155
  youngest winner, 9
operation, longest, 178
Oscars, 61, 64, 112
  most consecutive nominations, 94
Pacific, fastest crossing, 31
prizes, 112–113
Pulitzer Prizes, 113
rescues, 36–37

safety belt, most lives saved, 37
seat belt, most lives saved, 37
sitting, longest time, 22
standing, longest time, 22
St. Bernard, most lives saved, 37
  telethon, most money raised, 61
TV awards, 113
UN ambassador, youngest, 8
tree, longest time in, 22
wall, longest time sitting against, 22
wheelchair journey, longest, 32

Danger

accidents, 34–35
acid rain, 181
adventures, 30–33
air, worst disasters, 34
air force, biggest, 50
animal, most dangerous, 174
army, biggest, 50
  most multinational, 51
atomic bombs, 132
  most people killed, 50
attic, longest time in, 24
Avian flu, worst outbreak, 176
bacterium, deadliest, 153
ballooning, worst disaster, 34
bombs, 132, 133
burn, longest full-body, 116
cancer, fewest deaths, 177
  most deaths, 177
  most survivable, 177
cannon, heaviest, 132
car crash, youngest survivor, 36
carbon dioxide, highest emissions, 180
crime, 52–53
cyclones, 184
demolition, fastest bare-handed, 29
death rates, highest and lowest, 40, 41
disasters, 34–35, 184–185
diseases, 174–177
  commonest, 175
  deadliest, 177

fastest-growing, 176
  most resurgent, 176
  oldest, 176
dog, most lives saved, 37
droughts, 185
E Coli, deadliest outbreak, 176
earthquakes, 184, 185
  longest feline survival, 37
elevator, accidents, 36
  worst disaster, 34
endangered species, 182, 183
endurance, 22–25
execution, 53
explosion, worst disaster, 34
falls, 36
famine, 185
ferryboat, worst disaster, 34
fire, worst disasters, 34, 35
firearms, 133
fireworks, worst disaster, 35
fish, most poisonous, 163
floods, 184
flu, deadliest outbreak, 176
fluke, most adaptable, 175
flying doctor service,
  most successful, 37
fungus, most poisonous, 166
geysers, 185
guerrilla, youngest leaders, 51
guns, 132, 133
hailstorms, 184
helicopter, worst disaster, 34
hurricanes, 184, 185
ice storms, 185
infectious disease, commonest, 174
influenza, deadliest outbreak, 176
insect, most destructive, 165
jellyfish, most venomous, 165
joss sticks, worst disaster, 35
journeys, 30–33
landslides, 185
law and order, 52–53
leprosy, highest prevalence, 176
life expectancy, highest and lowest, 40
lifeguard, oldest, 37
lifesavers, 36–37
lightning strike, most survived, 36
machine guns, 133

malaria, most epidemics, 177
marine pollution, worst, 180
midair collison, worst, 34
missiles, 132
monsoons, 185
mortars, 132
motorcycle jumps, 116
Mount Everest, fastest ascent, 32
mountaineer, most successful, 31
mountaineering,
  longest fall survived, 36
  worst disaster, 34
mugging, 52
murderers, 52–53
navy, biggest, 50
nerve gas, 153
nuclear bomb, heaviest, 132
nuclear reactor, worst disaster, 181
operations, most, 179
ozone levels, lowest, 180
pandemic, deadliest, 176
parachute escapes, 36
parasites, 174–175
  biggest, 174
  longest-living, 174
  most bloodthirsty, 174
parasitic nematode, biggest, 174
polar expeditions, 30, 31, 33
pollution, 180–181
prison, most secure, 53
  most transfers, 52
rain, most acidic, 181
rattlesnakes, most in bathtub, 22
rescues, 36–37
rifles, 133
road tunnel, worst disaster, 34
robbery, 52
safety belt, most lives saved, 37
seat belt, most lives saved, 37
serial killer, most prolific, 52
ski lift, worst disaster, 34
skin infection, commonest, 17
smog, most lethal, 181
soldiers, youngest, 9
Space, worst disaster, 34
space walk, 39
speed, greatest attained by humans, 38

sport, worst disasters, 35
St. Bernard, most lives saved, 37
storms, 184
stunts, 116–117
submarine, worst disaster, 34
suicide, worst mass, 35
suicide rates, highest and lowest, 41
survivors, 36–37
tanker disaster, worst, 180
tanks, 132
terrorism, worst attack, 51
tightrope, longest time on, 22
torpedoes, 133
toxic cloud, biggest, 181
toxicity, 152
train, worst disasters, 34
tsunamis, 184
typhoons, 184
underground train, worst disaster, 34
virus, newest, 176
volcanoes, 185
wall of death, longest ride, 116
  oldest rider, 116
war, 50–51, 132–133
weapons, 132–133
weed, most damaging, 166

Moon, first people on, 38
most travelled man, 32
motorcycle circumnavigation, 32
Mount Everest, fastest ascent, 32
mountaineer, most successful, 31
North Pole, 30, 33
orbit, longest time, 38
Pacific, fastest crossing, 31
  fastest solar-powered crossing, 33
polar expeditions, 30, 31, 33
Shuttle, Space, 39
  biggest payload, 145
  longest flight, 144
snowmobile, longest journey, 31
South Pole, 31, 33
Space, 38–39, 144–145
spacecraft, 144–145
  fastest, 144
  smallest, 144
speed, greatest attained by humans, 38
telescope, most expensive, 145

⊕

Discovery

adventures, 30–33
altitude, greatest, 38
Antarctic, 31, 33
Arctic, 30, 33
Atlantic, fastest crossing, 31
ballooning, circumnavigation, 30
Cape Town-to-Cairo, running, 31
car journey, longest, 32
circumnavigation, 30, 31, 32
cycling, 33
horse-drawn trailer, 33
hovercraft, longest journey, 31
journeys, 30–33
lawn mower, longest journey, 30
microlight, circumnavigation, 31

☺

Fun

aerobics, biggest display, 28
airplane sickbags,
  biggest collection, 80
alcohol, most expensive, 72
  strongest, 72
amusement parks, 86–87
angels, biggest collection, 81
applause, loudest, 29
bagel, biggest, 72
baked beans, most eaten, 75
balancing, 18
bar, longest, 75
barbecue, biggest, 75
Barbie dolls, biggest collection, 80
barrel jump, longest, 20
bathtub, longest journey, 24
  longest push, 24
  most rattlesnakes in, 22
beans, most eaten, 75
beer, strongest, 72

beer glass pushing, 18
beer mats, biggest collection, 80
  catching, 18
  flipping, 18
bingo, biggest game, 77
birthday party, biggest, 83
board games, 78
  most played, 77
botijos, biggest collection, 81
bottle openers, biggest collection, 80
bowling ball stacking, 18
breakfast, biggest, 74
breastfeeding, most babies, 29
brick, longest distance carrying, 24
bridge, most hands, 77
  most world titles, 77
bubblegum, biggest collection, 81
bubbles, most people blowing, 26
bucket chain, longest, 26
bunny hop, biggest, 27
burgers, most stuffed in mouth, 21
bus tickets, biggest collection, 80
cake, most candles, 73
camcorders, smallest, 130
candles, most on a cake, 73
candy, longest line, 75
car, longest push, 25
card throwing, 20
cards, house of, 20
  most in a fan, 20
cartoons, 94–95
champagne fountain,
  biggest, 75
chamber pots, biggest collection, 80
checkers, most opponents, 76
  most world titles, 77
chess, highest ratings, 77
chewing gum, biggest collection, 81
chicken dance, biggest, 28
children's party, biggest, 83
Chinese dumpling, biggest, 73
cigarette lighters, biggest collection, 80
clothespins clipping, 18
clothing tags, biggest collection, 80
clubbing, 82–83
coffee morning, biggest, 27
coin balancing, 18
collecting litter, most people, 26
collectors, 80–81
computer games, 120–121
conga, longest, 28
consoles, games, 120
cookie, biggest, 73

country line dance, biggest, 28
couples to have kissed, 27
crawls, longest, 24
cricket spitting, 20
custard pies, most thrown, 29
cyberpet, most downloaded, 124
cyberstar, most variations, 124
daisy chain, 26
dance party, longest, 82
dancing, 28
dancing dragon, longest, 29
demolition, fastest bare-handed, 29
Dinky toy, most valuable, 62
domino stacking, 18
dominoes, most toppled, 76
drink, 72–75
driving simulator, best-selling, 120
earrings, biggest collection, 81
Easter egg hunt, 27
eating, 72–75
endurance, 22–25
escalator, longest journey, 24
fake paintings, biggest collection, 80
festivals, 82–83
fish and chips, biggest portion, 75
flight simulator, best-selling, 121
food, 72–75
food fight, biggest annual 82
foot, longest time on one, 24
French knitting, longest, 20
friendship circle, biggest, 27
fruit stickers, biggest collection, 80
gambling, 76
games, 76–77, 78, 79
  computer, 120–121
garlic festival, biggest, 83
gay festivals, biggest, 83
GI Joe, most valuable, 67
Giga Pet, oldest, 121
glass pushing, 18
gnomes and pixies,
  biggest collection, 80
golf ball balancing, 18
golf balls, biggest collection, 80
gum, biggest collection, 81
gunging, most people, 27
haircutting (most scissors), 18
hairsplitting, 18
hamburgers, most stuffed in mouth, 21
home pages, 123
hopscotch, biggest grid, 76
  most games, 22
horse racing, gambling, 77

house of cards, most stories, 20
hug, biggest, 28
hula hoop spinning, 19
human centipede, longest, 27
human conveyor belt, longest, 27
human logo, biggest, 26
human rainbow, biggest, 27
ice cream sundae, biggest, 73
inflatable castle, biggest, 87
internet, 122–125
jackpots, biggest, 77
Jenga, fastest-built tower, 76
jigsaw puzzles, 78
kaleidoscope, most valuable, 67
key rings, biggest collection, 80
kiss, longest, 23
kites, 79
  longest flight, 25
knitting, French, 20
lawn mower, longest journey, 30
leapfrog, 24
Lego, biggest structures, 79
lighters, biggest collection, 80
line dance, biggest, 28
Lite-Brite, biggest picture, 79
litter, most people collecting, 27
lollipop, biggest, 73
lottery, most wins by a town, 76
  biggest jackpot, 77
M&M's flipping, 20
matchstick balancing, 18
meal, most expensive, 74
memory, 20
Mickey Mouse toy, most valuable, 67
milk squirting, 20
milking, cows, 20
  snakes, 20
millennium parties, 82
Mini Disc players, 130
Monopoly, most valuable, 78
mosquito killing, 19
motorcycle pyramid, biggest, 27
movies, longest marathon, 22
  most watched, 22
MP3 player, best-selling, 130
mugs, biggest collection, 81
musical chairs, biggest game, 26
nail clippers, biggest collection, 80
nightclub, biggest, 82,
  smallest, 83
noodle, longest, 75
numbers, most memorized, 20
observation wheel, biggest, 87

paper airplane, longest flight, 79
paper chain, longest, 26
paper clip chain, longest, 26
parking meters, biggest collection, 80
parties, 82–83
pass-the-parcel, biggest game, 76
peanut throwing, 20
Pez dispensers, most valuable, 66
pizza, biggest, 72
  longest delivery route, 75
playing card throwing, 20
playing cards, most in a fan, 20
  biggest, 78
pub, biggest, 75
pumpkin shooting, 21
refrigerator magnets,
  biggest collection, 80
rice, fastest eater, 75
rides, 86–87
ring-o'roses, biggest, 26
rock festival, biggest, 82
roller coasters, 86, 87
Rolls-Royces, most raffled, 77
rubber band shooting, 20
Rubik Cube, fastest, 20
runs, longest backward, 24
sancocho, biggest, 74
sausage, longest, 72
Scottish country dance, biggest, 28
Scrabble, highest scores, 76
scream, loudest, 29
shaving, most heads, 29
  most people, 18
sheepshearing, 18
shoes, most shined, 29
shot glasses, biggest collection, 81
sickbags, biggest collection, 80
sign language
  biggest hand-signing, 29
signed books, biggest collection, 81
skill, 18–21
skittles, highest scores, 76
slot machine, biggest jackpot, 77
snake milking, 20
solitaire, fastest game, 76
spaghetti firing, 21
spinning top, longest spin, 20
spitting, 20
stamps, most licked, 20
stuffed toy, longest, 79
sundae, biggest, 73
surfboard passing, 27
sushi roll, longest, 72

swear words, most in an animated
  movie, 95
tap dance, biggest, 28
  longest, 28
teamwork, 26–29
teddy bear, biggest, 79
  most valuable, 65
  smallest, 78
teddy bears' picnic, biggest, 83
teeth, most cleaned, 29
tequila slam, biggest, 75
theme parks, 86–87
thermometers, biggest collection, 81
tiddledywinks,
  highest and longest jumps, 76
toast, biggest, 74
toy retailer, biggest, 69
toys, 78–79
trees planted, 26
TV sets, 130
twins, biggest gathering, 29
Twister, biggest sheet, 78
typing, longest marathon, 25
unicycle, longest ride, 24
video camera, smallest, 130
walking, backward, 24
  on hands, 24
websites, 122, 123
whiskey, most expensive, 72
wine, most expensive, 72
world wide web, 122–125
worms, charming, 19
  eating, 21
YMCA, biggest dance, 28
yo-yo, biggest, 79
  most tricks, 21
Zorb ball, longest journey, 21

Hi-tech

apartment block, tallest, 146
aircraft, 142–143
  military, 132, 133
airliners, fastest, 142
airplanes, 142, 143
ambulances, biggest, 136
automobiles, 134–135
bicycles, 138–139, 232–233
bikes, 138-139, 232–233
bombs, 132, 133

building, tallest, 146
buildings, 146-149
buses, 136-137
cable suspension bridge, longest, 146
camcorders, smallest, 130
camera, fastest, 128
  smallest, 128
cars, 134–135, 230-231
  eco-friendly, 134, 182
cell phones, 128, 129
  biggest company, 58
  most expensive, 70
chess computer, 119
combat jet, fastest, 142
computer games, 120–121
computers, 118–119
concert, biggest on-line, 124
consoles, games, 120
cyberpet, most downloaded, 124
cyberstar, most variations, 124
domain names, 122, 125
dome, biggest, 148
driving simulator, best-selling, 120
earthmover, biggest, 136
e-commerce, 122, 123
e-mail, 119, 123, 125
escalator, longest ride, 148
  shortest, 148
fax machine, smallest, 129
flight simulator, best-selling, 121
forklift trucks, biggest, 136
gadgets, 128–131
games, computer, 120–121
Giga Pet, oldest, 121
hardware, 118–119
glasses, lightest, 128
golf, biggest on-line tournament, 124
helicopters, 142
home pages, 123
hotel, biggest, 147
  tallest, 147
house, most expensive, 146
hovercraft, 140
internet, 122–125
IT, 118–119
keyboard, smallest computer, 118
launch system, most reliable, 144
lighthouse, tallest, 148
loudspeakers, most expensive, 70
machine guns, 133
Mini Disc players, 130
monster trucks, 116
motorcycles, 138–139, 232–233

MP3, 125
  best-selling player, 130
newscaster, virtual, 125
observation wheel, biggest, 87
office, biggest, 147
office building, tallest, 146
optical fibers, narrowest, 129
phones, smallest, 128, 129
planes, 142,143
railroads, 136-137
robots, 126-127
rocket, most expensive, 144
  most powerful, 144
  most powerful engine, 145
scaffolding, tallest, 148
scanner, biggest, 118
search engines, 123
ships, 140-141
software, 118-119
spacecraft, 144-145
  fastest, 144
  smallest, 144
speakers, most expensive, 70
spiral staircase, longest, 148
streetcars, oldest, 137
structures, 146-149
  tallest, 147
submarines, 141
telephones, smallest, 128, 129
telescope, most expensive, 145
trains, 136-137
trucks, 136
tunnel, longest, 148
TV sets, 130
vacuum cleaner, most advanced, 126
vehicles, 136-137
video camera, smallest, 130
virus, computer, 119
weapons, 132-133
websites, 122, 123
windows, biggest, 148
world wide web, 122-125
worm, computer, 119

www.

Internet

concert, biggest on-line, 124
cyberpet, most downloaded, 124
cyberstar, most variations, 124
domain names, 122, 125

e-commerce, 122, 123
e-mail, 119, 123, 125
golf, biggest on-line tournament, 124
home pages, 123
internet, 122-125
MP3, 125
newscaster, virtual, 125
search engines, 123
virus, computer, 119
websites, 122, 123
world wide web, 122-125
worm, computer, 119

Media

Academy Awards, 61, 112
actors, 108, 112
  highest-earning, 98
  highest-grossing, 90
  shortest, 92
advertisements, TV, 59, 97
advertising, 59
  biggest agency, 58
African music, 105
albums, best-selling, 100
animated films, 94
animation, 94, 95
arcade machine, dance marathon, 23
audience, biggest, 99, 100, 106
authors, 111
  most filmed, 93
  youngest, 9
awards, 112-113
band, highest-paid, 55
  richest, 54
bhangra music, 104, 105
big beat music, 102
books, 110, 111, 113
  most expensive, 70
  most valuable, 64
Booker Prize, 113
bookstore, biggest, 69
box office, highest gross, 90, 92, 93
Brit awards, 113
businessmen, richest, 55
cartoons, 94-95
cello, most valuable, 63
Césars, 113
chorus line, oldest, 109
circus, 108

classical music, 106-107
clothes, 88-89
clubbing, 82-83
comedies, highest grossing, 92
comic, most valuable, 65
comic strips, 94, 95
commercials, TV, 59, 97
composers, 106
concert, biggest on-line, 124
conga, longest, 28
contract, TV, 99
costumes, most in a movie, 91
country music, 104, 105
crosswords, 110
dance music, 102-103
dancing, 28
  longest marathon, 23
designer, youngest, 9
designer label, fastest-growing, 88
diary, best-selling, 111
DJ, marathon, 23
  youngest, 8
documentaries, TV, 96
drama, TV, 96
drum 'n' bass, 103
Emmys, 113
extra, TV, most appearances, 99
fashion, 88-89
fashion designer, highest-earning, 54
  most at one show, 88
film producer, highest-earning, 54
flamenco dancer, fastest, 17
game shows, TV, 97
Grammys, 112
guitar, most valuable, 63
hip-hop, 102
horror movies, 93
human mobile, biggest, 109
jazz, 106-107
jazz-funk music, 103
Latin music, 104
letters to newspapers, 110
line dance, biggest, 28
live entertainment company,
  biggest, 59
lyrics, most valuable, 65
magazines, 110, 111
  most expensive, 70
media, 110-111
media tycoon, richest, 54
miniseries, TV, 96
modeling, longest career with one
  company, 88

movies, 90–93, 112, 113
  most watched, 22
  movie marathon, longest, 22
MP3, 125
music, 100–107
music awards, 112, 113
music charts, 100, 101
music manuscripts, most valuable, 107
music producer, richest, 55
music video, 96, 97
news broadcaster, highest-earning, 98
news organization, biggest, 85
newscaster, virtual, 125
newspapers, 110
nightclubs, 103
novels, 111
opera, 106, 107
opera singer, youngest, 9
orchestra, biggest, 107
  oldest, 106
Oscars, 61, 64, 112
  most consecutive nominations, 94
painting, most valuable, 64
pen and ink drawing, most valuable, 64
performance, 108–109
personal-problem solvers, 110
photograph, most valuable, 65
piano, most valuable, 63
play, longest , 109
  shortest, 109
pop music, 100–101
pop stars, 100–101
print runs, biggest, 111
prizes, 112–113
producers, TV, 99
programs, TV, 96–99
pseudonyms, 101
public relations company, biggest, 58
publishing, 110–111, 113
  biggest company, 59
Pulitzer Prizes, 113
Qawaali music, 104
quizzes, TV, 97
R&B, 103
raï music, 105
rap music, 102
record company, biggest, 56
reggae, 104
rock festival, biggest, 82
rock music, 100–101
salsa music, 104, 105
sampling, 103
sculpture, most valuable, 64

Shakespeare, longest play, 109
single, biggest-selling, 100
sitarist, longest career, 104
songwriters, 100
special effects, 116–117
stage, biggest , 108
studio, biggest, 90
swear words, most in an animated
  movie, 95
talk show host, highest-earning, 98
tap dance, biggest, 28
  fastest, 16
  longest, 28
theater, 108–109
theatrical production,
  highest-grossing, 109
  most expensive, 108
TV, 96–99
  awards, 113
TV show, most convulsions
  caused by, 95
video, 96, 97
video retailer, biggest, 97
vocal note, highest, 107
  lowest, 107
western, highest grossing, 92
world music, 104–105
writers, TV, 98
YMCA, biggest dance, 28
yodeler, fastest, 17

Money

actors, highest-earning, 98
  highest-grossing, 90
advertisements, TV, 97
advertising, 59
  biggest agency, 58
AGM, biggest attendance, 56
albums, best-selling, 100
alcohol, most expensive, 72
animal, most expensive, 70
atlas, most valuable, 65
auctions, 62–67
band, highest-paid, 55
  richest, 54
bank, biggest, 58
baseball, most valuable, 66
  most valuable glove, 66
bequest, biggest, 60

bicycle, most valuable, 66
big business, 56–59
bikini, most valuable, 67
billionaire, youngest, 55
bingo, biggest game, 77
book, most expensive, 70
  most valuable, 64
bookstore, biggest, 69
box office, highest gross, 90, 92, 93
boxer, highest-paid, 55
boxing memorabilia, most valuable, 67
bra, most expensive, 89
businessmen, richest, 55
camera, most valuable, 65
carpet, most valuable, 62
cat, most expensive, 71
cell phone, most expensive, 70
cell phone company, biggest, 58
cello, most valuable, 63
chairs, most valuable, 62
charitable foundation, biggest, 60
charities, 60–61
Chief Executive Officer,
  highest paid, 56,
  lowest paid, 57
cities, cheapest, 42
  most expensive, 42
clock, most valuable, 62
clothing brand, best-selling, 68
coin, most valuable, 62
cologne, most expensive, 70
comedies, highest grossing, 92
comic, most valuable, 65
commercials, TV, 59, 97
company, biggest, 58
cosmetics company, biggest, 59
cosmetics tycoons, richest, 54
countries, 40–43
credit cards, most, 69
cricketing memorabilia,
  most valuable, 66
currency, least valuable, 43
department store, biggest,68
designer label, fastest-growing, 88
diamond, most valuable, 62
Dinky toy, most valuable, 62
donation, biggest, 60
dress, most valuable, 66
e-commerce, 122, 123
economics, 40–43
electronics, biggest retailers, 69
employer, biggest, 58
family business, oldest, 56

fashion designer, highest-earning, 54
fashion retail chain, biggest, 68
film producer, highest-earning, 54
flea market, biggest, 68
flotation, biggest, 56
fragrance, most expensive, 70
gambling, 76
GI Joe, most valuable, 67
gifts, 60–61
gold, biggest reserves, 42
golden handshake, biggest, 56
golfers, highest-earning, 196, 197
gross national product, 43
guitar, most valuable, 63
hair, most valuable, 62
hat, most expensive designer, 88
head wear, most valuable, 66
health expenditure, highest, 42
  lowest, 42
helmet, most valuable, 66
house, most expensive, 146
illuminated manuscript,
  most valuable, 65
illustrated manuscript,
  most valuable, 67
income tax, 42
industrialization, 43
inflation, 42
insect, most expensive, 71
insurance company, biggest, 58
investment consultant, highest fees, 56
investor, richest, 56
jackpots, biggest, 77
jeans, most valuable, 66
jewel theft, biggest, 52
jewelry, most valuable, 62
jewelry box, most valuable, 62
kaleidoscope, most valuable, 67
law firm, biggest, 58
lecturing, highest fees, 57
legs, most valuable, 114
letters, most valuable, 64
live entertainment company,
  biggest, 59
lottery, most wins by a town, 76
  biggest jackpot, 77
loudspeakers, most expensive, 70
luxury goods tycoon, richest, 54
lyrics, most valuable, 65
magazine, most expensive, 70
mall, biggest, 68
market capitalization, biggest, 57
markets, biggest, 68

meal, most expensive, 74
media tycoon, richest, 54
Mickey Mouse toy, most valuable, 67
Mini, most expensive, 71
Monopoly, most valuable, 78
motor scooter, most expensive, 139
movie costume, most valuable, 64
movie poster, most valuable, 64
movie prop, most valuable, 64
music box, most valuable, 65
music manuscripts, most valuable, 107
music producer, richest, 55
news broadcaster, highest-earning, 98
NFL franchise, most valuable, 194
oil and energy company, biggest, 58
Oscar, most valuable, 64
painting, most valuable, 64
paperweight, most valuable, 63
pen, most expensive, 71
  most valuable, 62
pen and ink drawing, most valuable, 64
perfume, most expensive, 70
Pez dispensers, most valuable, 66
pharmaceutical company, biggest, 58
photograph, most valuable, 65
piano, most valuable, 63
pinball machine, most expensive, 70
poster, most valuable, 64
print, most valuable, 64
public relations company, biggest, 58
publishing company, biggest, 59
raffle, most Rolls-Royces, 77
record company, biggest, 56
richest people, 54–55
robbery, 52
rocket, most expensive, 144
royal, richest, 54
rummage sale, biggest, 69
salty snacks company, biggest, 59
sculpture, most valuable, 64
shares, biggest price change, 56
shawls, most expensive, 88
shipwreck, most valuable, 141
shoes, most expensive, 88
shopping, 68–71
shopping center, biggest, 68
single, biggest-selling, 100
skate shoes, best-selling, 89
skull, most valuable, 62
slot machine, biggest jackpot, 77
soaps and cosmetics company,
  biggest, 59
soccer players, most expensive, 187

soccer program, most valuable, 66
soccer shirt, most valuable, 66
speakers, most expensive, 70
spice, most expensive, 72
sponsored swims, most successful 61
sporting event, most money raised 60
sportswear, biggest brand, 69
Stock Exchange, oldest, 56
surfer, highest-earning, 228
surf wear, best-selling, 89
supermodels, richest, 114
Swatch, most expensive, 70
Swiss army knife, most expensive, 70
talk show host, highest-earning, 98
taxation, 42
teddy bear, most valuable, 65
telecommunications company,
  biggest, 58
telegram, most valuable, 64
telescope, most expensive, 145
telethon, most money raised, 61
tennis, highest earning sisters, 198
tennis racket, most valuable, 66
theatrical production,
  highest grossing, 109
  most expensive, 108
theft, 52
thimble, most valuable, 63
tiara, most expensive, 88
tobacco company, biggest, 59
tooth, most valuable, 62
toy retailer, biggest, 69
tree, most expensive, 71
TV commercials, most starring
  company founder, 59
typewriter, most valuable, 62
underwear, best-selling, 89
valuables, 62–67
video retailer, biggest, 97
wallet, most expensive, 70
watch, most expensive, 70
wax doll, most valuable, 67
wealth, 54–55
wedding dress,
  most expensive, 88
western,
  highest grossing, 92
wholesale market,
  biggest, 68
wool, most expensive, 70
wristwatch, most valuable, 63
Zippo lighter, most valuable, 66

Nature

amphibian, biggest, 164
  smallest, 164
animals, 19, 160–165
  biggest, 160, 169
  rarest, 182, 183
bird of prey, rarest, 183
birds, biggest, 162
  biggest egg, 162
  deepest dive, 162
  earliest, 169
  fastest, 162
  highest-flying, 162
  largest wingspan, 162
  longest feathers, 162
  smallest, 162
  talking, 162
butterfly, biggest, 165
cactus, tallest, 167
cave, biggest, 157
chelonian, oldest, 164
  smallest, 164
claws, biggest, 169
coldest places, 172
crocodilian, smallest, 165
crustacean, biggest, 164
cyclones, 184
desert, biggest, 156
dinosaurs, 168–169
dog, heaviest, 160
driest place, 173
droughts, 185
earthquakes, 184, 185
ecology, 180–183
endangered species, 182, 183
environment, 180–183
eyes, biggest, 165
famine, 185
fish, biggest, 162
  fastest, 163
  most eggs, 163
  most poisonous, 163
  oldest, 163
  slowest, 163
  smallest, 163
fjord, longest, 157
floods, 173, 184
flower, biggest, 166
  smelliest, 167
fungus, biggest, 167

most poisonous, 166
geysers, 185
hail, 172, 184
horses, 234–235, 244–245
  smallest, 161
hurricanes, 184, 185
ice storms, 185
insect, biggest eggs, 165
  fastest, 164
  most destructive, 165
island, biggest, 157
jellyfish, most venomous, 165
kangaroo, biggest, 161
lake, biggest, 157
  deepest, 156
landslides, 185
leaves, biggest, 167
lizard, smallest, 164
mammals, biggest land, 160
  fastest, 160
  flying, 161
  rarest, 183
  slowest, 160
  smallest, 160
  tallest, 160
mammoths, 168
monsoons, 185
mountains, biggest ranges, 156
  highest, 156
ocean, biggest, 157
  deepest point, 157
  smallest, 157
orchid, biggest, 167
organic farming, 182
plants, 166–167
pollution, 180–181
pregnancy, longest, 161
primate, smallest, 160
rabbit, longest ears, 161
rain, 172, 173
reef, longest, 157
reptile, biggest, 165
restaurant, biggest, 74
  most visited, 74
rivers, longest, 156
rodent, biggest, 161
roots, deepest, 166
  longest, 166
rosebush, biggest, 167
seaweed, longest, 166
seed, biggest, 167
  smallest, 167
snail, biggest, 165

snake, longest, 164
  oldest, 164
  smallest, 164
snow, 172
snowflake, biggest, 172
spider, biggest, 164
  biggest web, 164
  smallest, 164
storms, 172, 173, 184
storm chasing, 172, 173
sunflower, most heads, 167
  tallest, 167
sunshine, 172
temperature, highest, 172
  lowest, 172
thunder, 172
tornadoes, 172
tsunamis, 184
tree, deepest roots, 166
  fastest-growing, 166
  most massive, 166
  oldest, 166
  tallest, 166
typhoons, 184
volcanos, 185
  most active, 156
waterfall, highest, 157
weather, 172–173
weed, biggest, 166
  most damaging, 166
wind, fastest, 172

People

airplane passenger, oldest, 10
altar boy, oldest, 49
antiwar rally, biggest, 46
arrest, biggest mass, 53
arrests, most, 53
athlete, oldest, 10
author, youngest, 9
balloonist, oldest, 10
beard, longest, 159
  longest (woman), 159
billionaire, youngest, 55
birth, most premature, 178
birth rates, highest and lowest, 40
birthday party, biggest, 83
body, human, 158–159
body piercings, 114, 115

bodybuilding, 114, 115
book of signatures, biggest, 47
bride, oldest, 11
bridegroom, oldest, 10
Buddhist temple, biggest, 48
campaigns, 46–47
children, most, 178
children's party, biggest, 83
churches, 48, 49
cities, cheapest, 42
  most expensive, 42
civil disobedience march, biggest, 46
clubs, 84, 85
collectors, 80–81
conservation organization, biggest, 47
countries, 40–43
country, most visitors, 151
couturier, oldest, 11
crime, 52–53
criminal trial, 52
currency, least valuable, 43
death rates, highest and lowest, 40, 41
demonstration, biggest, 46
dental associations, biggest, 84
designer, oldest, 11
  youngest, 9
director, youngest, 9
diving, youngest world champion, 9
divorce rates, highest and lowest, 41
divorcing couple, oldest, 11
DJ, youngest, 8
doctor, youngest, 8
doctors, fewest and most, 41
driver, oldest, 10
economics, 40–43
environmental campaign,
  longest-running, 47
evacuations, biggest, 50
execution, 53
facial hair, 159
fan clubs, 84, 85
feet, biggest, 159
fingernails, longest, 158
Freemasons, 84
funeral, first Space, 38
gay rights march, biggest, 46
gold, biggest reserves, 42
golfer, youngest hole in one, 9
graduates, youngest, 8
groom, oldest, 10
gross national product, 43
guerrilla, youngest leaders, 51
heads of state, oldest, 44

shortest, 44
  youngest, 44
health expenditure, highest, 42
  lowest, 42
heaviest person, 158
  twins, 158
  woman, 158
Hindu temples, biggest, 48
hole-in-one, youngest, 9
hospitals, 43
hot-air balloonist, oldest, 10
human body, 158–159
human chain, longest, 46
human rights organization, biggest, 47
  oldest, 85
income tax, 42
industrialization, 43
inflation, 42
jewel theft, 52
judge, youngest, 8
king, youngest, 44
Koran, 49
leaders, 44–45
legs, most valuable, 114
life expectancy, highest and lowest, 40
lifesaving society, oldest, 85
lightest person, 158
magic societies, 84
majority, biggest, 45
marriage rates, highest and lowest, 41
married couple, oldest, 11
  youngest, 9
Masonic lodge, oldest, 84
men, biggest shortage, 40
ministers, most female, 45
monarchs, heaviest, 45
  youngest, 44
Mormon temple,
  biggest, 48
mosque, biggest, 48
mothers, oldest, 178
mustache, longest, 159
mugging, 52
multiple births, biggest, 178
murderers, 52–53
news organization, biggest, 85
Nobel Prize, youngest winner, 9
North Pole skier, oldest, 10
nurses, most per capita, 41
old age, 10–11, 158
oldest living man, 158
oldest living person, 158
oldest man, 158

oldest person, 158
operations, most, 179
organizations, 84–85
Orthodox cathedral, biggest, 48
parachutists, oldest, 10
parties, 82–83
petitions, 46, 47
philately, biggest organization, 84
physician, youngest, 8
piercings, body, 114, 115
pilot, oldest, 10
playwright, oldest, 11
politics, 44-47
premier, highest-paid, 45
  oldest, 44
  youngest, 44
presidents, oldest, 44
  youngest, 44
prime minister, highest-paid, 45
  oldest, 44
  youngest, 44
prison, most secure, 53
  most transfers, 52
prisoner of conscience, youngest, 46
  longest-held, 47
private housing, 43
professor, youngest, 9
psychologists, biggest organization, 84
queen, youngest, 44
racial equality rally, biggest, 46
racing driver, oldest, 11
  youngest, 11
reign, longest, 44
religion, 48–49
rented housing, 43
richest people, 54–55
robbery, 52
Rotary club, oldest, 84
school, biggest, 84
sentences, longest, 53
serial killer, most prolific, 52
sex discrimination,
  biggest settlement, 46
shortest man, 158
  twins, 159
  woman, 158
Siamese twins, oldest, 159
Sikhs, biggest gathering, 49
skull, biggest, 169
smallest waist, 159
snowboarder, oldest, 228
society, 40–43
soldiers, youngest, 9

stamp collectors, 4
supermarket, youngest consultant, 8
synagogue, biggest, 48
tallest man, 159
  UK, 75
tallest woman, 158
tattoos, 114
taxation, 42
temples, 48, 49
theft, 52
tightrope walker, oldest, 11
toenails, longest, 159
tourism, 151
tourists, highest-spending, 151
tuba player, oldest, 11
twins, 159
UN ambassador, youngest, 8
UN speech, longest, 45
unions, 84
worship, 48–49

Power

air force, biggest, 50
antiwar rally, biggest, 46
army, biggest, 50
  most multinational, 51
campaigns, 46–47
CEO, highest paid, 56,
  lowest paid, 57
Chief Executive Officer,
  highest paid, 56,
  lowest paid, 57
churches, 48, 49
civil-disobedience march,
  biggest, 46
crime, 52–53
demonstration,
  biggest, 46
environmental campaign,
  longest-running, 47
evacuations, biggest, 50
Freemasons, 84
gay rights march,
  biggest, 46
guerrillas,
  youngest leaders, 51
heads of state,
  oldest, 44
  shortest, 44

youngest, 44
human rights organization,
  biggest, 47
  oldest, 85
investor, richest, 56
king, youngest, 44
law and order, 52–53
leaders, 44–45
majority, biggest, 45
Masonic lodge, oldest, 84
military, 50–51
ministers, most female, 45
monarchs,
  heaviest, 45
  youngest, 44
peacekeeping, 51
petitions, 46, 47
politics, 44–47
premier,
  highest-paid, 45
  oldest, 44
  youngest, 44
presidents, oldest, 44
  youngest, 44
prime minister,
  highest-paid, 45
  oldest, 44
  youngest, 44
prison,
  most secure, 53
  most transfers, 52
prisoner of conscience,
  youngest, 46
  longest-held, 47
queen, youngest, 44
racial-equality rally,
  biggest, 46
reign, longest, 44
religion, 48–49
richest people, 54–55
royal, richest, 54
sentences, longest, 53
terrorism,
  worst attack, 51
trade unions, 84
treaty, oldest, 51
UN speech, longest, 45
unions, 84
war, 50–51
worship, 48–49

Science

acid, strongest, 153
acid rain, 181
amphibian, biggest, 164
  smallest, 164
animals, 160–165
  biggest, 160, 169
  biggest cloned, 153
  most dangerous, 174
  rarest, 182, 183
artifact, smallest, 154
asteroid, biggest, 171
  smallest, 171
astronomy, 170–171
bacterium, deadliest, 153
balance, finest, 155
beard, longest, 159
  longest (woman), 159
birds, biggest, 162
  biggest egg, 162
  deepest dive, 162
  earliest, 169
  fastest, 162
  highest-flying, 162
  largest wingspan, 162
  longest feathers, 162
  smallest, 162
  talking, 162
birth, most premature, 178
bitterest substances, 152
body, human, 158–159
butterfly, biggest, 165
cactus, tallest, 167
calculator, smallest, 154
carbon dioxide,
  highest emissions, 180
cancer, fewest deaths, 177
  most deaths, 177
  most survivable, 177
cave, biggest, 157
chelonian,
  oldest, 164
  smallest, 164
chromosomes, 152
cloning, 153
coldest places, 170, 172
driest place, 173
comet, biggest, 171
compound, most extracted, 154
computation, biggest, 155

constellation,
 biggest, 170
 smallest, 170
crocodilian, smallest, 165
crustacean, biggest, 164
death, commonest causes, 176
desert, biggest, 156
dinosaurs, 168–169
diseases, 174–177
 commonest, 175
 deadliest, 177
 fastest-growing, 176
 most resurgent, 176
 oldest, 176
dog, heaviest, 160
driest place, 173
earthquakes, 184, 185
eclipse, longest, 171
ecology, 180–183
elements,
 commonest, 152
 hardest, 152
 heaviest, 152
 newest, 152
electrical current,
 most powerful, 154
endangered species, 182, 183
energy, 134, 135, 182
environment, 180–183
eye, first artificial, 179
eyes, biggest, 165
facial hair, 159
feet, biggest, 159
fingernails, longest, 158
fish, biggest, 162
 fastest, 163
 most eggs, 163
 most poisonous, 163
 oldest, 163
 slowest, 163
 smallest, 163
fjord, longest, 157
flood, 173
flower, biggest, 166
 smelliest, 167
fuel efficiency, 134
fungus, biggest, 167
 most poisonous, 166
genetics, 152
hailstones, heaviest, 172
hand transplant, first, 179
heart transplant, earliest, 179
heaviest person, 158

twins, 158
 woman, 158
horse, smallest, 161
human body, 158–159
immunization,
 most successful campaign, 176
infectious disease, commonest, 174
insect, biggest eggs, 165
 fastest, 164
 most destructive, 165
island, biggest, 157
jellyfish, most venomous, 165
kangaroo, biggest, 161
lake, biggest, 157
 deepest, 156
leaves, biggest, 167
lightest person, 158
lizard, smallest, 164
mammals, biggest land, 160
 fastest, 160
 flying, 161
 slowest, 160
 smallest, 160
 tallest, 160
math problem, longest-standing, 154
medicine, 178–179
metallic element, most extracted, 154
meteor shower, greatest, 171
meteorite, biggest, 171
microbes, biggest, 153
mineral, softest, 152
mountains, biggest ranges, 156
 highest, 156, 171
multiple births, biggest, 178
nerve gas, 153
Nobel prize, most from one lab, 155
ocean, biggest, 157
 deepest point, 157
 smallest, 157
old age, 158
oldest living man, 158
 living person, 158
oldest man, 158
 person, 158
orchid, biggest, 167
organic farming, 182
ozone levels, lowest, 180
parasites, 174–175
 biggest, 174
 longest-living, 174
 most bloodthirsty, 174
pi, most accurate version, 155
planet, biggest, 171

brightest, 171
coldest, 171
hottest, 171
plants, 166–167
pollution, 180–181
pregnancy, longest, 161
primate, smallest, 160
prime number, highest-known, 155
protein, 153
rabbit, longest ears, 161
rain, 172, 173
recycling, 182
reef, longest, 157
reptile, biggest, 165
rivers, longest, 156
rodent, biggest, 161
roots, deepest, 166
 longest, 166
rosebush, biggest, 167
satellite, biggest, 171
 smallest, 170
seaweed, longest, 166
science, 152–155
seed, biggest, 167
 smallest, 167
shortest man, 158
 twins, 159
 woman, 158
Siamese twins, oldest, 159
skull, biggest, 169
smallest waist, 159
smelliest substance, 152
snail, biggest, 165
snake, longest, 164
 oldest, 164
 smallest, 164
snow, 172
snowflake, biggest, 172
solar energy, 182
spider, biggest, 164
 biggest web, 164
 smallest, 164
star, biggest, 170
 brightest, 170
 nearest, 170
 oldest, 170
 smallest, 170
 youngest, 170
storms, 172, 173, 184
sunflower, most heads, 167
 tallest, 167
sunshine, 172
sweetest substance, 152

tallest man, 159
  woman, 158
temperature, highest, 154, 172
  lowest, 154, 172
thunder, 172
toenails, longest, 159
tornadoes, 172
toxic cloud, biggest, 181
toxicity, 152
transistor, smallest, 154
transplant, most organs, 179
transplant, youngest patient, 179
tree, deepest roots, 166
  fastest-growing, 166
  oldest, 166
  most massive, 166
  tallest, 166
twins, 159
vets, most in one procedure, 178
virus, newest, 176
volcanos, 185
  most active, 156
waterfall, highest, 157
weather, 172–173
weed, biggest, 166
  most damaging, 166
wind, fastest, 172

Space

asteroid, biggest, 171
  smallest, 171
astronomy, 170–171
coldest place, 170
constellation, biggest, 170
  smallest, 170
eclipse, longest, 171
escape velocity, fastest, 145
launch, loudest, 145
launch system, least reliable, 144
  most reliable, 144
lunar hit, first, 145
man-made object, most remote, 144
meteor shower, greatest, 171
meteorite, biggest, 171
mountain, highest, 171
planet, biggest, 171
  brightest, 171
  coldest, 171
  hottest, 171

robots, 127
rocket, biggest, 144
  cheapest, 144
  most expensive, 144
  most powerful, 144
  most powerful engine, 145
  smallest, 144
satellite, biggest, 171
  oldest, 144
  smallest, 170
shuttle flight, longest, 144
shuttle payload, biggest, 145
spacecraft, 144–145
  fastest, 144
  smallest, 144
star, biggest, 170
  brightest, 170
  nearest, 170
  oldest, 170
  smallest, 170
  youngest, 170
telescope, most expensive, 145

Speed

aircraft, 142–143
airliners, fastest, 142
auto sports, 230–231
bathtub racer, fastest, 16
bed maker, fastest, 17
bicycles, 138–139, 232–233
bikes, 138–139, 232–233
birds, fastest, 162
boats, 140–141
buses, 136-137
cars, 134–135, 230-231
CN Tower, fastest pogo stick, 16
coconut tree, fastest climber, 17
combat jet, fastest, 142
drag racing, 230
Empire State Building,
  fastest run up, 17
fish, fastest, 163
flamenco dancer,
  fastest, 17
half-marathon, fastest pushing a baby
  buggy, 16
horse racing, 234–235
hovercraft, 140
insect, fastest, 164

kite, fastest, 17
knot tier, fastest, 16
land speed, highest, 134
mammals, fastest, 164
motorbikes, 138–139, 232–233
motorcycling, 138–139, 232–233
pantomime horse, fastest, 17
pole climbing, fastest, 16
baby buggy pushing, fastest, 16
racehorses, 234, 235
racing (horse), 234
rally driving, 230
sack racer, fastest, 16
ships, 140–141
spacecraft, fastest, 144
speed, 16–17
  greatest attained by humans, 38
spike driver, fastest, 16
stilt walker, fastest, 16
submarines, 141
talker, fastest, 17
tap dancer, fastest, 16
Tour de France, 232, 233
trains, 136, 137
treetopper, fastest, 16
trucks, 136
vehicles, 136–137
wheeled trash can, fastest, 16
window cleaner, fastest, 16
yodeler, fastest, 17

Sports

AFL, 204, 205
ATP tour (tennis), 199
Alpine skiing, 220
America's Cup, 214
archery, 249
athlete, oldest, 10
athletics, 208–211, 236–239
Australian Open (tennis), 199
Australian rules football, 204, 205
auto sports, 230–231
ball sports, 204–207
baseball, 200–201, 245–246
  most valuable, 66
  most valuable glove, 66
basketball, 190–191
bicycling, 232–233, 243–244
  down a glacier, 227

boats, 214
bobsled, 219
body boarding,
  most championships, 228
bowling, 205
bowls, 205
boxer, highest-paid, 55
boxing, 222, 223
  most valuable memorabilia, 67
bridge, most hands, 77
  most world titles, 77
bungee jumping, highest, 228
  most people, 228
butt boarding, 226
Canadian football, 195
CFL, 195
checkers, most opponents, 76
  most world titles, 77
chess, highest ratings, 77
combat sports, 222–225
Cresta Run, 219
cricket, 202–203, 248
  most valuable memorabilia, 66
cross-country running, 208
curling,
  most World Championships, 218
decathlon, 210, 237
discus, 237, 238
diving, 215
  youngest world champion, 9
drag racing, 230
equestrianism, 234–235
extreme sports, 226–229
fencing, 222
field hockey, 206
figure skating, 218, 219
football, 194–195, 246–248
  Australian rules, 204, 205
  Canadian, 195
Formula One, 230, 231
freefalls, biggest, 229
French Open (tennis), 199
goal, fastest (soccer), 186
golf, 196–197, 248
  biggest on-line tournament, 124
  youngest hole in one, 9
golfers, highest-earning, 196, 197
Grand Prix, 230, 231
Grand Slam (tennis), 198
gravity speed biking, 227
Grey Cup, 195
gymnastics, 212–213
hammer throw, 211, 237, 238

handball, 204
heptathlon, 211, 238
high jump, 236, 237, 238, 239
hockey, field, 206
  ice, 216-217
horse racing, 234–235, 244–245
hurdles, 208, 210, 236, 237, 238, 239
ice climbing, 227
ice hockey, 216–217
ice-skating, 218, 219
  longest race, 219
Indianapolis 500 race, 230, 231
in-line skating, 226
javelin, 210, 237, 238
jet skiing, most championships, 229
jockeys, 234
judo, 224, 225
karate, 225
kayaking, most titles, 228
knee boarding,
  most championships, 228
korfball, 204
lacrosse, 207
Le Mans 24-hour race, 230
long jump, 208, 211, 236, 237, 238, 239
lugeing, 219
marathons, 209
martial arts, 224–225
motorcycling, 232-233
mountain biking, 227
NFL, 194–195
  most valuable franchise, 194
NHL, 216–217
National Football League, 194–195
National Hockey League, 216–217
netball, 204
Nordic skiing, 220
Olympics, 189, 190, 191, 201, 207, 210,
  212, 213, 214, 215, 218, 219, 220, 221,
  222, 225, 232, 235
  oldest gold medallist, 10
  youngest medalists, 8
one-day internationals
  (cricket), 202, 203
parachute, 229
pelota, 206
pentathlon, 211
pole vault, 210, 211, 236, 237, 238, 239
pool, 207
racing (horse), 234
racketball, 206
racquetball, 206
rally driving, 230

relay races, 208, 210
rhythmic gymnastics, 213
roller hockey, 206
rugby, 192–193
running, 208–209, 236, 237, 238, 239
  backward, 24
Ryder Cup, 196
sand boarding, longest back flip, 228
shooting, 248–249
shot put, 237, 238, 239
show jumping, 235
skateboarding, 226, 227
  glossary, 227
skating (ice), 218, 219, 244
ski boarding, 227
skibob, 218
skiing, 220–221
ski jumping, 221
snooker, 207
snowboarder, oldest, 228
snowboarding, 220, 221, 227
soccer, 186–189
  most valuable program, 66
  most valuable shirt, 66
speed skating, 218, 219, 244
sport, worst disasters, 35
sporting event, most money raised, 60
sportswear, biggest brand, 69
squash, 206
Stanley Cup, 217
steeplechase, 236, 238
sumo, 224, 225
Super Bowl, 194, 195
Supercross, 232
surfer, highest-earning, 228
surfing, most championships, 228
swimming, 214, 215, 240–243
  longest ocean, 25
  underwater, 228
table tennis, 206
tae kwon do, 224, 225
tennis, 198–199
  most valuable racket, 66
tenpin bowling, 205
Test matches (cricket), 202, 203
Tour de France, 232, 233
track-and-field, 208–211, 236–239
trampolining, 213
transfer fee, highest (soccer), 187
triathlon, 210
triple jump, 237, 238, 239
US open (tennis), 198, 199
volleyball, 204

walking, 210, 239
  backward, 24
  on hands, 24
water polo, 215
water sports, 214–215
weight lifting, 212–213, 250–251
white–water kayaking, most titles, 228
Wimbledon (tennis), 198, 199
windsurfing, highest latitude, 228
winter sports, 216–221
World Cup (soccer), 188, 189
World Cup (rugby), 192
World Series (baseball), 200, 201
wrestling, 222
  sumo, 224, 225
  Turkish, 223
X-Games, 226, 227
yachting, 214

☆

Stars

Academy Awards, 112
actors, 90, 98, 108, 112
audience, biggest, 99, 106, 108
awards, 112–113
band, highest-paid, 55
  richest, 54
beauty pageants, 114, 115
big beat music, 102
boxer, highest-paid, 55
Brit awards, 113
Césars, 113
circus, 108
classical music, 106–107
dance music, 102–103
drum 'n' bass, 103
Emmys, 113
fashion designer, highest-earning, 54
  most at one show, 88
films, 112, 113
Grammys, 112
jazz, 106–107
jazz-funk music, 103
Miss World, 114, 115
model, catwalk, 114
modeling, longest career
  with one company, 88
movies, 112, 113
Mr. Olympia, 114
Ms. Olympia, 115

music awards, 112, 113
news broadcaster, highest earning, 98
opera, 106, 107
orchestra, biggest, 107
Oscars, 61, 64, 112
  most consecutive nominations, 94
performance, 108–109
play, longest , 109
  shortest, 109
pop stars, 100–101
prizes, 112–113
publishing, 113
R&B, 103
rap music, 102
sampling, 103
soccer players, most expensive, 187
supermodels, richest, 114
surfer, highest-earning, 228
talk show host, highest earning, 98
television awards, 113
tennis, highest–earning sisters, 198
theater, 108–109
theatrical production,
  highest-grossing, 109
most expensive, 108
TV awards, 113

🏢

Urban

apartment block, tallest, 146
building, tallest, 146
buildings, 146–149
bungee jumping, highest, 228
  most people, 228
buses, 136–137
bus route, longest, 150
cable suspension bridge,
  longest, 146
cars, 134–135, 230–231
cemetery, biggest, 148
  tallest, 148
crematory, biggest, 149
dome, biggest, 148
door, heaviest, 148
escalator, longest ride, 148
  shortest, 148
extreme sports, 226–229
hotel, biggest, 147
  oldest, 147
  tallest, 147

house, most expensive, 146
in-line skating, 226
office building, tallest, 146
office, biggest, 147
palace, biggest, 146
railroads, 136-137
  busiest, 151
railroad station, biggest, 150
orbital road, longest, 150
scaffolding, tallest, 148
skateboarding, 226, 227
skating glossary, 227
spiral staircase, longest, 148
square, biggest, 146
stairway, longest, 148
streetcar route, longest, 150
structures, 146–149
  tallest, 147
subway,
  most stations, 150
traffic jam, longest, 151
trains, 136–137
transportation, 150
travel, 150–151
tunnel, longest, 148
vehicles, 150–151
wall, longest, 148
walls, thickest, 148
windows, biggest, 148
X-Games, 226, 227

Picture credits

EDITORIAL TEAM

Managing Editor
Tim Footman

Senior Editor
Emma Dixon

Editors
Ken Campbell, Helen Dawson,
Jeff Probst

Keeper of the Records
Stewart Newport

Research Manager
Shelley Flacks

Researchers
Duncan Flett, Sammy Harris,
Lucy Holmes, Della Howes,
Rasila Kuntawala, Selina Lim, Shazia Mirza,
Manjushri Mitra, David Okomah, John Rattagan,
Bronwen Surman

Research Services Manager
Martin Downham

Records Research Co-ordinator
Amanda Sprague

Records Research Assistants
Ann Collins, Keely Hopkins, Jo Wildsmith

Editorial Consultant
Brian J Ford

Designer
Robert Hackett

Picture Editor
Beverley Hadfield

Assistant Designers
Yahya El-Droubie,
Lee Riches

Pre-Production Managers
Patricia Langton, Kate Pimm

Production Co-ordinator
Clair Savage

Production Director
Chris Lingard

Fulfilment
Mary Hill, Britta Aue

Technical Consultant (Cover)
Esteve Font Canadell

Colour Origination
Colour Systems, London, UK

Printing & Binding
Printer Industria Gráfica,
SA, Barcelona, Spain

Special thanks to: Ian Castello-Cortes; Lesley Horowitz and Dominic Sinesio at Office, NYC (design concepts);
Daniela Marceddu, Tamzin Pike, Julia Aldhamland, Sharon Southren (picture research); Ron Callow at Design 23, London, UK;
Roger Hawkins at Integrated Colour Editions; Andrzej Michalski; Nicky King; Dave McAleer; Emma Howcutt;
Mark C Young; Orla Langton; *Play* by Moby; *Songs Of Strength & Heartbreak* by The Mighty Wah!

Acknowledgments

Guinness World Records Ltd would like to thank the following for their contributions to the book.

Shanaaz Alexander
Amnesty International
Juan Arrieta
Dr Paul M Barrett, Dept of Zoology, University of Oxford, UK
Dr Iann Barron
Simon Baylis, Moore Stephens
Sean Blair
Jay Bowers, South London Press
James Basil Bradley
Aníbal Buonomo
Ashley Burford
Clive Carpenter
Alfredo Casero
Shirley Condon
Prof Timothy Beers, Michigan State University, USA
Simon Cavendish Brown
Prof Brian Chaboyer, Dartmouth College, USA.
Christie's
Stuart Claxton
Dr Simon Conway Morris, Dept of Earth Sciences, University of Cambridge, UK
Fernando Crespo
Kerry Dolan
Dr Wolfgang Drautz, German Embassy, UK
Andrew Durham, British Telecom
Ferdinand Edwards
Sir Sam Edwards, University of Cambridge, UK
Michael Feldman
Mike Foster, Jane's Information Group
Charlotte Freemantle, Carat Insight
Mark Freer, British Telecom

José García Domene
Lisa Gibbs
Simon 'Arsenal!' Gold
Greenpeace
Dr John Gribbin, Visiting Fellow in Astronomy, University of Sussex, UK
Michelle Gupta
Michael Feldman
John Hale, Demon Internet
John Hansen
David Hawksett
Neil Hayes
Louis Headland
Ron Hildebrant
Caroline Hoyle, Royal Geographical Society, UK
Prof Erich Ippen, MIT, USA
Sir Peter Johnson
Adam Kesek
Melanie Kirk
Roland Lawrence
Hein Le Roux
Roselle Le Sauteur
Prof Roger J Lederer, California State University, Chico, USA.
Joyce Lee
Claire Lieberman
Clair McFadden, World Circuit Records
Bruce McLaughlin
Norris & Ross McWhirter (founding compilers)
Leo Masliah
Lucille Mills
Trevor Morris
Dr Douglas Morrison, CERN, Switzerland
Scott Murray, Football Unlimited
Wendy Nathan
Gillian Nixon, WorldSport.com
Barry Norman
Uzo Obiorah

Xavier Penas
Matthew Petitt
Greg Phillimore
Dr Maxim Pshenichnikov, University of Groningen, Netherlands
Mariano Rao
Sir Martin Rees, Astronomer Royal, Cambridge University, UK
Nancy Richards
Jason Ringgold
David Roberts, Guinness Book Of British Hit Singles
David Roberts, Walnut Creek, USA
Malcolm Roughead
Jorge Ruhle
Gerard Sampaio
Rosemary Seagrief
Dr Jeff Sherwood, Dept of Energy, USA
Prof Sandro De Silvestri, Politecnico di Milano, Italy
Olivia Smales
Malcolm Smith
P Snodgrass
Sotheby's
Jo Steel
Gary Still, BP Amoco
Jessica Storey
Kim Stram
Kevin Street, Symantec Corporation
Elliott Sydney
Ben Thomas
Lyndsey Ward
Louise Whetter
Louise Wilson
Barry Wright
Rica Yamaguchi
Cathy Yarbrough, National Human Genome Research Institute, USA
Doree Zodrow, Baylor College of Medicine, USA

Guinness World Records – The Story

The roots of Guinness World Records go back to 1951, to a shooting party in County Wexford, Ireland. Sir Hugh Beaver, the managing director of the Guinness brewing company, was involved in a dispute as to whether the golden plover was Europe's fastest game bird. In 1954, another argument arose as to whether the grouse was faster than the golden plover. Sir Hugh realized that these sorts of questions probably arose among people in pubs all the time, and that a book which provided answers to them could be useful to pub owners.

The twins Norris and Ross McWhirter, then running a fact-finding agency in London, were commissioned to compile what became *The Guinness Book Of Records* and, after a busy year of research, the first copy of the 198-page book was bound on Aug. 27, 1955. It was an instant success and became the No. 1 best-seller in Britain before Christmas. The first US edition was published the following year, closely followed by French, German, and Japanese versions.

The English-language edition of the book is now distributed in 70 different countries, with another 22 editions in foreign languages. Sales of all editions passed 50 million in 1984, 75 million in 1994, and will reach the 100-million mark in the next few years.

Other successes include the *Guinness World Records* television shows, now watched in 35 countries around the world, and the Guinness World Records Experience attractions, including the new interactive center in Orlando, Florida, USA.

And now, 2000 sees the launch of guinnessworldrecords.com – all the wonder, spectacle, and excitement of the world of records and record-breaking, just a mouse-click away.

To recognize the fact that the company is no longer simply a book publishing concern, in July 1999 its name was changed from Guinness Publishing to Guinness World Records Ltd.

My Goodness My GUINNESS

⊙ GUINNESS ADVERTISING

The Guinness company dates from 1759, when its first brewery opened in Dublin, Ireland. By the middle of the 20th century the firm was renowned for its groundbreaking advertising, with innovative designs promoting its stout beer across the world. The example above dates from 1936.

→ THE BIRD THAT STARTED IT ALL

The golden plover (right) can reach speeds of 40.4 m.p.h. during migration, but the grouse has been timed at 43.5 m.p.h.